£26.99

Marketing Research

A ... Approach

We work with leading authors to develop the
strongest educational materials in marketing,
bringing cutting-edge thinking and best learning practice
to a global market.

Under a range of well-known imprints, including
Financial Times Prentice Hall, we craft high quality print and
electronic publications which help readers to understand
and apply their content, whether studying or at work.

To find out more about the complete range of our
publishing, please visit us on the World Wide Web at:
www.pearsoneduc.com

Marketing Research

An Integrated Approach

Alan Wilson
Department of Marketing, University of Strathclyde

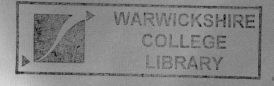

 Prentice Hall
FINANCIAL TIMES

An imprint of **Pearson Education**

Harlow, England · London · New York · Boston · San Francisco · Toronto · Sydney · Singapore · Hong Kong
Tokyo · Seoul · Taipei · New Delhi · Cape Town · Madrid · Mexico City · Amsterdam · Munich · Paris · Milan

**To my wife Sandra,
son Duncan,
and daughter Kirsty**

Pearson Education Limited
Edinburgh Gate
Harlow
Essex CM20 2JE

and Associated Companies throughout the world.

Visit us on the World Wide Web at:
www.pearsoneduc.com

First published 2003

ISBN 0 273 65113 7

British Library Cataloguing-in-Publication Data
A catalogue record for this book is available from the British Library

Library of Congress Cataloging-in-Publication Data
Wilson, Alan M.
     Marketing research : an integrated approach / Alan M. Wilson.
        p.   cm.
     Includes index.
     ISBN 0-273-65113-7 (alk. paper)
       1. Marketing research. I. Title.

     HF5415.2.W558 2002
     658.8′3--dc21   2002027894

10   9   8   7   6   5   4   3   2   1
07   06   05   04

Typeset in 10/12.5pt Sabon by 35
Printed by Ashford Colour Press Ltd., Gosport

Contents

Foreword

Effective progress in any area depends on many key factors, among them the ability to learn from the past and the ability to anticipate future needs and possibilities. In the field of marketing research, we realised long ago the power of using market information as an effective tool in business development. We have also looked constantly to the future, anticipating the needs of clients and the application to the marketing research process of developments in fields as diverse as psychology and technology.

For more than a century, the marketing research profession has sought to refine the processes through which organisations in all walks of life learn about their customers, their needs and their aspirations, and make decisions based on the information which they have gathered. The role of the researcher has grown in importance as markets have expanded and developed, and research itself is now a key component of the marketing process.

As Chairman of The Market Research Society (MRS), I have the privilege of leading the world's largest membership organisation for professional researchers and others engaged in market, social and opinion research. The MRS not only sets the standards for the profession, but also ensures that qualifications and training opportunities exist to enable those involved in marketing research to meet those standards. Through the safeguarding of standards and the promotion of learning, the MRS has helped place British marketing research at the forefront of our vital and dynamic profession.

As part of its ladder of qualifications, the MRS offers the Diploma in Market and Social Research Practice, designed for practising researchers who are keen to develop further their knowledge and skills. *Marketing Research – An Integrated Approach* supports that development through its focus on both the theoretical principles and the practical applications of the marketing research process. Through its use of case studies and current issues, it brings together a reflection on experience and the opportunity for individuals to consider the implications of that experience for their future development.

The marketing research profession in the United Kingdom rightly claims world leadership. The Market Research Society, in its commitment to enhancing that professionalism, seeks to support the development of marketing researchers, whatever the stage of their career. This book is further testament to that commitment to standards and development.

Sally Ford-Hutchinson
Chairman of The Market Research Society

Preface

Introduction

Whatever the type of organisation, market and customer information is critical if strategic goals are to be achieved and customer needs are to be met effectively. Successful managers take an orderly and logical approach to gathering information; they seek facts and undertake new marketing approaches on a systematic basis rather than simply through a procedure of trial and error.

Marketing research has always played a valuable role in providing a significant proportion of these facts and information. However, improvements in data capture and database management, as well as the advent of customer loyalty programmes and the Internet, have resulted in a growing number of managers combining marketing research with internally-held customer data and Internet resources to develop a more comprehensive view of their market place. Integrated information is critical to effective decision making. Marketing information sources can be thought of as separate jigsaw pieces; only when they are connected does the whole picture become clear. Taking decisions by looking at each of the pieces individually is not only inefficient but is likely to result in wrong assumptions and decisions being made.

Therefore the theme of this book is integration, and this is developed over five key dimensions:

- The integration of marketing research with other information sources such as customer databases, customer loyalty programmes and the Internet.

- The integration of marketing research and marketing decision making. Research should not be perceived as some tedious technical activity separate from the practice of marketing management. In reality, marketing research is rarely tedious, and an understanding of marketing research is critical to effective marketing decision making. It therefore needs to be explained in a manner which is both user-friendly and which demonstrates its application to real-life decisions.

- The integration of traditional marketing research approaches with newer developments in Internet-based surveys, computer-assisted interviewing, simulated test markets, mystery shopping, etc.

- The integration of knowledge of marketing research techniques with an understanding about the real world of marketing research, highlighting some of the current issues affecting the use of these techniques (declining response rates, representativeness, data protection issues, etc.).

- Finally, the book attempts to integrate the perspectives of practising marketing researchers, users of marketing research and academics, providing academic rigour with real-life practicality.

Audience

This book is intended for students who are taking their first course in marketing research. The content has been carefully chosen to benefit both those who will eventually be directly responsible for undertaking marketing research and also for those marketing or strategy personnel who will be managing, purchasing or overseeing a research project undertaken by others. To cater for this dual audience, the book is written in a non-technical yet authoritative style.

The book is also aimed at supporting the Marketing Research and Information module of The Market Research Society and the Chartered Institute of Marketing's professional qualifications. The relationship between the requirements of the module and the contents of this book is set out below.

Knowledge and Skill Requirements of the MRS/CIM Marketing Research and Information Module	Relevant Chapters
1 Information and research for decision-making (15%)	1 The Role of Marketing Research and Customer Information in Decision Making 2 The Marketing Research Process and case histories
2 Customer databases (15%)	3 Secondary Data and Customer Databases
3 Marketing research in context (25%)	1 The Role of Marketing Research and Customer Information in Decision Making 2 The Marketing Research Process and case histories/current issues
4 Research methodologies (30%)	3 Secondary Data and Customer Databases 4 Collecting Observation Data 5 Collecting and Analysing Qualitative Data 6 Collecting Quantitative Data 7 Designing Questionnaires 8 Sampling Methods and case histories
5 Presenting and evaluating information to develop business advantage (15%)	5 Collecting and Analysing Qualitative Data 9 Analysing Quantitative Data 10 Presenting the Research Results and case histories

Key features

The book is structured in ten chapters relating to the key aspects of marketing research, customer information and the main stages of the research process. Each chapter has the following features:

- **Opening vignettes**: each chapter starts with a mini case history related to how marketing research is used for 'real' in organisations such as MTV, Levi Strauss, London Underground and Eurostar.
- **Learning outcomes**: these set out the objectives for each chapter and provide a template of the outcomes that a student should be seeking from the chapter content.
- **Key words**: at the start of each chapter, the key words that will be used in the chapter are set out. These words also appear in the Glossary at the end of the book. Students find these key word lists particularly useful during their revision for exams.
- **Boxed features**: boxed features are used to show examples.
- **Researcher/client quotes**: quotes from real-life researchers and clients are used to reinforce some of the key messages in the text.
- **Discussion questions**: discussion questions allow students to check on their understanding at the end of each chapter and direct attention to the core concepts of the chapter.
- **Additional reading**: sources for additional reading that amplify the content are also listed at the end of each chapter.

In addition to these learning tools, the book also has:

- **Nine recent case histories**: these explain how marketing research has been used by leading organisations such as Skoda, AIR MILES, Carlsberg-Tetley and Allied Domecq. Each of these has been previously published in *Research* and is therefore very readable and practitioner oriented.

- **Nine articles on current issues in marketing research**: these articles relate to topics such as declining response rates, the growth in customer insight departments, researching difficult groups, etc. These have also appeared recently in *Research* and some take the form of discussions among key industry experts.

- **Internet sources of marketing information**: within Chapter 3 there is an extensive listing of Internet sources of information on customers and markets.

- **Glossary**: there is a glossary of all key terms at the end of the text, providing an ideal reference source.

Ancillary material

A lecturer's support package is available on the website **www.booksites.net/wilson**, consisting of:

- A *Lecturer's Manual* setting out suggested approaches and answers to the discussion questions, potential student projects and tasks to support the learning in each chapter, additional Internet sources, and suggestions as to how the case histories and research issues can be used for teaching purposes.

- **PowerPoint slides**: a comprehensive, fully integrated PowerPoint presentation for each chapter. This PowerPoint presentation gives the instructor the ability to completely integrate the classroom lecture with the chapter material.

Acknowledgements

My thanks go to the Market Research Society, and in particular to Ruth Martin and Bruce Love for their help and support during the writing of this book. My sincere appreciation also goes to Malcolm Rigg of BMRB, Heather Davison of The Chartered Institute of Marketing and the anonymous reviewers who generously provided suggestions for refining the finished work. I would also like to thank Justin Gutmann for his encouragement and support in the early stages of this project. Finally, a great hug of gratitude to my wife and children for their understanding and patience throughout this project (and, yes, you can now go back to using the computer for games!).

1

The role of marketing research and customer information in decision making

MTV – understanding the viewers

MTV, the largest international music television channel, integrates a variety of information from different sources and research techniques to develop an understanding of its viewers.

Like all television channels, MTV purchases the viewing figures for the industry. In the UK, these are produced by BARB (Broadcasters Audience Research Board, www.barb.co.uk) and provide audience statistics showing the number of viewers at different times of day and night. These figures are integrated and compared with information from a range of other marketing research techniques.

For example, the music channel conducts a fortnightly call-out tracker in the UK, Sweden, the Netherlands and Germany, whereby clips of music are played down the phone to a random sample of MTV's target market. Respondents are then asked questions as to the music's fit to the channel. They are also asked about 'burn' (a term relating to whether they have heard too much of a song).

Large-scale quantitative studies are also used to monitor the lifestyle of the target audience in terms of everything from political attitudes through to clubbing behaviour and even standards of personal hygiene. These lifestyle studies take place over six European countries, with 200 16–24 year olds being interviewed in each country. A yearly tracking study, called 'The Monitor' is also undertaken to check on perceptions and attitudes towards the channel.

These quantitative studies are augmented with group discussions and a variety of 'non-traditional' research: vox pops, event research, in-school and on-site interviewing, which might take place among participants of a programme at one of the studios. The channel is also utilising its website to test video clips and undertake surveys and focus groups online.

Information from all of these sources is integrated with data and knowledge held within MTV and its US parent Viacom (which also owns Nickelodeon in the US) to assist MTV defend its position as youth market leader and find new ways to make the most of its brand status.[1]

Learning outcomes

After reading this chapter you should:

- understand the need for an integrated approach to the collection, recording, analysing and interpreting of information on customers, competitors and markets;
- be able to define the terms marketing research and customer database;
- understand the need for marketing information and the marketing concept;
- be aware of some of the difficulties and limitations associated with the growing levels of information available;
- be able to describe the structure of the marketing research and database industry.

Key words

customer database	list brokers
data analysis services	marketing concept
data elements	marketing research
field agencies	profilers
full-service agencies	specialist service agencies
information explosion	triangulation

Introduction

This chapter introduces the concept of an integrated approach to marketing research and customer information/databases. It also places information and the marketing research industry in the context of marketing decision making.

An integrated approach

Traditionally information on customers, their behaviours, awareness levels and attitudes was only available to organisations through the utilisation of marketing research techniques where customers would be surveyed or observed. Organisations did hold limited information on their customers but what they held was frequently in the form of paper files, invoices and salespersons' reports. The material was generally difficult to access, patchy in its coverage and rarely up to date. Over the past ten years, significant improvements in computerisation, database management and data capture have meant that many organisations now hold significant amounts of data on their customers. For example, a grocery store operating a loyalty card scheme will have details on each cardholder relating to:

- their home address;
- the frequency with which they visit the store;
- the days and times they visit the store;
- the value of their weekly grocery shopping;
- the range of products purchased;
- the size of packages purchased;
- the frequency with which they use promotional coupons;
- the consistency with which they purchase specific brands;
- the extent to which they trial new products;
- the extent to which purchasing behaviour is influenced by the timing of advertising campaigns.

In addition, the range of products may indicate whether they live alone, have a family, have pets, are vegetarian or tend to eat ready-prepared meals.

The availability of such information has changed the role and nature of marketing research in many organisations. Nowadays research may focus more on awareness and attitudes rather than behaviour, or may focus more on potential rather than existing customers. Customer databases may also be used to assist in identifying potential respondents or topics for research. In addition, customers who are known to the organisation and have a specific relationship with them may be more willing to take part in research on a regular basis. Finally, budgets that were used solely for marketing research may now be split between the managing of a database and marketing research.

These interrelationships between customer databases and marketing research mean that many organisations are starting to adopt an integrated approach to the collection, recording, analysing and interpreting of information on customers, competitors and markets. However, care must be taken to ensure that marketing research is not involved in collecting personal data that will be used in selling or marketing activities directed at the individuals who have participated in a research survey. Marketing research is dependent on respondents voluntarily providing information on their behaviours and attitudes. Respondents may not provide such information if they think the information that they provide is likely to be misused for purposes other than research. Marketing researchers must therefore understand their professional duty of providing integrated information to marketing decision makers while protecting the rights of their main information resource, the respondent.

Marketing research: a definition

In defining marketing research, it is important to consider the key characteristics of the discipline:

- Marketing research provides commercial and non-commercial organisations with **information to aid marketing decision making.** The information will generally be externally focused, concentrating on customers, markets and competitors, although it may also report on issues relating to other stakeholders (e.g. employees and shareholders).
- Marketing research involves the **collection of information** using a wide range of sources and techniques. Information may be acquired from published sources, observing behaviours or through direct communication with the people being researched.
- Marketing research involves the **analysis of information.** Obtaining information is different from achieving understanding. Information needs to be analysed, developed and applied if it is to be actionable and relevant to the marketing decisions that need to be taken.
- Marketing research involves the **communication and dissemination of information.** The effective presentation of information transfers understanding of its content and implications to a wider audience of relevant decision makers and interested parties.

Taking these characteristics together, marketing research can be defined as:

> The collection, analysis and communication of information undertaken to assist decision making in marketing.

The customer database: a definition

The customer database can be defined as:

> A manual or computerised source of data relevant to marketing decision making about an organisation's customers.

This definition distinguishes the customer database from a computerised accounting or invoicing system as the data about customers has to be **relevant to marketing decision making.** The data in the customer database may be collected from many parts of the organisation and may be augmented by data from outside. Data is the basic raw material from which information and ultimately understanding are derived. A database consists of a store of data elements (see Table 1.1) that mean little independently but when combined provide information on a customer or group of customers. In other words, information is derived from the relationship between data

Table 1.1 Typical data elements held on retail and business consumers

Typical retail consumer data elements	Typical business data elements
Customer identification number/loyalty card number	Company number
Name	Industry type
Gender	Parent company
Postal address/post code	Number of employees
Telephone/e-mail	Postal address/postcode
Date of birth	Telephone/Fax/e-mail
Segmentation by lifestyle/demographic code	Credit limit
Relationship to other customers (i.e. same household)	Procurement manager
Date of first transaction	Turnover
Purchase history, including products purchased, date purchased, price paid, method of payment, promotional coupons used	Sales contact
	Purchase history, including products purchased, date purchased, price paid, method of payment
Mailings received	
Response to mailings/last promotion	

elements. For example, if an organisation wishes to know how long a particular customer has had a relationship with it, then the data elements associated with the current date and the customer's first transaction date have to be combined to calculate the relationship length.

The transaction record, which often identifies the item purchased, its value, customer name, address and postcode, is the building block for many databases. This may be supplemented with data customers provide directly, such as data on a warranty card, and by secondary data purchased from third parties. Several companies, such as CACI (www. CACI.co.uk) and Experian (www.experianintact.com), sell geodemographic profiling data that can be related to small geographic areas such as postcodes. Such data shows the profile of people within an area and is typically used for location planning and target marketing. Each postcode in the country is allocated a specific geodemographic coding which identifies the typical lifestyle of people living in that postal code area. For example in postcodes of:

ACORN Type 28 – *You are more likely to find the classic 'Mum, Dad and two children' household in these neighbourhoods than anywhere else in Britain. These are very stable, middle class areas with low levels of population mobility. They are found all over Britain, particularly in the suburbs of the major conurbations.*

ACORN Type 29 – *These are areas of mixed housing, but with a large elderly population. People are generally comfortably off, though there are some highly affluent people. They are located all over Britain, though the highest concentrations are in Sussex and Surrey.*

Researcher quote: *You can check out the ACORN profile for any postcode in the UK by going to www.upmystreet.com and typing in the postcode.*

In addition to physical transactions, databases can be created from virtual transactions. Web-based retailers and suppliers have a two-way electronic link with their customer. This is often done through the use of **cookies**, which are text files placed on a user's computer by the web retailer in order to identify the user when he or she next visits the website. They can record a customer's actions as they move through a website, noting not only the purchases but also the areas that the customer has browsed. This may indicate what the customer may buy on the next visit if the correct promotional offer is made. And unlike traditional retailers, an online retailer can alter the website in real time to test particular offers with specific potential customers.

Customer databases are generally developed for four main reasons:

1 **Personalisation of marketing communications:** to allow personalisation of direct marketing activity, with postal, telecommunication or electronic correspondence being addressed specifically to the individual customer. The offers being promoted can also be targeted at the specific needs of the individual. For example, a bank may be able to send out specific information on their student account offerings to the 16–18-year-old market segment.

2 **Improved customer service:** when a customer seeks service from a branch office or a call centre, the organisation is better able to provide that service if details about the past relationship/service history with the customer are known. For example, Amazon's book-selling website makes book suggestions to customers based on their previous purchases.

3 **Improved understanding of customer behaviour:** the organisation can better understand customer profiles for segmentation purposes and the development of new product/service offerings. For example, Sea France was able to categorise its customers into eight segments by analysing customer postcode data with variables such as ticket type, distance from the port, type of vehicle and frequency of travel. This was cross-tabulated with ticket values, allowing Sea France to determine which segments were of most value.

4 **Assessing the effectiveness of the organisation's marketing and service activities:** the organisation can monitor its own performance by observing the behaviour of its customers. For example, a supermarket may be able to check the effectiveness of different promotional offers by tracking the purchases made by specific target segments.

Although customer databases can fulfil these functions, it should be stressed that they tend to hold information only on existing and past customers; information on potential customers is generally incomplete or in some cases non-existent. This may limit their usefulness in providing a comprehensive view of market characteristics.

The marketing concept and the need for marketing information

The need for marketing information stems from the adoption of the marketing concept. Although there are many definitions of marketing, the basic concept of marketing is that the whole of the organisation should be driven by a constant concern for its customers, without whose business the organisation simply would not exist. In other words, the marketing concept requires an organisation to define who the customers or potential customers are, focus on their particular needs, then co-ordinate all of the activities that will affect customers, in order that the organisation achieves its financial and strategic objectives through the creation of satisfied customers.

> **The marketing concept:** The whole of the organisation should be driven by a goal of serving and satisfying customers in a manner which enables the organisation's financial and strategic objectives to be achieved.

The ethos of satisfying customers has to be spread throughout the whole organisation and not limited only to those who are in immediate or direct contact with the customer. The more the marketing concept can be spread through an organisation, the better will be the achievement of the organisation's commercial, charitable, political or social objectives.

This book uses the term customer in its widest sense, as some organisations may not sell products or services to consumers or companies but may still have similar types of stakeholder group that the organisation is seeking to satisfy. For example, charities may view their customers as being both the recipients of the charitable support and the donors. Political parties may view the electorate or their supporters as their customers. Even the prison service has stakeholders that may be classed as customers and these could be seen as being either the prisoners within the walls of the prisons or the general population that lives outside.

Whatever type of organisation, information is critical if the correct products, services and offerings are to be provided to the customers. In small organisations such as the village shop, the owner may personally know (a) the customer's buying habits and attitudes, (b) the competitors' activities and (c) the changes occurring in the local market (e.g. new houses being built). However, as an organisation becomes larger, the amount of direct contact the decision maker has with the customer becomes significantly less. As a result, management take decisions as to how best to serve their customers based on information that is gathered from a variety of sources rather than from personal experience.

In particular, effective marketing decisions are reliant on information in three main areas:

1 **Information on customers:** the marketing concept can only be realistically implemented when adequate information about customers is available. To find out what satisfies customers, marketers must identify who customers are, their characteristics and the main influences on what, where, when, and how they buy or use

a product or service. By gaining a better understanding of the factors that affect customer behaviour, marketers are in a better position to predict how customers will respond to an organisation's marketing activity.

2 **Information on other organisations:** if a commercial organisation wishes to maintain some form of advantage over competitors, it is essential that information is gathered on the actions of competitors. Comparison of performance relative to competitors helps managers recognise strengths and weaknesses in their own marketing strategies. Even in non-commercial organisations, gathering information on other charities, political parties or government departments can produce new ideas and practices that will allow the organisation to better serve its own customers.

3 **Information on the marketing environment:** the environment consists of a large number of variables, outside the control of an organisation, which have an influence on the marketing activities of the organisation. These variables, such as government policy, the economy, technological developments, changes in legislation and changes in the demographics of the population, have to be monitored continuously if an organisation is to keep pace with changing customer and market requirements.

Examples of changes in demographics within Europe

- A continuing decline in children of school age, a threat to producers of teenage magazines, confectionery, soft drinks, etc.
- An increasing proportion of older people (over 75), influencing the demand for retirement homes, hearing aids and special holidays.
- An increasing proportion of single-adult households, influencing the demand for smaller accommodation and food packaged in smaller portions.
- An increasing proportion of working women and the resultant demand for convenience foods, microwaves and child daycare centres.

All of the above information types have to be collated and their implications for an organisation's marketing activities have to be assessed. Although uncertainty is inherent in decision making, the gathering and interpretation of information can make the process more objective and systematic. Successful managers take an orderly and logical approach to gathering information; they seek facts and undertake new marketing approaches on a systematic basis rather than simply through a procedure of trial and error.

The key roles and application of marketing information

Information for marketing may have descriptive, comparative, diagnostic or predictive roles. Its **descriptive role** answers the 'What', 'Where' and 'When' questions that marketing managers may have, such as:

- **What, where** and **when** are customers buying?
- **What** level of donation is made to specific charities?

- **What** knowledge do customers have of a brand or range of products?
- **What** attitudes do customers have towards specific brands or products?
- **What** advertising and marketing communications have customers seen or been exposed to?

Its **comparative role** answers the 'How' questions used for performance measurement, such as:

- **How** did this service performance differ from previous experiences?
- **How** does our product compare with the competitors?
- **How** does this political party's policies compare with those of another party?

Information's **diagnostic role** answers the 'Why' questions and provides explanations:

- **Why** do customers believe that advertisement?
- **Why** do customers buy this product rather than one of the alternatives?
- **Why** are prisoners dissatisfied with the conditions?

The **predictive role** answers the '**What would happen?**' type of questions and helps to determine future trends:

- **What would happen** if the competitors reduced their prices?
- **What would happen** if this new product was launched?
- **What would happen** if government expenditure in this area was to reduce?

These descriptive, comparative, diagnostic and predictive roles result in information that addresses the key decision areas of an organisation's strategic and tactical marketing activities. In developing a strategy, the management team need to address marketing decisions such as:

- **The area of the market on which to focus**: specifically, what range of products or services should be produced and delivered? Which market segments should be targeted? What methods of delivery are required to reach these target segments? Information will assist organisations in answering these questions and determining the direction of their core business activities and their core customer segments. For example, an organisation such as Tesco may need to determine which European markets to enter or whether it should move into the selling of other non-grocery products such as cars or furniture.

- **The method of differentiation**: how will the organisation compete with other organisations? What will differentiate its offering from those of other organisations? How can the organisation better serve the needs of the target market? To answer these questions, marketers need to know which product or service benefits create most value for the potential customer. For example, when purchasing a car, is the target segment more interested in speed, comfort, economy or brand name? This may help determine the brand values that an organisation should adopt. These may go well beyond the physical features of the product; for example, the Virgin Airline brand values are associated with fun, innovation and quality service. Such brand values are developed as a result of researching the views of the target market and are refined or modified based on ongoing information on customer attitudes and competitor activities.

- **The establishment of objectives**: information is critical in determining the objectives for a product, a brand or for an organisation's marketing activities. Objectives may relate to market share, profit, revenue growth, awareness, levels of customer satisfaction or level of donations (for a charity). This is dependent on having information regarding the organisation's performance currently as well as answers to predictive-type questions about what is likely to happen in the market.

- **The development of the marketing programme**: at a tactical level, marketing information can provide detailed information to assist with decisions relating to:
  - product or service features;
  - packaging;
  - distribution channels;
  - ordering and delivery procedures;
  - pricing and discounting policies;
  - marketing communication approaches;
  - communication messages and media;
  - brand image and logo to be associated with the brand;
  - service support and complaint handling procedures;
  - design and location of retail or service outlets.

- **Implementation and the monitoring of performance**: marketing information is needed to determine whether elements of the marketing programme are meeting their objectives. Performance measurement is dependent on specific objectives having been set with marketing information providing the measures against these objectives. Are market share or sales targets being achieved? If not, why not? Should elements of the marketing programme be changed or continued? A company such as Ford will need to monitor which models of car are selling, as well as the optional extras that customers are buying, to determine how a model's specification will need to change in the future.

The information explosion

In the past, marketing managers often had difficulties in gathering sufficient information to make sound marketing decisions. Today's problems relate more to the filtering of relevant data from the explosion of information available in a wide range of formats from a wide range of sources. These sources may be internal to the organisation, coming from customer databases, performance reports and electronic barcode scanning devices, or they may be from the Internet or marketing research sources. More information does not always mean better decision making. It is important that the levels of information presented to the decision maker are kept to a manageable scale. Therefore marketing managers need to be specific about what information they need as well as the accuracy and reliability of the information they require. Decision makers need to be systematic in their use of information, if they are to fully understand its meaning and avoid going through the same information more than once.

> **Researcher quote:** *The main task isn't so much the finding of information; it is more to do with ensuring that the information is relevant and of a scale and format that is manageable.*

This also means that suppliers of information, whether marketing researchers or database managers, must develop a willingness to accommodate available information from each other. It has to be recognised that data obtained from several sources are likely to provide a more reliable guide for marketing decision making than data drawn from a single source. This is the concept of **triangulation**, where different sources of data are used to counterbalance the weaknesses in some sources with the strengths of others. The term triangulation is borrowed from the disciplines of navigation and surveying, where a minimum of three reference points are taken to check an object's location. As such, it is important that marketing managers are using information in an integrated manner rather than the piecemeal approach of databases separate from competitor intelligence separate from marketing research. This may mean that information professionals such as marketing researchers need to develop skills in integrating information from marketing research surveys with information from customer databases and Internet resources if they are to prove invaluable to the marketing decision maker. Such integration is more than simply pulling information together; it is also about deciding what information is worth accessing, what information should be rejected and what information should be stored.

The limitations of information

Information should not be seen as the ultimate panacea for poor marketing decision making. Decisions still have to be taken based on the judgement of the managers concerned. However, better informed judgement should result in better decisions. Wrong decisions may still be made but the incidence of these should reduce with the provision of relevant marketing research and customer information. Sometimes, research results may be ignored, particularly where the decision maker has an over-riding belief in the product or where a decision maker's reputation will suffer as a result of abandoning a new product development project or by taking a risk and launching. Occasionally the decision makers who ignore the research will be proved correct – the Dyson bagless vacuum cleaner and the Sony Walkman are examples of products that were launched contrary to marketing research recommendations. If the product concept is so unique and different from existing products, consumers and certain research approaches may provide misleading feedback. Therefore managers need to make judgements not only about the decisions that are to be taken but also with regard to the reliability of the information available.

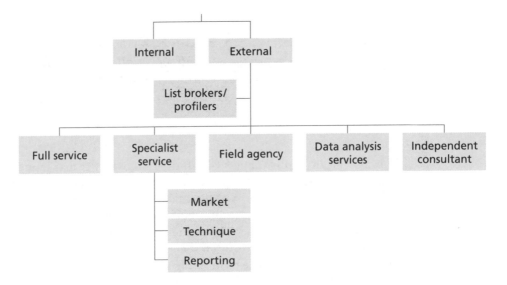

Figure 1.1 Information providers

The marketing research and database industry

Marketing research and customer database information can either be produced by employees internal to an organisation or can be outsourced from an external supplier. The internal supplier for marketing research is the marketing researcher or marketing research department. Such departments tend to be found only in larger organisations where there is a regular and possibly constant need for marketing research. Their incidence also tends to be greater in large organisations involved in consumer products or services rather than business-to-business products. Within some organisations (e.g. Britvic Soft Drinks, Ford, Van den Bergh, GuinnessUDV, Walker Snacks), internal marketing researchers have been renamed and are now called customer insight managers. This reflects a change from managers who simply managed the marketing research process to the creation of managers who manage information on an integrated basis from a variety of information sources. These managers may also be responsible for commissioning external suppliers to undertake marketing research or supply information. The external suppliers can be categorised as shown in Figure 1.1.

List brokers/profilers

List compilers and brokers capture lists of individuals and organisations and then sell them to companies that wish to augment their own customer databases and mailing lists. They capture names and other details from a wide range of sources, including:

- the names of shareholders and directors of public companies from public records;
- the names of subscribers to magazines;
- the names of people who replied to special promotions, direct mailings or competitions;

- the names of people replying to lifestyle questionnaires;
- warranty records for electrical products;
- the names of voters from the electoral role;
- a country's census records;
- data on bad debt from public records or by sharing data between credit providers.

Profilers are different from list brokers, inasmuch as their work will involve them directly interacting with an organisation's database, whereas a list broker will tend to simply sell an off-the shelf data file. Profilers such as CACI (www.CACI.co.uk) gather demographic and lifestyle information from many millions of individual consumers, which enables them to classify every neighbourhood in Great Britain into one of 17 groups and 54 subgroups. They then take this base information and combine it with the postal address information on an organisation's database to segment existing customers by factors such as lifestyle and income. This allows organisations to better target their offerings to existing customers. Profilers will also be able to identify additional prospective customers whose characteristics match those of an organisation's existing customers.

Full-service agencies

External suppliers of marketing research services can be classified as being full-service agencies or specialist service agencies. Full-service agencies offer the full range of marketing research services and techniques. They will be able to offer the entire range of qualitative and quantitative research approaches as well as be capable of undertaking every stage of the research, from research design through to analysis and report writing. Full-service agencies tend to be the larger research companies such as Taylor Nelson Sofres (www.tnsofres.com), BMRB (www.bmrb.co.uk), Ipsos-RSL (www.ipsos-rsl.com) and NOP (www.nopworld.com).

Specialist service agencies

These agencies do not offer a full range of services but tend to specialise in certain types of research. For example, a specialist agency may only do research in a specific market sector such as the automotive sector or children's products, or a geographic region such as the Middle East. Alternatively, the agency may be a specialist in terms of the research techniques and may only do qualitative research or telephone research. Some agencies may specialise in particular types of reporting approach. For example, certain agencies may only focus on syndicated reporting services, where, rather than carrying out a unique research project for a specific client, they research a market or product area and sell the resulting reports or data to a number of subscribing organisations. In some ways, these syndicated research suppliers are like publishers selling books as they sell the same report or data to a number of organisations. Examples of these agencies include Datamonitor (www.datamonitor.com), Key Note (www.keynote.co.uk) and Mintel (www.mintel.co.uk). Syndicated research is a major source of retail sales information and media consumption, such as television viewing and press readership.

Field agencies

As the name suggests, these agencies' primary activity is the field interviewing process, focusing on the collection of data through personal interviewers, telephone interviewers or postal surveys. Questionnaire and sample design as well as the analysis will therefore need to be undertaken by the client organisation itself or by another subcontractor.

Data analysis services

Small companies sometimes known as 'tab shops' (because they provide tabulations of data) provide coding and data analysis services. Their services include the coding of completed questionnaires, inputting the data from questionnaires into a computer and the provision of sophisticated data analysis using advanced statistical techniques. Within this grouping of organisations there are also individuals or small companies that transcribe tape recordings of qualitative research depth interviews or group discussions.

Independent consultants

There are a large number of independent consultants in the marketing research and customer information sector who undertake small surveys, particularly in business-to-business markets, manage individual parts of the marketing research process or advise on information collection, storage or retrieval.

The professional bodies and associations in the marketing research industry

There are a number of international and national associations and professional bodies representing the interests of marketing researchers and the marketing research industry.

The largest bodies are the Market Research Society (MRS) and ESOMAR. The MRS (www.mrs.org.uk) is based in the UK and has over 8,000 members in more than 50 countries. It is the world's largest international membership organisation for professional researchers and others engaged or interested in market, social and opinion research. It has a diverse membership of individual researchers within agencies, independent consultancies, client-side organisations and the academic community, and from all levels of seniority and job functions. All members of the Society agree to comply with the MRS Code of Conduct, which ensures that marketing research is undertaken in a professional and ethical manner. The MRS also offers various training programmes and is the official awarding body in the UK for vocational qualifications in marketing research. ESOMAR (www.esomar.nl) was founded in 1948 as the European Society for Opinion and Marketing Research. Its membership now reflects a more global positioning as it unites over 4,000 members (users and providers of research in 100 countries). Other associations and professional bodies are listed in Table 1.2.

Table 1.2 Professional bodies and associations representing marketing research

Name	Representing	Country	Website
The Market Research Society	Marketing research professionals	International (UK based)	www.mrs.org.uk
Chartered Institute of Marketing	Marketing professionals	International (UK based)	www.cim.co.uk
ESOMAR	Marketing research professionals	International (Netherlands based)	www.esomar.nl
AEMRI	European marketing research institutes	Europe (UK based)	www.aemri.org
EFAMRO	European marketing research associations	Europe (UK based)	www.efamro.org
VMÖ	Marketing research professionals	Austria	www.vmoe.at
FEBELMAR	Marketing research bureaux	Belgium	www.febelmar.be
Danish Marketing Association – The Market Research Club	Marketing research professionals	Denmark	www.d-m-f.dk
FMD	Marketing research institutes	Denmark	www.fmd.dk
FAMRA	Marketing research institutes	Finland	www.smtl.fi
The Finnish Marketing Federation	Marketing research professionals	Finland	www.mark.fi
ADETEM	Marketing research professionals	France	www.adetem.org
ADM	Marketing research agencies	Germany	www.adm-ev.de
BVM	Marketing research professionals	Germany	www.bvm.org
AGMORC	Marketing research agencies and professionals	Greece	www.sedea.gr
AIMRO	Marketing research agencies	Ireland	
Markt Onderzoek Associatie	Marketing research professionals	Netherlands	www.marktonderzoekassociatie.nl
Norwegian Marketing Research Association	Marketing research professionals	Norway	www.nmf-org.no
FSM	Marketing research institutes	Sweden	www.fsm.a.se
SMUF	Buyers of marketing research	Sweden	www.smuf.com
Swedish Market Research Society	Marketing research professionals	Sweden	
ASC	Survey computing professionals	UK	www.asc.org.uk
AQR	Qualitative research professionals	UK	www.aqrp.co.uk
AURA	Users of marketing research agencies	UK	www.aura.org.uk
BMRA	Marketing research agencies	UK	www.bmra.org.uk

Maintaining the distinction between marketing research and direct marketing

Marketing research is dependent on the willing co-operation of both the public and organisations to provide information of value to marketing decision makers. Such co-operation is likely to be prejudiced by suspicion about the purpose of research projects and concerns about the validity of the guarantees of confidentiality which are given to respondents. As highlighted in the codes of conduct of both the MRS and ESOMAR, as well as the 1995 European Union Directive on the Protection of Personal Data, information collected for marketing research purposes cannot be used for developing marketing databases that will be used for direct marketing or direct sales approaches. The principle of transparency is the key consideration in all dealings with respondents. It must be made clear to respondents that all personal data collected during a research project will be treated confidentially for genuine marketing research purposes and that no attempt will be made to sell something to the respondent as a result of their having taken part in the research. Also, direct marketing activity should not imply to the customer that it is some form of marketing research – any questionnaires or other data collection methods used for direct marketing should make clear at the time of collection that the information provided may be used for sales or sales promotion purposes. As such, the use of questionnaires as part of a database-building exercise for direct marketing purposes cannot be described as marketing research and should not be combined in the same data collection exercise. Where the results of a marketing research project are to be used to enrich and extend the information held on a marketing database, then personal data is not allowed to be used in a respondent-identifiable basis by the various professional codes of conduct. This means that research data being added to a database should not be in the form of personal data but instead should be anonymous and partly-aggregated data. For example, consumer profiles built up from aggregated research data may be used to categorise all consumers in a database, whereas personal information relating to individual respondents should not be used.

Therefore the integration perspective upon which this book is based refers to the marketing researchers managing the information outputs coming from sources such as customer databases rather than managing the inputs to such databases or managing the databases for other (non-marketing-research) purposes.

Summary

The marketing concept promotes the idea that the whole of the organisation should be driven by the goal of serving and satisfying customers in a manner which enables the organisation's financial and strategic objectives to be achieved. It is obvious that marketing decision makers require the best customer, competitor and market information available when deciding on future courses of action for their products and organisations. As such, the source of the information is less important than the quality of information. Marketing researchers need to adapt to these changing circumstances and be willing to integrate information from a range of sources, such as customer databases and the Internet, as well as from marketing research itself, in order to develop better knowledge of market conditions.

The definition of marketing research in this book reinforces this need by stating that marketing research is the collection, analysis and communication of information undertaken to assist decision making in marketing. The type of information is not specified apart from the fact that it should assist decision making in marketing. Therefore customer databases should be seen as an appropriate source of information to be included within the remit of marketing researchers. Such information can be used to assist decision making in descriptive, comparative, diagnostic and predictive roles. However, information does not in itself make decisions; it simply enables better-informed decision making to take place. Managers still need to use judgement and intuition when assessing information, and with the growth in information sources as a result of computerisation and the Internet, managers need more guidance and help in selecting the most appropriate information to access and use. Guidance of this type must take account of the manner in which the information was collected and analysed. The marketing research industry, involving many different types of information supplier, should be best qualified to do this.

Discussion questions

1   Marketing research has traditionally been associated with consumer goods. Today an increasing number of non-profit organisations (charities, government departments) are using marketing research. Why do you think this is the case?

2   Explain the importance of marketing research to the implementation of the marketing concept.

3   Using the upmystreet.com website, enter a postcode (it may be your own) and look at the detailed ACORN profile for that postcode. Report on the contents of the profile in class.

4   Consider a frequent flyer programme for an airline. What type of information is such a programme likely to hold on each of its members?

5   Why do organisations maintain customer databases?

6   Considering the demographic changes mentioned on page 8. What are the likely implications of these changes for a manufacturer of tinned baked beans?

7   Explain the meaning of each of the following information roles: descriptive, comparative, diagnostic and predictive.

8   What is meant by the term information explosion and what are its implications?

9   When Sony first undertook research into the potential for the Walkman, the results suggested that the product would be a failure. Why do you think that was?

10   Why are marketing research departments in many large organisations changing their names to customer insight departments? To justify this change, what activities should the renamed department be involved in?

Additional reading

Boddy, C. (2001) Perceived reasons for the success of the UK market research industry. *International Journal of Market Research*, **43**(1), pp. 29–41.

Culkin, N., Smith, D. and Fletcher, J. (1999) Meeting the information needs of marketing in the twenty-first century. *Marketing Intelligence and Planning*, **17**(1), pp. 6–12.

Leventhal, B. (1997) An approach to fusing market research with database marketing. *Journal of the Market Research Society*, **39**(4), pp. 545–58.

Smith, D. and Culkin, N. (2001) Making sense of information: a new role for the marketing researcher? *Marketing Intelligence and Planning*, **19**(4), pp. 263–72.

Smith, D.V.L. and Fletcher, J.H. (2001) *Inside Information: Making Sense of Marketing Data*. John Wiley, Chichester.

Reference

[1] Adapted from Etienne, S. (1999) I want my MTV, *Research*, 397, June, and published with the permission of The Market Research Society.

2
The marketing research process

Eurostar – staying on the rails

When Eurostar started in 1994, the ability to get from London to Paris by train in three hours, and to Brussels even faster, was an attractive selling point. Now the novelty's worn off and competition has increased with the spread of low-cost airlines.

Faced with these commercial pressures, Eurostar is keen to target business travellers. The business sector pushes up train occupancy, but it's a market that was out of reach when the service first began with only four trains a day. Now the company runs approximately 20 trains a day to Paris and 10 to Brussels, and can regard itself as a serious contender for corporate travel budgets. Another incentive is that business travellers will increase financial yield per train, as they are known to pay a premium price for a quality transport service. Eurostar's research requirement was to identify the needs of business travellers and examine how these differed from the needs of leisure travellers. An international qualitative marketing research study was undertaken involving more than 30 group discussions. The responses from the three countries (Belgium, France and the UK) were essentially similar: the business traveller wanted to eliminate wasted time and travel in an environment in which they could either work or relax.

As a direct result of the research, Eurostar embarked on a programme of enhancements for business travellers, such as a fast track through the terminal, faster access to taxis and speeding up of ticket exchange procedures. These actions are only part of a much larger programme of work to speed up the handling of business travellers and improve the quality of the travelling environment.[1]

Learning outcomes

After reading this chapter you should:

- understand the key steps in the marketing research process;
- be aware of the importance of the research brief and its contents;
- understand the process involved and the criteria used in selecting marketing research agencies;
- be aware of the importance of the research proposal and its contents;
- appreciate the broad types of research design;
- understand the need for an ethical and professional approach towards marketing research;
- be aware of relevant data protection legislation and professional codes of conduct.

Key words

'beauty parades'	marketing research process
causal research	observation
critical path method	primary data
cross-sectional research	professional codes of conduct
data protection legislation	programme evaluation and review technique (PERT)
descriptive research	qualitative research
experimental research	quantitative research
exploratory research	research brief
GANTT chart	research proposal
longitudinal research	secondary data

Introduction

This chapter is designed to introduce you to the key steps involved in undertaking a marketing research project. These steps represent the **marketing research process**, the sequence of activities and events that require to be addressed if a marketing research project is to provide information that is valuable to the marketing decision maker. This process will also provide the basic framework for the structure of the remainder of the book, with individual chapters examining some specific aspect of the process. The marketing research process is shown in Figure 2.1.

Stage 1: identification of problems and opportunities

The marketing environment is constantly changing and therefore marketing managers have to address new issues which may create opportunities or problems for their organisations. For example, the development of a new product may offer potential

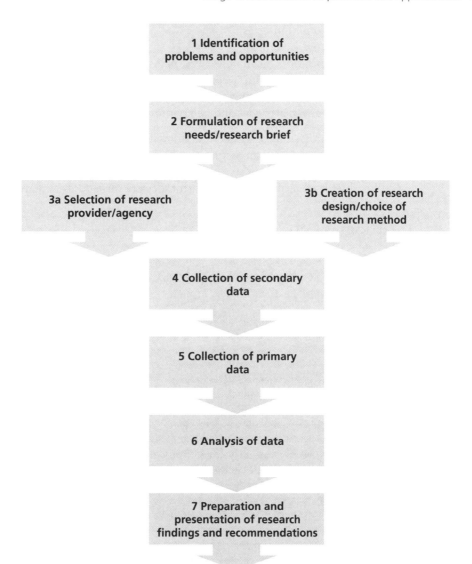

Figure 2.1 The marketing research process

opportunities to develop business or may simply result in major costs in terms of finance and corporate reputation. A drop in sales may mean that the product range is out of date and needing an expensive revamp, or it may have come about as a result of short-term price-cutting by the competition. Issues such as these raise questions that need to be answered before decisions can be made. Marketing research may provide the answers to some of these questions.

The precise definition of the problem aids in understanding the information that will be needed and therefore helps in identifying the research objectives. The organisation should assess the nature or 'symptoms' of the issue that it is currently facing. These may stem from what is known about:

- market conditions;
- competitors' actions;
- the organisation's own objectives, plans and capabilities;
- previous marketing initiatives and their effectiveness;
- the nature of the existing and new products or services;
- the awareness, attitudes and behaviour of customers.

It is critical that this assessment is done in as objective a manner as possible and is based on fact rather than assumption and hearsay. Any gaps in the information may also indicate areas where research is needed. The example of Thomas Cook (see box) illustrates how problems and opportunities are turned into research needs.

Thomas Cook

Thomas Cook is a large and well-known international travel company, operating travel agencies, charter airlines and foreign currency bureaux. Smaller and less well known is its profitable commercial foreign exchange business, which, as the name suggests, provides foreign currency payment services for businesses.

The problem/opportunity

The commercial foreign exchange business (CFX) was charged with significantly increasing the size of its share of the market. A quick look at its existing customer profile soon revealed that a small number of top customers accounted for a disproportionately large amount of its total revenue. As it could not sell more to these customers, it recognised that the most effective way to significantly increase revenue was to get more top customers. But to do this effectively it needed to improve its sales prospecting.

The questions

Before Thomas Cook could develop a more effective sales strategy it needed marketing research to answer questions such as:

- What types of company offer the greatest potential?
- How do we target these companies?
- What approaches should we use?
- What messages should we communicate?
- What pricing offers should we employ to win their business?[2]

It is arguably better to make plans and take decisions based on data gathered from objective marketing research rather than based on subjective feelings, 'hunches' and assumptions. There are no guarantees that decisions based on marketing research will always be correct and result in success, but there is a higher likelihood of success if research is used to verify or discount these feelings, 'hunches' and assumptions.

Stage 2: formulation of research needs/research brief

In formulating the specific research needs of a project, it is important to consult all of the managers and departments that will be involved in making and implementing the decisions that will flow from the research results. Their input at this early stage will reduce the likelihood of individuals or departments complaining at the end of the project that the wrong questions have been asked or that the research is worthless, as it simply replicates information already held within the organisation.

This can be managed by establishing a small project team which represents all of the interested parties within the organisation (for example, it may include representatives from marketing, operations, research and development, distribution, sales, corporate strategy, etc.). Alternatively, where the number of interested parties is large, it is generally more manageable to have a small core team who have discussions and meetings with all of the interested parties, and who then filter the information from these meetings and determine the specific research requirements. It may be necessary to appoint a senior manager as sponsor of the team in order to ensure full co-operation from the various departments.

This team would also be responsible for determining what information already exists within the organisation. It often seems easier and more interesting to develop new information than to delve through old reports and data files. However, if relevant data does exist it can reduce the cost and time involved in undertaking the research and it may also help to formulate the specific information targets and the most appropriate respondents for the research.

The research brief

The project team should also develop a written research brief setting out the organisation's requirements. This will provide the specification against which the researchers will design the research project. A written brief in comparison with a verbal briefing of the researchers allows the specifics of the briefing to be circulated and verified by all of those involved in or affected by the specific area of decision making. In particular, it enables all of the interested parties within the organisation to:

1 verify that the need for the research is genuine and is not simply:
   - a way of using up this year's marketing research budget, in order to guarantee the same level of funding on marketing research next year;
   - supporting a decision that has already been made as a way of reassuring the management team that they have made the correct decision;
   - a way of stalling a decision that management do not wish to make;
   - reiterating information that already exists within the organisation.
2 ensure that the information obtained will be relevant and of sufficient scope for the decisions that need to be taken;
3 ensure that the time scales and reporting procedures are compatible with the internal decision-making processes and timings.

Unfortunately, given the natural desire of managers to move things forward and the short time frame that is often set aside for marketing research, the development of

Table 2.1 Contents of the research brief

The research brief

1 Background
  • the organisation, its products and its markets
2 Project rationale
  • origin and development of research need
  • decision areas to be addressed by research
3 Objectives
  • definition of discrete areas of problem and opportunity that have to be explored
4 Outline of possible method
5 Reporting and presentational requirements
6 Timing

the brief is often not given proper attention. The tendency to short circuit the formulation of the research needs is unfortunate, as it can be very costly. A considerable amount of time, money and effort can be wasted in pursuit of the wrong research questions.

> **Researcher quote:** *I regularly experience presentations of research findings at the end of a project where members of the client organisation, who were not involved in the original briefing, ask why certain research questions were or were not asked. Surely this should have been sorted out by the organisation at the start of the project!*

The contents of the research brief are therefore very important; the typical structure for such a brief is set out in Table 2.1.

Considering each of the sections of the brief, the following guidelines should be followed:

1 Background: this section should set out a brief explanation of what is happening within the organisation, the nature of its products or services as well as current market trends. This will enable the researchers to understand the context within which the problem or opportunity and the research need exists. It will also assist in the design of the research method and may actually speed up the research process, as less time is spent researching information that is already known. To augment the information in this section, the organisation may provide the researcher with copies of annual reports, brochures, previous research studies, etc.

2 Project rationale: this section sets out the reasons for the research being required. What areas of decision will be addressed by the research and what are the implications of these decisions to the organisation? This will enable the researchers to identify the priorities and also to develop recommendations at the end of the research project which will directly assist the organisation's decision making.

3 **Objectives**: the objectives set out the precise information needed to assist marketing management with the problem or opportunity. They should be clear and unambiguous, leaving little doubt as to what is required. Some organisations may also list the specific information targets under each objective to ensure that there is no misunderstanding. For example, the following objective from a study for computer printers, considers attitudes towards the operation of a printer and uses information targets such as 'speed of printing' to highlight the specific areas of attitude to be examined.

> To examine customer attitudes towards the operation of the new computer printer in terms of:
>
> * speed of printing
> * quality of printing
> * use of the printer control panel
> * procedures for loading paper
> * procedures for installing print cartridges

In developing the objectives, it is critical that the brief includes only those objectives that relate to what the organisation 'needs' to know rather than to information areas that would be 'nice to know'. In other words, the findings from the research should be 'actionable' and provide decision-making information rather than simply being 'interesting'.

4 **Outline of possible method**: at this stage in the research process, this section should only give a broad indication of the approach to be undertaken in the research. The researcher, once briefed, should be allowed to use his or her experience to develop the most appropriate research design. Therefore, this section of the brief should simply highlight the parameters within which the design can take place. It should indicate the types of respondents or market segments to be included in the research. It should also indicate whether the study should be large scale and statistically significant with a large amount of quantitative information or whether it should provide more detailed qualitative information on a much smaller scale. Ultimately the organisation will need to consider the trade-offs that are involved – for example, the trade-off between costs or time and the scale of the research. The larger the project, the more expensive and time consuming it will be.

5 **Reporting and presentational requirements**: this section of the brief sets out the organisation's requirements in terms of the nature of the written documents required from the researchers such as the research proposal, any interim reports produced during the research and the final report. It should also highlight what formal stand-up presentations will be required when the proposals are submitted and also for the final results at the end of the project.

6 **Timing**: the brief should also set out the time scales for the submission of the proposal and the completion of the research.

The budget available for the project is rarely included within the brief. This is to ensure that the research is tailored to the needs of the organisation rather than the size of the budget. However, management should establish a maximum budget and keep this in mind when selecting the research provider or agency.

Stage 3a: selection of research provider/agency

The next stage of the research process is the selection of the researchers who are to do the research. The research could be undertaken by the in-house marketing research department within the organisation or by an external research agency. Larger organisations are more likely to have formal marketing research departments. Moreover, the incidence of such departments has been found to be higher in consumer products and services than in business-to-business products.

In many organisations, the marketing research department primarily manages the research activity of external agencies rather than undertaking projects on its own. Many related considerations influence the decision to go outside and use external agencies:

- Internal personnel may not have the necessary skills or experience. Few but the very largest companies can afford to have specialists in the full range of research techniques.
- It may be cheaper to go to an agency that has encountered similar studies with other clients and is therefore more likely to be more efficient at tackling the research.
- Agencies may have special facilities or competencies (a national fieldforce; group discussion facility with one-way mirrors; a telephone research call centre) which would be costly to duplicate for a single study.
- Internal politics within the organisation (e.g. the product under investigation is the pet project of a particular senior manager) may dictate the use of an objective outside agency whose credentials are acceptable to all parties involved in an internal dispute. The internal research department may be well advised to avoid being on one side or the other of a sensitive issue.
- If the research is to be undertaken on an anonymous basis without the name of the sponsoring organisation being divulged then an external agency may need to be used.

The research tends to be undertaken by the internal marketing research department if the research project is relatively small, or where time is critical, or if product knowledge is important. Otherwise an external agency will be selected to undertake all or part (e.g. the fieldwork) of the project.

International projects

Where a multi-country international marketing research project is undertaken (for example if Nokia wished to examine and compare customer attitudes towards its mobile phone brand across 10 countries) then more than one agency may be used to undertake the project. International research is more complex as a result of factors such as differences in language, culture, marketing research practices, privacy and data protection legislation. Therefore the management of the agencies and the research is also more complex. As such, there are a number of options available to organisations:

1 They can appoint different agencies in each of the countries that they are research-ing. This ensures that the researchers have local knowledge of the country being researched, the marketing research practices of the country and the local lan-guage. However, the selection process becomes more complex, with the client organisation having to shortlist, brief and select a separate agency in each country. This may be particularly difficult if the organisation has no experience of agencies in these countries. The management of the relationship with a number of agencies throughout the project may also be very onerous.

2 They can appoint one agency to do the project in all of the countries. This reduces the workload placed on the management of the client organisation and provides greater consistency in quality control over all the countries being researched. However, the agency may lack detailed knowledge of the markets and the accepted marketing research practices of the individual countries.

3 They can appoint one of the large multinational agencies to undertake the research. These would use their own subsidiaries in each of the countries being researched. There should be consistency in quality control and the individual subsidiaries should have local knowledge. The suitability of this option will depend on the countries being researched, as these agencies are only likely to have subsidiaries in the major markets of the world.

4 They can use one marketing research agency as the project manager responsible for a consortium of research agencies. This provides the client organisation with one point of contact. The day-to-day management is the responsibility of the project-managing agency, which briefs, selects agencies and manages their quality. In certain cases the project management agency may use overseas agencies that it has had a previous relationship with. The drawback of this approach is that some marketing research agencies may be good at undertaking research but less good at managing and co-ordinating the research of other agencies.

Whichever approach is adopted, agencies are almost always selected using the pro-cedures outlined in the following subsections.

Selection of external research agencies

It is first necessary to identify a shortlist of three or four agencies which will be briefed on the organisation's research requirements. Without prior experience, it is difficult to prejudge the effectiveness and likely research output of an agency. Like any service, there are few tangible cues to assist in the selection of the shortlist.

Therefore decision makers within organisations tend to rely either on their own personal experience or the experience of others such as colleagues in other depart-ments or other companies. Some may also seek recommendations from the trade association for their own industry (pharmaceuticals, toys, cars, etc.), or from bodies such as the Market Research Society, ESOMAR or the Chartered Institute of Marketing. In the UK, the Market Research Society also produces an annual Research Buyer's guide which lists agencies and their expertise.

The shortlist is normally drawn up on the basis of the following factors:

- previous experience in appropriate market sector (cars, groceries, advertising, etc.);
- previous experience in appropriate geographical market (for international research);
- appropriate technical capabilities (e.g. able to undertake telephone research);
- appropriate research facilities and fieldforce (e.g. call centre, national fieldforce, group discussion facilities);
- reputation for quality of work and keeping to time scales;
- communication skills (both written and verbal);
- financially stable/well established.

Once a shortlist of three or four agencies has been established, briefing of each of the agencies should take place using the written brief supported by a meeting between the organisation's project team and the agency. This should enable the agency personnel to fully understand the organisation's requirements, allowing them to develop a research proposal.

The research proposal

The research proposal is the submission prepared by the research agency for a potential client specifying the research to be undertaken. On the basis of the research proposal, the client will select an agency to undertake the research. The proposal then becomes the contract between the agency and the client company. In many respects, the proposal is as important as the research brief – if not more important. The typical structure for such a research proposal is set out in Table 2.2.

Researcher quote: *The proposal is the most important part of the whole research project. It provides both the template and the contract for all of the subsequent research.*

Table 2.2 Contents of the research proposal

The research proposal

1 Background
2 Objectives
3 Approach and method
4 Reporting and presentation procedures
5 Timing
6 Fees
7 Personal CVs
8 Related experience and references
9 Contract details

1 Background

Smith Brothers are agents for a range of professional grass cutting machinery and small industrial engines.

In the grass cutting sector, the company has specialised in the Atlas range of products in terms of both product sales and parts and service support.

In the small engine market, the company holds agencies for several major manufacturers of petrol engines (from 3 hp. to 20 hp.) for use in a variety of applications including mowers, cultivators, pumps and generators, etc.

The company is particularly strong in the municipal authority and golf course sectors and now wishes to increase sales by market expansion and increasing sales of grass cutting and horticultural equipment to other market sectors.

Prior to developing a marketing strategy, Smith Brothers would like to obtain a much better understanding of the opportunities and the requirements for horticultural machinery in the following market sectors:

❑ *Leisure*
- *hotels with extensive grounds*
- *caravan sites*

❑ *Institutions/government bodies*
- *hospitals (public and private)*
- *universities*
- *private schools*
- *government departments*
- *utilities (gas/electricity)*

❑ *Major landowners*
- *private estates (stately homes, zoos, etc.)*
- *factories, private companies*

❑ *Contractors*
- *landscape and building contractors*
- *suppliers of contract maintenance*

Figure 2.2 Example of background section in a proposal

The content of the various sections is similar to the research brief.

1 Background: the background section puts the research into context by briefly describing the client organisation, its markets and products, and the rationale for doing the research. Figure 2.2 sets out the background section for an organisation which was seeking research into horticultural equipment.

2 Objectives: the objectives are similar to those in the brief, although they may in certain cases be more precisely defined. The following example of an objective relates to the project set out in Figure 2.2.

To investigate the horticultural machinery needs of the four market sectors under consideration (leisure, institutions/government bodies, major landowners, contractors) in terms of:

- types of machinery currently used
- makes of machinery currently used
- age of current machinery
- source of supply
- level of expenditure on machinery during last 12 months
- maintenance provision

3 Approach and method: this section sets out the methodology of the research approach, highlighting the types of research to be used, the sample, the method of analysis and any limitations of the proposed approach.

4 Reporting and presentation procedures: this section highlights the structure of the report and the agency's proposals for interim and final presentations.

5 Timing: this should set out the time the project will take from time of commissioning and highlight any proposed break points between different phases of the research.

6 Fees: this should set out the total fees for the project. Expenses (e.g. travel, room hire, etc.) may be charged separately or be incorporated into the fees. Client organisations must pay particular attention to this section of the proposal and ensure that they are aware of the charging structure and that there is a ceiling put on additional expenses.

7 Personal CVs: this section sets out details about the background and experience of the key researchers who will be involved in this project.

8 Related experience and references: this section sets out the background on the research agency, outlining what experience it has had in projects similar to or relevant to this one. Certain clients may also require the agency to provide references from previous clients.

9 Contract details: if the proposal is accepted by the client, it will become the contract for the research that is to be carried out. As such, it is common for contractual details to be enclosed at the end of the proposal.

'Beauty parades'

In addition to the written proposal, agencies will generally be asked to present their proposals verbally in a form of 'beauty parade'. From the client organisation's perspective, this has three major benefits. First, it demonstrates the competence of the individuals in the agency. Second, it provides a check on the quality of their presentational skills and materials. This obviously gives an indication of their communication skills, which will be important in the presentation of the final research results, but in addition it gives an impression of the care and attention that they put into their work. Finally it allows the organisation to use questioning to check on the agency's understanding of the organisation's research need.

Client quote: *You learn a great deal about an agency in the presentation, particularly with regard to whether their understanding is superficial or detailed.*

Selection criteria to determine the successful agency

Agencies will be judged on a whole range of criteria, but the core criteria that tend to be used are as follows:

1 the agency's ability to comprehend the research brief and translate it into a comprehensive proposal;
2 the compatibility of the agency staff with the members of the project team (as they are going to have to work together on this project);
3 evidence of innovative thinking in the proposal (the research has been designed for this client and is not a standard off-the-shelf solution);
4 evidence of the agency understanding both the market in which the client organisation operates and the specific problem facing the organisation;
5 sound and appropriate methodology for the specific research needs;
6 meeting the organisation's requirements in terms of time scale and budgets;
7 relevant past experience and references.

Once the successful agency has been selected, the agency and client organisation will confirm that the proposal meets the client's needs or make minor adjustments where they are required. The proposal will then become the contract for the completion of the research.

Stage 3b: creation of research design/choice of research method

In developing the research proposal, the agency will have been involved in designing the formal research project and identifying the appropriate sources of data for the study. Where the research is being undertaken by a marketing research department, the process of research design will also have to be undertaken. In determining the design, it is important to be aware of a combination of both the broad types of information required and the resultant decisions to be made. There are three main categories of marketing research that can be undertaken:

1 exploratory research;
2 conclusive – descriptive research;
3 conclusive – causal research.

Exploratory research

Exploratory research is research intended to develop initial ideas or insights and to provide direction for any further research needed. It is a preliminary investigation of a situation involving a minimum expenditure of cost and time. Typically, there is little prior knowledge on which to build. It may be used to help define detailed object-ives for a subsequent marketing research programme, or to examine whether it is valuable to undertake further research at all. The research may be aimed at exploring whether there is any interest in a new product idea or at examining a new market that an organisation wishes to enter. Exploratory research is also useful for establishing priorities among research questions and for learning about the practical problems of carrying out further research. What questions will respondents be willing to answer? What respondents should be included in a further study? Such questions may be able to be answered by examining published data (see Chapter 3) or through a small pro-gramme of qualitative research (see Chapter 5) or even telephone research.

Conclusive research

All other research that is not exploratory in nature and that is aimed at evaluating alternative courses of action or measuring and monitoring the organisation's perform-ance is described as **conclusive research**. Conclusive research can provide information that is inherently descriptive in nature or causal in nature.

Looking first at descriptive information about a market, examples are:

- the proportion of the population reading a particular section of a daily newspaper;
- the customers' attitudes towards an organisation's products;
- the level of awareness of a particular advertising campaign;
- the extent to which customers are satisfied with the service they receive.

Descriptive information of this type is gathered through *descriptive research*. It pro-vides the answers to the **who, what, where, how and when** of marketing research. The findings describe what is happening; they generally do not explain why it is happening. Descriptive research is appropriate when the research objectives include the description of the characteristics of marketing phenomena, determination of the frequency of occurrence, or the prediction of the occurrence of specific marketing phenomena.

Descriptive research of this type may be required in relation to one point in time. This is called a **cross-sectional study** and involves the research being undertaken once to explore what is happening at that single point in time. Alternatively, the organisa-tion may wish to measure trends in awareness, attitudes or behaviour over time. Such repeat measurement studies are called **longitudinal studies**. This may involve asking the same questions on a number of occasions of either the same respondents or of respondents with similar characteristics.

> **Descriptive research:** studies that describe what is happening in a market.

> **Cross-sectional research:** a study involving data collection at a single point in time, providing a 'snapshot' of the specific situation.

> **Longitudinal research:** a study involving data collection at several periods in time which enables trends over time to be examined.

Descriptive research can tell us that two variables seem to be somehow associated, such as advertising and sales, but cannot provide reasonable proof that high levels of advertising cause high sales. Research that does examine information on relationships and the impact of one variable on another is called **causal research**. This addresses research questions such as:

- the relationship between family income and expenditure on groceries;
- the relationship between time spent watching the MTV cable channel and expenditure on CDs;
- the relationship between advertising awareness and purchasing behaviour.

> **Causal research:** research that examines whether one variable causes or determines the value of another variable.

Causal research provides the type of evidence necessary for making inferences about relationships between variables; for example, whether one variable causes or determines the value of another variable.

Causal research and descriptive research should not be seen as mutually exclusive, as some studies will incorporate elements of both causal and descriptive research. Conclusive projects should be seen as falling along a research continuum with 'purely descriptive with no specific testing of the relationship between variables' at one extreme and 'purely causal with strict manipulation and testing of relationships' at the other. Virtually all marketing research projects fall somewhere along this continuum, although the point where descriptive ends and causal begins is subjective and somewhat arbitrary.

> **Experimental research:** research that measures causality and involves the researcher changing one variable (e.g. price, packaging, shelf display, etc.), while observing the effects of those changes on another variable (e.g. sales) and controlling the extraneous variables.

Studies that are nearer to the causal end of the continuum will require an experimental research design in comparison to more standard data gathering for a descriptive study. Experimental research allows changes in behaviour or attitudes to be measured while systematically manipulating one marketing variable (e.g. price) and holding all other variables constant.

For example, Lyons Tetley Tea, when launching the round tea bag, experimented by analysing purchasing behaviour while altering the shape of the tea bag, all other variables, such as price, packaging, advertising, etc., being kept constant. This was

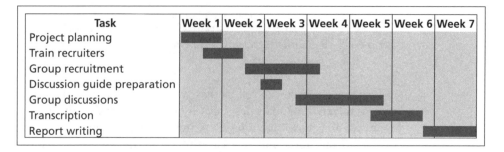

Task	Week 1	Week 2	Week 3	Week 4	Week 5	Week 6	Week 7
Project planning							
Train recruiters							
Group recruitment							
Discussion guide preparation							
Group discussions							
Transcription							
Report writing							

Figure 2.3 GANTT chart: qualitative project planning

done by recruiting a panel of tea drinkers who had to make all their tea and beverage purchases from an interviewer who called at their homes once a week (see page 199).

The distinction between descriptive and experimental research designs is more a matter of degree than of kind. While descriptive survey data may merely suggest causation (through, say, a positive correlation between price and sales), data generated through experimental research will increase the degree of confidence one can have in any suggested relationship. Although in pure science a completely controlled experiment can indicate for sure whether something is caused by something else, in marketing practice complete control is rarely possible. Therefore seldom can causation be conclusively established in practical settings, although most experimental research designs will provide reasonable establishment.

In addition to the determination of the data collection method, the research design phase will also consider the nature and number of respondents (sampling) to be included in the research. Timing, scheduling and project planning are also important at this stage.

Several managerial tools can be used for scheduling a research project. The most frequently used techniques are (1) the **critical path method** (CPM), (2) the **programme evaluation and review technique** (PERT) and (3) **GANTT charts**. CPM is a network approach that involves dividing the research project into its various components and estimating the time required to complete each component activity. PERT is a probability-based scheduling approach that recognises and measures the uncertainty of project completion times. A GANTT chart is a form of flowchart that provides a schematic representation incorporating the activity, time and personnel requirements for a given research project. An example of the use of a GANTT chart is shown in Figure 2.3.

Stage 4: collection of secondary data

Secondary data is information that has been previously gathered for some purpose other than the current research project. There are two basic sources of secondary data: data available within the organisation (internal data) and information available from published and electronic sources originating outside the organisation (external data). Internal data may include sales reports, information from customer loyalty cards and information in the internal marketing information system. External data may include government reports, newspapers, the Internet and published research reports. More detailed discussion of secondary data and its use is set out in Chapter 3.

Secondary data is used in many studies because it can be obtained at a fraction of the cost and time involved in primary data collection. It is most commonly obtained prior to the primary research as it:

- can help to clarify or redefine the research requirements as part of a programme of exploratory research. Internal data held on customers may provide more information on the detail of customer behaviour and may therefore clarify which customers or which behaviours should be researched further;

- may actually satisfy the research needs without the requirement for further primary research. Someone else, within or external to the organisation, may have already addressed identical or very similar research questions;

- may alert the marketing researcher to potential problems or difficulties. Secondary information about previous research studies may identify difficulties in accessing respondents through, for example, the telephone and therefore may persuade a researcher to switch to some other data collection method.

There are a number of weaknesses relating to the accuracy of the data and its relevance to the research project, which are discussed in more detail in Chapter 3.

Stage 5: collection of primary data

Primary data will be collected by a programme of observation, qualitative or quantitative research, either separately or in combination. Each of these types of research and their application will be discussed in detail in later chapters. At this stage, it is sufficient to signpost their existence and define them:

> **Observation research** is a data gathering approach where information is collected on the behaviour of people, objects and organisations without any questions being asked of the participants.

> **Qualitative research** uses an unstructured research approach with a small number of carefully selected individuals to produce non-quantifiable insights into behaviour, motivations and attitudes.

> **Quantitative research** uses a structured approach with a sample of the population to produce quantifiable insights into behaviour, motivations and attitudes.

Depending on the type of research being carried out, this phase is also likely to involve the development of data collection forms, the determination of the sample of respondents to take part in the research and the actual collection of the data.

Developing data collection forms

Primary data is frequently collected through questionnaires, but in some instances, it is also gathered through observation (see Chapter 4) and through qualitative research (see Chapter 5). Regardless of the data collection method used, some instrument or form must be designed to record the information being collected. This is a skilled task requiring careful thought and planning (see Chapter 7). A poorly designed questionnaire can jeopardise response rates and provide incomplete or inaccurate data. With the growth of computer-assisted interviewing where respondents' answers are fed directly into a computer terminal or through the Internet, computing skills may also be critical.

Determination of the sample

Determining the sample involves clearly specifying the types of respondent to be included in the research, the numbers of respondent required and the method by which individual respondents will be selected. There are a large number of sampling approaches (see Chapter 8) and their selection is influenced by factors such as the level of accuracy required, the nature of the project, the characteristics of the potential respondents, and time and cost constraints.

Collection of the data

Once the data collection form and the sample design are prepared, the data can be collected. If the research involves observation, then different types of equipment may be used (see Chapter 4). If it is qualitative, researchers need to use specific skills and techniques to gather detailed information from respondents (see Chapter 5). Quantitative research may require significant logistical management activity to co-ordinate the dispatch of large postal surveys, the operations of a telephone call centre or the management of geographically dispersed fieldforce interviewers (see Chapter 6). Quality control is critical at this stage to ensure that the research approach is implemented in a manner which is complete, consistent and adheres to any prespecified instructions.

Stage 6: analysis of data

The types of analysis undertaken in a project depend on the nature of the data and the specific data collection method used, as well as on the use to be made of the findings. In particular, there are significant differences between the analysis approaches adopted for qualitative research (see Chapter 5) and those used for quantitative research (see Chapter 9). The data may need to be prepared for data analysis, which may involve validation, editing and computer data entry. It may then be tabulated or analysed using a wide variety of statistical and non-statistical techniques before being fed into any presentation of the research results.

Stage 7: preparation and presentation of research findings and recommendations

Generally most projects would be completed by the research team preparing a formal written report and an oral presentation. Often the presentation and communication of the research findings is as important, if not more important, than is the research itself. It is difficult for client organisations to take research findings seriously if they are confusing, inaccurate or lack relevance to the key marketing decision makers. There is a need to understand the requirements of the audience for any research report or presentation, and to develop quality materials to match these needs (see Chapter 10).

Managing the client/agency relationship

Throughout the marketing research process, it is important that the project team in the client organisation and the researchers work as a team in order to maintain the quality and relevance of the research. This means that the project team should seek regular meetings during the project in order to maintain their awareness of what is going on and also to suggest alternative courses of action if the research is encountering problems, such as high refusal rates among respondents or the sample lists provided by the client being inaccurate. It may be worthwhile phasing the research into different stages and having interim presentations at various points throughout the research. At these presentations, decisions could be taken as to whether to continue with the proposed research, make amendments to the research design or abort the project. Certainly the project team should be involved throughout the project and not simply at the beginning and end, if they are going to maximise the benefits derived from the marketing research.

Ethics in marketing research

Marketing research ethics refers to the moral guidelines or principles that govern the conduct of behaviour in the marketing research industry. Ethics is particularly important in marketing research, as the industry is dependent on:

- **Goodwill**: the goodwill of the individual respondents for their willingness to volunteer information on their awareness, attitudes and behaviours. Any practice that erodes that goodwill makes future marketing research studies more difficult to undertake.
- **Trust**: marketing decision makers trust researchers to provide accurate information that has been collected in a professional manner. Researchers also trust decision makers to divulge all information that may have an impact on the completion of a marketing research study.

- **Professionalism**: if respondents are to answer questionnaires in a serious and thoughtful manner, they have to feel that the research is going to be used in a professional manner.

- **Confidentiality**: respondents are more willing to express their views and opinions, if they know that the information is going to be used in a confidential manner (in other words, taking part in marketing research will not result in the respondent becoming subject to sales calls, political lobbying or fund raising).

The behaviour of marketing researchers is controlled by the data protection laws enforced by the government of the country in which the research is being carried out and also by the relevant self-regulatory codes of conduct drawn up by the professional bodies that represent the marketing research industry.

Data protection legislation

Individual European countries each have their own national legislation on data protection. These all tend to fit within the framework of the European Union Directive on Data Protection. This Directive was passed in 1995 and required Member States to implement the Directive into national legislation during 1998. Although the intention was to have a common data protection law for Europe, each country has added to or changed the detailed meaning of some parts. This means that researchers undertaking research in non-domestic markets should always check the specific laws of the country in which they are researching.

Despite the different nuances of the different laws, the guiding principles are common and these are:

- **Transparency**: individuals should have a very clear and unambiguous understanding as to why their personal data (i.e. data that identifies a living, individual, natural person) is being collected and for what purpose it will be used.

- **Consent**: at the time when their personal data is being collected, individuals must give their consent to it being collected and they should also, at this time, have the opportunity to opt out of any subsequent uses of their personal data.

It is important to note that data protection legislation only covers data (including audio and video records) that identifies a living, individual, natural person. Once any identifiers linking data to a specific person have been removed then it no longer constitutes 'personal data' and is therefore not covered by the legislation. Information about companies is also outwith the remit of the legislation unless it identifies information about individuals within the companies.

The UK Data Protection Act (1998)[3] is relatively typical of data protection legislation in most countries and has the following eight data protection principles, which form the fundamental basis of the legislation.

1 Personal data shall be processed fairly and lawfully and, in particular, shall not be processed unless the individual agrees to the processing (some exemptions exist – but none relate to marketing research).

2 Personal data shall be obtained only for one or more specified and lawful purposes, and shall not be further processed in any manner incompatible with that purpose or other purposes.

3 Personal data shall be adequate, relevant and not excessive in relation to the purpose or purposes for which they are processed.

4 Personal data shall be accurate and, where necessary, kept up to date (with every reasonable step being taken to ensure that data that are inaccurate or incomplete, having regard to the purpose(s) for which they were collected or for which they are being further processed, are erased or rectified).

5 Personal data processed for any purpose or purposes shall not be kept for longer than is necessary for that purpose or those purposes.

6 Personal data shall be processed in accordance with the rights of data subjects under this Act.

7 Appropriate technical and organisational measures shall be taken against unauthorised or unlawful processing of personal data and against accidental loss or destruction of, or damage to, personal data.

8 Personal data shall not be transferred to a country or territory outside the European Economic Area unless that country or territory ensures an adequate level of protection for the rights and freedoms of data subjects in relation to the processing of personal data.

Researcher quote: *Too often researchers receive demands by sales or marketing personnel for access to results and the names and telephone numbers of respondents. Thankfully, the Data Protection Act now makes it crystal clear that this is not allowed without the prior permission of the respondent!*

The Act provides for various exemptions in respect of the processing of data for marketing research purposes:

- Personal data collected for research can be reprocessed, provided that this is not incompatible with what was described to respondents initially.

- Personal data can be kept indefinitely for certain types of projects involving longitudinal research, such as panels (note that in all cases where further interviews with a respondent may be required, consent for the subsequent interviews must be gained during the initial interview and not retrospectively). If personal data is removed then the anonymised elements of the data can be kept indefinitely with no restrictions.

- The rights of respondents to request access to the personal data held about them does not apply once any personal identifiers (e.g. name and address, telephone numbers, e-mail addresses, reference numbers, etc.) have been removed from the data. This means that respondents can request a copy of the primary data record (e.g. a questionnaire) only as long as it contains information that identifies the respondent.

> **Researcher quote:** *The data protection legislation means that every organisation must ensure that one individual in the organisation is made responsible for the area of data protection – it is a critical area!*

However, these exemptions apply only if the data is used exclusively for research purposes and if the following conditions are met:

- the data are not processed to support measures or decisions with respect to the particular individuals;
- the data are not processed in such a way that substantial damage or substantial distress is, or likely to be, caused to any data subject.

In addition to data protection legislation, the human rights legislation being introduced in many countries may have an impact on marketing research. Such legislation does cover wider ground than data protection, for example in the area of respect for private and family life, but the exact impact at present is unclear.

Codes of marketing and social research practice

In addition to legislation, there are professional codes of marketing and social research practice. These are self-regulatory codes of conduct developed by the professional bodies responsible for the research industry. The first such code was published in 1948 by the European Society for Opinion and Marketing Research. In the UK, the Market Research Society Code of Conduct was first introduced in 1954. Other national marketing research societies and the International Chamber of Commerce (ICC), which represents the international marketing community, produced their own codes. In 1976, ESOMAR and the ICC produced a single international code instead of two differing ones, and the joint ICC/ESOMAR code was established. This has been revised on a number of occasions since. National organisations such as the MRS in the UK have also been revising their own codes during this time, to the extent that most European national codes are now fully compatible with the ICC/ESOMAR International Code of Marketing and Social Research Practice.

Before considering the detail of the ICC/ESOMAR code, it is important to note that these codes are self-regulatory and are not controlled by law. Breaches of these codes can only result in disciplinary action relating to an individual's membership of the relevant professional body. Such disciplinary action may involve membership being withdrawn, demoted or suspended and the publication of information about such actions.

ICC/ESOMAR International Code of Marketing and Social Research Practice[4]

Rules

A. General

> **Researcher quote:** *This section of the code relates to the need for objective research in which clients can trust and also which complies with the necessary and relevant legislation relating to privacy, data protection, human rights, etc.*

1 Marketing research must always be carried out objectively and in accordance with established scientific principles.
2 Marketing research must always conform to the national and international legislation which applies in those countries involved in a given research project.

B. The Rights of Respondents

> **Researcher quote:** *This section of the code relates to protecting respondents when they agree to take part in marketing research. For example, it states clearly that researchers cannot secure co-operation by misleading respondents regarding information such as the purpose of the research, the likely length of the interview or the possibilities of being reinterviewed. It also covers rules relating to the research of children. The definitions of children may vary by country, with some countries in Europe defining children as 'under 14' (in the UK, it is under 16). There is also a rule about the recording of respondents by use of either video or audio.*

3 Respondents' cooperation in a marketing research project is entirely voluntary at all stages. They must not be misled when being asked for their cooperation.
4 Respondents' anonymity must be strictly preserved. If the Respondent on request from the Researcher has given permission for data to be passed on in a form which allows that respondent to be personally identified:

(a) the Respondent must first have been told to whom the information would be supplied and the purposes for which it will be used.

(b) the Researcher must ensure that the information will not be used for any non-research purpose and that the recipient of the information has agreed to conform to the requirements of this Code.

5 The Researcher must take all reasonable precautions to ensure that Respondents are in no way directly harmed or adversely affected as a result of their participation in a marketing research project.

6 The Researcher must take special care when interviewing children and young people. The informed consent of the parent or responsible adult must first be obtained for interviews with children.

7 Respondents must be told (normally at the beginning of the interview) if observation techniques or recording equipment are being used, except where these are used in a public place. If a Respondent so wishes, the record or relevant section of it must be destroyed or deleted. Respondents' anonymity must not be infringed by the use of such methods.

8 Respondents must be enabled to check without difficulty the identity and bona fides of the Researcher.

C. The Professional Responsibilities of Researchers

Researcher quote: *This section of rules is aimed at maintaining the general public's confidence in the integrity of marketing researchers. One particularly important rule in this section relates to the undertaking of non-research activities. Researchers or clients should not be involved in undertaking non-research activities (e.g. development of mailing lists, sales activity, debt collecting, fund raising, obtaining information for political or legal purposes) under the guise of marketing research.*

9 Researchers must not, whether knowingly or negligently, act in any way which could bring discredit on the marketing research profession or lead to a loss of public confidence in it.

10 Researchers must not make false claims about their skills and experience or about those of their organisation.

11 Researchers must not unjustifiably criticise or disparage other Researchers.

12 Researchers must always strive to design research which is cost-efficient and of adequate quality, and then to carry this out to the specification agreed with the Client.

13 Researchers must ensure the security of all research records in their possession.

14 Researchers must not knowingly allow the dissemination of conclusions from a marketing research project which are not adequately supported by the data. They must always be prepared to make available the technical information necessary to assess the validity of any published findings.

15 When acting in their capacity as Researchers the latter must not undertake any non-research activities, for example database marketing involving data about individuals which will be used for direct marketing and promotional activities. Any such non-research activities must always, in the way they are organised and carried out, be clearly differentiated from marketing research activities.

D. The Mutual Rights and Responsibilities of Researchers and Clients

Researcher quote: *This final section of Rules regulates the business relationships between researchers and clients. For most marketing research projects, these matters will be regulated by the contractual details included within the marketing research proposal. The section deals mainly with the transparency of working relationships and the ownership of materials (briefs, proposals, reports and data).*

16 These rights and responsibilities will normally be governed by a written Contract between the Researcher and the Client. Marketing research must also always be conducted according to the principles of fair competition, as generally understood and accepted.

17 The Researcher must inform the Client if the work to be carried out for that Client is to be combined or syndicated in the same project with work for other Clients but must not disclose the identity of such Clients.

18 The Researcher must inform the Client as soon as possible in advance when any part of the work for that Client is to be subcontracted outside the Researcher's own organisation (including the use of any outside consultants). On request the Client must be told the identity of any such subcontractor.

19 The Client does not have the right, without prior agreement between the parties involved, to exclusive use of the Researcher's services or those of his organisation, whether in whole or in part. In carrying out work for different Clients, however, the Researcher must endeavour to avoid possible clashes of interest between the services provided to those Clients.

20 The following Records remain the property of the Client and must not be disclosed by the Researcher to any third party without the Client's permission:

(a) marketing research briefs, specifications and other information provided by the Client

(b) the research data and findings from a marketing research project (except in the case of syndicated or multi-client projects or services where the same data are available to more than one Client).

The Client has, however, no right to know the names or addresses of Respondents unless the latter's explicit permission for this has first been obtained by the Researcher.

21 Unless it is specifically agreed to the contrary, the following Records remain the property of the Researcher:

(a) marketing research proposals and cost quotations (unless these have been paid for by the Client). They must not be disclosed by the Client to any third party, other than to a consultant working for the Client on that project (with the exception of any consultant working also for a competitor of the Researcher). In particular, they must not be used by the Client to influence research proposals or cost quotations from other Researchers.

(b) the contents of a report in the case of syndicated research and/or multi-client projects or services where the same data are available to more than one Client and where it is clearly understood that the resulting reports are available for general purchase or subscription. The Client may not disclose the findings of such research to any third party (other than to his own consultants and advisors for use in connection with his business) without the permission of the Researcher.

(c) all other research Records prepared by the Researcher (with the exception in the case of non-syndicated projects of the report to the Client, and also the research design and questionnaire where the costs of developing these are covered by the charges paid by the Client).

22 The Researcher must conform to currently agreed professional practice relating to the keeping of such records for an appropriate period of time after the end of the project. [In default of any agreement to the contrary, the normal period for which primary field records should be retained is one year with the research data being stored for possible further analysis for at least two years.] On request the Researcher must supply the Client with duplicate copies of such Records provided that such duplicates do not breach anonymity and confidentiality requirements (Rule 4); that the request is made within the agreed time limit for keeping the Records; and that the Client pays the reasonable costs of providing the duplicates.

23 The Researcher must not disclose the identity of the Client (provided there is no legal obligation to do so), or any confidential information about the latter's business, to any third party without the Client's permission.

24 The Researcher must, on request, allow the Client to arrange for checks on the quality of fieldwork and data preparation provided that the Client pays any additional costs involved in this.

25 The Researcher must provide the Client with all appropriate technical details of any research project carried out for that Client.

26 When reporting on the results of a marketing research project the Researcher must make a clear distinction between the findings as such, the Researcher's interpretation of these and any recommendations based on them.

27 Where any of the findings of a research project are published by the Client, the latter has a responsibility to ensure that these are not misleading. The Researcher must be consulted and agree in advance the form and content of publication, and must take action to correct any misleading statements about the research and its findings.

28 Researchers must not allow their names to be used in connection with any research project as an assurance that the latter has been carried out in conformity with this Code unless they are confident that the project has in all respects met the Code's requirements.

29 Researchers must ensure that Clients are aware of the existence of this Code and of the need to comply with its requirements.

In addition to the formal code of conduct, ESOMAR, MRS and other national marketing research societies provide written guidelines to their members on specific areas and issues involving the practice of marketing research such as:

- Internet research;
- research among children and young people;
- qualitative research;
- mystery shopping research;
- the use of free prize draws;
- questionnaire design;
- maintaining distinctions between marketing research and direct marketing.

These are regularly updated and can be obtained from the MRS (www.mrs.org.uk) and ESOMAR (www.esomar.nl) websites.

Summary

The research process consists of a series of stages that guide the research project from conception through to final recommendations. Care must be taken in the early stages of a project to formulate what is expected from the research, and a research brief should be written to act as a specification against which researchers will be able to design the research project.

The research proposal is the submission prepared by the researchers for a potential client specifying the research to be undertaken. The proposal is also critical in the agency selection process. In developing the research proposal, the research design is determined by the nature of the research required. This may be exploratory in nature or conclusive research. This chapter has defined these, along with descriptive and causal research.

The later sections of the research process, such as collection of primary research, analysis of data and the presentation of research findings, will be examined in more detail in later chapters. Secondary research is discussed in the next chapter.

Finally, marketing research is dependent on the goodwill of the individual respondents for their willingness to volunteer information on their awareness, attitudes and behaviours. It is therefore important that the whole of the marketing research process is undertaken in an ethical and professional manner. This requires researchers to conform to their professional codes of conduct and relevant data protection legislation.

Discussion questions

1   Why should a team rather than an individual be used to develop a research brief?

2   How should one go about selecting a marketing research agency?

3   What role does exploratory research play in the marketing research process?

4   Describe the various ways that a multi-country research project can be managed.

5   Discuss the proposition that the research proposal is the most important part of the whole marketing research project.

6   Explain the difference between cross-sectional studies and longitudinal studies. Give examples of studies for which each may be appropriate.

7   What is the relationship between exploratory, descriptive and causal research?

8   Why is ethics particularly important for the marketing research industry?

9   Explain the difference between a marketing research code of conduct and data protection legislation.

10   What are the key rights of marketing research respondents?

Additional reading

Baskin, M. and Coburn, N. (2001) Two tribes divided by a common language? The true nature of the divide between account planners and market researchers. *International Journal of Market Research*, **43**(2), pp. 137–69.

Butler, P. (1994) Marketing problems: from analysis to decision. *Marketing Intelligence and Planning*, **12**(2), pp. 4–13.

Chapman, R.G. (1989) Problem definition in marketing research studies. *Journal of Services Marketing*, **3**(3), pp. 51–9.

Moorman, C., Desphande, R. and Zaltman, G. (1993) Factors affecting trust in market research relationships. *Journal of Marketing*, **57**(1), pp. 81–102.

References

[1] Adapted from Gofton, K. (2000) Staying on the rails, *Research*, 408, May, pp. 28–9, and published with the permission of The Market Research Society.

[2] Adapted from Adams, G. and Bunt, K. (2000) B2B travel takes off, *Research*, 408, May, pp. 34–5, and published with the permission of The Market Research Society.

[3] A basic guide to the Data Protection Act 1998 for marketing researchers is available from the MRS website (www.mrs.org.uk).

[4] The ICC/ESOMAR International Code of Marketing and Social Research Practice can be obtained from the ESOMAR (www.esomar.nl) or MRS (www.mrs.org.uk) websites.

3
Secondary data and customer databases

Wal-Mart's data warehouse

At over 24 terabytes, Wal-Mart's data warehouse is the largest in the world. It contains point-of sale, inventory, products in transit, market statistics, customer demographics, finance, product returns, and supplier performance data from Wal-Mart's 2,900 stores in the US. The data is analysed in three broad areas of decision support: analysing trends, managing inventory and understanding customers. By examining individual items for individual stores, the system can create a seasonal sales profile of each item. In terms of marketing research, the company can analyse relationships and patterns in customer purchases. This can lead to the creation of linked promotions as well as improved floor and shelving layouts. This type of data warehouse will be rolled out to its stores in Germany and its Asda stores in the UK.

Learning outcomes

After reading this chapter you should:

- understand the benefits and limitations of secondary data;
- understand how to evaluate secondary data;
- be aware of how to assess the accuracy of secondary data;
- be aware of the various sources of secondary data available inside and outside the organisation;
- be aware of the value of customer databases and the manner in which they can be used for generating marketing information;
- be aware of the components of a marketing decision support system.

Key words

cookies
database
data conversion
data mining
deduplication
directories
external data

geodemographic profiling
internal data
lifestyle databases
marketing decision support system
newsgroups
search engines
secondary data

Introduction

With the growing capabilities of computers and the Internet, there is a large amount of secondary data within customer databases and external sources available to the marketing researcher. However, this data is only of value if it is relevant to the objectives of a particular research project. Marketing researchers should therefore be aware of the vast array of secondary data available and the factors to consider in evaluating the quality and worth of the data. This chapter will consider these issues within the context of a rapidly changing digital age.

The uses, benefits and limitations of secondary data

Secondary data is information that has been previously gathered for some purpose other than the current research project. The data is available either free or at a cost and can be delivered electronically by computer or in printed hard-copy format.

Benefits of secondary data

Secondary data is almost always faster and less expensive to acquire than primary data. This is particularly true when electronic retrieval is used to access digitally stored data. From the Internet alone, information can often be found on market size and trends, competitor activity, distributors, ownership patterns, environmental trends, etc. Gathering such information from primary research would be very expensive and time consuming. Here is an example of data available at a touch of a button on the UK fast food and takeaway market from Key Note, an organisation that provides market reports in electronic and physical format:

Takeways and fast-food outlets have become part of the lifestyle of the young and much of the marketing and promotional efforts of the leading chains are aimed at younger age groups, from young children through to teenagers and young families. Purchases of takeaway foods are biased towards the young, with penetration levels of 93.2 per cent in the 15–24 age band. Penetration levels continue to be high up to age of 54 and then they fall off dramatically, with takeaways used by only 59 per cent of adults in the 55–64 age group and by only 33.2 per cent in the over 65s age group. In the latter age groups, the fish and chips takeaway may still be popular, but newer takeaway concepts, particularly pizzas and ethnic foods, are largely ignored. In 1998, 64.2 per cent of all users of takeaways were found in the 15–44 age band. Men are more likely to use takeaways than women and penetration is high across virtually all social grades and regions.[1]

Such information may:

1 help to clarify or redefine the definition of the organisation's research requirements (for example, if research is required into new ethnic takeaway concepts, it would be appropriate to focus the research on the 15–44 age band);
2 answer some or all of the organisation's research needs (for example, if the research is simply aimed at highlighting the trends in the takeaway market);
3 assist in the research design, highlighting aspects such as who to interview, where to interview (outside which types of takeaway restaurants) and the most appropriate questions or multiple response answers;
4 enable researchers to interpret primary data with more insight, letting them see the broader picture of what the data means in the context of other current or historical developments in the market (for example, a research finding that shows price sensitivity in the pizza market may be explained by the age profile of the customers for takeaway pizzas);
5 provide a source of comparative data to check on the reliability of data gathered from primary research;
6 provide information that cannot be obtained using primary research such as government spending, export figures, etc.

Researcher quote: *There is often so much secondary information, you don't know where to start. At least the Internet is making the searching process far quicker.*

Limitations of secondary data

Despite the main advantages of secondary data, it has limitations. These limitations stem from the fact that the information was not designed specifically to meet the researchers' needs, and relate to the availability, applicability, accuracy and comparability of the data.

Availability

For some research questions, there will be no available source of data. If SAS airlines wishes to evaluate customer attitudes towards a new seat design, it may find information about aircraft seats but there will be no specific secondary data which will provide information on attitudes towards the new seat design. If IKEA wants to consider the levels of awareness of its brand and product range in Belgium, it may have to undertake primary research. Overall, questions that relate to awareness and attitudes are unlikely to be answered by secondary data, whereas, information on market size, market conditions and buying behaviour may be more likely to be available from secondary research sources.

Applicability

It is not uncommon for secondary data to be expressed in units or measures that cannot be used by the researcher. This is commonly called a 'data-fit' problem. Philips may wish to determine the number of mobile phones sold in Norway per annum but may find that government and other secondary sources only publish the total value of mobile phones sold in Norway rather than the volume. In some countries, data about mobile phones may not be distinguished from data for all types of telecommunication equipment.

The manner in which information is classified by size may also cause problems. For example, a researcher may want to know the Irish market for 5–10 mm steel tube but may find that official sources classify and publish information on tubes in the following categories: 0–25 mm, 26–50 mm and over 50 mm. None of these directly matches the information requirements of the researcher.

When secondary data is reported in a format that does not exactly meet the researcher's needs, it may be possible to undertake **data conversion**. This involves reworking the original form of the data to a format that allows estimates to be made to meet the researcher's needs. For example, by considering the value of mobile phones sold in Norway and the average price of a phone, it should be possible to estimate the overall volume of phones sold.

> **Data Conversion:** the reworking of data into a format that allows estimates to be made to meet the researcher's needs.

In addition to problems with the units of measurement, the information may also fail to be applicable if it is out of date or does not match the time frame that the researcher is interested in.

Accuracy

As the researcher was not involved in the original collection of data, there is also no control over the accuracy of the secondary data. Research conducted by other persons may be biased to support the vested interest of the source. For example, companies and pressure groups (e.g. the anti-smoking lobby, environmental groups and even shampoo companies) often undertake and publish surveys to raise awareness of their products or their causes. The researcher must assess the reputation of the organisation that gathered the data and critically assess the research objectives and the research design to determine whether the research is unbiased. In order to do this, it is important that the researcher goes back to the original source for information rather than relying on Internet or newspaper reports of the research findings. By going back to the original source, there is a higher likelihood of obtaining details of the research design, and the complete set of the research results. Where the researcher cannot access the original source, the data should be treated with a great deal of caution.

An assessment of accuracy should take account of factors such as:

1 **The nature of the organisation undertaking the research.** The source of the secondary data is often a key to its accuracy. Government departments and large commercial marketing research agencies are liable to be more reliable than research being undertaken by a relatively unknown research organisation or by a company not normally associated with research. In less-developed countries, the researcher needs to be aware that even government research may be biased as it may be used to support certain political postures.

> **Researcher quote:** *You get to know which sources to trust. It is usually a good sign if there is information about the size of the sample, response rates and the statistical significance.*

2 **The purpose of the research and the sponsors of the research.** Understanding the motivation for the research can provide clues in assessing the quality of the data. Surveys can often be undertaken by organisations for public relations purposes, with an interesting or humorous topic being researched in order to gain wide coverage for a brand name in the media. Pressure groups such as those involved in campaigning on environmental issues or smoking may bias research and the manner in which it is undertaken to produce evidence to support their cause.

3 **The number and types of respondents involved in the research.** Information about the size of the sample, response rates and the statistical significance of results will also provide an indication of the rigour with which the research was undertaken. The types of respondent included in the research may also highlight whether there was any bias in the sample selection.

4 **The research instrument used to collect the information.** Was the research undertaken by self-completion means (i.e. responding to a postal survey or phoning a freephone number) or did the respondents get selected and screened by telephone or personal interviewers. Self-selection methods may result in bias towards only those respondents who have strong views on a particular subject.

The accuracy may be able to be checked by using multiple sources and comparing data from one source with data from another. When the data is not consistent, the researcher should attempt to identify reasons for the differences or determine the risks in using any of the data.

Accuracy problems can also occur when using time series data to analyse trends in data over time. The definition of the categories being measured may have been changed and therefore data from earlier time periods may not be directly comparable with current data.

Comparability

Comparability is often a problem when integrating and examining data from different sources. This is particularly the case where information is being collected from a number of countries for an international marketing research project. Differences may occur in

1 **The reliability of the information.** In developing countries, where a substantial proportion of the population may be illiterate or difficult to access, population or economic data may be based on estimates, or rudimentary data collection procedures. For example, the population census may be based on personal interviews conducted with the head of a village rather than with individual households. Even in some European countries, business statistics and income data are affected by the taxation structure and level of tax evasion. Production and sales statistics for small family businesses are often very inaccurate.

2 **The frequency of studies.** The frequency with which surveys are undertaken may also vary from country to country. While in the UK a population census is undertaken every 10 years, in some countries it may be more than 30 years since a complete census was undertaken.

3 **Measurement units.** These are not necessarily equivalent from country to country. For example in Germany, the purchase of a television is included as an expenditure for recreation and entertainment, while in the US this is included as furniture, furnishing and household equipment.

4 **Differences in circumstances.** Even where data may seem to be comparable, there may be differences in the circumstances that lie behind the data. If a researcher was to undertake a comparison of GNP per capita data of Sweden and UK, the information may prove misleading. The high per capita income figures for Sweden, which suggest a high standard of living, do not take account of the much higher levels of Swedish taxation linked to the state's provision of social services.

Figure 3.1 sets out a flowchart that a researcher should therefore follow when evaluating secondary data.

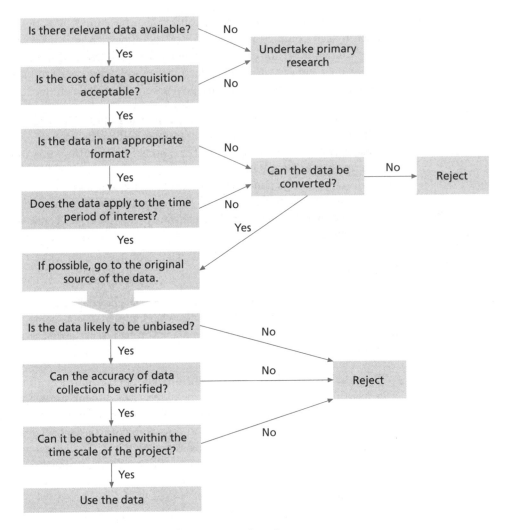

Figure 3.1 A flowchart for evaluating secondary data

Sources of secondary data

Secondary data may be sourced from within the organisation requiring the research to be conducted (internal data) or from outside the organisation (external data). Whether it is internal or external, it should still be evaluated using the questions in Figure 3.1. Simply because information is present within the organisation does not mean it is accurate, reliable and able to be accessed in a short time scale. Data which is available in internal invoicing and accounting systems may require considerable processing before it is useful to the researcher.

However, it is always worth evaluating and collecting internal secondary data before seeking external secondary data.

Internal data: data available within the organisation that has the research need.

External data: data that originates outside the organisation that has the research need.

Internal secondary data

Any organisation will hold information on its customers, the customers' buying behaviour and the performance of the organisation. This information may be part of an organisation's customer database or it may simply be hidden within invoicing and sales reporting systems.

The customer database

At the most basic level, a customer database may simply be a card index system. For example, a small opticians selling glasses and contact lenses may have a card index listing customers' names, addresses, the products purchased, the dates of their past visits to the optician and the date of their next check-up. Information about the products purchased from suppliers and costs and margins for these products may also be held within the optician's accounts and bookkeeping data.

A database is simply an organisation's memory bank, a collection of related information that can be accessed and manipulated quickly using computers.

Such basic data could be analysed in terms of:

- geographical spread of customers;
- frequency of spectacles and contact lenses replacement;
- frequency of visit;
- future trends in appointments;
- rates of retention (do customers come back after their purchase for future purchases?);
- product trends and future sales forecasts;
- price sensitivity of customers;
- profitability of individual customers and individual products.

To undertake such analyses may be time consuming where the information is spread over ledgers, computer files and paper-based files or card indexes. But in a larger chain of opticians, a computerised customer database may be held which would allow information and analysis of this type to be accessed at the touch of a few keystrokes. Such databases can be extremely complex. For example, the information gathered through loyalty cards in grocery stores such as Tesco sets out details of every individual purchase made by a cardholder, the frequency of their visits to the stores, their redemption of promotional coupons, and the typical value of their grocery shop. Such information can indicate whether individuals have pets, children, are vegetarian, their size of household and even their lifestyles (based on their purchases of convenience foods, alcohol, toiletries, etc.).

These complex data volumes are often so large that management do not have the time or ability to make sense of the data. The solution to this is **data mining**, where highly powerful computers are used to dig through volumes of data to discover patterns about an organisation's customers and products. Data can be mined to identify which products or promotions should be offered to attract particular customers to the store, which products should be linked in promotional offers, and which customers are the most profitable and worth retaining. It can also be used to identify customers for marketing research purposes. For example, if Tesco wished to test customer reactions to a new cat food product, it could use the database to identify large users of cat food and their shopping characteristics.

Types of customer data

There are four main types of customer data used to construct a database. These are:

1 Behavioural data. This type of data is derived directly from the actual behaviour of the customer and the interactions between the customer and the organisation. The data may come from a wide range of sources, including:

- advertising coupon responses;
- order forms;
- enquiries;
- letters;
- competition entries;
- telephone calls;
- sales order processing systems;
- accounting systems;
- payments;
- complaints.

2 Volunteered data. This is data that customers have volunteered by filling in a form or questionnaire (note that this is not a marketing research questionnaire) with the intention of updating the information that an organisation holds about them. They may do this to ensure that they get regular information about products or services that are of specific interest to them. An organisation will use such information to fill in missing fields within a database and also to provide triggers for future marketing campaigns.

3 Profile data. This is obtained by linking the data with other sources such as:

- **Geodemographic profiling systems** (e.g. Super Profiles, ACORN, MOSAIC), sourced from bureaux, such as CACI and Experian. The neighbourhood type data is linked to database addresses via the postcode. CACI started geodemographic profiling with ACORN, which clusters addresses according to census and electoral roll data. The census provides information on small groups of houses, which are then clustered with others according to common characteristics and given a particular ACORN label (see page 5). MOSAIC is a similar system, which has 58 postcode types built out of 54 variables such as average time of residence, household age, occupational groups, financial data and housing standards.

- **Lifestyle databases** (e.g. Clarita, ICD, Lifestyle Database): such data is derived from questionnaire responses to 'lifestyle surveys'. Such surveys rely on questionnaires being distributed in magazines and respondents being recruited through the offer of prizes or shopping vouchers. Such surveys should make it clear to respondents that the data is being collected for the creation of a database rather than for marketing research purposes. The information from such lifestyle databases can be used to predict the behaviour or characteristics of an organisation's customers based on the extent to which their profile matches those on the lifestyle database.

- **Company databases** (e.g. Dunn & Bradstreet): profiling of organisations can be undertaken using information relating to number of employees or the Standard Industrial Classification (SIC), which sets out the industry sector that the organisation is involved in.

An example of profiling: Dawes Cycles

Dawes, a UK manufacturer of bicycles, produces a full range of cycles that are sold directly into independent cycle shops. Following a recent management buyout, Dawes challenged CACI to help it to focus its limited sales and marketing resources onto those areas of greatest return.

As part of a new customer loyalty scheme, Dawes was collating customer information through cycle guarantee cards. The postcodes on these were profiled with CACI's consumer classification ACORN. Built using census data, ACORN segments the UK population into groups which share similar lifestyle and demographic characteristics.

The resulting profile enabled Dawes to determine the profile of its current consumer base and helped it to understand who its consumers were. It also helped to reshape the sales process. By analysing the catchment areas of each of the independent cycle shops using ACORN and overlaying this with typical consumer profiles and sales information, Dawes was able to rank the cycle shops to highlight those retailers that offered the greatest potential for growth. This also helped Dawes to decide on the sales team's call frequencies necessary for each cycle shop.[2]

4 Attributed data. Although marketing research respondents' identities are confidential and cannot be used to add to customer databases directly, the results from a marketing research study (for example, people who are in their 20s are more likely to have an MP3 player) can be extrapolated throughout the customer file. Therefore each person within this age category will have an entry on the database saying 'high likelihood of MP3 ownership'.

Processing data

Wherever the data originates, it is important that it is processed and stored in a methodical manner. Data capture needs to be disciplined, with data entered into prescribed fields and validated with software. The customer record is broken into fields, with each field holding an item of data such as surname, product number, time of purchase, telephone number, etc.

Any raw data being entered into a database by a call centre operator, a typist or from some external data file needs to go through a number of steps before it goes live on the database. These are described in the following subsections.

Formatting

Formatting aims to remove the inconsistencies and data 'noise' that appears within incoming data. Data should be in the correct sequence and length to fit within the various fields of the customer record. This may mean that punctuation and spaces may need to be removed. Lower-case data may also need to be converted to upper case. Abbreviations may also be substituted for longer or common words (e.g. *Limited* may become *Ltd*). Where the databases are international and therefore cover a number of countries, the database must take account of the different conventions in terms of addresses. For example, in France, the number of the house may be listed after the street name rather than before it, as is the case in the UK.

Validation

Software will be used to validate the accuracy of the information. Validation involves checking that the data is complete, appropriate and consistent, and may occur as the data is being entered or once the data is in the system. The database software will be able to identify fields where there are missing or invalid values. For example, the computer is likely to check name prefixes against a table of reference data such as:

01	Mr
02	Mrs
03	Master
04	Miss
05	Sir
06	Lord
07	Lady
08	Dr
09	Rev
10	Admiral
11	General
12	Major
13	Viscount
14	Hon.
15	Professor

Similar tables of reference data can be used to check job titles, brands of products, models of cars, etc. Addresses are checked against the national Postcode Address

File (PAF) for completeness and accuracy. The PAF in each country will hold the full postal address and postcode for each property in the country and also for large organisations that have their own unique postcode. The file can be obtained either free or for a small charge from the national post office in each country.

> In the UK the Postcode Address File (PAF) is the official Post Office file of postcodes and addresses. It includes over 26 million addresses and approximately 1.7 million postcodes. The PAF contains no data about the occupants of these addresses. It is available on CD-ROM with quarterly updates.

The data fields may also be subject to a rejection process which recognises spurious data or names given by pranksters such as Mickey Mouse and Donald Duck, although care must be taken to ensure that no real Mr M. Mouse or Mr D. Duck is wrongly branded a prankster. Software can also be used to identify consistency in the data; for example, if a file suggests that an individual does not have a mobile phone but the contact details give a mobile phone number.

Deduplication

Once the data has been entered into the database and validated, the process of deduplication will be undertaken. Deduplication is the process through which data belonging to different transactions or service events are united for a particular customer. Duplication may occur because address data is incomplete or entered in slightly different styles such as:

Mr David P. Jackson Valley Green Gatehouse Abbeyfield Grampian AB12 4ZT	Mr P. Jackson The Gatehouse Valley Green Abbeyfield Grampian AB12 4ZT
Mr & Mrs Jackson V. G. Gatehouse Abeyfield Near Aberdeen AB12 4ST	Mr D.P. Jakson The Gatehouse Valley Green Road Abbeyfield AB12

In order to maintain the integrity of a customer database, the software should either automatically eliminate duplicates or identify potential duplicates that require a manual inspection and a decision to be taken. Where the process is done automatically, the sophisticated software is adjusted to opt for overkill or underkill. Overkill is the technical term to describe the situation where the system removes all entries that may potentially be duplicates. Underkill is where the system may fail to detect duplicates as it only removes entries where the likelihood of duplication is very high. Overkill would be chosen by a credit card company to ensure a customer does not open two accounts by pretending to be two people. Underkill would be chosen where an organisation wanted to have as many prospects as possible on its database. Deduplication is more difficult in business-to-business databases as a result of organisations using multiple trading names, multiple locations, PO boxes and various abbreviations.

Deduplication needs to be undertaken each time data is added to a database and particularly when data files are merged as a result of corporate takeovers or the purchasing of external databases or mailing lists.

A database as a source of marketing intelligence

The database can provide information on the full universe of an organisation's customers rather than from just a sample as would be the case in most marketing research. The information available can be categorised into the following groupings:

- information on purchasing behaviour (products and services purchased, timing and method of purchase, trends);
- information on customer loyalty (relationship length, value, profitability);
- information on customer response (to marketing communications, new products, price changes, etc.).

However, there are weaknesses in such information:

- Database information only describes what has happened and not why. There is usually no information on why behaviour has changed or why customers have responded in the way that they have.
- Database information provides historical data and does not communicate customers' likely actions in the future. Trends that the database identifies may not continue in the future as a result of changing tastes, economic conditions, etc.
- Database information does not depict the whole market. A database only represents current customers and prospects; it provides no information on non-customers. It also provides no information on customers' behaviour with other suppliers.

Using a database for testing

Where database information has a major strength, it is in the area of tracking customer reactions to different service and product offerings. Direct marketing campaigns may have been used to obtain a direct one-to-one comparison between two marketing options, e.g. between a product with new features and an unchanged product. By presenting the two different offers to identical samples of the target audience, a measure of the selling power of each offer can be obtained.

Sample 1	New product features
Sample 2	Existing product features

The results of such a test (i.e. how many customers buy each option and what are their specific characteristics) can be stored on the customer database. It can provide an objective and measurable assessment of customers' behaviour in a true-life marketing environment. The data will show what a customer actually does when confronted by an actual proposition that has to be responded to or ignored. It can therefore provide an indication of what is likely to happen when a new offering is provided to the whole market.

Using a database for forecasting

The impact of past promotional campaigns can be used to forecast the outcome of future campaigns. By examining past buying behaviour of recipients of direct mail or promotional vouchers, it may be possible to predict which segments of a database are likely to respond to similar offers in the future. Software can be used for forecasting by modelling the impact of different offerings aimed at different groups of customers. For example, software using a tree segmentation approach is frequently used to determine the specific customer characteristics on which response rate depends. The long-term value of individual customer types can also be forecast based on their historical behaviour in terms of frequency of purchase, value of purchases and level of repeat purchase. The costs of servicing these customers would also be considered in determining the likely future value of different customer groups. The company can then determine which customers it is worth focusing future marketing campaigns upon.

Data mining

Data mining is the process of selecting, exploring and modelling large amounts of data to uncover previously unknown relationships and patterns of behaviour. With complex databases, it can often be difficult for managers to think up all of the possible hypotheses and questions to test with the data when looking for patterns and relationships. Data mining software can overcome this by highlighting and reporting on all possible trends and patterns among the data elements. Such software uses probabilities and statistics to determine which relationships are least likely to have occurred by chance and can be considered as being significant. There is a danger with data mining that it can waste more time than it saves as it can distract attention by highlighting patterns that have no commercial relevance. Therefore, managers must be ruthless in determining which patterns to investigate further and which to discard.

Data protection

In most countries and also within the European Union (EU) there are data protection laws. The key elements of EU legislation are discussed in Chapter 2. In addition to meeting the various laws relating to data protection, organisations should consider the following general principles.

An organisation should:

- never hold data about someone who does not want you to: it should give that person an opt out;
- not write to people who do not want to be written to;
- not hold less data than it needs to be effective, nor more than is acceptable: in particular, it should avoid sensitive areas such as racial and religious data;
- make sure the data is accurate and up to date;
- make very sure that the collection methods are honest and fair – information should not be collected under false pretences (for example, claiming that information is needed for a survey when it is actually being used for a mailing list);
- allow customers to see their data at little or no charge;
- be responsible for its own data: even if it is rented out, the organisation should ensure that it is going to a reputable organisation;
- be responsible for the data that is used: even if it is rented, the organisation should ensure that it came from a reputable source;
- protect the data that it holds;
- make sure the database records the customer's permission to use the data, and when it was given (or not);
- use any scheme such as Britain's Mailing Preference Scheme, which allows consumers to indicate a wish for a blanket suppression of direct mail from any source.[3]

Marketing decision support systems

Marketing decision support system: an interactive computerised information source designed to assist in marketing decision making.

In the larger more sophisticated organisations, the customer database will only be one part of the marketing decision support system (MDSS) available within the organisation. The purpose of an MDSS is to combine marketing information from diverse sources into a single source which marketing staff can enter interactively to quickly identify problems and obtain standard reports as well as answers to specific analytical questions. The MDSS system may also include other internal measures of:

- sales;
- operational measures (in grocery stores, these may include the speed at which items are scanned through the checkout, wastage, the frequency of products being out of stock, queue length);

- customer satisfaction scores and mystery shopping scores (see Chapter 4);
- advertising spend;
- customer complaints;
- the effectiveness of previous promotional campaigns;
- marketing research reports from studies undertaken in the past.

The MDSS will also contain external information on competitors, market trends and other environmental factors impacting on an organisation's market. A typical MDSS is assembled from three main components:

1 **Data storage:** this involves storage of data from all sources, stored in a sufficiently disaggregated way so that it can be analysed in relation to different parameters. It offers an instantaneous response to managers' requests for information without the need for a computer programmer.

2 **Reports and displays:** the capabilities of a MDSS range from simple ad hoc or regular tables and reports to real-time delivery of information alerts to a marketing manager's computer when critical incidents happen.

3 **Analysis and modelling:** the MDSS should be able to make calculations such as averages, develop trend data and undertake standard statistical procedures such as regression, correlation and factor analysis. The MDSS also allows modelling of 'what if' questions. For example: What are the likely implications of a 3 per cent price rise? What is the likely return from an advertising spend of 'x'? What is the ideal size for the salesforce? The models used to address these questions can range from straightforward forecasts to complex simulations representing the relationship between marketing input and output variables.

Whether internal data is held in a complex marketing decision support system or in a basic cardfile, the information that is available within the organisation should be examined first before researching external sources. The internal information may not answer the research questions, but it may provide pointers to where or how the information could be obtained through primary research or further secondary research. It may also provide lists of potential marketing research respondents as well as raising more precise information targets for the research.

External secondary information

With regard to external sources of secondary information, this can be obtained in hard copy format in the form of newspapers, trade journals, published reports, directories, books and government statistics. Alternatively, with the growth of the Internet, a large proportion of secondary information is now available in electronic format. Even if the information itself is unavailable electronically, the source and type of data available can frequently be identified by electronic means.

Finding secondary information on the Internet

If you know the web address or URL (uniform resource locator) of the website that contains the secondary data you are searching for, you can type the address into the web browser (Netscape Navigator and Microsoft Internet Explorer are the dominant browsers). If you do not know the specific web address, you can use a search engine. These can take the form of **single search engines**, each of which contains collections of links to sites throughout the world and an indexing system to help you find the relevant sites, or they can be **multiple search engines**, which allow you to search several search engines simultaneously from the one site.

These search engines allow you to enter one or more key words relating to specific products, markets, countries or companies, and in return the search engine returns a list of sites that have information relating to these key words. It is important to be as specific as possible with the key words used, otherwise the search engine may return a list of many thousands of sites. For example, if secondary information was required on the car market in Denmark, a search on AltaVista using the key words 'cars' and 'Denmark' returns a list of over one million sites, whereas a search using the words 'Cars', 'Denmark' and 'market' produces a list of 11,000 sites. This may still seem a lot but the sites that most accurately match the key words are always listed first.

The best-known search engines

Single search engines

AltaVista
Search tool owned by CMGI Inc. and Compaq. Indexes about 250 million web pages. You can select the language of the retrieved pages (e.g. search only for pages in German). There are many localised versions of AltaVista for different countries in Europe, the Asia–Pacific region and the Americas.
www.altavista.com

Ask Jeeves
You input a question (e.g. What size is the market for family cars in Denmark?) and the engine tries to match it with a list of questions it calculates may be similar to yours, and you choose the nearest.
www.ask.com

Business Suchdienst (German language)
Human-compiled searchable directory of sites.
www.business-suchdienst.de

EuroFerret
UK-based search engine, with 35 million web pages indexed.
www.euroferret.com

EuroSeek
Interfaces in numerous languages. You can restrict search to specific country domains or languages.
euroseek.net

Google
Examines over two billion web pages, and offers additional features such as automatic translation.
www.google.com

Hotbot
About 120 million pages are indexed. Full text is indexed. There are simple and advanced search options.
www.hotbot.lycos.com

Infoseek
There are Infoseek linkups in Denmark, Germany, Spain (Spanish language), France, Italy, the Netherlands, Sweden, and the UK.
infoseek.go.com

LookSmart
Manually compiled database of about 600,000 sites. Browsable by subject. There is also LookSmart UK and LookSmart Netherlands.
www.looksmart.com

Lycos
Indexes about 50 million pages. There are also localised versions for many European countries, including Germany, France, the UK, Belgium, Sweden, etc. You may get routed automatically to the one with the same country code as you.
www.lycos.com

Northern Light
About 205 million pages. As well as the usual searchable database of web sites, there is also a 'Special Collection' of journals, magazines, newswire, etc., databases, which you can search for free, but you pay to see the full text.
www.northernlight.com

Voila (French language)
Operated by France Telecom. Indexes 6 million French pages and 100 million worldwide.
www.voila.fr

Web.de – Deutschland im Internet (German language)
Directory of German web sites, which can be searched or browsed. Business section has news headlines, information from stock exchange.
web.de

Yahoo!
Yahoo! has local versions (e.g. Yahoo! UK & Ireland, Yahoo Deutschland, Yahoo! France, etc.).
www.yahoo.com

Multiple search engines

All4one
Searches AltaVista, Excite, Lycos and Hotbot.
www.all4one.com

Apollo 7
A German meta search engine searching 11 engines, mainly German.
www.apollo7.de

Dogpile
Defaults to search LookSmart, GoTo.com, Dogpile Web Catalog, Dogpile Open Directory, Direct Hit, About.com, InfoSeek, Real Names, AltaVista, Lycos and Yahoo!.
www.dogpile.com

ixquick
Searches 12 search engines, including All the Web, LookSmart, Hotbot, Netscape and Overture.
www.ixquick.com

Multimeta
Searches some major international and German search engines: Entireweb, AltaVista, Voila, Excite, Hotbot, Lycos, MSN, Yahoo! (Germany) and Yahoo! (USA).
www.multimeta.com

Directories of search engines

In order to identify other search engines, the following websites list available search engines as well as sources of business information:

Searchability
Describes various search engines, grouped by category.
www.searchability.com

Virtual Search Engines
Links to 1,000 search engines and directories, arranged by category.
www.virtualfreesites.com/search.html

Directories

In addition to search engines, there are a range of electronic directories available to the marketing researcher. Directories are helpful for identifying individuals or organisations relevant to a particular research study. They may be available in printed format, CD-ROMs or on the Internet. Some of the directories available on the Internet are listed in the box.

International directories

Trade Partners UK: websites for exporters
A good list of sites, including a large number of directories. List by country, region.
www.tradepartners.gov.UK

Dun & Bradstreet
Site includes a worldwide directory of 26 million companies and a UK Directory. Charges are made for detailed listings from the directories.
www.dnb.com

Financial Times company briefings
A subscription service giving basic details plus some financials of 18,000 major companies in 50 countries.
www.ft.com

Kompass
Directory of 1.5 million companies in 61 countries worldwide. Search by product or company. You get address, phone and telephone number free for all companies, and for selected companies you can get a more detailed profile.
www.kompass.com

Telephone Directories on the Web
Listing of yellow pages sites worldwide.
www.teldir.com

Austria: Compnet.at
Directory of 160,000 Austrian companies.
www.compnet.at

Austria: Herold gelbe Seiten im Internet (German language)
Austrian yellow pages directory of 290,000 firms.
www.gelbeseiten.at

Belgium: Top Business (German or English language)
Directory of Belgian companies, associations and professionals.
www.topbusiness.be

Denmark: Publicom (Danish language)
Official register of Danish companies.
www.publi-com.dk

Europages: The European Business Directory (multilingual)
Includes well-established directory of basic details of 500,000 companies from
30 European countries, searchable by name or product.
www.europages.com/home-en.html

Europe: Thomas Register of European Manufacturers
Directory of 207,000 companies in 17 countries in Europe.
www.tremnet.com

Europe: Wer liefert was? (multilingual)
WLW is a directory of 305,000 firms and their products. Covers Belgium,
Finland, Germany, Italy, Croatia, Luxembourg, the Netherlands, Austria,
Sweden, Switzerland, the Czech Republic, Slovenia, Slovakia, the UK, and
France.
www.wlw.de

Finland: Finnish yellow pages (Finnish language)
Finnish yellow pages directory.
www.keltaisetsivut.fi

France: Bottin (French language)
Directory of French companies.
www.bottin.fr

France: Les pages jaunes (French or English language)
Yellow pages directory, white pages and trademark pages.
www.pagesjaunes.fr

France: Pages Pro (French or English language)
Directory of 600,000 businesses from France Telecom.
www.pagespro.com

France: Telexport (French or English language)
Directory of 40,000 French exporters and importers, from the Paris Chamber
of Commerce and Industry.
www.telexport.tm.fr

Germany: Alleco (German language)
Complete registers of companies in Germany and Austria. Searching free, pay
for company details.
www.alleco.de

Germany: Teleauskunft (German, French or English language)
German white pages directory and yellow pages telephone directory.
www.teleauskunft.de

Greece: Everesi
An English-language directory of Greek companies with websites.
www.evresi.gr

Greece: Greek Telephone Directories
Includes yellow pages directory in Greek or English and white pages in Greek only.
www.hellasyellow.gr

Ireland: Golden Pages
Yellow page directory.
www.goldenpages.ie

Italy: Pagine gialle online (multilingual)
Directory has basic details of 3 million Italian businesses, with simple product classification. Searchable by name, address, product category, etc.
www.paginegialle.it

Netherlands: Gouden Gids online (Dutch language)
Yellow pages directory, including web links where available.
www.goudengids.nl

Spain industry (multilingual)
A directory which covers 160,000 companies. Includes line of business, products imported and exported, employee numbers, web link.
www.spainindustry.com

Spain: Paginas amarillas multimedia (Spanish language)
Yellow pages directory listing 1.6 million businesses and professionals.
www.paginas-amarillas.es

Sweden: StorTele (Swedish language)
Yellow pages directory of Swedish companies.
www.stortele.se

UK: Ask Alix
Directory of 1.8 million UK companies. Search by keyword, name or town. Companies that have purchased priority listings get higher ranking. Linked to Multimap.Com location maps.
www.askalix.com/uk

UK: Companies House
Search company database by company name or registration number.
www.companies-house.gov.uk

UK: Electronic Yellow Pages
An electronic version of BT's Yellow Pages directory, listing contact details of over 1.6 million UK businesses.
search.yell.com

UK: Kelly's
Directory of 143,000 companies
www.kellys.reedinfo.co.uk

UK: ThomWeb
Directory of 2 million UK firms, produced by Thomson Directories.
www.thomweb.co.uk

UK: ICC Information
Information on British and Irish companies, directors and shareholders.
www.icc.co.uk

Country information

The Internet is particularly useful for gathering information on countries. Governments provide a large amount of statistical information. In addition to general population censuses, national statistical offices produce an array of data on social conditions, consumer expenditure, industrial production, tourism, international trade, energy, agriculture, retailing and transport. The main categories of statistical information available from the UK government are:

- agriculture, fishing and forestry;
- commerce, energy and industry;
- crime and justice;
- economy;
- education and training;
- health and care;
- labour market;
- natural and built environment;
- population and migration;
- social and welfare;
- transport, travel and tourism.

A large proportion of government data can be sourced or at least identified on the government and regional websites listed in the boxes.

International information

Global information is available from the following sources:

CIA World Factbook
The CIA World Factbook is available at the Central Intelligence Agency site. The factbook has basic data on the countries of the world, produced by the CIA.
www.cia.gov/cia/publications/factbook/index.html

Europe: Eurochambres
Site of the Association for European Chambers of Commerce.
www.eurochambres.be

Europe: Market Access Database
A European Commission site, aimed at exporters. It has a database of commentary and market data on a variety of sectors in each of the European countries, together with general information about trade in the country concerned.
mkaccdb.eu.int

Europa: Public Opinion analysis
The European Commission's monitoring survey, it is posted onto their website (with surveys on attitudes to and awareness of various topics).
europa.eu.int/comm/public_opinion

United Nations
There is free access to selected social indicators (e.g. literacy rates, unemployment) and selected reference tools and reports.
www.un.org

World Bank
Includes press releases, information on publications, and selected country and region reports.
www.worldbank.org

Country-specific information supplied by national governments

These are the official sites of the statistics departments of the various national governments.

Germany: Federal Statistical Office
Statistics on the economy (including industry) and press releases.
www.destatis.de/e_home.htm

Italy: National Institute of Statistics
Statistics on the economy (Italian and English language).
petra.istat.it

Netherlands: Statistics Netherland (Dutch or English language)
Key statistics for the Netherlands, economic indicators, text of informative press releases and the searchable Statline statistical database.
www.cbs.nl

Norway: Statistics Norway (Norwegian or English language)
Statistical reports, arranged by subject.
www.ssb.no

Spain: **Instituto Nacional de Estadística** (Spanish or English language)
Press releases, publications catalogue etc. from the national statistics office.
www.ine.es

UK: **Government Information Service**
Links to many UK government department sites and local authority sites.
www.ukonline.gov.uk

UK: **Official statistics**
The UK Office for National Statistics site
www.statistics.gov.uk

Compilations of published marketing research

In addition to government data, research agencies and organisations sell reports and data on specific markets. The best known of these are listed in the box.

Marketing research reports

Datamonitor
Produces reports on industrial and consumer markets, worldwide but with emphasis on Europe.
www.datamonitor.com

Euromonitor
Produces reports on European markets.
www.euromonitor.com

Frost & Sullivan
Reports on industrial and consumer research, worldwide.
www.frost.com

Key Note
Produces market research reports, primarily about UK consumer markets, but with some coverage of European markets and business-to-business markets.
www.keynote.co.uk

Mintel
Produces reports on consumer markets both electronically and in print.
www.mintel.co.uk

Some agencies may also sell the data they gather from their regular audits, panels (see pages 82 and 139 for an explanation of these terms) and surveys. These can provide information on market shares, TV viewing patterns, newspaper and magazine readerships, awareness levels and purchasing behaviour. The best-known suppliers in the

UK are Neilson and BMRB, although a number of the major retailers such as Tesco and Boots are now also offering their suppliers data about market shares within their Stores.

News sources

Many broadcasting companies and newspapers provide very detailed websites providing press cuttings as well as information on companies and markets (see box).

Sites listing multiple sources

Euroseek Media guide
A set of links to news sites (newspapers, etc.) particularly for Europe.
euroseek.net

UN Wire
Daily free worldwide news, compiled by the United Nations, concentrates on issues such as peace, health and humanitarian issues. Provides hyperlinks, or references, to sources. E-mail delivery of headlines. Archive on website.
www.unfoundation.org/unwire

Individual sites

Belgium: De Financieel-Economische Tijd
Flemish-language Tijdnet ('de website van ondernemend Belgie'). It includes daily news from financial markets and Belgian companies.
www.tijd.be/nieuws

Europe: CBNC Europe
From NBC and Dow Jones. Recent news headlines.
www.cnbceurope.com

Europe: Euromoney
Has news from *Euromoney* magazine, worldwide directory of country reports.
www.euromoney.com

Europe: Week in Europe
Produced by the European Commission, it gives summaries of European news.
www.cec.org.uk/pubs/we/index.htm

France: *Le Monde* and *Le Monde Diplomatique*
Free daily news stories from *Le Monde*. French language.
www.lemonde.fr

Ireland: RTE
News from Ireland's broadcaster RTE.
www.rte.ie/news

Italy: ANSA
News from the Agenzia Nazionale Stampa Associata.
www.ansa.it

Italy: RCS online (Italian language)
Includes *Corriere della Sera* and various other papers from the same publisher, e.g. *Gazzetta dello Sport*, *Il Mondo*, *Capital*, and searchable archive.
www.rcs.it

Netherlands: NRC Handelsblad (Dutch language)
Business news updated daily.
www.nrc.nl

Norway: Aftenposten (Norwegian or English language)
Economic and business news.
www.aftenposten.no

Scandinavia Now online
Selected business news from Denmark, Norway, Iceland, Finland and Sweden.
www.scandinavianow.com

Sweden: Affärs Världen (Swedish language)
Business news from Sweden. Includes data on companies listed on the stock exchange.
www.afv.se

BBC news
News and business stories, with hypertext links to relevant sites. Searchable archive.
www.bbc.co.uk

Electronic Telegraph
From the publishers of the *Daily Telegraph*. Has a City section with news stories, market prices and commentary. Searchable archive.
www.telegraph.co.uk

Financial Times
News stories, company information, country information and market reports. Current and archive information.
www.ft.com

ITN
News, including business section, from this UK broadcasting company. Also archive search available.
www.itn.co.uk

The Times and *Sunday Times*
News and business section.
www.timesonline.co.uk

Newsgroups and discussion lists

There are also newsgroups (also known as discussion lists) which function much like bulletin boards for a particular topic. With over 300,000 newsgroups currently in existence, there is a newsgroup/discussion list for almost every hobby, profession and lifestyle. Most Internet browsers come with newsgroup readers. These newsgroups involve people posting views, questions and information on the site. Then discussions may occur between two or more people on a topic. The discussions are threaded, allowing any participant to follow the thread of a discussion relating to a particular topic. Newsgroups are often useful for identifying sources of information or getting people's initial reactions to a new idea or concept. The box lists some of the many newsgroups in existence.

Newsgroups

Directory of newsgroups
www.cyberfiber.com

Google Groups
Archives approximately 80,000 usenet newsgroups and discussion fora, mostly going back to 1995 (formerly Dejanews).
groups.google.com

Summary

Secondary information is important in the early stages of a marketing research project. It can save a lot of wasted time and effort in the primary research phase of a project. The Internet has made secondary information far more visible and accessible to the researcher. It is therefore important that the limitations of secondary data are known and care is taken in the selection of information used. This is true of both information that is available within an organisation and information that is obtained from external sources.

Customer databases can provide a significant amount of information about the behaviour and characteristics of an organisation's customers. However, they do need to be carefully designed and managed if their full value is to be realised.

This chapter has set out the main sources of information available within and outside an organisation. The sources listed are not exhaustive and this whole area is changing rapidly; however, this chapter should certainly give an indication of what is available.

Discussion questions

1 Why should an organisation spend time gathering secondary data prior to undertaking primary research?

2 Describe the key limitations of secondary data. How can the effect of these be minimised?

3   For each of the following products and services, which industry associations would you contact for secondary data? (a) Glass bottles, (b) farm machinery, (c) plumbing services, (d) photographic equipment, (e) games software.

4   What is the difference between internal and external secondary data?

5   Similar to the table of reference data on page 58, produce a table of reference data for job titles in your company or industry.

6   Describe the weaknesses of database information.

7   Enter your postcode into the www.upmystreet.com website and assess the accuracy of the ACORN profile for your neighbourhood.

8   List the possible contents of a marketing decision support system and explain their value to a marketing decision maker.

9   Explain what data mining is and where it may be useful.

10   Use five different search engines to find 'Marketing Research: An Integrated Approach'. Which of the search engines is best at finding an information source on this book?

Additional reading

Fletcher, K. and Peters L. (1996) Issues in customer information management. *Journal of the Market Research Society*, **38**(2), pp. 145–60.

Jackson, P. (1994) *Desk Research*. Kogan Page, London.

Jacob, H. (1984) *Using Published Data: Errors and Remedies*. Sage, Beverly Hills, CA.

Jenkinson, A. (1995) *Valuing your Customers*. McGraw-Hill, Maidenhead.

Leventhal, B. (1997) An approach to fusing market research with database marketing. *Journal of the Market Research Society*, **39**(4), October, pp. 545–61.

Macfarlane, P. (2002) Structuring and measuring the size of business markets. *International Journal of Market Research*, **44**, Quarter 1, pp. 7–30.

Stewart, D.W. and Kamins, M.A. (1993) *Secondary Research: Information Sources and Methods* (Applied Social Research Methods Series, Vol. 4). Sage, Newbury Park, CA.

Websites

CIO Data Warehouse Research Center: www.cio.com/research/data
Datawarehousing.com: www.datawarehousing.com
DataWarehousingonline.com: www.datawarehousingonline.com
The Data Warehousing Information Center: www.dwinfocenter.org

References

[1] See Key Note website for other examples (www.keynote.co.uk).

[2] Adapted from CACI case history on CACI website (www.CACI.co.uk).

[3] Adapted from Jenkinson, A. (1995) *Valuing your Customers*, McGraw-Hill, Maidenhead, p. 237.

4
Collecting observation data

London Underground – observing the service

London Underground is part of London Transport and is responsible for managing and operating the underground public transport network in and around London. Over 772 million passenger journeys are made on the network each year. London Underground uses mystery shopping for monitoring and measuring the level and consistency of the underground's tangible and intangible service performance.

It uses trained independent customer service auditors (mystery shoppers) to act as anonymous travelling customers. Four times per year, teams of these mystery shoppers travel around the network in pairs. They follow strictly specified routes, assessing 26 train measures and 116 station measures relating to the following attributes:

Stations	Trains
Cleanliness and environment	Cleanliness and environment
Lighting and brightness	Brightness and comfort
Temporary and short-term information	Maps and information
Permanent and long-term information	Permanent and long-term information
Electric and electronic information	Electric and electronic information
Comfort factors	Public address
Customer facilities	Staff
Ticket purchase and use	Safety
Staff	General impression
Customer mobility and access	Personal safety

The shoppers' routes are organised such that in each quarter, at least seven visits are made to each platform of the 246 London Underground stations. A typical mystery shopper's route consists of six station visits with five train assessments taking place while travelling between the stations. Each pair of shoppers is supplied with a questionnaire which includes descriptions of the rating scale to be used for each service measure together with a short statement explaining what the measure covers. The survey is designed to allow shoppers enough time to complete the train measures between station visits. When shoppers arrive at the nominated station, they move from the platform, along a routeway, through the booking hall and then exit the building. The shoppers then retrace their steps to a designated platform and move on to the next station in the assignment, carrying out a train assessment en route. All of the areas where responses are required are highly structured to minimise the impact of the shoppers' own individual preferences in terms of areas such as service or cleanliness. Shoppers are often shown videos or photographs of service environments or encounters to illustrate the appropriate rating for a specific type of encounter.

In terms of output, mystery shopping reports providing feedback on lines and individual stations are distributed after each wave of the research to over 100 users within London Underground. The majority of users are responsible for the operational management of stations and tracks. They use the mystery shopping scores for setting targets for staff and contractors as well as for developing appropriate action plans to improve performance. Line development managers and corporate planning also use the mystery shopping data to develop business cases for capital investment.[1]

Learning outcomes

After reading this chapter you should:

- understand the value of observational research;
- be aware of the different categories and types of observation research;
- in particular, understand the nature of audits and mystery shopping research;
- be aware of some of the ethical issues associated with observation research.

Key words

audits	observation
content analysis	one-way mirrors
contrived observation	participant observation
hidden observation	scanner-based research
Internet monitoring	stand-out equipment
mechanised observation	structured observation
mystery shopping	television viewing measurement

Introduction

Observation is an important methodology in all forms of research into behaviour. Whether a scientist is examining the behaviour of animals or chemicals, observation using the human eye or with measuring equipment is the traditional scientific approach. The behaviour of markets, customers and organisations can also be observed. This chapter looks at how observation is used in marketing research.

Observation research defined

Observation is a data gathering approach where information on the behaviour of people, objects and organisations is collected without any questions being asked of the participants. The researcher becomes the witness of behaviour and events rather than the collector of information second-hand from others about their perceptions and recollections of behaviour and events. Events may be witnessed by human observers or using equipment.

Observation only measures behaviour – it cannot investigate reasons behind behaviour, it cannot assess the participant's attitudes towards the behaviour and it cannot measure the likelihood of the participant repeating the behaviour. Also, only public behaviour is observed; private behaviour in people's homes or offices is generally beyond the scope of observation studies. The types of behaviour that can be measured are physical actions such as shopping patterns or television viewing, verbal behaviour such as conversations with customer service personnel, spatial patterns such as traffic flows on roads and in-store, temporal patterns such as the amount of time spent queuing, and physical objects such as the brands of products in a consumer's bathroom cabinet (see Table 4.1).

Table 4.1 Examples of what can be observed

In-store	At home	On the road
Arrival time in store	TV viewing patterns	Use of public transport
Shopper's movement pattern in store	Family purchasing behaviour	Driving routes taken
Browsing behaviour	Brands of products owned	Behaviour while driving (e.g. use of car seat belts, mobile phones, etc.)
Time spent shopping/queuing	Children's behaviour with a new toy	
Behaviour/expressions when queuing		
Interaction with service personnel		
Products purchased		
Payment methods used		

> **Researcher quote:** *Observation tells you what people are doing but it doesn't tell you why they are doing it.*

Observation allows the researcher to overcome some of the potential weaknesses of interviewing and survey research. These weaknesses include:

- There can be a discrepancy between real and verbal behaviour. Occasionally statements are made in interviews which are not a true reflection of the behaviour of the interviewed persons.
- Often facts are only brought to light by means of natural settings only. The interviewee is not conscious of them and they are therefore not easy to get at by questioning.
- The verbal capabilities of the interviewed person can limit the quality and quantity of information gathered.

The major advantage of observation research over surveys of respondents is that the data that is collected does not have distortions or inaccuracies as a result of memory error or social desirability bias. The data that is recorded is the actual behaviour that took place. For example, if a video rental outlet wanted to identify the most frequently rented videos over the last six months, in surveying its members, it would find that the respondents would be unlikely to remember all the videos that they rented and/or would miss out those videos that they now feel embarrassed about having rented. The computers in the video outlet, on the other hand, could count the number of times each video is borrowed and therefore give a true representation of rental behaviour.

Observation overcomes the high refusal rates that may exist for some survey research. Respondents may be willing to provide their attitudes in a survey but may be less willing to spend a large amount of time listing their behaviours and purchases. Much of the observation can go on without inconveniencing the participant and in certain cases without the participant being aware that it is happening.

Categories of observation

Observation studies can be categorised along the following five key dimensions:

- natural versus contrived;
- visible versus hidden;
- structured versus unstructured;
- mechanised versus human;
- participant versus non-participant.

   1 Natural versus contrived observation. Consumers may be observed in their natural setting when they are going around the supermarket, queuing in banks or driving along the road. Those being observed are going about their normal activities and are unlikely to be aware that they are being observed. Alternatively, a researcher might recruit mothers with young children to be observed playing with new toys. In this case, the recruited people will know that they are participating in a study. The research may take place in a room with video cameras or one-way mirrors. It is therefore a contrived environment as the children may behave differently from the way they do in the natural setting (i.e. at home). However, the contrived environment tends to speed up the observation data-gathering process. The researcher does not have to wait until certain events happen; instead the researcher can manipulate the situation and the participant to meet the research objectives.

2 Visible versus hidden observation. Visible observation is where people know they are being observed, because they can see either the observer or the camera, or because a poster at a shop door may actually tell them that observation research is being undertaken in the store. If people know they are being observed, they may behave differently than normal so hidden observation methods such as one-way mirrors and security cameras are often used for research. However, if the research is being undertaken in an environment where people would not expect to be videoed or observed then organisations will be expected to inform them that observation research is being undertaken.

3 Structured versus unstructured observation. The recording of observations can range from being very structured to being very unstructured. At the very structured end of the scale, observers may simply count phenomena and keep a tally on a record sheet. For example, traffic counts will normally involve observers using hand-held counters and a paper record sheet. Other structured observation may involve the observer filling out a form similar to a questionnaire on each person being observed. Unstructured observation would involve an observer watching the actions of people either in person or on a video and making notes on behaviour.

4 Mechanised versus human observation. Where observation involves the counting of the frequency of behaviour, mechanised observation may be more appropriate than employing human observers. This can include automated traffic counting devices, which can count the number of cars crossing a sensor in a section of road or the number of people exiting or entering a shop, bank, museum or post office. Equipment can be installed in people's homes to monitor their television viewing patterns or to scan all the purchases that they bring home from a supermarket. In the supermarkets themselves, electronic scanners can accurately monitor the purchases being made as well as the speed at which checkout assistants are handling each item. Where the behaviour being monitored is more complex, human observers are required.

5 Participant versus non-participant. Where service quality and staff performance are being measured using **mystery shopping** (see the London Transport example at the start of this chapter), the observer may actually participate in the transaction that is being observed. The use of participant observation, where the researcher interacts with the subject or subjects being observed, stems from the field of cultural anthropology. Anthropologists would take part in a tribe's daily life in order to understand the norms, attitudes and behaviours that were neither documented nor communicable via language. In mystery shopping, the observer will communicate with the service provider as part of the transaction but will not communicate the fact that observation is being undertaken. Most other forms of observation do not involve any participation.

Specific observation methods

Audits and scanner-based research

An audit is an examination and verification of the movement and sale of a product. There are three main types of audit: (1) wholesale audits, which measure product sales from wholesalers to retailers and caterers, (2) retail audits, which measure sales to the final consumer, and (3) home audits, which measure purchases by the final consumer.

Retail audits were introduced by ACNielsen in 1933 in the USA. They are now an international activity, with ACNielsen (www.acnielsen.com) alone undertaking regular retail audits in more than 80 countries over 6 continents. Originally they involved a team of auditors from a research firm visiting a representative sample of food stores every two months to count the inventory of the store and record deliveries to the store since the last visit. For each product category (including brands, sizes, package types, flavours, etc.) national and regional sales figures per store type were then produced. Additional information such as prices, allocated display space and in-store promotional activity would also be collected. With the growing use of electronic scanners at the checkouts of the larger multiple retailers, much of this information is now gathered electronically, with auditors only being required to visit the smaller independent stores. Scanners have enabled data to be gathered more quickly and accurately, as well as providing the opportunity to study very short time periods of sales activity. The information from retail audits is provided to the food, household, health and beauty, durables, confectionery and beverage products industries, where it helps management gauge product penetration, market share, overall product performance, distribution, promotion effectiveness and price sensitivity.

Wholesale audits work in a similar fashion. For example, the ACNielsen Catering Wholesale Service, a continuous tracking service, offers manufacturers detailed, weekly sales and marketing information on the wholesale sector within foodservice.

It offers manufacturers detailed analysis of trends by individual sector and product category, and customer segment. The customer segments include the workplace, education, health, hotels, pubs, restaurants, fast-food environments, travel and leisure. The data comes from the six largest operators in the catering wholesale sector: 3663, Brake Bros, Watson & Philips Foodservice, dbc Foodservice, Cearns & Brown and Glanbia Foodservice. Together, these six operators represent up to 70 per cent of leading manufacturers' deliveries into the UK foodservice market.

Home audits involve a panel of households who have been issued with a diary or an electronic scanner for installation in their kitchens to record all of their purchases across every outlet type, from warehouse clubs to convenience stores and from supermarkets to pharmacists and mass merchandisers. The diary needs to be completed on a continuous basis by the panel members and is then returned at regular intervals to the marketing research agency. Information from electronic scanners will be returned automatically overnight down the telephone line (see details of the Taylor Nelson Sofres Superpanel on page 140).

Knowledge of purchases makes it possible to analyse:

- heavy buyers and their associated characteristics;
- brand loyalty and brand switching rates;
- repeat purchases for new products.

Such information is more comprehensive than that produced from retailer's loyalty card schemes as it relates to all of the shops that a customer visits.

Television viewing measurement

In all countries where there is television advertising, the measurement of audience size is critical to the charges made for advertising slots and the scheduling of programmes.

In the UK, the Broadcasters Audience Research Board (www.barb.co.uk) uses professional research suppliers to conduct and report on audience research. A survey takes place based on a sample of about twenty thousand households structured by postal code areas within ITV areas. The questions are designed to determine patterns of television usage across the country and to ensure that the audience measurement panel is an up-to-date representation of the population.

The results of the survey, together with government census data, are then used to select a fully representative sample of homes in terms of viewing habits, TV equipment ownership, family composition, demographics, etc., to take part in the audience measurement panel. Three thousand homes take part in the panel and are given a nominal incentive payment for their services.

Electronic meters are attached to the television sets and register when the set is turned on and off, and which channel is tuned. In addition, each household has a control with eight numbered buttons on it, and each member of the household has his or her own number. Each person presses their number whenever they are watching the television, and again when they stop. This data is fed into the meter. Video cassette recorders have a separate meter attached to them that records when they are recording a programme, and when they are playing a tape. The electronic meter can collect data from up to nine television sets in one household. All the information about what channel the set was tuned to and who was watching is retrieved automatically by a computer via the local telephone system.

Internet monitoring

It is possible for web-based retailers and suppliers to monitor the number of times different pages on their site are accessed, what search engines brought people to the site, and what service provider browsers are using as well as tracking the peak times at which people access the site. With cookies, a text file is placed on a user's computer by the web retailer, making it possible to identify when users revisit the site and the sections of the site that they visit. For example, an organisation such as Amazon (www.amazon.co.uk) can monitor the types of book that particular customers are interested in and whether the customers spend time reading the review of the books or considering alternatives. Cookies give web retailers an advantage over traditional retailers as they can provide information on browsers (the equivalent of window shoppers) as well as customers.

One-way mirror observations[2]

In many focus groups used in qualitative marketing research, one-way mirrors are used to enable clients and researchers to view respondent behaviour during a discussion. Behind the mirror is the viewing room, which consists of chairs for the observers and video cameras to record the proceedings. An alternative to the mirror is to televise the proceedings to a separate viewing room.

Although transcripts of what is said in a discussion are normally prepared, the one-way mirrors allow the observers to see facial expressions and non-verbal reaction to a product or concept. The way in which people handle a product in a group or the manner in which children play with a new toy can all be observed through a one-way mirror. A first-hand view of customer reaction to a product can be very useful to clients, particularly during the early development stages of a new product.

> **Client quote:** *The data comes alive, when you can see the people actually saying the words.*

In-store observation

Observation studies within retail outlets are commonplace. The prevalent use of security cameras in stores has provided a mechanism for monitoring behaviour. That behaviour can relate to the route customers take through the store, the products that are looked at, the time spent in the store and the interaction between shoppers and sales personnel. Security cameras have all but replaced the human observers who used to follow customers around the store.

Stand-out equipment

Stand-out equipment or shelf impact testing is a contrived form of observation used with new packaging to determine the visual impact of new packaging when placed on shelves next to competitors' products. Respondents are shown projected pictures (either 35 mm slides or computer-generated graphics) of shelving displays. They are asked to press a button when they see a particular brand. Measuring the elapsed time between the picture being shown and the button being pressed can provide an indication of the impact of the packaging. Different packaging colours and formats can be compared prior to the relaunch and repackaging of a product.

Mystery shoppers

Mystery shopping, a form of participant observation, uses researchers to act as customers or potential customers to monitor the processes and procedures used in the delivery of a service. In the UK, mystery shopping is used quite extensively by organisations in financial services, retailing, motor dealerships, hotels and catering, passenger transportation, public utilities and government departments (see Table 4.2).

Table 4.2 Major sectors using mystery shopping

Sector	Examples
Financial services	Banks, building societies, life companies, general/motor insurance, estate agents
Leisure/travel	Travel agents, tourist offices, hotels, restaurants, car hire, public houses
Transport/utilities	Airports, underground, rail, airlines, electricity, gas, water
Motoring	Motoring organisations, car manufacturers, petrol stations
Retail	Grocery, department stores, electrical, fashion, Post Office
Government departments	Benefits Agency, Vehicle Licensing, Passport Office, Inland Revenue

Unlike customer satisfaction surveys, the mystery shopping approach is being used to measure the process rather than the outcomes of a service encounter. The emphasis is on the service experience as it unfolds, looking at which activities and procedures do or do not happen rather than gathering opinions about the service experience. Customer satisfaction surveys on their own do not provide sufficiently detailed information to allow management to identify and correct weaknesses in the service delivery process.

> **Client quote:** *I need to know if staff are saying and doing everything according to our stated standards of quality. Only mystery shopping can tell me if this is happening.*

Mystery shopping studies are used for three main purposes:

- to act as a diagnostic tool, identifying failings and weak points in an organisation's service delivery;
- to encourage, develop and motivate service personnel by linking with appraisal, training and reward mechanisms;
- to assess the competitiveness of an organisation's service provision by benchmarking it against the offerings of others in an industry.

Mystery shopping aims to collect facts rather than perceptions. These facts can relate to basic enquiries, purchases and transactions covering topics such as:

- How many rings before the phone was answered?
- How long was the queue?
- What form of greeting was used?

They can also relate to more complex encounters such as in the purchase of a mortgage where the procedures adopted in a two-hour fact-finding meeting can be assessed in terms of service quality and financial compliance.

Table 4.3 Rating scale used by London Underground

Politeness of staff

Score	Comment
10	Excellent – very courteous
9	–
8	Good – polite
7	–
6	–
5	Acceptable – business like
4	–
3	–
2	Poor – brusque
1	–
0	Unacceptable – short or rude

In terms of any research approach, the reliability of a technique can be defined as the extent to which similar observations made by different researchers would provide the same results. This is a very important issue if mystery shopping results are to be taken seriously and particularly if staff are to be rewarded on the results. Attempts are made to maximise the reliability of mystery shopping through the use of objective measurement and the careful selection and training of the shoppers.

Objective measurement is clearly possible in verifying whether an activity did or did not happen (e.g. whether the customer's name was used), and also where attributes can be counted (e.g. the number of checkouts that are open and queue length). However, judgements on the appearance of the premises and staff as well as the actions of staff in terms of politeness, product knowledge and helpfulness are slightly more subjective. Users and agencies attempt to minimise this subjectivity by using rating scales with descriptive labels (Table 4.3). This is often supported by verbatim comments from shoppers to justify their rating selection.

All of the areas where responses are required are highly structured to minimise the impact of the shoppers' own preferences in terms of areas such as service or cleanliness. Shoppers are often shown videos or photographs of service environments or encounters to illustrate the appropriate rating for a specific type of encounter.

An encounter involves interaction, and the quality of that interaction is as dependent on the customer as it is on the service provider. How does mystery shopping reduce the impact of the shopper's personal characteristics such as sex, age, accent, looks, ethnic background and personality? Great care is taken in the selection of mystery shoppers. The shoppers must match a customer profile that is appropriate for the scenario that they are being asked to enact. This becomes more important and more difficult as the encounter becomes more complex. Selecting passengers for public transport may require less rigorous procedures than selecting a customer for a mortgage or investment product. For these complex products, the agencies are of the opinion that the shopper should invent the absolute minimum by using their own financial details and personal circumstances. This can clearly cause difficulties, particularly where a customer's details are entered onto a centralised computer (e.g. during a fact-find for a financial product). That shopper may not be able to approach the financial organisation again, and with the use of credit scoring agencies, there may also be problems when approaching other financial institutions. Similar problems occur in purchasing an item such as a car, in that a shopper cannot enter a showroom and ask about a sports car, then reappear weeks later and enquire about a family car. Therefore agencies have to continually recruit and maintain a bank of credible shoppers. This can be difficult – one car manufacturer cancelled a mystery shopping programme because the agency was having difficulty continually recruiting new and credible car purchasers. Credibility may require shoppers to be existing customers of the organisation, and where the purchase is normally a joint purchase, husband and wife teams may need to be recruited.

Selection is also important with regard to the personality of the shopper. Most situations require the shopper to adopt a neutral rather than an aggressive or defensive approach in the service encounter. In traditional marketing research, a field supervisor would be able to check the suitability of an interviewer by accompanying and observing them during their first interviews. With the exception of situations where the shopper is relatively anonymous such as in a train or a grocery store, it is difficult to accompany and supervise the shopper. Each encounter may vary, so a repeat visit will not be able to verify the accuracy and reliability of the shopper's observations. Agencies have to rely on edit checks of completed evaluation forms, looking at the trends of a particular shopper's observations as well as checking the logic of the evaluation.

Training is also important, particularly with regard to the briefing of shoppers on their circumstances and needs but also in terms of data collection skills. Shoppers receive a detailed briefing on the scenario that they are to enact, focusing on their personal characteristics, the questions they should ask and the behaviours they should adopt. They are then tested on these elements to ensure that the service encounter is realistic and to reduce the opportunity for the true identity of the mystery shopper to be detected by the service personnel.

> **Researcher quote:** *We want 'natural' encounters; we don't want to use mystery shoppers who simply want to play the part of an awkward customer.*

The training of data collection skills focuses on identifying the elements of the service to be observed as well as the retention and recording of the information. Retention and recording of information is particularly important, as the shoppers cannot complete an assessment form during the service encounter. Therefore shoppers receive memory testing and training. In certain situations they may be able to use *aides-mémoire* to record and retain data (e.g. writing on a shopping list or making notes about a holiday or financial product) but otherwise the information must be memorised until the encounter is complete and the shopper has left the premises. On a two-hour fact-finding interview for an investment product, there can be a large amount to remember.

In traditional survey research, the reliability of a research approach is often judged on sample size. In mystery shopping, an outlet may only be shopped once or possibly twice in any wave of the research. For example, if a hotel chain undertakes a mystery shopping exercise three times per year, during each phase of the research, individual hotels will receive an assessment based on one visit from a mystery shopper. Where an outlet offers a range of different types of product, slightly more visits may be necessary (e.g. a bank branch may receive three or four separate visits and telephone enquiries about mortgages, savings products and transaction products). The service organisations justify such limited numbers of visits by stating that every service encounter is critical and the quality of service delivery should be identical in each encounter. This has an implication for the results generated from these studies. An organisation may find that the average mystery shopping score for all of its outlets may follow a certain trend but the scores for individual outlets may fluctuate from month to month depending on the specific circumstances at the time of the visit. The aim of the service companies is to standardise the quality of all service encounters; the fluctuations provide a measure of the extent to which standardisation of service is being achieved.

Content analysis

Content analysis involves the analysis of the content of any form of communication, whether it is advertisements, newspaper articles, television programmes or taped conversations. For example, the content of advertisements might be investigated to evaluate their use of words or themes or characters. Equal opportunity groups may carry out a study to look at the number of times women or ethnic minorities appear in mass media advertising. Companies may study the images or messages used by competitors as an input to the design of their own promotional materials. The content of annual reports, corporate statements and speeches can all be analysed in the same manner. Study of the content of communications can be more sophisticated than simply counting the items – the communication is broken into meaningful units using carefully applied rules. Further discussion of this technique is covered in Chapter 5, as it is a method that is frequently used for analysing qualitative data.

Ethical issues in observation research

Observation methods introduce a number of ethical issues. The use of cameras and other hidden observation methods impact upon the respondent's right to privacy. Chapter 2 details the manner in which the marketing research codes of conduct deal with observation. However, the general rule of thumb is that consumer behaviour can only be observed and videotaped without the participant's permission when the behaviour occurs in a public place (e.g. in a street or a retail store). If the observation is undertaken in any other location or where the participant would not expect to be observed by others, then permission must be sought. Therefore in any contrived environment or interviewing situation (e.g. focus groups), the participants must be told that they will be observed or videotaped. Deception is not an acceptable practice.

Summary

Observation is an important marketing research tool. It allows the researcher to overcome some of the potential weaknesses of interviewing and survey research by providing a more detailed and accurate record of behaviour. The researcher is not dependent on the willingness or the memory of respondents to recall factual information.

However, observation only measures behaviour – it cannot identify reasons for behaviour or respondents' attitudes towards the behaviour. It can answer questions such as what, where, when and how but it cannot determine why someone behaves in the way that they do.

Observation can take many forms and can be categorised according to the following key dimensions:

- natural versus contrived;
- visible versus hidden;
- structured versus unstructured;
- mechanised versus human;
- participant versus non-participant.

Observation does not necessarily have to focus on the behaviour of customers: mystery shopping examines the performance of organisations and their service personnel. Mystery shopping, a form of participant observation, has become a major activity of the marketing research industry as a result of the increasing emphasis being put on service quality and service standards.

In addition, the long-established observation methods such as audits, traffic counts, television viewing measurement, one-way mirrors, content analysis and stand-out equipment have been augmented as a result of improved technology by the more recent developments in scanner-based research, Internet monitoring and video recording. With more and more enquiries and purchases being handled by telephone call centres and computer links, mechanical or technological methods of observing behaviour are likely to become even more important.

Discussion questions

1   What are the biggest limitations of observation research?

2   What advantages does observation research have over interviewing and survey research?

3   In what type of situations would contrived observation be more appropriate than natural observation?

4   In the past week, how many of your actions or behaviours do you think have been observed mechanically?

5 What advantages does mystery shopping have over the sending of a manager around various service outlets to see what is happening?

6 Describe the workings of a retail audit.

7 How do web-based retailers and suppliers monitor your actions on their sites?

8 What attempts are made to make mystery shopping as objective as possible?

9 What training do you need to become a mystery shopper?

10 Is observation for marketing research purposes ethical? Justify your answer.

Additional reading

Dawson, J. and Hillier, J. (1995) Competitor mystery shopping: methodological considerations and implications for the MRS Code of Conduct. *Journal of the Market Research Society*, 37(4), pp. 417–27.

Grove, S.J. and Fisks, R. (1992) Observational data collection methods for services marketing: an overview. *Journal of the Academy of Marketing Science*, 20(3), pp. 217–24.

Morrison, L.J., Colman, A.M. and Preston, C.C. (1997) Mystery customer research: cognitive processes affecting accuracy. *Journal of the Market Research Society*, 39(2), pp. 349–62.

Wilson, A.M. (1998) The use of mystery shopping in the measurement of service delivery. *Service Industries Journal*, 18(3), pp. 148–63.

Wilson, A. and Gutmann, J. (1998) Public transport: the role of mystery shopping in investment decisions. *Journal of the Market Research Society*, 40(4), October, pp. 285–94.

References

[1] Adapted from Wilson, A. and Gutmann, J. (1998) Public transport: the role of mystery shopping in investment decisions, *Journal of the Market Research Society*, 40(4), October, pp. 285–94.

[2] An example of a viewing facility for group discussions can be seen at: www.researchhouse.co.uk.

5
Collecting and analysing qualitative data

Sizzle and Stir – researching a new concept

Since the introduction of the Chicken Tonight product in 1993, the UK market for cook-in sauces has grown enormously and become highly competitive. Van den Bergh, part of the Unilever group and the maker of Chicken Tonight, wished to grow the brand and develop the product's differentiation from the competition. The company needed to understand: What was going on in the home? What was the cook thinking, feeling, and wanting during the meal preparation process? How would a busy mother, with kids on the go, want to prepare a chicken korma? A series of group discussions were used to look at packaging, label design, flavour delivery, benefits, attitudes, occasions of use, etc. From these, the concept of a two-step cooking product was developed with packaging which con-

sisted of two jars. The top jar held a paste of spices for the meat, with the bottom jar holding the cook-in sauce, the aim being to offer the customer a curry or oriental dish that tasted as good as a takeaway. Even the name 'Sizzle and Stir' came from a respondent at a group discussion. Consumers liked the name because it told you exactly what the function of the product was and it was fun, catchy and lively. In the first year of production, sales of Chicken Tonight Sizzle and Stir exceeded the company's most optimistic estimate.[1]

Learning outcomes

After reading this chapter you should:

- be able to identify the types of research most suited to qualitative research;
- be aware of the key characteristics of individual depth interviews;
- understand the key tasks involved in undertaking group discussions;
- appreciate the main types of projective technique;
- be aware of the influence of technology on the future of group discussions;
- understand the processes and procedures involved in analysing qualitative data.

Key words

accompanied shopping	paired interviews
animatics	photo sorts
brand mapping	projective questioning
brand personalities	projective techniques
cartoon completion	role playing
chat rooms	screening questionnaire
concept boards	sentence completion
content analysis	spider-type diagrams
content analysis software	stimulus materials
cut and paste method of analysis	story boards
discussion guide	tabular method of analysis
focus group	text analysis software
group discussions	topic list
group dynamics	video conferencing
group moderator	viewing rooms
individual depth interview	word association tests

Introduction

This chapter is designed to introduce you to the principal methods used to gather qualitative data. It discusses the two most commonly used qualitative research approaches, these being the individual depth interview and the group discussion (also known as the focus group or group depth interview). Techniques such as projective techniques that are used to enhance the productivity of the qualitative approach will also be discussed.

Qualitative research defined

Qualitative research can be defined as research which is undertaken using an unstructured research approach with a small number of carefully selected individuals to produce non-quantifiable insights into behaviour, motivations and attitudes. Taking the key components of this definition:

- the data gathering process is **less structured** and more flexible than quantitative research and does not rely on the predefined question and answer format associated with questionnaires;
- it involves **small samples** of individuals who are not necessarily representative of larger populations;
- although the sampling process may lack the statistical rigour of more representative studies, great **care is taken in the selection of respondents** owing to the time and effort that will be spent on researching the views of each of them;
- the data produced is **not quantifiable** and is not statistically valid – qualitative research is concerned with understanding things rather than with measuring them;
- the researcher obtains **deeper and more penetrating insights** into topics than would be the case with a questionnaire or a more structured interview.

It is a mistake to consider qualitative and quantitative research as two distinctly separate bodies of research – many studies encompass both approaches, with qualitative research being used to explore and understand attitudes and behaviour, and quantitative research being used to measure how widespread these attitudes and behaviours are.

> **Researcher quote:** *A study which combines qualitative and quantitative methods gives you depth of understanding as well as information about the general representativeness of that understanding.*

Types of research most suited to qualitative research

There are three main areas where qualitative research is most commonly used; these are exploratory research, new product development and creative development research.

Exploratory research

Exploratory research will be used when an organisation's management wishes to increase its understanding of customer attitudes, emotions, preferences and behaviours. As such, qualitative research may be required to obtain an initial understanding of:

- **Consumer perceptions of a product field.** For example: *Do consumers consider muesli bars as competing in the biscuit market, the cake market or the confectionery market? Is flavoured fromage frais exclusively a children's product?*
- **Consumer segments.** For example: *How should users of mobile phones be segmented? How can beer drinkers be segmented?*
- **Dimensions which differentiate brands.** For example: *Why do consumers buy Coca-Cola rather than Pepsi? What training shoe brands are considered to be suitable for the sports enthusiast rather than the fashion conscious?*
- **The decision-making process.** For example: *What do consumers think about when selecting birthday cards? How do people go about planning their annual holiday?*
- **Product usage patterns and behaviour.** For example: *What emotions do different decor and colour schemes in a hotel trigger? What would make customers change their mobile phone network?*
- **Identifying service or product improvements.** For example: *What improvements would customers like to see in the service they receive from a bank? How could the design of railway carriages be improved?*

Such exploratory research will assist in determining whether an organisation should undertake further research as well as helping to define the objectives, information targets and sample for a programme of more extensive research.

New product development

Qualitative research is particularly suited to obtaining reactions to new product concepts and designs where consumers are presented with an idea or innovation that they have not experienced before. During the new product development process there is usually a stage where a concept has been developed in a communicable form but no tangible usable product is available for testing. Qualitative research can help to determine if the concept warrants further development and provide guidance on how it might be improved and refined. By exposing people to the concept and getting their reactions, it is possible to identify:

- perceived benefits of the concept;
- weaknesses in the concept;
- likely interest in the concept;
- potential target market for the concept;
- suggested improvements or developments of the concept.

Qualitative research can also be used in the later stages of the product development process to assess reactions to mock-ups or prototypes of new products and their packaging.

> **Client quote:** *Qualitative research can give you confidence that the product concept you are creating is as exciting as you think it is.*

Creative development research

Qualitative research can assist in the development of the message and creative execution of advertising and promotional activity. It can also be used to pre-test the chosen execution to determine whether it achieves an organisation's communication objectives.

During the development stage, qualitative research can enable 'the creatives' from an advertising agency to understand the consumer's relationship with the product group and individual brands. All promotion involves the encoding of a message to accomplish an organisation's communication objectives. Encoding is the process of translating messages into a symbolic form through the use of words, symbols and non-verbal elements that have meaning for and can be interpreted by the target audience. Qualitative research can assist in this process of encoding by providing information on the language that consumers use when talking about products, the lifestyles that they associate with different brands and the perceived value they place on different product attributes during brand selection.

Qualitative research also plays a role in the pre-testing of promotional material before it is launched to ensure that it is communicating the intended message to the target audience. The intention is not to judge whether the respondents like the advertising or promotional material but is instead aimed at analysing the campaign's effectiveness at correctly communicating the intended message.

The individual depth interview

Individual depth interviews are interviews that are conducted face-to-face, in which the subject matter of the interview is explored in detail using an unstructured and flexible approach. As with all qualitative research, depth interviews are used to develop a deeper understanding of consumer attitudes and the reasons behind specific behaviours. This understanding is achieved through responding to an individual's comments with extensive probing. The flexibility of this probing sets this interview approach apart from other questionnaire-type interviews. Although there is an agenda of topics (topic list) to be covered, the interviewers will use their knowledge of the research objectives, the information gained from other interviews and the comments of the respondent to select which parts of the dialogue with the respondent to explore further, which to ignore, and which to return to later in the interview. Not only is the depth interview flexible, it is also evolutionary in nature. The interview content and the topics raised may change over a series of interviews as the level of understanding increases.

Researcher quote: *You really obtain an understanding of a subject when you listen to people in depth.*

Key characteristics

Length

In-depth interviews tend to be longer than traditional questionnaire-based interviews, with many lasting within the region of 60–90 minutes. The research industry also undertakes mini-depth interviews, which are less wide ranging in the areas covered and tend to last up to a maximum of 30 minutes. Mini-depth interviews are often combined with other research techniques such as hall tests (see page 135) or tests in places where respondents may not be available for a longer period (e.g. at an airport or railway station).

Information collection

Almost all depth interviews are tape recorded. This enables the conversation to flow, eye contact to be maintained and interaction to occur. On some occasions video recording may be undertaken, particularly where the style of the individual respondent and/or non-verbal reaction to a subject is required.

Topic list

A topic list or interviewer guide is used which outlines the broad agenda of issues to be explored and indicates at which points stimulus material or projective techniques should be introduced. It must be stressed that a topic list contains a list of topics or issues and does not consist of predetermined questions. The format of a topic list is similar to the group discussion guide shown in Figure 5.2 (page 103).

Location

Interviews are normally undertaken in the respondent's own home or office, although this can sometimes result in interruptions from telephones, children or work colleagues. However, this threat of interruption has to be balanced against the opportunity for the interviewer to experience the context of the respondent. From an office it may be possible to determine the seniority of the respondent and the extent to which the respondent uses technology such as computers, as well as the nature and size of the respondent's employer. In the home, the neighbourhood, the street, the house and the interior will help to provide background on the lifestyle of the respondent.

Using the respondent's premises also allows the researcher to access additional materials for the interview such as files and brochures in an office or bills and the contents of the kitchen cupboard at home. Alternatively, interviews can be undertaken in central locations such as hotels, cafes and bars where the number of possible interruptions can be reduced and refreshments can be provided to put the respondent at ease. Overall, interviews are carried out wherever it is convenient for the respondent and may include retirement homes, prisons, airports, etc.

Paired interviews

Although many in-depth interviews involve one respondent, it may be necessary to undertake the interview with a pair of people such as a married couple, a mother and child, two business partners or even teenage friends. This allows the interviewer to assess how the two respondents influence each other's attitudes and behaviour. However, it should only be used where both individuals are jointly involved or where each has an influence on the actions of the other in the area under investigation; for example:

- **Married couple:** purchasing mortgages, electrical white goods, DIY products, contraception methods, etc.
- **Mother and child:** purchasing clothes, toys, confectionery; television viewing habits.
- **Teenage friends:** Attitudes towards music, fashion, entertainment activities.
- **Business partners:** Attitudes towards financing arrangements, technology, government support.

The development of rapport

The development of rapport is critical to the success of an in-depth interview: respondents will only open up and express their true feelings and opinions if they feel comfortable with the interviewer. Rapport is not automatic and has to be worked at during an interview. Interviewers can attempt to ensure that they dress in a manner which is not too dissonant from the respondent, for example dressing smartly when interviewing a businessperson or dressing casually when interviewing students or young people.

> **Researcher quote:** *If people aren't relaxed, they won't open up and it can feel like an interrogation rather than a conversation.*

Body language

Frequently the interviewer may mirror the body language of the respondent in terms of posture, hand movements and expressions. This is similar to our own actions when me meet friends and assists in the building of rapport. As long as it is done in a relatively natural manner it should put the respondent at their ease. A depth interviewer needs to visually demonstrate an interest in what the respondent is saying through behaviours such as nodding agreement, smiling and maintaining eye contact. Silence can be used to demonstrate an interviewer's willingness to learn by allowing the respondent to think rather than filling a pause in the interview with further questions.

The skills of the interviewer

The flexibility of the in-depth approach means that the skill of the interviewer is critical to the quality of information obtained from the interviews. A standard fieldforce interviewer is trained to administer questionnaires in a relatively mechanical manner by asking questions accurately and quickly. This is very different from the conceptual thinking required of an in-depth interviewer, who has to establish a rapport with the respondent while keeping his or her own opinions concealed and encouraging the respondent to develop points and summarise his or her views. Where a questionnaire-based interview can often seem like an interrogation, a depth interview should seem like a free-flowing conversation. The Qualitative Research Study Group (1979) suggested that a good qualitative interviewer needs to demonstrate the following qualities:

- intellectual ability plus common sense;
- imagination plus logic;
- conceptual ability plus an eye for detail;
- detachedness plus involvement;
- neutral self-projection plus instant empathy;
- non-stereotypical thinking plus a capacity to identify the typical;
- expertise with words plus a good listener;
- literary flair/style plus capacity to summarise concisely;
- analytical thinking plus tolerance of disorder.[2]

> **Researcher quote:** *The quality of the research output depends on the research input and that input is the interviewer. The skills of the qualitative interviewer will determine the level and depth of information obtained.*

Specialised in-depth interviews

Accompanied shopping is a specialist type of in-depth interview, which involves respondents being interviewed while they shop in a retail store and combines observation with detailed questioning. The interviewer obtains the agreement of respondents to accompany them on a shopping trip. Purchases and the selection process are then observed, with the interviewer asking how certain decisions and purchases are arrived at as they occur. This enables the interviewer to witness the impact of displays, packaging and point-of-sale material on *real behaviour* rather than recalled behaviour. Owing to the time and cost involved, the number of accompanied shops is usually small. There are also concerns among some researchers that the interviewer's presence may bias behaviour, with respondents choosing healthier or more environmentally friendly products when they are being observed.

Group discussions

Group discussions (also known as focus groups or group depth interviews) are depth interviews undertaken with a group of respondents. In addition to the increased number of respondents, they differ from individual interviews in that they involve interaction between the participants. The views or contribution of one person may become the stimulus for another person's contribution or may initiate discussion, debate and even arguments. The interaction between group members, commonly called **group dynamics**, is critical to their success and is their principal asset. Group discussions developed out of the group therapy approach used by psychiatrists to tackle areas such as addiction and behavioural problems in patients. Psychiatrists found that patients were more willing to talk about a topic if they were aware that other people had similar experiences and attitudes as themselves. They would also talk about a topic in more detail if they were in discussion with other group members than if they were to respond to direct questioning. This is the case whether the subject matter relates to psychologically oriented problems such as alcohol dependency or to marketing research issues relating to brand image, new packaging and advertising messages. Group discussions can provide the researcher with a richer and more detailed knowledge of a subject. It can also highlight the dynamics of attitudes, by showing how participants change their opinions in response to information or stimulus introduced by others. Information about the triggers that change opinions is of particular importance to advertisers.

Group discussions were first used for marketing research in the mid-1950s, when they were termed motivational research. Since then, their use has grown dramatically, not only for research on commercial products but also for governments and political parties. They take the form of a moderator holding an in-depth discussion with 8–12 participants on one particular topic. However, this description belies the complexity of the tasks involved in managing and running a successful focus group. The following subsections set out the detail of the tasks involved.

Recruitment of participants

Recruitment involves ensuring that appropriate respondents are identified, invited to participate and ultimately turn up prepared to take part in the group discussion. Recruitment is a very critical element of group discussions and has long been a major quality control issue in the UK marketing research industry. Group discussions are unlikely to achieve their research objectives if the wrong types of participant are recruited, all of the invited participants do not turn up, or they turn up with erroneous preconceptions or expectations.

The research proposal will set out the type of participants required for a group discussion and based upon this the research manager will produce a specification for the recruiting interviewers. For example, if Colgate is researching a new type of toothpaste for sensitive teeth, the specification may request adults between the ages of 18 and 45 who regularly purchase and use specific brands of toothpaste for sensitive teeth. Care must be taken to ensure that the specification is not so tightly defined that it becomes a very difficult task to find appropriate participants within the short time scales that are frequently imposed. The participants would normally be recruited in street interviews or in doorstep interviews, although telephone interviews or interviews in stores (or in this case, in dentists' waiting rooms) could also be used. Members of the public will be screened for their appropriateness using a screening questionnaire similar to the one set out in Figure 5.1.

In addition to assessing appropriateness to the topic, a screening questionnaire will be used to screen out those potential participants who work in or have some connection with toothpaste manufacturers or the marketing research industry. It will also aim to identify and screen out 'the professional group discussion participant'. These are individuals, sometimes members of the recruiter's family or friends who can often be co-opted by less than professional recruiters into groups on a regular

Name:	Date:
Address:	Phone:
Time:	Interviewer:

Good morning/afternoon,

I am _____ from _____ Market Research Services. We are planning a group discussion on the topic of toothpaste and sensitive teeth. Would you be interested in participating in such a session on _____ at _____

(IF 'NO', TERMINATE AND TALLY)

1 Do you regularly purchase any of the following brands of toothpaste? (SHOW LIST OF TOOTHPASTE BRANDS)

     YES................. 1 CONTINUE
     NO.................. 2 TERMINATE AND TALLY

2 Are you between the ages of 25 and 64?

     YES................. 1 CONTINUE
     NO.................. 2 TERMINATE AND TALLY

3 Do you live in the Glasgow area?

     YES................. 1 CONTINUE
     NO.................. 2 TERMINATE AND TALLY

4 Do you or any member of your family work for an advertising agency, a marketing research firm or a company which makes, sells or distributes toothpaste?

     YES................. 1 TERMINATE AND TALLY
     NO.................. 2 CONTINUE

5 When, if ever, did you last attend a marketing research group? _____
(IF LESS THAN 6 MONTHS AGO, TERMINATE AND TALLY)

Figure 5.1 Sample screening questionnaire to recruit group participants

basis to make up the numbers and ease the scale of the recruiter's task. However, by attending many group discussions, they become atypical and respond differently to stimuli and therefore do not accurately reflect the attitudes and behaviours of the market segment under investigation. The increase in respondent refusal rates can tempt recruiters to co-opt these tame participants. It is therefore important that screening questionnaires are used to ensure that appropriate standards of recruitment are maintained. However, it is also important that the researcher makes the recruiter's job as straightforward as possible by keeping the screening questionnaire short and simple rather than trying to use it to gather large amounts of additional material on each of the potential participants.

New 'group discussion' concerns

A significant number of group discussion participants are repeat attendees, according to a new study that raises questions over how some groups are recruited. The BMRB survey found that one in 10 people who had taken part in a group over the past 12 months had done so at least three times that year, while one in 100 had clocked up 16 or more visits. The findings suggest that almost one-third of an eight-person group will have attended at least four groups in the past year, with one person having attended at least 16. The figures may be overly high, BMRB said, as they suggest more groups are being run in Britain than current estimates. However, they still raise concerns over repeat attendance, the firm added.[3]

If a respondent meets the criteria on the screening questionnaire, they will then be invited to participate in the group discussion, which may take place anything up to a week after recruitment. If the recruit accepts the invitation they will often be given an invitation card setting out the venue, time, contact numbers, etc. However, this does not guarantee that the recruit will attend the group. One of the biggest problems in undertaking group discussions is the high incidence of 'no-shows'. People say they will attend, but then fail to appear because they have something more interesting to do or experience 'cold feet' about attending the group. Why does this happen? In trying to understand people's attitudes towards why they do or do not take part in a group discussion, it is useful to consider the typical negative attitudes that a potential participant may have:

- I am worried that it is all a con-trick.
- I won't have anything useful to say.
- I am going to feel embarrassed.
- I am worried that they are going to try and sell me something.
- I don't know anybody there and I don't know what is going to happen.
- Why should I spend my valuable time helping with research?
- It will probably be very boring.
- I did one before and I didn't enjoy the experience.
- I might be the only person there.

It is the role of the recruiter to reassure the potential participant that it is vitally important that they attend as their input will be crucial to improving the particular product or service in question. Incentives of financial rewards or gifts and vouchers will frequently be offered to demonstrate the value put on the participant's contribution in both input and time. This would be promised at the recruitment stage and given to the participant when they attend the group discussion. Recruiters should also explain what will happen, the typical number of people attending and the type of relaxed atmosphere that will exist. The legitimacy of the exercise can be communicated through explaining the links of the recruiter to professional bodies such as the Market Research Society and through using a respectable or high profile venue.

Selection of group discussion venue

Traditionally, group discussions were held in locations where participants felt most comfortable, such as individual homes located in the same area as the respondents or hotels for business people. These locations have no special facilities apart from the researcher using an audio tape recorder. Although the majority of group discussions are still undertaken in such venues, there are also a growing number of specialist viewing rooms or viewing facilities in cities and large towns throughout Europe. Some are owned by research agencies, but the majority are independent and available to anyone willing to pay their hourly room-hire rates.

These specialist facilities are set out in the form of a boardroom or living-room setting with video cameras or a large one-way mirror built into one wall. Behind the mirror or in a room linked to the video cameras there is a viewing room, which holds chairs and note-taking benches or tables for the clients and researchers. The participants' comments, body language and reactions can be watched from these rooms without inhibiting the activities of the group discussion participants. This is not the only opportunity that the clients or researchers have, as the action is also videotaped or audio taped for later viewing or analysis. However, live viewing does allow the marketing, research and advertising people to view together and discuss the implications of what they see and hear. It also allows young researchers to observe and learn about group dynamics, content, structure and the role of the moderator.

The group discussion participants will be told that they are being watched or taped but this rarely inhibits them, particularly after the discussion has been running for a few minutes. Refreshments and food or snacks will also be commonly provided to assist in relaxing the atmosphere.

Scheduling and the number of group discussions

In scheduling group discussions, the needs of the participants, the research team and the clients must be considered. For the participants, it relates to times at which the people in the target group are likely to be available, e.g. outside working hours, around school times for parents, times of available public transport, etc. For the research team, if multiple group discussions are being undertaken with more than one moderator, the logistics of moving videos and other support material between the groups as well as travel times need to be considered. For clients, if they want to attend, the timing of group discussions must fit with their diaries and availability.

With regard to the number of groups, three or four group discussions are sometimes sufficient, particularly if there is consensus in the findings obtained from each group. The moderator tends to learn a great deal from the first two discussions. Frequently the third and fourth sessions only help to confirm the findings of the first two as much of what is said in these groups has been said before. More groups may be needed if the researcher is seeking information about regional differences or differences between different segments of the target population. Undertaking only one or two groups can be dangerous as there is always the chance that you get a group whose views are atypical of the target population.

Creation of a discussion guide

Similar to the topic list in individual depth interviews, a discussion guide is used which outlines the broad agenda of issues to be explored and indicates at which points stimulus material or projective techniques (see pages 106 and 107) should be introduced. The discussion guide is generated by the research team based on the research objectives and client information needs. The guide tends to break the group discussion into three phases:

- The introduction phase:
  - the objectives of the session;
  - the nature of a group discussion is explained;
  - the general agenda of topics that will be followed;
  - prompts for the participants to introduce themselves.

- The discussive phase:
  - general topic areas to be discussed;
  - potential prompts and stimulus material.

- The summarising phase:
  - prompts for summarising what has been discussed;
  - thanks to participants.

Figure 5.2 shows an actual discussion guide used by a moderator to explore hotel guests' attitudes towards the various attributes provided by a hotel during a weekend break.

Introduction (10–12 minutes)

- ❏ Welcome and explain nature of group discussions
- ❏ Explanation of research project, objectives, sponsors, etc.
- ❏ Format of session
- ❏ Introductions: first name, home town, length of stay
- ❏ Reasons for coming to this (a) destination (b) hotel

Ease of obtaining information / booking prior to arrival (10 minutes)

- ❏ Type and source of information used and required prior to booking
- ❏ Means of contact: telephone / answering machines / Internet / correspondence / coupon response / travel agent
- ❏ Expectations of a brochure – what can make it useful / useless
- ❏ Central reservations versus individual establishment versus travel agent
- ❏ Information required over the telephone and with confirmation
- ❏ Ask for examples of good contact and examples of disappointing contact

Figure 5.2 Discussion guide on hotel attributes

Figure 5.2 *continued*

Quality of accommodation (40 minutes)

What makes a good impact / bad impact (obtain examples):

1 On arrival and prior to entering hotel

2 On entering the reception area

3 The bedroom

   ❐ What makes a bedroom comfortable?
   ❐ If not mentioned, ask about bathroom, bed, bedding, cleanliness, control of
      temperature, television, radio, lighting, mini-bar, cupboard space, telephone,
      decor, security, tea/coffee facilities, toiletries, etc.)
   ❐ Expectations of room service
   ❐ Provide examples of bedrooms which have failed to reach or exceeded
      expectations

4 Dining and bar facilities

   ❐ What enhances/spoils the experience?
   ❐ Cover areas such as:
      ❐ service (efficiency versus friendliness)
      ❐ decor/ambience
      ❐ quality of offering
      ❐ range of offering
   ❐ Do these vary according to the meal being taken (e.g. breakfast versus dinner)
   ❐ Provide examples of good and bad experiences

5 Leisure facilities

   ❐ Importance of leisure facilities – what is required and service expected/level of use

6 Departure

   ❐ Obtain good and bad experiences of checking out – summarise important issues

7 Other features relating to accommodation

Overall value for money (10 minutes)

❐ Perceptions of what this means
❐ Understanding of hotel grading system (crowns/commended, etc.)

Summary of satisfaction criteria (10 minutes)

❐ So overall what are the key things that affect satisfaction (prerequisites versus
   desirables)?
❐ Check to see if anything left unsaid that is important

Thanks for your participation

Moderating the group

The skill of the moderator is critical to the success of a group discussion. The moderator has to bring together a group of strangers, build a rapport between them, focus their discussions on the appropriate topics, and ensure that they all have an equal opportunity to contribute, as well as control any participants who would like to dominate the group. They must do all of this in a supportive rather than a dominating manner – the client does not want to hear the moderator's views: instead, he or she wants to hear what the participants have to say.

> **Researcher quote:** *Every group is different, you don't know how it is going to go. You need to stay alert and be ready to react to every situation.*

No two group discussions run in exactly the same manner, as the personalities of the participants are different in each group. Some groups work well with a great deal of co-operation, participation and a willingness to listen to each participant's point of view. Others can result in tension, defensiveness and general hostility. It is important for a moderator to understand the thinking process of the group participants.

1 **Seeking understanding:** many participants will turn up in a slightly anxious state, unsure about what is going to happen and possibly uncertain about the exact topic, the length of time they will be there and what is expected of them. This will make them defensive and relatively quiet and subdued until they can work out what is going on. This situation can be eased partially by the recruiter and also by the interviewer in the introduction phase of the group discussion. The recruiter should be clearly informing the participants about the topic area, the nature of a group discussion and the time that they will need to set aside for the exercise. The moderator should reinforce this in the early stages of the group discussion. It is also important for the moderator to share the broad agenda for the discussion, so that the participants have some knowledge of what is likely to be discussed next rather than being anxious about what or how much is yet to come. The moderator may also wish to 'surface' any anxieties by asking the group during the introduction phase what they expected to happen prior to arriving at the venue.

2 **Wish to feel included:** a participant will be anxious until they make a contribution to the discussion. This anxiety will increase, the longer the period of non-contribution. It is important for the moderator to involve all participants at a very early stage in the group discussion. Getting participants to introduce themselves, should not be seen as addressing this issue. Although introductions help, particularly where participants introduce the person sitting next to them rather than themselves, there is a need for some input on the topic from each participant early on in the discussion. Projective techniques, discussed on page 107, may be one way of doing this.

3 **Seeking to communicate my status/experience:** it is quite normal, particularly in the early stages of a group discussion, for participants to try to communicate their status relative to the others in the group. This may take the form of communicating

their extensive experience or knowledge of the topics being discussed (e.g. 'I have a brother who works in the car industry and he says . . .'); alternatively, they may communicate an air of aloofness (e.g. 'I don't have time when I go shopping to notice the type of packaging on a product'). This is all to do with positioning within the groups and will tend to die down as the group discussion progresses. If it does get out of hand, with one individual attempting to dominate the discussion, the moderator may need to interrupt and ask what the others in the group think about a particular topic.

4 **Wish to relate to others:** once members have established their status within the group, they will tend to settle down to co-operate on the tasks of the group, telling of experiences, anecdotes, attitudes, etc. The body language of the group becomes much more positive, with participants mirroring each other's language and gestures. They are willing to listen to each other and agree or accept each other's viewpoint. At this stage the moderator should play a very passive role, becoming involved only to maintain the discussion on relevant subject areas. The moderator should be happy to allow silences rather than filling them with a battery of questions; it is even possible to offer up the silence for discussion: 'That seems to have killed the discussion. Any thoughts about why?'.

5 **Wish to be seen as having valuable opinions/views:** throughout a group discussion, participants are keen to see that people are listening to them and what they are saying. The moderator's role is to show that he or she is listening by maintaining eye contact, nodding, and smiling or frowning at appropriate times, probing for further information and mirroring the body language of the contributor.

6 **Wish to leave:** the moderator must realise that the participants are unlikely to be as interested in the topic as the research team, so it is important to bring the group to an end before the participants start becoming edgy and thinking about things they are going to be doing after the group has finished. It is therefore good practice to 'signpost' to the group when fidgeting occurs that it is almost time for winding up. Participants are then more likely to remain committed to the activity if they know that there is not much longer to go. The last few minutes should allow the participants to add any comments that they feel should have been covered in the discussion.

Good moderators need to develop an awareness of the changing moods and feelings in a group as the discussion progresses. Such an awareness can help in the planning and handling of each group discussion.

Stimulus material

Stimulus material is used to communicate the marketer's or advertiser's latest creative thinking for a product, its packaging or its advertising. By using such material it is possible to get the participants' reactions to the creative ideas. The material may take many forms, ranging from complete advertisements on video to a set of concepts sketched out on a flip chart or board. Care must be taken in interpreting participants' reactions to stimulus materials as the setting and the semi-complete state of the materials may result in participants being more critical of the concepts. The most common types of stimulus material are:

• **Concept boards:** a set of boards on which different product, advertising or pack designs or attributes are illustrated.

- **Storyboards:** key frames for a television advertisement are drawn consecutively, like a comic strip. Storyboards can also be presented on different pages of a flip chart – to avoid group participants reading ahead.
- **Animatics:** key frames for a television advertisement are drawn or computer generated and then filmed with an accompanying sound track. Actual photographs can also be used to improve the presentation.
- **Mock-up packs or products:** a 3D mock-up of a new packaging or product design.
- **Completed advertisements:** these may be in the form of videos, press ads, etc.

Projective techniques

Projective techniques are techniques used in group discussions and in-depth interviews to facilitate a deeper exploration of a respondent's attitudes towards a concept, product or situation. They involve respondents projecting their feelings into a particular task or situation, enabling them to express attitudes that they find difficult to verbalise. As such, a projective technique may gather 'richer' data than do standard questioning and discussion. Although the results of projective techniques are sometimes difficult to interpret, they provide a useful framework to get respondents to start exploring and talking about a subject in more depth.

> **Researcher quote:** *Projective techniques really get the respondents talking and laughing . . . but you need that to get to the bottom of a subject!*

There is a very wide range of potential techniques, although the most frequently used for marketing research are projective questioning, word association, brand personalities, brand mapping, photo sorts, sentence completion, cartoon completion and role playing. Other well-known techniques such as the Thematic Apperception Test (TAT) the Rorschach inkblot test and psychodramas are more common in the field of pyschoanalysis than in marketing research.

Projective questioning

Projective questioning, sometimes known as third-party techniques, is probably the most straightforward of projective techniques. It involves putting the respondent 'in somebody else's shoes' and asking questions such as:

- 'What do you think the average person thinks about when selecting a bank for a savings account?'
- 'What do you think people in your street would think if they saw a BMW parked in your driveway?'
- 'A lot of people seem very negative about McDonald's fast food. Why do you think that is the case?'

Answers to such questions will usually reflect the opinions of the respondent without causing them any embarrassment at having to express their own feelings overtly. Questions such as the McDonald's question may also help to reassure the respondent that other people have opinions similar to themselves. By looking at something from a different perspective, respondents may identify attitudes or concerns that they were not aware they had.

Word association tests

The clinical application of word association tests in psychoanalysis dates back to the late nineteenth century when they were used to analyse the human thinking process. In marketing research, word association is typically used in conjunction with brand names or celebrity endorsers. With brand names it highlights not only the products that the brand is associated with but it also identifies the values associated with a particular brand or corporate identity. This can assist marketers in developing communication objectives and strategies to position or differentiate their brands from those of competitors. Similarly, in selecting a celebrity to endorse a product in an advertising campaign or in a sponsorship deal, it is useful to determine what values are associated with the celebrity.

Examples of word association tests

What is the first thing that comes to mind when I say chocolate?

Write down the first ten things that come to mind when I say IBM?

What is the first thing that comes to mind when I say Tiger Woods?

Answers can either be reported verbally or written down. The moderator would not stop after the respondents have identified one word but instead would probe respondents for further words. So for 'chocolate', respondents might give answers such as 'Cadbury's', 'biscuit', 'bar', 'treat', 'luxury', 'temptation', etc.

Respondents can then be asked why they associate chocolate with each of these words. For example: what is the link between chocolate and temptation? The answer may help in the development of advertisements similar to the ones used for Cadbury's Flake.

In addition to the direct outputs of word association, the technique is also very useful as a way of warming up a group by getting everybody contributing and involved. Most people find it fun and it is a very straightforward task for respondents to undertake.

Brand personalities

Brand personalities involve respondents imagining a brand as a person and describing their looks, their clothes, their lifestyles, employment, etc. For example: 'If Nokia was a person, what type of person would he or she be?' might result in answers such as:

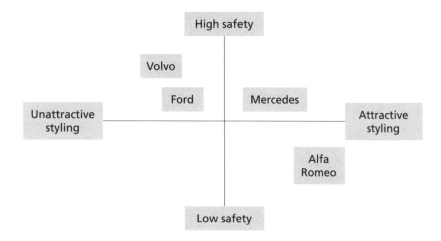

Figure 5.3 Brand map

A modern, relatively young slightly quirky male, who is small in size, reasonably attractive and interesting to know. Probably into pop music and outdoor pursuits.

This could compare with Philips:

A slightly older family-oriented person who is pretty dependable and slightly boring. Probably into classical music and golf.

Alternatively, respondents can also be asked to imagine the brand as another product; for example: 'If British Airways was a car what type of car would it be and how would this compare with SAS or easyJet?' Whichever approach is taken, developing brand personification can help to verbalise the imagery and vocabulary associated with the brand.

Brand mapping

Brand mapping involves presenting a set of competing brand names to respondents and getting them to group them into categories based on certain dimensions such as innovativeness, value for money, service quality and product range. This can be done by giving the names verbally and allowing the respondents to use a flip chart or by putting them on cards and allowing the respondents to sort the cards into groups. Sometimes axes relating to different dimensions (see Figure 5.3) are provided to enable direct comparisons to be made between different groups and respondents.

Brand mapping is a useful technique for discovering how consumers segment a market and also for understanding a brand's positioning. Respondents can also be shown new advertising or packaging designs to see if this changes the positioning of the brand in any way.

Photo sorts

Photo sorts can be done either by using a set of photographs on individual cards or by using a collage of photographs on a display board or flip chart. The photographs would tend to depict different types of people of varying ages, lifestyles, employment types, etc. Respondents are then asked to connect the individuals in the photographs with the brands they think they would use. For example, in research undertaken for Manpower recruitment, respondents had to match pictures of different types of office staff with different temp. agency brands. Similar to brand mapping, photo sorts allow the researcher to understand how consumers perceive a brand and its positioning.

Sentence completion

In sentence completion, the respondent is given an incomplete sentence or group of sentences and is then asked to complete them. This helps to highlight attitudes that lie just below the surface. Examples of incomplete sentences are as follows:

- 'People who eat Pot Noodle are . . .'
- 'I think people who buy products from mail order catalogues are . . .'
- 'Tesco, as a supermarket, is . . .'

Once a respondent has completed the sentence, they can then be probed to find out why they said what they did. In many ways, sentence completion is similar to word association although it can enable researchers to put more of a context on the respondent's thinking process.

Cartoon completion

Cartoon completion is a pictorial version of sentence completion. The cartoon usually shows two characters with balloons for dialogue or thoughts similar to those seen in comic books. One of the balloons sets out what one of the characters is thinking or saying, while the other is left empty for the respondent to complete. An example is shown in Figure 5.4. The faces of the figures are usually expressionless so that the respondent is not influenced to respond in a particular manner. A variation on this approach is to have a cartoon of a character using a particular brand or facing a particular situation and asking the respondent to verbalise what the character is thinking.

Role playing

Role playing is another route of obtaining information about brands without directly asking questions of the respondent. Respondents are asked to act out the brand. For example, a lawn mower manufacturer needed information on consumer perceptions

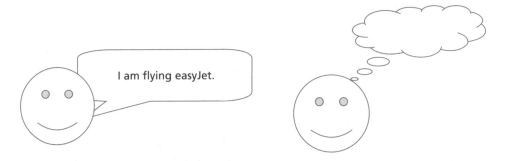

Figure 5.4 Cartoon completion

of differing competitor brands. In the group discussions, respondents were asked to move across the room as different brands of lawn mower (e.g. as an Atco, as a Flymo, as a Black & Decker). Such role playing can often be difficult to interpret, although respondents are generally asked to explain what they are doing and why. Respondents can also be asked to play the part of a particular brand and sell themselves to other members of the group (for example, an instruction may be: 'Play the part of Huggies nappies and try to persuade a new mother why she should buy you rather than a competitor'). As role play involves an element of exhibitionism, it will only work with people who are relatively extrovert and relaxed.

Technological developments in qualitative research

The Internet and improvements in telecommunications have led to agencies and companies experimenting with alternative ways of running and viewing group discussions. In terms of viewing, there is the potential for clients to watch a group discussion over their company's in-house broadcasting network or through video streaming on the Internet. This can allow more people to be involved in observing the research, particularly if it is being carried out in a different region or country. Pieces of the video broadcast can also be incorporated into e-mails or PowerPoint presentations to demonstrate the points being made.

In terms of running groups, improved telecommunications have enabled groups to be run by video conferencing. This has tended to be used with businesspeople who may find it difficult to attend a group discussion in one location as they are situated in various locations throughout the world. The screen facing each participant can be split so that they can view the facial expressions of the moderator and all of the other participants. This is an expensive way of running group discussions but may be appropriate for subjects such as high-value industrial products or first class air travel.

A cheaper version is online focus groups or private chat rooms where a group is recruited who are willing to discuss a subject online usually using text. Participants react to questions or topics posed by the moderator and type in their perceptions or comments on other participants' inputs. As people are typing in responses, it can often be difficult to develop any real group dynamics and it is impossible to see people's non-verbal inputs (facial expressions, etc.). The ability to type fast is also quite critical, particularly if interaction is sought. However, such chat rooms may be useful for discussing high technology topics with people who would be unwilling to attend a group discussion because of their geographical dispersal or their introverted nature. In the longer-term improvements in modems, bandwidth and computer connections may offer greater opportunities to use webcams and voice in Internet group discussions.

Analysis of qualitative data

As the researcher is often intimately intertwined with the gathering of qualitative research, it may be assumed that he or she will be able to analyse and interpret the data as it is collected. However, there are difficulties in attempting to short-cut the analysis in this manner. While the data is being gathered, the researcher is often more concerned with the process of doing the research rather than the detail of the content. The content that is generally recalled is the contact that supports the researcher's or the client's own point of view. The comments of particularly vociferous or articulate respondents may be recalled more easily than others.

Taking stock at the end of the project is therefore preferable as the researcher can be re-immersed in all of the data gathered and can organise the content into a form that directly answers the research objectives. This type of analysis is called **content analysis** because it analyses the content of the tapes and transcripts that represent the output of the qualitative research. Content analysis involves two main components:

1 organisation of the data: the structuring and ordering of the data using manual or computerised procedures;
2 interpretation of the data: determining what the data says with regard to the research objectives.

Organisation of the data

The data from qualitative research will take the form of tapes or videos of the depth interviews or group discussions. Although some researchers may undertake analysis directly from these media, the majority obtain typed transcripts of the interviews or discussions to work from, as it is extremely difficult to analyse segments of different interviews and groups when the researcher is having to move back and forward between different sections of different tapes. The videos and tapes should not be discarded as they will be useful in highlighting different points to clients at the end of the study and they also help to determine the strengths of respondents' feelings through highlighting the expressions and tone of voice used when certain points were made.

Therefore, from transcripts, it is probably easier to establish order and patterns in the data. The most common manual approaches to doing this are:

- the tabular method;
- the cut and paste method;
- spider-type diagrams;
- the annotation method.

The tabular method

This normally takes the form of a large sheet of paper divided into boxes (similar to a very large Excel spreadsheet) with the two or three most important respondent characteristics (users, non-users; smokers, non-smokers; male, female) being put in the column headings. The row headings are the most important issues relating to the research objectives for the project (see Figure 5.5). The researcher then transfers the content (in the form of verbatim quotes, interpretation or a précis of behaviour and attitudes) into the relevant boxes. When all the groups or depth interviews are structured in this manner, it becomes easier to compare and contrast the data collected.

This form of tabular approach ensures that each transcript is treated in the same way and therefore can allow two or more researchers to undertake the task simulta-

	Users	Non-users
Attitudes towards quality	'The quality is fine – it is certainly no worse than any of the other brands' 'Good quality' 'Reliable / dependable'	'I feel less confident about the build quality of the product' 'adequate – not impressive'
Attitudes towards price	'It is quite a bit cheaper than the competing brands' 'Good value for money'	'It is cheaper but that reflects the quality' 'Cheap'
Attitudes towards typical users	'The average person' 'Sensible not flash'	'Downmarket – somebody concerned about price more than style' 'Somebody who shops at a discount store'

Figure 5.5 Example of a tabular approach to qualitative analysis

neously. This is very important as it can take a considerable amount of time to go through each transcript, particularly when it relates to a group discussion of up to two hours in length.

On the negative side, it has the disadvantage of being inflexible in that information, which does not fit into the framework, is often ignored even though it may be valuable in another manner to the research and the client. It can also be quite a laborious exercise copying over material into the grid of boxes.

The cut and paste method

The cut and paste method is similar to the tabular approach, except rather than data being copied across to a grid, the material is cut and pasted from the original transcript into separate sections or tables relating to each topic. This can be done by either physically cutting up copies of the transcript and sticking them onto separate sheets relating to a range of separate categories or alternately by computer. Most word processing packages will allow such cut and paste activities to be undertaken in a virtual form without scissors and glue before printing out the recategorised data.

Spider-type diagrams

Some researchers may use spider-type diagrams (also known as Mind Mapping®) to organise the data. These set out each of the issues at the centre of a diagram with the key responses emanating from the centre like a spider's web, highlighting the links between different issues (Figure 5.6). The interconnections are therefore much clearer to the researcher and the client than is the case in the tabular format. However, it is often difficult for more than one researcher to undertake the task simultaneously as they are unlikely to categorise the linkages in the same manner.

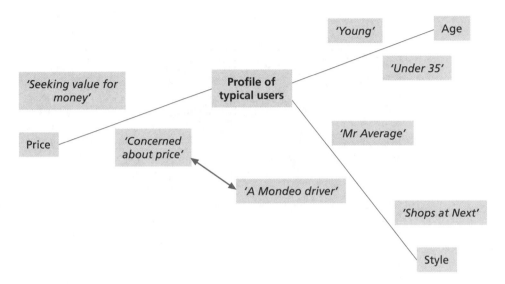

Figure 5.6 Typical spider-type diagram

The annotation method

The annotation method involves the researcher reading through the transcripts and annotating the margins with codes or comments to categorise the points being made by respondents. These can sometimes be colour coded to highlight commonalties between different transcripts more clearly. The researcher then reads down the margins at the end of the process to undertake the interpretation and identify which verbatim quotes are to be used in the final report. This method has the benefit of allowing the respondents' comments to be assessed in their context (taking account of what was said before and after the comments were made) rather than looking at individual parts of a discussion in isolation. However, it can end up becoming quite messy and requires the researcher to have a tidy mind as well as a tidy pen. The editing toolbar on many word processing packages can often allow such annotation to be done in a clearer manner.

Computerised programs

Data analysis programs can also be used to categorise and order the data. Computers can assist with the sheer volume of data that can be collected. The two main broad groups of programs are content analysis software and text analysis/theory building software.

Content analysis software

Content analysis software basically counts the number of times that prespecified words appear in text, for example, the number of times that 'efficiency' is mentioned in interviews about selection criteria for choosing process equipment. The software can often do various operations with what it finds, such as marking or sorting the found text into new files and the production of text frequency distributions. The text frequency distributions that are produced can provide initial comparisons between transcripts to determine the main topics or themes that they share. However, analysis of this type is very crude and is only of value in giving a broad first feel of the data rather than any form of detailed analysis.

Text analysis/theory building software

These packages, such as QSR NUD*IST, The Ethnograph and QSR NVivo,[4] help the researcher divide the data into chunks or segments, attach codes to the segments and then find and display all of the segments with a given code (or combination of codes). For example the word 'efficiency' may not be directly mentioned but segments of text on 'cost effectiveness', 'speed of production', etc., could all be categorised within the same coding. The researcher can then retrieve data where one category or topic is discussed in relation to another. Patterns and relationships within the data may then be identified through using the software's system of rules and hypothesis testing features, which are frequently based on formal and Boolean searching logic. (Boolean requests relate to 'and/or/not' requests; for example, cost effectiveness AND production, effectiveness OR production, effectiveness NOT production.) Some programs will search for overlapping or nested segments. For example, they would find where a segment coded 'efficiency' overlaps with 'speed of production'. NUD*IST, which stands for Non-numerical Unstructured Data Indexing Searching and Theorising, is a programme which allows the researcher to build up a complex categorisation system to classify the data. The software allows the researcher to build up tree displays of categories which can be continually altered as the researcher refines the categories and the relationships between them.

In selecting software for qualitative analysis, the following factors should be taken into consideration:

1 **Data entry**: does the program allow the researcher to format text in any format or does the text need to be formatted along strict rules relating to numbers of characters per line and delineation of blocks of text?

2 **Data storage**: can the data be stored in the original word-processed format or does it need to be split into separate files, making it difficult to change or add to the text?

3 **Coding**: can the coding be done on-screen or does it require the researcher to work with a hard copy to assign the codes before entering them into the computer? How complex can the coding be? Does it allow multiple codes or nesting of codes on a single block of text? Does it allow the researcher to make marginal notes and annotations? (This is particularly important when a team of researchers is involved in doing the analysis as it ensures that the reasons given for assigning specific codes are made explicit.)

4 **Search and retrieval**: how fast can the package search for and retrieve appropriate strings of data? (This may relate as much to computer hardware as it does to software.) What information does it display on the results of searches (the text only or the text and details about the context in which the text appears)? Does it maintain a record of all searches done?

Interpretation of the data

Although some of these computer packages and content analysis procedures can be very sophisticated, it should be noted that they are only capable of organising the data: they do not interpret what it means. The researcher needs to interpret what was said, determine what it all means and identify the implications for marketing decisions. The researcher needs to think through the manner in which things were said to determine what messages the respondents were trying to communicate, either consciously or subconsciously. A researcher's understanding of this increases with experience of qualitative research but also from personal experience of socially interactive situations in everyday life. In our day-to-day social interactions, we do more than listen to others: we interpret their commitment, belief and enthusiasm in what they are saying. We notice inconsistencies, uncertainty, fear and incomprehension. We can often recognise the boasting, bluffing and disguising that people do to cover up their true opinions and behaviour. Combining these intuitive skills with an understanding of the literature on group dynamics can go a long way to providing the researcher with the necessary toolkit to understand respondents in qualitative research. Such understanding will make it possible for the researcher to determine the implications for the research objectives and ultimately for the marketing decisions that have to be made.

Summary

Qualitative research provides researchers with detailed information on the behaviour, motivations and attitudes of respondents. It is most commonly used for exploratory research, new product development and creative development. The main approaches in qualitative research are the individual depth interview and the group discussion. The interactive nature of both of these approaches means that their success is dependent on the skills of the interviewer or the moderator. The relative merits of each approach are set out below.

Advantages of depth interviews over group discussions:

- The respondent is the centre of attention and can therefore be probed at length to explore remarks made which may provide critical insights into the main issue. The respondent cannot hide behind other people's comments or discussions and does not have to compete for time to talk.
- Group pressure is eliminated, so the respondent reveals what he or she actually thinks rather than what is acceptable to the rest of the group.
- Respondents may be willing to talk about sensitive topics that they would hesitate to discuss in front of other people.
- Recruitment is a less complex process.
- Group facilities are not required and the interviews can be undertaken in the respondent's home or office.
- Depth interviews are necessary where group participation is difficult because respondents are geographically dispersed or have very busy diaries.

> **Advantages of group discussions over depth interviews:**
>
> - Depth interviews are more expensive than focus groups when viewed on a per-interview basis.
> - Depth interviews are more time consuming. A typical depth interviewer will undertake a maximum of 4 interviews per day, whereas a moderator could do 2 groups involving 16–20 people in the same time scale.
> - Group discussions allow interaction between participants, providing a stimulus to each participant.
> - Group discussions highlight the dynamics of attitudes by showing how participants change their opinions in reaction to the views of others.

Projective techniques such as word association and sentence completion can be used to enhance the quantity and quality of material produced by both individual depth interviews and group discussions.

At the end of a qualitative project the researcher needs to be re-immersed in all of the data gathered and organise the content into a form that directly answers the research objectives. This type of analysis is called content analysis and involves the twin activities of data organisation and data interpretation.

Finally, it is important to reiterate that it is a mistake to consider qualitative and quantitative research as two distinctly separate bodies of research; many studies incorporate both approaches. Together they can provide a far clearer picture of a market and its characteristics.

Discussion questions

1   Describe the skills that you think a moderator of a group discussion should have.

2   In the Screening Questionnaire (Figure 5.1), the interviewer is asked to tally the people who are rejected. Why do you think this is?

3   Why are group discussions widely used in the development of advertising?

4   Why is qualitative research particularly suited to the early stages of new product development?

5   Describe the key characteristics of an individual depth interview.

6   Why is the development of rapport so critical to qualitative research?

7   The interviewer or moderator is critical to the success of qualitative research. Discuss.

8   What is a projective technique?

9   Why would you run a group discussion by video conferencing or over the Internet?

10 Explain the most common approaches to the analysis of qualitative data.

Additional reading

Catterall, M. and Maclaran, P. (1998) Using computer software for the analysis of qualitative market research data. *Journal of the Market Research Society*, **40**(3), pp. 207–22.

Cowley, J.C.P. (1999) Strategic qualitative focus group research – define and articulate our skills or we will be replaced by others. *International Journal of Market Research*, **42**(1), pp. 17–38.

Gordon, W. (2000) *Goodthinking – A Guide to Qualitative Research*. Admap Publications, London.

Gordon, W. and Langmaid, R. (1988) *Qualitative Market Research: A Practitioner's Guide*. Gower, London.

Krueger, R.A. (1998) *Analysing and Reporting Focus Group Results*. Sage, Newbury Park, CA.

Marks, L. (2000) *Qualitative Research in Context*. Admap Publications, London.

Robson, S. and Foster, A. (eds) (1989) *Qualitative Research in Action*. Arnold, London.

Website

Computer Assisted Qualitative Data Analysis Software Networking Project: caqdas.soc.surrey.ac.uk

References

[1] Townsend, M. and Donaldson, S. (2000) Recipe for success. *Research*, **412**, September, p. 44.

[2] Market Research Society, R&D Society Sub-Committee on Qualitative Research (1979) Qualitative Research – a Summary of the Concepts Involved.

[3] Cervi, B. (2001) New 'focus groupie' concerns. *Research*, January, p. 8.

[4] QSR NUD*IST and QSR NVivo: www.qsrinternational.com. The Ethnograph: www.scolari.co.uk.

6
Collecting quantitative data

The National Readership Survey

The UK National Readership Survey is funded by the Institute of Practitioners in Advertising (IPA), the Newspaper Publishers Association (NPA) and the Periodical Publishers Association (PPA). The survey is aimed at assessing the effectiveness of different types of printed media for advertisers, advertising agencies and publishers. This large-scale programme of quantitative research is contracted out to the research agency Ipsos-RSL Ltd and costs around £3 million to undertake. The research is carried out continuously throughout the year with over 35,500 respondents interviewed each year. The computer-assisted personal interviews (CAPI) are carried out by interviewers using lap-top computers. Interviewers visit houses selected using a multi-stage probability sample derived from the Postcode Address File, and one individual is selected for interview within each household based on a strict sampling selection process.

Respondents are asked about 270 publications using 50 prompt cards with 6 titles on each. For any of the publications that they have seen in the last year, they are asked specific questions about the recency and frequency of readership. Results are weighted to produce estimates of the number and type of readers in the general population for each of the publications. Organisations which subscribe to the NRS can obtain detailed information on the readers of each publication covering aspects such as demographics, shopping behaviour, income levels, household composition, house ownership, ownership/usage of various forms of technology, leisure pursuits, education, TV viewing habits, etc. Advertisers can use such information to improve the placing of advertisements to match the target audience that is being sought. Also publishers use it to determine what rates to charge and optimal advertisers to sell space to.[1]

Learning outcomes

After reading this chapter you should:

- be aware of the characteristics of the main quantitative survey methods;
- appreciate how technology is being used to undertake these methods;
- understand the application of these methods within omnibus surveys and experimental techniques (hall tests, placement tests and simulated test markets).

Key words

CAPI
CATI
e-mail surveys
executive interviewing
face-to-face survey
hall tests
in-home/doorstep interviewing
omnibus surveys
panel research

placement tests
postal surveys
quantitative research
self-administered surveys
simulated test markets
street interviewing
telephone interviewing
web surveys

Introduction

This chapter is designed to introduce you to the principal methods used to gather quantitative data. To be quantifiable, data needs to be collected in an ordered and structured manner. The most popular structured approach to data collection in marketing research is the survey method. There are as many forms of survey method as there are different forms of communication. The advent of e-mail and the world wide web has added to the more traditional survey forms of telephone and personal interviews. This chapter will look at the various survey methods available as well as the application of these approaches within the specialist areas of omnibus surveys, hall tests, placement tests, simulated test markets and panels.

Quantitative research defined

Quantitative research can be defined as research which is undertaken using a structured research approach with a sample of the population to produce quantifiable insights into behaviour, motivations and attitudes. Taking the key components of this definition:

- the data gathering is **more structured** and less flexible than qualitative research as it tends to use predefined questions that are consistently used with all respondents;

- the research tends to involve **larger samples** of individuals than would be used in qualitative research. While some quantitative studies may involve as many as tens of thousands of respondents, many involve samples in the region of 100 to 200 individuals;
- in comparison with qualitative studies, quantitative studies can be **more easily replicated** and direct comparisons can be made between the results;
- the data gathered provides answers that can **quantify the incidence** of particular behaviours, motivations and attitudes in the population under investigation;
- analysis of quantitative studies will tend to be **statistical** in nature and will commonly be undertaken with the help of computer software.

However, in considering quantitative research, it is important to re-emphasise the point made on page 93 – that is, many studies encompass both qualitative and quantitative approaches, with qualitative research being used to explore and understand attitudes and behaviour and quantitative research being used in a conclusive or confirmatory manner to measure how widespread these attitudes and behaviours are.

Survey methods

Surveying involves the structured questioning of participants and the recording of responses. These tasks can be undertaken verbally, in writing or via computer-based technology. An interviewer may be used to administer the survey or the respondent may complete the survey on his or her own. This second type of survey is known as a self-completion or self-administered survey. Interviewer-administered questionnaires are generally undertaken over the telephone or through face-to-face contact in the home, street or place of work. They may involve the use of paper-based questionnaires or computer terminals (lap-tops and notepads). Self-completion surveys can be delivered and collected from respondents by post, by hand, by fax, by the Internet, by e-mail or potentially by a web-enabled WAP phone. The various survey methods are shown in Figure 6.1.

Face-to-face methods

Face-to-face or personal interviewing methods can be categorised into in-home/doorstep, executive and street. They involve meeting the respondent face-to-face and interviewing them using a paper-based questionnaire, a lap-top computer or an electronic notepad. Face-to-face contact of this type has the following advantages over more remote approaches such as telephone and self-completion methods because it is generally easier to:

- motivate a respondent to take part and answer difficult questions when there is direct face-to-face interaction;
- convince the respondent that the research and the interviewer are genuine;
- check and ensure respondent eligibility before the interview is conducted;
- assist a respondent with a more complex questionnaire or set of questions;

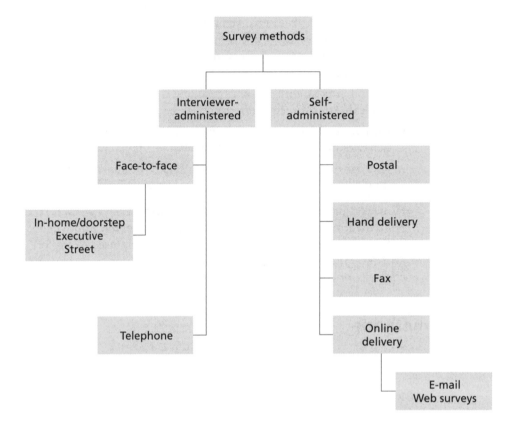

Figure 6.1 A classification of survey methods

- judge the interest, impatience and the seriousness with which a respondent is answering a questionnaire;
- improve understanding of the interviewer and the respondent through non-verbal communication;
- control the visual elements of the questionnaire (showcards and photographs will be shown at the correct point in the questionnaire, unlike self-completion methods where everything is seen at once or telephone where visuals are impossible to use).

Balanced against this are the drawbacks of personal interviewing:

- it is generally seen as being a more costly and time consuming approach;
- interviews need to be clustered within specific geographical areas (e.g. cities, town centres, etc.) if interviewers are to be used efficiently. People in more remote locations are less likely to be interviewed;
- the training and briefing of interviewers can be more difficult as a result of their geographical dispersal;
- quality control is more difficult as supervisors have to travel around a dispersed set of interviewers to ensure that proper interviewing standards are being met;
- it is more difficult to motivate interviewers than is the case in a centralised telephone call centre.

Interviewer bias can also be more prevalent in personal interviewing and can take various forms. It can bias who is interviewed, with interviewers choosing houses or respondents that they feel more comfortable about approaching. It can also happen as a result of the way the interviewer asks a question and also the manner in which the interviewer responds facially and verbally to an answer. Finally it can happen as a result of the manner in which the interviewer records the answer. All of these elements of bias are more difficult to monitor when an interviewer is in somebody's house/office or is in the street in comparison to being in a centralised telephone call centre.

In-home/doorstep interviews

Interviews undertaken at the respondent's place of residence either within the house or more often on the doorstep of the house were the traditional form of interviewing undertaken in consumer markets. Questions about grocery products, soap powders and the like were regularly asked of housewives by interviewers with clipboards. In many developed countries, this form of interviewing has declined significantly as the increase in the number of working women has resulted in fewer women being at home during the day when interviewers call. This makes interviewing more time consuming, particularly as many interviewers are unwilling to go around knocking on doors outside daylight hours. The increased time it takes to get the interviews and the larger number of houses requiring to be visited has resulted in these home-based interviews becoming significantly more expensive than street or telephone-based interviews. However, they are still used where the type of house or neighbourhood is critical to the research design. In developing countries, they may be the only way of getting to respondents, particularly where telephone ownership is low. They also have the advantage of being able to put the respondents at their ease in a familiar environment as well as enabling the interviewer to use visual material (e.g. pictures or lists of names) to speed up the interview and improve data quality.

> **Researcher quote:** *It is becoming more and more difficult to get the desired sample from doorstep interviews as there are some inner-city areas where interviewers are unwilling to go after 5 p.m. and there are also a growing number of people (particularly the elderly) who are unwilling to open their doors to strangers.*

Executive interviews

Executive interviews are the business-to-business version of in-home/doorstep interviews. This type of survey involves interviewing businesspeople at their place of work about industrial or business products and services. The term businesspeople should be seen in its broadest sense as it may involve interviewing factory managers about lubricants or machinery, office managers about stationery and photocopiers, architects about building materials, shopkeepers about delivery services, doctors about pharmaceuticals, farmers about tractors, and teachers about books.

Interviewing of this type is expensive because the interviewer needs to be more skilled to remain credible and successfully undertake interviews in these areas where they may have little detailed knowledge or understanding in comparison to doing research on consumer products. It is also more expensive because the process of interviewing is more complex. First, the individuals responsible for purchasing or specifying the products need to be identified and located. This usually involves phoning organisations and being passed around many departments and individuals until the correct person is found. Sometimes lists can be obtained, but these are not always accurate or up to date. Once the correct person has been identified, it is necessary for the interviewer to get them to agree to be interviewed. If the interviewer can speak to the target respondent directly then this may not be too difficult. However, when he or she is shielded behind secretaries and receptionists, the task can become time consuming and difficult.

> **Researcher quote:** *Receptionists come out with: 'he's busy', 'he's in a meeting', 'he doesn't do marketing research', 'he wouldn't have time to see you', 'phone back in a couple of months'. However, when you do eventually manage to get hold of the target you usually find that they are really keen to talk to somebody about topics related to their work.*

An appointment must then be made for the interview and the interviewer needs to travel to the respondent's workplace to undertake the research.

Street interviews

Street interviews, known as mall intercept interviews in North America, involve respondents being approached while they are shopping in town centres. They are then interviewed on the spot or asked to come to a hall test (see page 135).

In Europe, unlike North America, most street interviews are undertaken in the open air rather than in shopping malls or centres as many shopping centre managers view interviewing as an unnecessary nuisance to shoppers. Some shopping centres do allow interviews but charge a fee and must be booked in advance.

Interviewing in the open air can adversely affect the quality of the data obtained. A respondent being interviewed in wet, cold or even very hot weather may not be as attentive to the questions being asked as would someone located in the comfort of their own house or even a shopping mall. Distractions from passers by, traffic and the general noise of a busy shopping street can make interviewing very difficult. There may also be difficulties in recruiting respondents as shoppers frequently avoid interviewers holding clipboards because they are in a hurry or are preoccupied with their shopping activities. Street interviewing also severely limits the length of the interview as it is unlikely that a respondent will be willing to answer questions for more than 10 minutes while standing holding shopping bags in a busy main street.

Researcher quote: *There is nothing worse than standing in the rain with your questionnaires watching people crossing the road to avoid you!*

Even with these difficulties, street interviews are still very popular as they are significantly less expensive than in-home interviews. Interviewers do not need to spend time visiting houses where no one is at home as the respondents come to the interviewer rather than the other way around.

Derivatives of street interviews are exit surveys where respondents are interviewed as they exit an exhibition or venue (e.g. a sports centre, a tourist attraction, a theme park) about their attitudes towards the facilities and their experiences within the venue. Major retailers and transport operators also carry out this type of research within their outlets, asking questions about their brand of products or services.

British Airports Authority, which owns airports in the UK, Italy, Australia and North America, interviews travellers within its airports about customer satisfaction levels with check-in procedures, retail outlets, car-parking, restaurant and toilet facilities. Questions will relate to the range of facilities, ease of use, speed of service, cleanliness, helpfulness of staff, clarity of signage, etc. Interviews are carried out with travellers as they wait in lounges and as they browse the airport shops.

Computer-assisted personal interviewing (CAPI)

More and more large marketing research agencies are using computer-assisted methods for their personal interviewing rather than paper-based questionnaires. This either involves using a lap-top computer for indoor (in-home or executive) interviewing or a 'penpad' for outdoor use (a touchscreen computer where an 'electronic pen' is used to point at answer boxes and which has the ability to write directly onto the screen for verbatim responses) for outdoor use. Computers of this type allow direct data entry, doing away with the need for the collection of paper-based questionnaires from all of the interviewers and the laborious task associated with transferring the information from the questionnaires to a computer. The computer also routes the interviewer through the questionnaire, showing one question at a time in response to the answers given to previous questions. This results in interviews that flow more smoothly as interviewers no longer have to shuffle through the questionnaire to find the next appropriate question. The computer also edits the input for incorrect and incompatible replies; instructions are then given to the interviewer to reduce any inconsistencies. At the end of a day's interviewing, the data can be downloaded to the researcher's central computer, allowing for immediate analysis.

Telephone interviews

Telephone interviews are used for business-to-business and consumer-type research. The majority of the interviews are undertaken from a centralised call centre location, although a small number involve interviewers using their own home-based telephones. The main benefit of the centralised location is control. The interviewers can be briefed and trained in one location. Their calls can be monitored using unobtrusive monitoring equipment that allows supervisors to listen in on interviews and correct or replace interviewers who are interviewing incorrectly. Quality control checks can be done on the questionnaires immediately after they have been completed. The cost of calls can also be logged accurately. Finally, interviewers need to clock in and out of work, allowing control of the timing of the interviews and ensuring that interviewers work sufficient hours regularly.

Unlike personal interviews, the interviewers do not need to be located near the respondents and the need for interviewer travelling time and expenses is eliminated. Interviews can be undertaken nationally or internationally from one central location, with many of these locations being situated outside major cities where office rental costs and staff costs are much less. Some of the interviewer bias that may exist with personal interviewers is also reduced, first, through the tighter supervision, which ensures that questions are asked correctly and responses are recorded accurately, and second, through the interviewer's selection of respondents being dictated by the names and/or numbers supplied rather than the approachability of different types of respondent. The telephone also has the advantage of reaching people who otherwise may be difficult to reach through any other means, such as businesspeople travelling around or people who live in flats with entry-phones.

The other major benefit of telephone interviews is speed. Interviewers can be briefed and be conducting interviews within hours of the questionnaire being developed. It would take much longer to brief a team of personal interviewers. This speed can mean that interviewing can be timed to happen immediately after a specific event. For example, an advertisement or an electioneering party political broadcast may appear on television at 7 p.m., and interviewers can then be phoning viewers to seek their attitudes towards the broadcast by 7.05 p.m.

The telephone survey does have some inherent disadvantages. The biggest disadvantage relates to respondent attitudes towards the telephone. Over the past 15 years, there has been a major growth of telephone usage for telemarketing purposes throughout Europe. Home improvement companies, financial service organisations, catalogue marketers and even charities use the telephone to generate sales/funds, either directly or by arranging for a sales representative to visit prospective purchasers. Many are persistent and relatively aggressive callers and in certain situations some disguise their approach as being marketing research. This activity is called 'sugging' (selling under the guise of research) by the marketing research industry. As a result, many members of the public are confused about the difference between marketing research, where the confidentiality of the respondent is maintained, and telemarketing, where names and data will be used for selling purposes, either directly or by selling the information onto other companies. Refusal rates are therefore increasing and consumer concerns in certain countries have led to legislative controls on unsolicited calls for telemarketing or telephone research (e.g. in Germany and parts of the USA). Consumers are also using equipment such as answering machines to screen their calls before answering them. The Market Research Society in the UK provides a freephone service for respondents to phone in order to check that the research is bona fide. However, this is only of benefit to those who are willing to spend time checking on the credentials of the agency and the research; many respondents will take the easier option of simply refusing to take part.

> **Researcher quote:** *You get home improvement companies who phone up saying they are doing marketing research. They usually only ask one question about whether the respondent has double glazing. If the respondent says no, they proceed immediately into a sales pitch. They make telephone surveys so difficult for the rest of us!*

Although some telephone interviews can last 25–30 minutes, they are normally much shorter and certainly shorter than face-to-face interviews. Respondents lose interest quicker when they only have their sense of hearing stimulated (no visual or tactile cues to occupy the other senses) and it is easy for them to hang up the phone when they become bored. Certain types of question such as complex ranking questions or questions with a large number of multiple-choice responses are also more difficult to undertake over the phone.

In international telephone surveys, there may be specific problems in undertaking interviews. One of these relates to low levels of telephone ownership, particularly in many of the developing countries in Africa and Asia. This can result in telephone samples in these countries being biased towards particular types of consumer (especially in the professional classes). Even in developed countries there may be problems relating to the coverage of telephone networks owing to the growth of the use of mobile phones and people choosing to rely solely on mobile rather than land line networks (e.g. students, people on low incomes, professional-type people, countries with poor public networks). Even if respondents can be accessed through the telephone network, different cultures will react differently towards a telephone survey. For example Mediterranean and Arabic peoples are reluctant to divulge personal details over the telephone whereas North Americans and northern Europeans are more open towards providing information over the telephone.

Computer-assisted telephone interviewing (CATI)

In the mid- to late 1980s telephone research agencies were starting to provide interviewers with a computer so that they used a paper-based questionnaire to ask questions but typed the responses directly into the computer. This was superseded by computer software, which put the questions on the monitor, allowing the interviewer to enter the response for each question, with the computer automatically routing the interview to the next appropriate question. For example a 'Yes' answer to one question may lead to a further set of questions whereas a 'No' answer should be routed onto the next topic area.

CATI also allows for customisation of questionnaires. For example, at the start of an interview, we might ask respondents their name and the age of their children. Later in the interview, questions might be asked about each child. This may appear on the screen as follows: 'Mr Wilson, regarding your 10-year-old son, what breakfast cereal does he eat?'. Other questions about this child and other children would appear in similar fashion. In international research, questionnaires can be switched to different languages. Many CATI systems also allow for the direct recording of verbatim comments given to open-ended questions.

Such systems also eliminate inconsistencies in responses. For example, if a respondent states that he does not drive but later answers that he has a car, the computer would ask the interviewer to clarify this.

In terms of managing the interviewing process, today's CATI systems are frequently linked to the telephone dialling process so that as soon as one interview is finished, the computer is dialling the next number. Such dialling can also be set up so that it predicts (predictive dialling) when an interview is likely to finish and starts dialling before the previous questionnaire is fully completed. ISDN technology allows the equipment to detect busy signals and no answers, immediately dialling other respondents to minimise interviewer waiting time.

In the USA, a number of organisations are experimenting with completely automated telephone interviews (CATS) which use interactive voice technology. Instead of a human interviewer, questions are asked by the recorded voice of an interviewer with respondents answering the closed-ended questions using their touch-tone phone. It is proving to be more successful with in-bound calls where respondents are recruited through a mail shot and are then asked to phone a freephone number to complete the survey. Such an approach can be useful for basic customer satisfaction research and limited research linked to specific loyalty programmes, warranty registration, etc.

Self-administered surveys

Self-administered surveys differ from the above methods, in that no interviewer, either live or recorded is involved. Although this means that there is no interviewer available to bias or influence the data gathered from the respondent, it also means that there is no interviewer available to clarify questions or responses. The survey form or questionnaire must be able to clearly communicate the questions being posed and provide a straightforward approach to respond. It must also be able to motivate the respondent to complete all of the questions. The design of self-administered questionnaires is discussed in Chapter 7. Their delivery can be accomplished via the mail (postal surveys), by hand, by fax or online (e-mail, web surveys).

Postal surveys

In postal surveys, questionnaires are mailed to pre-selected respondents along with a return envelope, a covering letter and possibly an incentive. The respondents complete and return the questionnaire. Although postal surveys have been around for many years, their importance has grown as a result of the prevalence of customer databases and customer satisfaction measurement.

Postal surveys are superficially attractive on account of their cost relative to other methods using interviewers, but this has to be balanced against the low response rates associated with postal surveys. Response rates associated with postal surveys are variable and depend on the respondents' level of interest in the subject, the relationship between the respondent and the researching firm, the accuracy of the mailing list and the incentive offered. Typical response rates for well-executed surveys are around 40–50 per cent (i.e. for every 1,000 questionnaires, only 400–500 completed questionnaires are returned). However, it is not uncommon for some surveys to receive less than a 20 per cent response rate.

> **Researcher quote:** *In designing a good postal survey, you have to look at the survey from the respondent's point of view. Why will they bother replying?*

Response rates may be improved by addressing the following:

- **Accuracy of the mailing list**: the accuracy of the mailing list and the extent to which it can be segmented into the most relevant targeted groups is critical to the success of postal surveys. The source of the list is therefore important: lists that relate to customers who are regularly interacting with an organisation are likely to be more accurate and detailed than lists relating to customers who have only made a one-off purchase or lists that have been purchased from an external list-broker.

- **Pre-contact**: prior contact with the research organisation, where respondents have taken part in previous research and have agreed to being recontacted, usually results in a higher response rate. There is also some evidence to suggest that pre-notification of the survey by telephoning, e-mailing or writing to potential respondents also improves the response rate.

- **Part of an existing relationship**: postal surveys are also more likely to be effective when there is some form of relationship between the researcher and the respondent (e.g. between companies and their customers, account holders, subscribers or loyalty card members). Relationships such as these are likely to mean that the respondent is more interested in the subject and has at least a perception that taking part in the survey will improve the relationship or service received in the future.

- **The covering letter**: The letter which accompanies the questionnaire needs to sell the benefits of the survey to potential respondents and should encourage them to respond. Generally, the letter should be personalised and should help to reassure recipients that the research is genuine and will follow research industry guidelines.

The Market Research Society in the UK has a symbol which can be put on the letter. In addition, the letter should cover the following:

- the purpose of the research;
- reasons why people should respond;
- the ease of completion and the short time needed to complete;
- an assurance of confidentiality;
- the manner in which recipients were selected;
- a contact number for more information;
- the time scale for return and the manner in which it should be returned;
- a thank-you.

The envelope in which the covering letter and questionnaire is despatched should also look distinct from a typical direct mail envelope. An official-looking envelope is likely to be taken more seriously. There are conflicting views about whether the return envelope should have a stamp or a pre-paid format. Respondents may feel obliged to return an envelope with a stamp; however, this should be balanced against the increased cost of putting postage stamps on every envelope as the use of the pre-paid format only involves paying the postage for envelopes that are actually returned.

- **Incentives**: incentives such as an entry into a prize draw can be effective in increasing response rates; they may also speed up the response if a closing date is given. Other incentives such as discount vouchers can also be used. The impact of sending pens and pencils with the questionnaire has dropped as a result of many charities sending these items with their fund-raising mail shots.

- **Reminders**: sending out reminders around 10 days after the questionnaire is posted out is quite effective, and telephone calls can also be used as a second or final follow-up. This raises the cost of the survey. It may also mean that questionnaires will need to be numbered so that the researcher can recognise who has and has not responded. This may lead to fears of loss of anonymity on the part of the respondent – the covering letter may need to reassure respondents about the purpose of any such numbers or identification marks.

- **Questionnaire design**: questionnaire design also has an important influence on response rates. This is discussed further in Chapter 7.

Advantages and disadvantages of postal surveys

Advantages

- **National and international coverage**: can be sent to a geographically dispersed sample.
- **Low cost**: for each completed questionnaire from a geographically dispersed sample, postal surveys are likely to be around one third of the cost of a typical telephone survey and less than a ninth of the cost of a typical face-to-face interview.
- **No interviewer bias.**

- **Respondent convenience:** the respondents can complete the questionnaire at their own speed when they want. They can confer with other members of their household or refer to files, documents, etc.
- **Piggybacking:** the questionnaire can piggyback on the back of other correspondence such as bank statements, warranty registrations and newsletters, reducing the cost further.

Disadvantages

- **Low response rate.**
- **Biased response:** those who respond may not be representative of the population. It may be that only those who have strong opinions or have links with the organisation being researched take the time and effort to complete the questionnaire.
- **Lack of control of questioning:** it is difficult to control the manner in which the questionnaire is completed. As a result sections may be left blank.
- **Lack of control of respondent:** it is difficult to ensure that the named recipient answers the questions. It is not unknown for managers to get their secretaries or parents to get their children to complete the questionnaires.
- **Limited open-ended questions:** it is difficult to get respondents to write down full answers to open-ended verbatim-type questions. Therefore most questions should simply involve ticking boxes, and open-ended questions should be limited to a very small proportion of the total.
- **Pre-reading of questionnaire:** care must be taken in designing the questionnaire as the respondent can read the whole questionnaire in advance of completing it. This has implications for awareness and attitude type questions.
- **Response time:** from time of despatch, it can take two to three weeks until all completed questionnaires are returned. There may even be the odd questionnaire drifting in up to 10 weeks after the survey was despatched. Postal or telephone reminders may be needed to get respondents to return questionnaires.

Hand delivery of survey

Self-administered questionnaires may be handed to potential respondents or left for their collection rather than posted. Where the audience is captive such as in an aeroplane, in a hotel, in a car hire office or in a restaurant, this approach is inexpensive and can produce a high response rate. In an aeroplane, the cabin crew hand out the questionnaire to passengers in selected seats during a flight and collect them before the plane lands. In hotels, questionnaires about service delivery are traditionally left in the bedrooms for guests to complete. However, research has shown that response rates tend to be higher when the questionnaire is personally handed to guests by reception staff. Some restaurants also have a brief questionnaire on the back of their bills. If staff rewards are tied in with the responses to these questionnaires, care must be taken to ensure that real customers rather than staff are completing them – it is not unknown for staff to pretend they are customers to improve their own situation.

> **Researcher quote:** *If you leave a questionnaire in a hotel room to be completed, the average person won't fill it in. You need to hand it to guests or you will only hear feedback from those who are very dissatisfied or very satisfied.*

Fax surveys

Sending questionnaires by fax is only really effective where potential respondents are prewarned by telephone or e-mail and their agreement is sought prior to sending. Fax surveys are most appropriate for business or professional respondents and can be faster and cheaper to implement than postal surveys. However, the quality of the presentation of the questionnaire can vary dramatically depending on the quality of the potential respondent's fax machine. Missing pages and questions appearing on a curled up thermal paper roll may be less than user friendly and result in poor response rates.

Online surveys

The two main online methods available to researchers are e-mail surveys and web surveys. They can both deliver a questionnaire to potential respondents through desk-based PCs but also through portables, digital television and WAP (web-enabled) mobile phones. E-mail surveys are similar in many ways to postal surveys with the exception that they are delivered electronically. Web surveys on the other hand are the equivalent of taking a postal survey and turning it into a computer-assisted research tool.

E-mail surveys

There are two main types of e-mail survey: those where the questionnaire appears as text within the e-mail and those where the questionnaire is sent as an attachment (either as a word processor document or as a piece of software which runs the questionnaire).

Where the questionnaire simply appears in the text with tick boxes and spaces for response, the respondent simply scrolls down the e-mail entering text or checking boxes and then sends the questionnaire back to the researcher by using the 'reply' facility. If the questionnaire is produced by one of the many specialised Windows-based software tools that are available, then the system will automatically collate the data and produce tables and graphs. The questionnaire will also look like a traditional self-completion survey. However, if it is produced on standard e-mail software, the questionnaire will look far less professional and the researcher will need to manually transfer responses to a data processing package.

If attachments are used, these can simply be word processor documents that the potential respondent can open with their own software, enter responses and return. Care must be taken to ensure that the document will be compatible with the various versions of software that potential respondents are likely to have. Alternatively, executable e-mail questionnaires are questionnaire programs sent as a file attachment. Once received, the respondent clicks on the attachment, the first question appears on the screen and the program routes the respondent through a series of questions depending on the answers given. The attachment is then e-mailed back on completion. This has the advantage that a more complex questionnaire can be used than is the case with the other e-mail approaches. However, its complexity also means that the file size of the attachment can be quite large and can cause problems when sending by e-mail. As a result, this type of approach is more commonly used for staff surveys within organisations using the company's intranet network.

Whichever e-mail method is used, the research will tend to be cheaper and faster to implement than is the case for postal surveys. Respondents may also give more detailed responses to open-ended questions than with postal surveys as they have a keyboard in front of them and are used to producing short, structured responses using the e-mail medium. Against this there are the difficulties in developing a representative sample when using e-mail as, first, there is no comprehensive list of e-mail addresses and second, there are still large segments of the population who do not have access to the Internet and do not have an e-mail address.

The amount of spam (unsolicited 'junk' e-mails) being sent to computer users is growing, which may make it difficult for e-mail surveys. The sending out of unsolicited surveys should therefore be avoided and a prenotification should be sent first, inviting respondents to take part. Researchers should also be aware that respondents may be concerned about confidentiality as the returned questionnaire is likely to have the respondent's e-mail address attached. It is important that the researcher emphasises that the confidentiality of the respondent will be protected.

Web surveys

Web surveys take a number of forms but the most common are the standard questionnaire format and the interactive questionnaire. The standard questionnaire format has the questionnaire appearing on the page as it would on paper. The respondent scrolls down the page completing each question. The interactive questionnaire is similar to those used in CAPI and CATI systems, with questions appearing on the screen one at a time. The respondent submits their answer and then the computer shows a new question dependent upon the answer to the previous questions.

The standard format is cheaper to produce and suitable for relatively straightforward questionnaires, whereas the interactive questionnaire is more suitable for complex questionnaires that require routing and skip patterns in the questioning. The fact that the interactive questionnaires download questions one at a time means that the respondents' answers will not be influenced by them seeing the full set of questions; however, this may be extremely annoying for users with slow modems as they wait for each question to download. Respondents also have to complete all questions correctly before they are allowed to proceed and their answers are submitted, which can infuriate respondents who do not want to answer a particular question or have an answer that does not match those on a predefined list.

Web surveys are still at their early stages but are proving effective for research into monitoring web usage and attitudes towards web sites, as well as feedback on computers and technology in general. The fact that respondents are all Internet users means that they are not typical of consumers in general; however, this may not matter when the research objectives are linked to technology and technology usage. Potential respondents can be invited to take part through e-mails or by a link through a company's website or intranet site. Once again, this may mean that the sample is particularly biased towards e-mail users and those with an interest in the specific company and web pages.

> **Researcher quote:** *In the future, web-based surveys will replace a significant number of postal surveys.*

Omnibus surveys

Omnibus research is a data collection approach that is undertaken at regular intervals for a changing group of clients who share the costs involved in the survey's set-up, sampling and interviewing. Basically, an omnibus survey consists of a series of short question sets, with each set belonging to a different client. For a fee, each client purchases space on the survey's questionnaire, either on a one-off basis or regularly each time the survey operates. A number of research agencies in the UK and across Europe undertake omnibus surveys with a particular type of respondent on a regular timetabled basis. Some of the best-known omnibus surveys include:

- **Omnimas,** operated by Taylor Nelson Sofres,[2] interviews 2,100 different adults aged 16+ per week. The sample is selected to be nationally representative, and is interviewed face-to-face in the respondents' own homes using CAPI pen technology.

- **CAPIBUS,** operated by Ipsos-RSL,[3] uses CAPI in a weekly omnibus survey covering a high-quality sample of 2,000 adults aged 15+ each week of the year, with results available in just 10 days. A similar weekly service, CAPIBUS-Europe, covering the UK, France, Germany, Italy and Spain, is also available.

- **Telebus,** operated by NOP,[4] undertakes a computer-assisted telephone interview omnibus of 1,000 UK adults twice per week. If clients deliver the questions to the agency by Tuesday or Friday, the results are returned to the client on Thursday or Monday.

There are also specialist omnibus surveys, such as **Motorbus** (NOP), which interviews 500 motorists each weekend, **Access to Internet** (BMRB[5]), which interviews 500 adult Internet users weekly, and the **Small Business Omnibus** (NOP), which interviews 500 senior managers in small businesses bi-monthly.

These are just a few of the many omnibus surveys that are available; they enable companies to get fast results to a small number of questions from a relatively large sample at a relatively low cost. The charges for inclusion in a survey normally consist of a joining fee, a cost per individual question, a cost per coded answer and a charge for any special analysis required. For a small number of questions, these charges will be significantly cheaper than undertaking an ad hoc survey to reach the same size of sample. This is unlikely to be so where the number of questions is large and the type of questions is complex.

In addition to using omnibus surveys to obtain a 'snapshot' of awareness, attitudes or behaviour, a client can subscribe to a survey on a regular basis, enabling these attributes to be tracked over time. This is particularly useful for monitoring the effectiveness of promotional activities such as advertising or sponsorship.

There are two drawbacks to omnibus surveys. The first of these is inflexibility – a client cannot change the nature of the sample being interviewed as this would adversely affect other clients who are using the survey as a tracking study. There is also inflexibility in the type and number of questions that any client can ask within a particular wave of the survey. Questions have to be relatively straightforward with no one subject or product area being allowed to dominate the questionnaire. Clients also tend to be concerned about the position in which their questions appear in the questionnaire. They have two basic fears: (1) that other questions will bias the answers to their own questions and (2) that the respondent will lose interest nearer the end of the questionnaire. Many would like to have their questions appear at the beginning of the questionnaire, but this would be impossible to do for all clients, so similar sets of questions tend to be grouped together (e.g. questions about grocery products, then questions about financial services, then holidays and travel, etc.).

There are many omnibus surveys available; clients need to select carefully, taking account of the following considerations:

- population covered;
- method of data collection;
- frequency of fieldwork;
- reputation of supplier for quality research;
- pricing;
- speed of reporting;
- sample composition and size.

Hall tests

Hall tests are so called because they involve hiring a hall, hotel room or other venue in a central location, usually next to a shopping area. Respondents are recruited into the hall by interviewers stationed on the main pedestrian thoroughfares nearby. They are screened in the street to ascertain their suitability relative to the sample required (usually a quota sample) before being taken or directed to the hall. In the hall, researchers test respondent's initial reactions to a product or package or concept. They may be asked to taste a new drink, smell a new perfume, look at a new design for a car, or open and close a new form of packaging for milk. The emphasis is very much on people's initial reactions to these aspects as they will only be in the hall for a very short period of time (10–20 minutes). Hall tests are not very appropriate for evaluating the longer term usage of a product. For example, a hall test may show people's initial reactions to the look of a new vacuum cleaner but attitudes towards the cleaning ability of the cleaner could only be gauged by testing in people's homes (placement tests). However, many products, such as groceries, are selected in retail stores on the basis of first impressions; analysing these impressions is therefore very important to marketers.

In planning hall tests, there is a need for care and common sense. For example, the type of venue and the time of day may adversely influence the test. Undertaking a taste test for alcohol in a church hall or very early in the morning may provide very different results than if the test was undertaken in the evening in the function room of a hotel or bar.

Products can be tested on their own (a monadic test) but are more frequently tested against one or two other products (a multiple test). Some packaging tests may include all the competitors' products within a given range. Having tasted, smelt, touched or looked at the product, respondents will be interviewed by an interviewer using a structured or semi-structured questionnaire. Such research is normally quantitative, although some studies may require a qualitative dimension to be added. To satisfy this, depth interviews may be undertaken with a subsample of respondents who complete the main questionnaire.

In terms of scale, it is usual to carry out hall tests in a number of locations to overcome regional bias, with samples of around 100–400 people being interviewed in a typical project. The throughput at each venue will depend on the number of interviewers, the complexity of the quota of respondents being sought and the number of people shopping, but a target of between 50 and 100 respondents per day per hall is not uncommon. Clients can often attend the hall to observe respondents' reactions and obtain a feel for the likely results.

Placement tests

Not all products are appropriate for testing in halls. Products that need to be tested over a period of time such as vacuum cleaners, cars, photocopiers and anti-dandruff shampoos are better tested where they are used; that is, in the home, in the office or on the road. Home testing is also appropriate where products need to be prepared by the consumer, such as a cake mix, or where the whole family is involved with the product (e.g. a new type of tomato sauce). Testing of products in the home and where they are to be used is called **placement testing**.

In placement testing, respondents who match the target population are recruited, often from omnibus surveys or street interviews. They are then given a new product to test in their own home or in their office. Information about their experiences with and attitudes towards the products are then collected by either a questionnaire (self-completion or interviewer administered) or by a self-completion diary. The diary involves completing information on specific question areas about the product on a daily or weekly basis. The information is then sent back to the researcher by post or by electronic means.

Products may be tested in this way for anything from 3 weeks for a new electrical product to 6–12 months for a new car or office equipment. Ford gets a sample of organisations that have company car fleets to test new models for periods of up to 12 months before launching a new car in the market place. There is a risk that competitors will see the product during the test, but that may be less of a problem than launching a product that does not meet customer needs.

> **Researcher quote:** *It is amazing what you find out when real people in their own homes test a product rather than it being tested by R&D people in a lab.*

Placement tests can be expensive to organise and undertake as sufficient numbers of products in their finished format need to be produced for testing. More respondents may also need to be recruited than are actually required as people may drop out of the exercise before the test is complete, either because they do not like the product or because they lose interest in filling out the diary.

Simulated test markets

Test markets or store tests were traditionally used to assist marketers in predicting the potential results of a product launch and to experiment with changes to different elements of a product's marketing mix. Using different commercial television transmission areas, it was possible to compare a control area where the product offering remained unchanged against an area where a new product, a new promotional campaign or a new pricing policy was introduced. Products would appear on retail shelves beside competing products and the consumers would be unaware that a test was being undertaken. The thinking behind such a test was that national sales could be extrapolated from a test area that was representative (in miniature) of the national market and where the marketing activities could be undertaken without interference or contamination from external variables. The television transmission areas were important because the advertising seen in a local area could be controlled and changed. This is more difficult with the advent of satellite and cable television, where the population may be watching multiple national and international channels. This change, along with the following difficulties associated with attempting to control the many variables in a test area, has resulted in the virtual disappearance of traditional area and store testing in favour of simulated test marketing:

- **Isolation:** increasing difficulty in isolating an area with overlapping television regions, newspaper circulation areas, satellite and cable TV advertising, as well as the growth in national retailers and people commuting longer distances to work and shop.
- **Timing:** to be accurate, test markets may need to run for periods of up to six months. It is becoming more difficult to control variables for that length of time

with rapid changes occurring in market conditions and competitor activity. Test markets of this length also enable competitors to prepare their own plans to tackle the new product.

- **Competitor spoiling**: it is not uncommon for competitors to spoil a test market by flooding an area with their own products or promotions. In certain circumstances, they may buy up the new products to give a false impression of their success.
- **Area selection**: it is often difficult to identify areas that truly reflect the demographic make-up of a nation.
- **Cost**: running a test market with associated advertising and finished products can be a very expensive activity.

As traditional test markets have declined, there has been a corresponding increase in the use of simulated test markets. Simulated test markets rely on simulated or laboratory type testing and mathematical modelling. A typical simulated test market involves the following steps:

1 Recruiting participants using street, doorstep or telephone interviews. Participants would be screened to ensure that they were members of the target population (for example, in a programme of research prior to the launch of the round tea bag, Lyons Tetley sought participants who were heavy tea drinkers; see page 199).

2 Those who qualify are exposed to the product concept or prototype and in many cases the packaging, promotion and advertising for the new product. This is frequently done at the same time as the participants are exposed to competing products and advertising.

3 Participants are then given an opportunity to buy a product from the product range under investigation (i.e. the new product and competing products) from the researcher or interviewer. Frequently this is done using a catalogue of the products with respondents being given freedom of choice.

4 If the product is one that is consumed and repurchased (e.g. a food or soap powder), respondents would be asked to only buy this type of product from the researcher. Researchers would then visit each week over a period of time and the respondents would be asked to repurchase from the catalogue of products available. Customers would use their own money when purchasing. Questionnaires may also be used to examine participants' experience of using their chosen product and the reasons for purchasing it.

5 The trial and repeat purchase information developed from these activities would be used as the input to a computerised simulation program that is used to project share or volume for the product if it were distributed on a national basis.

Undertaking tests on this basis is quicker and requires no complex negotiations with local retailers and media suppliers. Competitors are also less likely to adversely impact on a test and are less likely to know that a test is being conducted. On the negative side, participants may still be influenced by the national media and advertising that they are exposed to. Some participants may also alter their behaviour as a result of being part of the test (e.g. they do not buy the cheapest product as they normally do but instead buy products in order to impress the researcher with their expensive or cosmopolitan taste). However, having said this, most simulated test markets are seen as being as accurate if not more accurate than the traditional store testing.

Panels

A panel (sometimes known as a longitudinal survey) is a form of survey from which comparative data is collected from the sampling units on more than one occasion. Panels can consist of individuals, households or organisations, and can provide dynamic information on:

- broad trends in a market (e.g. Are people moving from buying white bread to brown bread? Which television programmes are more or less popular than previously?);
- case histories of specific respondents (e.g. level of repeat purchases, brand switching, reaction to special offers and advertising);
- attitudes and reactions over time to particular products or services (a placement test is a type of panel where people's reaction to a new type of vacuum cleaner or car can be measured over time).

Information may be gathered by questionnaire, telephone interviews, diaries (documents where the respondent records their behaviour and purchases over a period such as a week or a month), barcode readers or through the Internet. The best-known examples of panel research are the consumer purchase panels monitoring individual or household buyer behaviour in the areas of grocery, food and drink, and toiletries. However, the retail audits described in Chapter 4 are produced from panels of retailers.

Although panel research design is similar to that of any quantitative survey design in terms of sampling, data collection and data analysis, it is different in that it has to be designed for long-term consistency. Purchasers of trend data from panel research need data series (possibly stretching back over many years) that are reliable and that have not been affected by methodological problems or changes. Ongoing control is therefore critical in panel research. Such control is particularly important with regard to the recruitment and maintenance of panel members. The key tasks involved are:

- **Recruitment of a representative sample of the population that is willing and capable of doing the task**: panels require more of a commitment from their members than is the case with one-off surveys. Ease of recruitment will vary depending on the perceptions of potential respondents towards the commitment required in terms of both time and effort, balanced against their perception of the value of the research and any specific incentives or rewards offered. For example, a computer expert may require little reward and be quite willing to regularly spend time filling in a questionnaire on new software and technology, whereas, a busy household may require significant prizes or payments to regularly report on their grocery shopping. Recruitment also requires panel member training as the success of the research is dependent on the skill of the panellists in completing the task (e.g. noting purchases made, using a barcode scanner on their purchases or completing a diary).
- **Maintaining the members of the panel once recruited**: the goal is to hold onto as many panel members as possible in order to maintain consistency of reporting and

also to get the full return from the costs of recruitment and training. Panellists will be offered incentives to undertake their tasks and also to encourage longer panel membership. This usually involves some kind of loyalty reward scheme similar to a loyalty card for a supermarket, where points can be saved for a future purchase or product discount. Newsletters, prize draws, mystery gifts and regular telephone calls are also frequently used to maintain the link between the research agency and the panellist and to sustain their interest in the task.

- **Replacing panel members who leave with similar respondents to maintain consistency**: there will always be some level of turnover of panel members, although hopefully this will be kept to a minimum. People move house, their circumstances change or they lose interest in taking part in the research. Researchers must always have a group of trained up panellists to replace them. Replacement is on a like-for-like basis, not only in terms of demographic subgroup but also in terms of behavioural characteristics. For larger panels, recruitment of panel members is often an ongoing activity, with recruits being put onto a back-up or substitute panel for a period of time before being brought into the main panel as replacements. Their performance as potential panellists can therefore be monitored before they go live and impact on the 'real' panel data.

- **Quality control**: computer software is frequently used to check on the consistency of data coming from a panel member. Are the panellists undertaking the correct task when they should and are they doing it consistently? Abnormal purchasing patterns or potential errors in data entry can be identified and queried with the panellist.

As refusal rates in other forms of marketing research increase, panels of committed respondents may become more important in the gathering of market information. Panels are obviously advantageous as they provide measurement of change over time. The increased commitment of the panellists can also enhance the quality of the data collected. On the other hand, panel members may not be totally representative of the population as a whole in the fact that they are interested in the topic being investigated and are therefore willing to spend time and effort noting their purchases and behaviour. They may also alter their behaviour because they know that their behaviour is being recorded (e.g. they may buy less chocolate, ready prepared meals, discount items, etc.).

Taylor Nelson Sofres Superpanel (www.tnagb.com)

The Taylor Nelson Sofres Superpanel provides purchasing information on British grocery markets and consists of 15,000 households which are demographically and regionally balanced to offer a representative picture of the market place. Data is collected twice weekly via electronic terminals in the home, with purchases being recorded via home scanning technology. The sample is drawn from all individuals aged 5 to 79 who are resident in domestic households on mainland Great Britain and the Isle of Wight and who are in telephone owning households. Recruitment involves the main shopper in a selected household being contacted by telephone and then having the Superpanel service described to them, together with an outline of the personal task involved, the characteristics of the equipment used and the incentivisation package. If the household agrees, a complete package is despatched to them, including the electronic terminal, instructions and a demonstration video, so that the household can install the equipment themselves. All household members, including children, record details of their purchases and the shops visited by scanning on-pack barcodes using a specially designed computerised scanner together with a code book. The code book is used for non-barcoded fresh food products. The data is transferred by a modem overnight to the Taylor Nelson Sofres headquarters. Panellists receive monthly incentives and six monthly bonuses for taking part. These can be accumulated and redeemed for a selection of gifts from a catalogue. A monthly newsletter is also sent out to maintain communication and announce winners for monthly prize draws.[6]

Summary

This chapter has set out the wide range of quantitative techniques that are available to marketing researchers. Survey research is the most popular marketing research technique and can be implemented through interactive methods, such as personal or telephone interviewing, or with no direct contact through self-administered methods delivered by post, by hand or by electronic means. Where interaction occurs, it is critical to stress the importance of the interviewer. In telephone and personal interviews, the interviewers are the main interface with respondents and are, therefore, a vital link to consumer co-operation. With refusal rates increasing, good interviewer training and induction programmes are critical to the future success of these methods. Computers are assisting the interviewing process through computer-assisted personal and telephone interviews (CAPI and CATI) and to a lesser extent through completely automated telephone surveys (CATS).

Postal surveys and surveys that are handed to respondents have traditionally made up the bulk of self-administered surveys. However, the advent of the Internet has resulted in the development of e-mail and web-based surveys. These have the advantages of being fast and cheap with the potential of reaching a large number of people. The surveys can also incorporate multimedia graphics and potentially audio. Currently, web users are not representative of the population as a whole, but this is likely to change, with digital television and web-enabled phones providing access to a wider audience. Until then such surveys are likely to focus on specialised audiences and web/technology-based topics.

Some of the key factors that determine the broad choice of survey method are set out in Table 6.1 for each of the approaches. This chapter has also described derivatives of these survey methods. Omnibus surveys, which can be face-to-face or telephone, are surveys that are undertaken at regular intervals for a changing group of clients who share the costs involved in the set-up, sampling and interviewing processes. They can provide access on a continuous or ad hoc basis to a large sample in a

Table 6.1 A comparison of survey approaches

	Face-to-face	Telephone	Self-administered
Cost	High	Medium	Low
Speed	Medium	High	Low
Suitability for geographically dispersed sample	Low	High	High
Control over interviewing process	Medium	High	Medium
Questionnaire length	High	Medium	Medium
Diversity of questions	High	Low	Medium
Positive public perceptions	Medium	Low	High
Ability to motivate respondents	High	Medium	Low
Suitability for sensitive or taboo subjects	Medium	Low	High
Ability to probe and clarify	High	High	Low
Response rates	High	Medium	Low
Scope for further use of computers	Medium	Medium	High

very short time scale for a client who wishes to ask only a limited number of questions. Survey methods can also be used within the testing of new products, new product attributes and new packaging. Such testing can take the form of hall tests, where initial reactions are assessed, placement tests, where products that need to be tested over a period of time are assessed, or simulated test markets, where the likely impact of a product launch is assessed. These testing or experimentation methods are all generally quantitative in nature and rely on survey-type instruments and sampling procedures to collect data.

Discussion questions

1 How does quantitative research differ from qualitative research?

2 What advantages does personal interviewing have over telephone interviewing?

3 What does interviewer bias mean and how can it impact on personal interviewing?

4 What are the advantages of using computers to assist in the undertaking of personal or telephone interviews?

5 Why are response rates for telephone interviewing on the decline?

6 How can the response rates of postal surveys be improved?

7 Discuss the proposition that e-mail surveys will soon replace all postal surveys.

8 Describe the workings of an omnibus survey and explain why a client may use one.

9 In what circumstances would you use a placement test rather than a hall test?

10 Describe the workings of a panel and explain why a panel may be used instead of a one-off survey.

Additional reading

Cobanoglu, C., Warde, B. and Moreo, P.J. (2001) A comparison of mail, fax and web-based survey methods. *International Journal of Market Research*, **43**(4), pp. 441–52.

Curasi, C.F. (2001) A critical exploration of face-to-face interviewing vs. computer mediated interviewing. *International Journal of Market Research*, **43**(4), pp. 361–75.

Dommeyer, C.J. and Moriarty, E. (1999) Comparing two forms of an e-mail survey: embedded vs. attached. *International Journal of Market Research*, **42**(1), pp. 39–50.

Mehta, R. and Sivadas, E. (1995) Comparing response rates and response content in mail versus electronic mail surveys. *Journal of the Market Research Society*, **37**(4), pp. 429–39.

Page, K. (2000) New developments in readership research. *International Journal of Market Research*, **42**(4), pp. 367–94.

Taylor, H. (1997) The very different methods used to conduct telephone surveys of the public. *Journal of the Market Research Society*, **39**(3), pp. 421–32.

Taylor, H. (1999) Does Internet research work? *International Journal of Market Research*, **42**(1), pp. 51–63.

Tse, A.C.B. (1998) Comparing the response rate, response speed, and response quality of two methods of sending questionnaires: e-mail vs. mail. *Journal of the Market Research Society*, **40**(4), pp. 353–61.

Weible, R. and Wallace, J. (1998) Cyber research: the impact of the Internet on data collection. *Marketing Research*, **10**(3), pp. 19–31.

Whitlark, D. and Gearts, M. (1998) Phone surveys: how well do respondents represent average Americans? *Marketing Research*, Fall, pp. 13–17.

Wilcox, S. (2000) Sampling and controlling a TV audience measurement panel. *International Journal of Market Research*, **42**(4), pp. 413–30.

References

[1] For more information see www.nrs.co.uk.

[2] For more information see www.tnagb.com.

[3] For more information see www.ipsos-rsl.com.

[4] For more information see www.nop.co.uk.

[5] For more information see www.bmrb.co.uk.

[6] For more on the Taylor Nelson Sofres Superpanel, see www.tnagb.com.

7
Designing questionnaires

The Target Group Index

The Target Group Index (TGI) is a sub-scription service operated by BMRB in 38 countries for advertisers, advertising agencies and media owners. It is aimed at improving the effectiveness of promotional activity by identifying and describing target groups of consumers and their media exposure. Each year, 25,000 people complete a self-administered questionnaire on their purchasing behaviour, media exposure and lifestyles. Respondents are recruited through personal interview and then given the questionnaire to complete and send back to BMRB. The effective response rate is 60 per cent of those who are recruited. That high level of response is dependent on the time and effort put into developing and testing of the questionnaire, not only to ensure that it collects accurate data but also that it is attractive, clear and interesting to potential respondents.[1]

Learning outcomes

After reading this chapter you should:

- understand the sequential stages involved in designing a questionnaire for quantitative research;
- be aware of the three main types of question (open, closed and scaled response) and their usage;
- understand the most commonly used scaling approaches (constant sum, Likert, semantic differential, stapel and purchase intent scales);
- be aware of the guidelines regarding the wording, sequencing, layout and pilot testing of questionnaires.

Key words

closed questions	pilot testing
constant sum scales	purchase intent scales
dichotomous questions	questionnaire design process
Likert scales	scaling questions
multiple-choice questions	semantic differential scales
open-ended questions	stapel scales

Introduction

In survey research, a questionnaire is the research instrument designed to generate the data necessary for accomplishing a project's research objectives. It standardises the wording and sequence of questions in order that each respondent is asked to provide information in exactly the same manner. This control ensures the validity of any comparison being made between different respondents' answers, as well as providing data in a form that can easily be analysed. Questionnaires provide the critical communication link between the researcher and the respondent. A questionnaire must:

1 communicate to the respondent what the researcher is asking for;
2 communicate to the researcher what the respondent has to say.

The primary objective of questionnaire design is to try to reduce the 'noise' or distortion in that two-way communication, in order that each party correctly understands what the other is saying (Figure 7.1). Questions that are difficult to interpret or answers that are either incomplete or confusing are examples of the noise that can hinder clear communication. Creating a questionnaire that provides a good communication vehicle is a difficult task, which requires a structured and systematic approach. This chapter identifies the critical activities involved in each stage of a questionnaire's design. As part of this the different types of questioning and scaling approaches will be discussed.

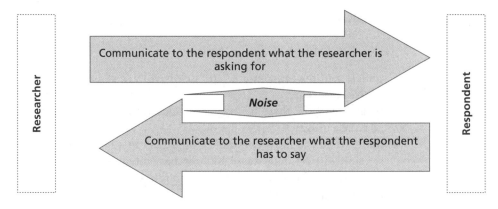

Figure 7.1 Questionnaire design: two-way communication

> **Researcher quote:** *Questionnaire design is all about effective two-way communication.*

The questionnaire design process

If you have never designed a questionnaire before, you may think it is simply a matter of writing down questions similar to those that you would have in a normal conversation. However, in conversations, misunderstandings are commonplace. People answer questions that are different from those that are asked. People use facial expressions, hand actions and clarifying words to further explain their questions or answers. People also interrupt each other to clarify misunderstandings, yet people talking at cross-purposes is still a common phenomenon. Therefore clarity of communication is not as simple an activity as it seems. Another example of this is illustrated by the following question from a recent survey about student finance:

Do you encounter any difficulties in paying the rent for your accommodation?

Yes ___ No_____

The researcher was looking at the financial difficulties that students were facing and at face value, there appears to be little wrong with the question. However, many students answered the question in relation to the *process* of paying rent rather than the difficulties associated with the actual *raising of the finance* to pay rent. The question therefore attracted more 'No's than expected because people found payment simple because they paid by direct debit or standing order or because the landlord regularly came round for the money. One respondent even stated that he had no difficulties because his landlord lived in the flat upstairs from him. This demonstrates that people can read different meanings into questions. Therefore questionnaire design should not be taken lightly as improper design can lead to inaccurate information, incomplete data and may result in research moneys being wasted. It is therefore

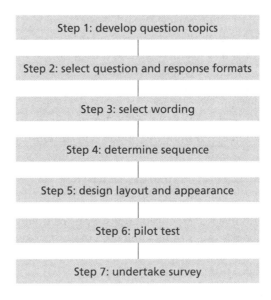

Figure 7.2 The questionnaire design process

advisable to adopt the stepped approach outlined in Figure 7.2 for the questionnaire design process.

Although these steps are shown as sequential steps, one should not see them as totally discrete. The steps are interrelated, as questionnaire design is an interactive process, with many drafts of a questionnaire being produced before a final version is completed. Changes in one of the later steps may result in the researcher having to make changes to elements involved in one of the earlier steps. For example, a proposed change in the layout and appearance may need a researcher to rethink response formats or question sequence. Problems identified when the questionnaire is pilot tested may also impact on any of the preceding steps. So although the tasks should be tackled in the sequence shown, each step will remain incomplete until the final questionnaire is approved for use on the survey.

The tasks involved in each of these interrelated steps will now be described in detail in the following sections.

Step 1: develop question topics

In developing the question topics, researchers should take account of the project's research objectives, the findings of any exploratory qualitative research undertaken and the characteristics of the respondents.

Research objectives

The research objectives should be seen as the key driver of questionnaire design. Which topics need to be included to provide the required information to fully satisfy the research objectives? Which topics are of critical importance and which are of secondary importance? What level of detail is required? What classification information is needed about the respondent? How will the results from the research be presented and used? Answers to these types of question will help to determine the topics to be covered, the weighting to be given to each topic and the broad manner in which the information should be collected. They will also help in determining which information is truly needed in comparison to information that is simply 'nice to know'. Such 'nice to know' information may add significantly to the length of a questionnaire, resulting in higher refusal/non-response rates among respondents.

Qualitative research findings

If a programme of exploratory primary research has been undertaken prior to the quantitative research, the findings can be used to clarify what should be asked and also the best ways of tackling each topic. The qualitative research should also help in determining the most relevant wording for questions and the statements to be used in rating scales.

Characteristics of respondents

Respondents must be able and willing to provide the information requested. Ability is based on the respondents having knowledge of the subject in question: Will they be able to recall how many shoes they tried on the last time they visited a shoe retailer? (*It is unlikely unless they visited a shoe retailer very recently.*) Will they be able to accurately recall how long they stood in the supermarket queue during their last visit? (*They will probably only remember if the length of time was excessive or something unusual happened.*)

In determining the topics, the researcher needs to put him/herself in the position of the respondent and determine what subjects the respondent is likely to have sufficient knowledge or memory of. Even where the respondents have knowledge they may be unwilling to answer questions on a particular topic, either because they think it is a sensitive and private matter or because they find the subject boring or uninteresting. Private subjects may relate to areas such as financial matters, earnings, personal hygiene products or contraceptives for consumers, or profits, future plans or supplier details for organisations. The researcher needs to consider how much information is needed in such areas and how the specific subjects should be tackled.

The level of interest respondents have in a subject is likely to have an impact on the potential number of questions that can be asked in a survey. If the respondents perceive the topic as having limited relevance to them, they may fail to complete self-administered questionnaires, hang up during a telephone interview or simply give any set of answers in order to finish the interview. The environment in which the respondent is interviewed can exacerbate this further. For example, it may be very difficult to maintain the attention of a respondent in an uninteresting subject during a street interview where there may be many other distractions. Therefore in determining the topics, care must be taken to identify how they can be made to seem interesting and relevant to potential respondents. There is a need to look at the topics from the respondent's perspective: are they concise, relevant and interesting?

Having taken these three inputs into account, the researcher should develop a rough set of topics/question areas to be addressed that can then be fitted into specific question formats.

Step 2: select question and response formats

There are basically three main forms of questions based on their format for capturing responses. These are open-ended (response) questions, closed (response) questions and scaling (response) questions.

Open-ended questions

Open-ended questions (sometimes known as unstructured questions) are those in which the respondents can reply in their own words. There are no pre-set choices of answers and the respondent can decide whether to provide a brief one-word answer or something very detailed and long. In the examples below, one-word answers may be all that is required (e.g. for question 1); however, for the other questions, more detailed answers may be more useful. Respondents may need to be encouraged to elaborate on a short answer by the use of probes such as 'Is there anything else?', 'In what way?', 'Can you expand on that?'.

> **Typical open-ended questions**
>
> 1 *Which country do you come from?*_____
>
> 2 *What did you enjoy most about your flight?*_____
>
> 3 *Why did you choose to fly by British Airways?*_____
>
> 4 *What is your opinion of the proposed merger between British Airways and Airline X?* _____

Open-ended questions are frequently used because the range of potential answers is very wide (for example, question 1 in the example) or where the research team feel that they lack sufficient knowledge about the subject to provide an exhaustive list of potential answers. Open-ended questions may uncover reasons why people fly British Airways that researchers had not recognised before. Such questions can provide researchers with a large amount of information that would not be available from a predetermined list of responses. The respondents answer from their own frame of reference using their own phrases and terminology. Such information may be particularly useful for copywriters designing advertising copy using the consumers' language.

Open-ended questions may also help to explain the answers to other types of question appearing in a questionnaire. For example, attitude rating scales may show a person's dissatisfaction with an organisation but an explanation for this may only come from an open-ended question about reasons for satisfaction/dissatisfaction.

Table 7.1 Coding of open-ended responses

3 Why did you choose to fly by British Airways?_____	
Category	Code
Executive Club member	1
Times of flights	2
In-flight catering	3
Service	4
Price	5
Connections	6
Out of habit	7
No choice	8
Other	9

Answers may be more honest in open-ended questions instead of simply being appropriate and matched to the set of responses provided.

Open-ended questions do have their drawbacks. One of the most significant is their analysis and interpretation. This involves editing and coding, where editing involves the reduction of the many responses into a number of categories and then coding each of the answers into one of these categories (see Table 7.1). If there are too many categories, it may be difficult to identify patterns or determine the relationships with answers given to other questions; too few categories lead to the categories being too broad and relatively meaningless. This is a time consuming process and generally has to be undertaken manually even if the data has been collected using computer-assisted interviewing. Unusual or complex answers may need to be interpreted by the researcher and forced into a category that does not exactly match (e.g. where should the researcher put: 'I have had bad experiences flying Lufthansa on that route regarding reliability').

The depth of information may vary dramatically between respondents depending on the ability of the interviewer to fully probe the subject and also the ability of the respondent to articulate their views. Shy or inarticulate respondents may provide the bare minimum of information. Open-ended questions are particularly difficult in self-administered questionnaires where the respondents do not have an interviewer to probe further. When respondents are on their own, they frequently write brief, incomplete answers which are of limited value to the researcher. However, it should be stressed that not all interviewers are good at recording answers verbatim and many simply summarise what respondents say, potentially missing out key points.

Some of these problems can be partially overcome in interviewer-administered questionnaires by pre-coding (before the interviews) rather than post-coding (after the interviews) potential responses. Although the question will still be asked in an open-ended manner, a list of answers will appear on the questionnaire along with an 'other' category for non-conforming answers. Interviews then tick the pre-printed answer that most closely matches what the respondent says. This makes the recording of the answers straightforward and reduces the analysis time. However, it loses the detail of the phrases and terminology used by respondents and it requires the researcher to have sufficient knowledge of the subject to anticipate most of the potential answers. It should be noted that pre-coded open-ended questions are different from closed or multiple-choice questions; although probing may occur, the list of answers is never read out. Respondents can respond in any way that they think fit. In contrast, multiple-choice questions require the alternative answers to be read or shown to the respondent.

Closed questions

A closed question is one that requires the respondent to make a selection from a predefined list of responses. There are two main types of closed questions: dichotomous questions with only two potential responses and multiple response questions with more than two. With each, the question is asked and the response alternatives are read out (or read by the respondent) before the most appropriate response is selected. Unlike open-ended questions, all respondents provide the same level of depth and interviewers only need to tick the selected box instead of summarising or recording responses verbatim. Analysis and the data entry process are also far simpler.

Dichotomous questions

Dichotomous questions are the simplest form of closed question as the respondent is limited to two fixed alternatives.

> 1 Have you shopped at Tesco before?
>   Yes   1
>   No   2
>
> 2 Each week, are you visiting this Tesco store more often or less often than last year?
>   More often   1
>   Less often   2

Some respondents may have difficulty choosing between the two options so a 'don't know' category is often added to address such situations. Dichotomous questions do not provide much detail. For example, question 1 tells us nothing about how frequently the respondent visits the store or whether their most recent visit was yesterday or 5 years ago. Question 2 does not distinguish between those who are visiting much more often and those who are visiting only slightly more often. Respondents may also have difficulty in answering a question with polarised alternatives. For example a respondent who visits Tesco with the same frequency as last year may have difficulty answering question 2. However, even with these weaknesses, dichotomous questions are useful as screening-type questions to determine whether a respondent should be asked further questions on a particular topic.

Multiple-choice questions

Multiple-choice questions provide respondents with a choice of potential responses to a question. The respondents are asked either to give one alternative that correctly expresses their viewpoint or to indicate all responses that apply.

The responses available to the respondent need to be mutually exclusive and collectively exhaustive.

Mutually exclusive means that each of the responses should be distinct, with no overlap between the categories. Problems are often seen with this in multiple-choice questions that relate to numerical values.

Within which of the following age brackets are you located?

15–20 years ☐
20–35 years ☐
35–50 years ☐   ✗   Incorrect!
Older than 50 years ☐

With this question where do respondents who are 20, 35 or 50 place their tick? The categories are not mutually exclusive. This causes confusion and results in the collection of incorrect data.

Collectively exhaustive means that all potential responses are listed. This means that the researcher needs to know all or most of the answers during the questionnaire design phase. This is relatively straightforward for factual information (such as newspapers read, brands of dog food purchased, European countries visited) where there is a relatively finite list. It is more difficult for factors relating to attitudes and opinions (although a qualitative research phase that has been undertaken prior to the quantitative research or a previous research study may help). Even where the research team think they know all the potential answers, it is often best to include an 'other' category enabling an alternative answer to be written in.

Which national newspaper do you read on a regular basis?

The Times ☐
The Daily Telegraph ☐
Financial Times ☐
The Guardian ☐
The Sun ☐
Daily Express ☐
Daily Mirror ☐
Other (please specify) _____

The optimum number of response categories in a question will be dependent on the manner in which the questionnaire is to be administered. Too many categories in a self-administered questionnaire will add to the overall length of the questionnaire, impacting on response rates and also potentially on mailing costs for postal surveys. In such cases the list should be limited to those responses that are considered to be most likely, supporting these with an 'other' category. In telephone and personal surveys, where the various categories need to be read out to respondents, long lists can increase interview time and try respondent patience. Respondents may also have difficulty remembering all of the categories by the time the interviewer gets to the end of the list. In personal interviews this can be overcome by putting the list on a 'show-card'. Rather than the interviewer reading out the options, the respondent is given the showcard and asked to select from it. In telephone interviews, where no visual options are available, the list may need to be reduced similar to self-administered questionnaires. If long lists of response category are essential to the research, personal interviewing may be the only option.

> **Researcher quote:** *It frequently takes longer to generate the response categories than it does to design the questions.*

The ordering of potential responses is important as it can influence a respondent's choice, especially when they are slightly unsure as to what answer to give. This is particularly the case when the responses are in the form of words, phrases and statements rather than numbers. Research has shown that respondents are more likely to choose the statements at the beginning or end of a list rather than those appearing in the middle. To reduce the impact of this, interviewers are frequently asked to rotate the sequence of categories from one questionnaire to the next. So, for the question on newspapers set out above, the interviewer would start the list of potential responses with *The Times* for respondent 1, with *The Daily Telegraph* for respondent 2, and so on. If this is done systematically, each response category will occupy various positions within the sequence, reducing the impact of position bias when considered across all respondents. This may be difficult in self-administered questionnaires, as many versions of a questionnaire would need to be produced, adding to the costs of the survey.

Scaling questions

Scaling in marketing research normally refers to procedures for the assignment of numerical measures to subjective concepts such as attitudes, opinions and feelings. The assignment of numbers enables the information from different groups of the population to be more easily compared and summarised. Statistical techniques can also be used to manipulate and analyse the data obtained. In designing scales there are a number of different dimensions that need to be considered: unidimensional versus multidimensional assessment; graphic versus itemised rating formats; comparative versus non-comparative; forced versus non-forced scales; balanced versus unbalanced scales. Design issues also exist with regard to the number of scale positions and the labelling/pictorial representation of positions.

Unidimensional versus multidimensional assessment

Scales can be unidimensional or multidimensional. Unidimensional scaling focuses on only one attribute, for example satisfaction. Respondents would be asked to rate their satisfaction with a particular product or service. Multidimensional scaling looks at a variety of dimensions, so a questionnaire about an overnight stay in a hotel may look at attitudes towards a range of items such as the comfort of the bedroom, the quality of the food, the helpfulness of reception staff, the range of amenities, etc.

Graphic versus itemised rating formats

Graphic rating scales (sometimes known as continuous rating scales) present respondents with a continuum, in the form of a straight line anchored between two extremes:

Respondents are asked to place a tick or cross on the line to represent the level of quality that they associate with the product under investigation. With regard to analysis, a score is assigned by dividing the line into categories and assigning the score based on the category within which the mark has been placed. For example, if the line was 15 cm long, each 2.5 cm could equal one category starting at 0 for low quality to 6 for high quality. A potential drawback of a graphic rating scale of this type is that coding and analysis takes a significant amount of time as physical distances have to be measured and interpreted for each attribute being assessed. Also, respondents may find it difficult to translate their feelings into distances on a line. To overcome this, some scales provide more structure to the respondent by assigning numbers along the scale while still allowing the respondent to mark the line at any point between the values identified:

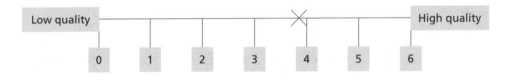

Although graphic rating scales suggest greater precision than other forms of scale, the precision is generally considered to be spurious owing to the difficulties respondents have in visualising attitudes as a distance along a line and in determining the fine distinctions between different points on the line. As a result graphic rating scales are used significantly less frequently than are itemised rating scales.

Itemised rating scales have a finite set of distinct response choices. The respondent chooses the rating or score that best reflects their view of the subject. These can take a variety of numerical and non-numerical forms, as can be seen in the following example from customer satisfaction questionnaires for hotel guests.

Indicate your overall opinion about the quality of the hotel bedroom using a scale from 1 to 5, where 1 is very low quality and 5 is very high quality.

| Very low quality | 1 | 2 | 3 | 4 | 5 | Very high quality |

Or

Which of the following best describes your overall opinion of the quality of the hotel bedroom?

Very low quality	Low quality	Neither low nor high quality	High quality	Very high quality
___	___	___	___	___

Respondents tend to find that itemised rating scales are generally easier than graphic rating scales. They are also much easier to analyse.

Comparative versus non-comparative assessments

Comparative rating scales ask respondents to compare the organisation or issue in relation to a common frame of reference. Everybody is comparing like with like. In contrast, a non-comparative rating scale does not provide a standard frame of reference and allows respondents to select their own frame of reference or even to use no frame of reference at all. For example, respondents in the following question may be comparing Asda eggs with eggs from other supermarkets, or with eggs they had as a child, or eggs they had in France on holiday or with eggs that they buy from the local farmers market.

Non-comparative rating scale

Rate the quality of the eggs that you have previously purchased from Asda using a rating scale where 1 is very poor quality and 5 is very high quality.

| Very poor quality | 1 | 2 | 3 | 4 | 5 | Very high quality |

This compares with the following questions, which provide a frame of reference within which the respondent positions the eggs from Asda.

Comparative rating scales

1 *In comparison to the eggs that you have previously bought from Tesco, rate the quality of the eggs from Asda using a rating scale where 1 is significantly lower quality and 5 is significantly higher quality.*

Much lower quality than Tesco	Lower quality than Tesco	About the same quality	Higher quality than Tesco	Significantly higher quality than Tesco
1	2	3	4	5

2 *Rank the following retailers for the quality of their eggs by placing a 1 beside the best, a 2 beside the store you think is second best, and so on.*

Tesco	___
Asda	___
Sainsburys	___
Marks & Spencer	___
Safeway	___

The first of these questions compares one object directly against another so the frame of reference is Asda eggs compared with Tesco eggs. The second uses a rank-order scale, which places the items (in this case, stores) in order. Rank-order scales are attractive because they reflect the way most people look at items, suppliers, etc., by placing them in an order (first choice, second choice, third choice, etc.) rather than attaching scores to things. Ranking and comparative rating scales in general do have the disadvantage that they are dependent on the respondent having knowledge of the subject with which the comparison is being made. Some Asda egg buyers may never have tasted Tesco eggs and therefore would have difficulty answering question 1 and they would only be able to partially complete question 2. The second specific problem with rank-order scales is that the researcher only receives ordinal or order data. Nothing is known about the relative difference between the factors being ranked. Do the retailers' eggs only vary slightly in quality or are one or two retailers significantly better than the others? This makes it difficult for a company to know how much they need to improve to alter their ranked position. This may not be an important weakness where the research is trying to assess aspects such as purchasing priorities. For example, a ranking approach may be very useful for a car manufacturer trying to identify customers' priorities in terms of standard and optional car features.

Overall the choice of comparative versus non-comparative formats is dependent on both the likely breadth of knowledge held by respondents, which may or may not enable them to make comparisons, and the specific purpose for which the client organisation wants the data.

Forced versus non-forced scales

A forced-choice scale does not allow respondents the option of selecting a neutral rather than a positive or negative view about an attribute. In general, a rating scale with an even number of categories is forced whereas an odd number of categories allows for a middle/neutral option.

Example of forced-choice scale

Indicate your overall opinion of the cost of IKEA furniture by ticking one of the following categories.

Very inexpensive	*Inexpensive*	*Expensive*	*Very expensive*
_____	_____	_____	_____

Example of non-forced-choice scale

Indicate your overall opinion of the cost of IKEA furniture by ticking one of the following categories.

Very inexpensive	*Inexpensive*	*Neither expensive nor inexpensive*	*Expensive*	*Very expensive*
_____	_____	_____	_____	_____

There is no clear agreement on whether forced-response choices provide information that is superior to scales where a neutral option is available. Forcing respondents to take a positive or negative view when they do not have any significant opinion on a subject may result in a set of spurious data. On the other hand, providing a neutral option may result in certain respondents selecting it in order to hide their true feelings or because they simply do not want to put the effort into examining what they do think. It is certainly the case that the majority of scales used in marketing research in the UK use an odd number of positions, which incorporate a neutral response. However, forced scales should not be rejected out of hand but should be considered for subjects where the researcher feels that there are likely to be very few people with neutral attitudes. For example, if an airline was to ask their passengers about the comfort of their seats, the appropriateness of including a neither comfortable nor uncomfortable category is questionable.

Balanced versus unbalanced scales

A balanced scale is one that has an equal number of positive and negative response choices. Most scales are balanced, as there is a danger of biasing respondents to answer in a certain manner if there are more positive than negative categories or vice versa. The only exception to this is where **end-piling** is expected; that is, where almost all responses appear in a few categories at one end of a measurement scale. This can occur if a scale is looking at the importance of features in a product. For example, motorists could be asked to rate the following car attributes: fuel efficiency, comfort, safety, ease of handling. All of these are unlikely to be considered as unimportant; however, their relative importance may vary. An unbalanced scale in which a majority of the choices favour one side, such as the one below, may be more effective at determining the relative differences in importance.

Unimportant	Important	Very important	Critical
( )	( )	( )	( )

The number of scale positions

The number of categories to include in a rating scale is linked to the forced/ non-forced and balanced/unbalanced issues. It is a topic that is controversial, with different researchers preferring different numbers, in many cases with limited justification for their choice. The majority of surveys use rating scales with typically between 5 and 9 categories. Sometimes scores out of 10 are used as people have tended to become accustomed to this type of scoring while progressing through their formal education at school. At face value, the larger the number of categories, the more precise the measurement. However, this will only be the case if respondents are able to make the fine distinctions between the categories when assessing what is being measured. What is the actual difference between a 7 and an 8 on a 9-point scale? Therefore the capabilities of the respondents should be considered when selecting the number of positions, as should the method of administering (fewer positions in telephone interviews) and the nature of the attribute being examined (it may be easier to use more categories when looking at an attribute such as performance in comparison to looking at satisfaction).

Labelling and pictorial representation of positions

Most rating scales will have a pair of anchor labels that define the extremes of a scale. However, researchers will often put intermediate labels in the form of words and numbers on the scales. There are no hard and fast rule as to the number or form these labels should take. However, it is generally better to leave a category unlabelled than to make up a label that does not fit with the other labels. Labels tend to become more difficult to develop when there are more than five or six in a scale (for example, what category does one put between 'good' and 'very good' or between 'poor' and 'very poor'). So generally in scales involving more than seven categories, a number of the categories will be unlabelled.

Very weak		Weak		Neither weak nor strong		Strong		Very strong
(1)	(2)	(3)	(4)	(5)	(6)	(7)	(8)	(9)

Picture labels can also be used to help respondents understand the categories and distinguish between them. These can be particularly useful in surveying children or people from different ethnic backgrounds. McDonald's uses faces similar to the ones below to assess customer satisfaction with its service.

Commonly-used scaling approaches

Constant sum scales

Constant sum scales requires the respondent to divide a given number of points, usually 100, among a number of attributes based on their importance to the individual (Figure 7.3). This has advantages over a standard rank-order scale in that the researcher not only obtains the ranked importance of each attribute but also the scale of difference that the respondent perceives as existing between the different variables. Two attributes can also be awarded equal values, which may be difficult in a ranking question. The principal weakness of this approach is that the number of attributes has to be relatively limited otherwise the respondents have difficulty allocating the points to total 100. Ten is most commonly seen as being the maximum number as respondents generally have difficulty in dividing by any number greater than 10.

Likert scale

The Likert scale is based on a format originally developed by Renis Likert in 1932. The scale involves respondents being asked to state their level of agreement with a series of statements about a product, organisation or concept. The scores are then

Below are five characteristics of food processors. Please allocate 100 points among the characteristics in a manner that represents the importance of each characteristic to you. The more points that you allocate to a characteristic, the more important it is to you. If a characteristic is totally unimportant, you should allocate 0 points to it. Please make sure the total points that you allocate adds up to 100.

Characteristics of food processors	Number of points
Has many accessories	
Is made by a well-known manufacturer	
Is easy to clean	
Is stylish	
Is quiet to operate	
	100 points

Figure 7.3 A constant sum scale used in a food processor study

I would now like to find out your attitudes towards this model of phone. Therefore, for each of the following statements, please tell me if you strongly agree, agree, neither agree nor disagree, disagree, or strongly disagree.

	Strongly agree	Agree	Neither agree nor disagree	Disagree	Strongly disagree
The phone is easy to use					
The phone's design is stylish					
The keys are too small					
The phone is better than the one I currently use					
The functions and commands are confusing					
I would look good with a phone like this					
The phone looks as if it is built to last					
I don't need a phone like this					

Figure 7.4 An example of Likert scale items

totalled to measure the respondent's attitude. The number of statements included in the scale may vary from study to study, depending on how many characteristics are relevant to the subject under investigation. Each statement expresses either a favourable or unfavourable attitude towards the concept under study. The respondent indicates agreement by selecting one of the following descriptors: strongly agree, agree, neither agree nor disagree, disagree, strongly disagree. Figure 7.4 presents eight illustrative statements that a mobile phone manufacturer can use to measure attitudes towards one of its products.

As Figure 7.4 shows, a typical feature of Likert scales is that there is normally a good balance of statements that are favourable and unfavourable towards the product or concept. Such a mix of statements will reduce the chances of respondents simply agreeing with all statements. After the scale has been administered, numbers are assigned to the responses, usually using the numbers 1 through to 5 (occasionally the number set −2, −1, 0, +1, +2 is used). As some of the statements will be favourable and others unfavourable, the allocation of numbers will have to vary accordingly. With favourable statements, 1 would be allocated to strongly disagree,

2 to disagree, 3 to neither agree or disagree, 4 to agree and 5 to strongly agree. The allocation of numbers would be reversed for unfavourable statements. Then each respondent's overall attitude is measured by summing his or her numerical ratings on the statements making up the scale. On a 20-item scale, the maximum favourable score would be 100, therefore a person scoring in the 80s or 90s would be considered as having a positive attitude to the product or company being assessed. However, in addition to the summing of the scores, it is important to look at the components of the overall attitude as respondents with the same total may rate individual attributes differently. Some respondents may be positive about the functionality of the mobile phone whereas others may be more positive about its style. Information such as this may explain why a phone is or is not selling and may also identify what attributes are attractive to particular market segments.

The overall value of the Likert scale depends on the care with which the statements making up the scale are selected. Designing a good Likert scale involves generating a large pool of statements (possibly up to 100 statements for a final scale of 20) and then sifting through these to arrive at the final statements used in the survey. The sifting process is usually undertaken using a pre-test of the statements with a small sample of the population to be researched. Statements are rejected if respondents consider them to be unclear or ambiguous. They are also rejected if they fail to discriminate between respondents with differing attitudes. This is determined by comparing respondents' scores for each individual statement with their total score for all statements. The statements on which the respondents' scores correlate positively or negatively with the respondents' total scores are better indicators of attitudes and are hence more useful for inclusion. Therefore, of the original pool of statements, the 20 or 30 statements that are unambiguous and have the highest correlations with the total attitude scores will be selected. Care taken in the selection and sifting of the statements is critical if the Likert scale is to be considered reliable and sensitive. Of all of the scales available, the Likert scale is probably the one that is most commonly used in commercial marketing research.

Semantic differential scale

Although the semantic differential scale plays a similar role to a Likert scale, its construction is more complex. The researcher selects a set of bipolar adjectives or phrases (e.g. helpful and unhelpful; friendly and unfriendly) that could be used to describe the product, company, brand or concept. Each pair of adjectives is separated by a seven-category scale with neither numerical nor verbal labels. Respondents are asked to rate the brand or concept for each pair of adjectives (Figure 7.5).

The location of the positive statements should be randomly placed on the right and left of the scale, in order to force the respondents to think about the adjectives before responding, otherwise respondents may simply go down the attributes giving the same rating to all. Care is also required in selecting the pairs of adjectives/phrases and these should be chosen in a systematic manner similar to that used for Likert scales.

In terms of analysis, the seven categories can be numerically coded using a scale of 1, 2, 3, 4, 5, 6, 7 or −3, −2, −1, 0, 1, 2, 3 and overall attitude scores can be obtained for the combined attributes as well as the individual descriptors (making sure that negative descriptors are reversed). Commonly a pictorial profile of semantic

Now consider your attitudes towards Adidas. Listed below are pairs of statements that could describe a sports brand. For each pair, mark an X between the two statements in a position that best reflects your view of Adidas.

Expensive	:___:___:___:___:___:___:	*Inexpensive*
The choice of professionals	:___:___:___:___:___:___:	*The choice of amateurs*
Old fashioned	:___:___:___:___:___:___:	*Modern*
A market leader	:___:___:___:___:___:___:	*A market follower*
High quality	:___:___:___:___:___:___:	*Low quality*

Figure 7.5 An example of a semantic differential scale

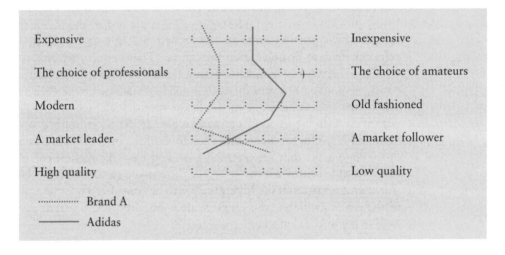

Figure 7.6 A semantic differential profile

differential results is produced (see Figure 7.6). Note that to facilitate interpretation of the information, all of the favourable descriptors are placed on the same side of the profile.

Such a profile can provide a quick and efficient means of identifying differences between different brands, companies, concepts, etc. According to Figure 7.6, Adidas has a higher rating for quality than brand A but in all other respects brand A has a superior image. Such ease of comparison has resulted in semantic differential scales being regularly used for corporate image research.

Stapel scale

The stapel scale is a variation of the semantic differential scale which uses a single descriptor rather than a pair of opposite descriptors. The scale is a forced-choice scale with 10 response categories and no verbal labels (Figure 7.7).

For the following statements relating to freight transport, indicate with your first impression how accurately the statements on the left-hand side represent Railfreight.
The more accurately you think the word describes Railfreight, the larger the plus number you should choose. The less accurately you think a phrase describes Railfreight, the larger the minus number you should choose. You can select any number from +5 for words you think are very accurate to –5 for words you think are very inaccurate.

	+5		+5		+5		+5
	+4		+4		+4		+4
	+3		+3		+3		+3
	+2		+2		+2		+2
Reliable	+1	*Competitive*	+1	*Fast transit*	+1	*Good record for*	+1
deliveries	–1	*in price*	–1	*times*	–1	*loss and damage*	–1
	–2		–2		–2		–2
	–3		–3		–3		–3
	–4		–4		–4		–4
	–5		–5		–5		–5

Figure 7.7 A stapel scale used for assessing attitudes towards Railfreight

The data obtained from stapel scales can be analysed in much the same way as for the semantic differential scale with overall attitude scores and pictorial profiles based on the mean scores.

The principal advantage of the stapel scale is that the researcher does not have to go through the arduous task of identifying bipolar adjective pairs. However, the layout of the scales can sometimes make it difficult for all respondents to understand what is required of them. It also takes up more space in a questionnaire, adding to questionnaire length and refusal rates. As a result, the stapel scale is used to a much lesser extent in commercial marketing research than either semantic differential or Likert scales.

Purchase intent scales

The purchase intent scale is used to measure a respondent's intention to buy a product or potential product. It is frequently viewed as a multiple-choice question rather than a scale. However, as it attempts to quantify a subjective measure, it will appear here as a scaling technique. The purchase intent scale is generally asked during the concept testing stages of new product development and also when companies are considering revisions to their products or services. The scale is very straightforward – consumers are simply asked to make a subjective judgement about their buying intentions (see Figure 7.8).

Many companies use the purchase intent scale to make go/no-go decisions in product development by adding together the definitely buy and probably buy categories and comparing this total against a predetermined go/no-go threshold (say, for example, 70 per cent of respondents answering in these categories). Using past data from previous product launches, some organisations may be able to forecast the expected market share based on patterns of purchasing intentions.

1 *If new product X sold for £2.75 and was available in the stores where you normally shop, would you:*

Definitely buy product X [SKIP to Q3]	1
Probably buy	2
Probably not buy [ASK Q2]	3
Definitely not buy [ASK Q2]	4

2 *What if the product was priced at £1.99? Would you:*

Definitely buy product X	1
Probably buy	2
Probably not buy	3
Definitely not buy	4

Figure 7.8 A purchase intent scale

Step 3: select wording

Whatever form of question or scaling technique is used, care must be taken in the words that are used and the phrasing that is adopted. The complexity and style of the wording will be specific to the topic and the respondents involved. The overriding principle should be that wording and phrasing should be as simple and straightforward as possible. There are certain errors that researchers should be aware of and avoid. These are discussed in the following subsections.

Ambiguous questions

Respondents and researchers may read different meanings into questions, resulting in inappropriate or unexpected answers.

In a survey with children:

When will you leave school?

To this question, should they answer with the age when they leave school for good or should they give the time of day that the school closes?

In a survey for a paint manufacturer:

What did you decorate last?

One respondent gave the reply : 'the Christmas tree'.

To avoid such confusion and surprises, questions should be tested with a small group of potential respondents to check that their understanding of the questions is similar to that of the researcher.

> **Researcher quote:** *It always amazes me, how many different meanings people can read into a very simple, straightforward question.*

Double-barrelled questions

Double-barrelled questions are questions where two topics are raised within one question. Such questions can cause difficulty for the respondent because they do not know which of the topics to address, particularly if they have different views about each. They also cause difficulty for the researcher team, as they are unclear as to which topic the respondent is addressing. For example:

> *Have you seen an improvement in the quality of this hotel's food and accommodation?*
>
> *Yes_____ No_____ Don't know _____*

This relates to the two separate issues of accommodation and also food. A 'no' response from the respondent could mean:

(a) there has been no improvement in either food or accommodation;
(b) there has been an improvement in food but not in accommodation;
(c) there has been an improvement in accommodation but not in food.

Only the respondent will know what he or she means. This type of problem can be overcome by breaking the question into two or more questions and rewording the questions to focus on only one issue at a time (i.e. one focusing on food and the other focusing on accommodation).

Leading or loaded questions

Leading or loaded questions are questions that tend to steer respondents toward a certain answer, particularly where the respondents are unsure as to their true feelings. For example:

> 1 Don't you think smoking is antisocial?
>
> Yes ___ No ___
>
> 2 How often do you buy goods from cheap or discount type stores such as TK Max?
>
> Very frequently ___
> Frequently ___
> Occasionally ___
> Never ___
>
> 3 Do you think students like government policies?
>
> Yes ___ No ___ Don't know ___

Because of the phrasing 'don't you think', respondents are more likely to answer 'yes' to question 1. Also, emphasising the 'cheap or discount' aspect of the TK Max store in question 2 may make respondents less willing to say frequently or very frequently. In question 3, does the answer 'no' mean that the students dislike government policies or does it mean that they do not have any strong views about government policies? This question is one sided in its current format; if the answers are to have any value it should be written as:

> Do you think students like or dislike government policies?
>
> Like ___ Dislike ___ Neither like nor dislike ___ Don't know ___

Although leading questions are sometimes used by unethical groups to gain feedback to further their particular cause or ideas, the majority are developed unknowingly by researchers who have not maintained a totally objective viewpoint throughout the questionnaire design process. Researchers must therefore take care to construct questions in as neutral a fashion as possible.

Implicit assumptions

Questions with implicit assumptions are questions where the researcher and the respondent are using different frames of reference as a result of assumptions that both parties make about the questions being asked. These have similar outcomes to ambiguous questions; the difference is that the question is clear and it is the assumptions that underlie it that are ambiguous.

> Do you use the memory keys on your phone when making calls?
>
> Yes ___ No ___

This question makes several implicit assumptions. First, it is not clear whether the researcher is asking about the respondent's mobile phone or landline phone (or even a phone at work). The answer is likely to vary depending on what the respondent assumes. The researcher also assumes that the respondent's phone has memory keys and that the respondent knows what they are. It is necessary to state the frame of reference with more clarity or ensure that the respondent is qualified to answer the question by using one or more filter questions. A filter question is a question that tests to see whether a respondent qualifies for or has experience relevant to a subsequent question. The following filter questions could be used to ensure that the same frame of reference is being used for the above question:

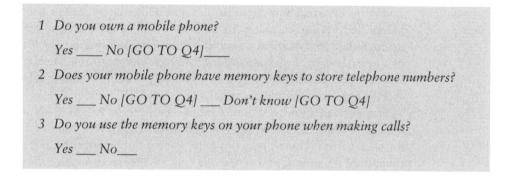

1 *Do you own a mobile phone?*

Yes ____ No [GO TO Q4]____

2 *Does your mobile phone have memory keys to store telephone numbers?*

Yes ___ No [GO TO Q4] ___ Don't know [GO TO Q4]

3 *Do you use the memory keys on your phone when making calls?*

Yes ___ No___

Filter questions are particularly important at the start of a questionnaire to screen out respondents who are inappropriate to the study being undertaken. Care must be taken with the number of filter questions as they can unnecessarily add to the length of the questionnaire and can sometimes try the patience of the respondent. In some cases it may be more appropriate to place a 'not applicable' response category in a question rather than adding an additional question as a filter.

Researcher quote: *I was always told to be careful about making assumptions. If you **assume**, it can make an **ASS** of **U** and **ME**!*

When undertaking international research, the wording may need to be changed for each country not only due to language differences but also as a result of cultural and environmental factors. Direct translation of a questionnaire may not communicate the same meaning to different nationalities of respondents. The questionnaire should be adapted to the individual environments in which it will be used and should not be biased in terms of any one culture. For example, the interpretation of scaling questions is different with different nationalities. In many Asian cultures, people are unwilling to give negative ratings about individuals or organisations. Assumptions should not be made about purchasing behaviour as the role and position of women, family members and retailers may differ significantly. Literacy rates may also vary, resulting in difficulties with open-ended questions or complex wording.

Step 4: determine sequence

In sequencing questions in a questionnaire, it is often best to think from the respondent's point of view: what sequence will respondents perceive as being interesting and logical? If respondents feel that they are jumping from subject to subject, the questioning can feel more like an interrogation than a relaxed marketing research survey. Therefore questions on similar topics should be clustered together within the questionnaire, allowing respondents to maintain their train of thought on one topic before moving on to the next.

One of the most controversial issues in sequencing is the positioning of classification questions and whether they should appear at the start or end of a questionnaire. Classification questions are questions that appear in almost all questionnaires and are concerned with gathering data on the respondent's personal or demographic characteristics. Such classification questions may be located at the start of a questionnaire if they are needed to screen (accept or reject) people for interview. For example, this may be necessary where respondents are being selected to meet the specific requirements of a quota sample.

However, in all other circumstances classification questions should be located at the end of a questionnaire. Interest and rapport must be established at the start of a questionnaire if the respondent is to complete the questions in a thorough and thoughtful manner. Questions at the start of the questionnaire should therefore be interesting and relatively straightforward both in terms of content and question format. Classification questions and questions on sensitive subjects (potentially embarrassing or private topics) should be avoided until nearer the end when rapport and interest have been established. Respondents may also feel more obliged to answer these questions at the end because they have already taken time and effort to answer all of the earlier questions.

Questions should follow a **funnel sequence**, moving from the generalities of a topic to the specifics. For example, if a survey was looking at attitudes towards shoppers' car parking facilities in a city centre, the funnel approach would probably move through the order shown in Figure 7.9.

Funnel sequencing is particularly critical where answers to earlier specific questions could bias the answers to later questions. It is also important where the researcher wishes to ensure that respondents are only asked questions that are specifically relevant to them. Some of the general questions at the start of the funnel sequence may act as skip questions that determine what specific questions are asked of a particular respondent further down the funnel. For example, if the respondent in the car parking questionnaire stated that he or she only used one particular car park, then the respondent would only be asked about the features that relate to that car park. Traditionally, skip patterns involving respondents being asked different numbers of questions in different sequences needed to be as straightforward as possible if interviewers or self-administered respondents were not to become confused. This is less of a problem where computer-assisted interviewing is used as the computer package can be programmed to move around the virtual questionnaire in any way that the researcher feels to be appropriate.

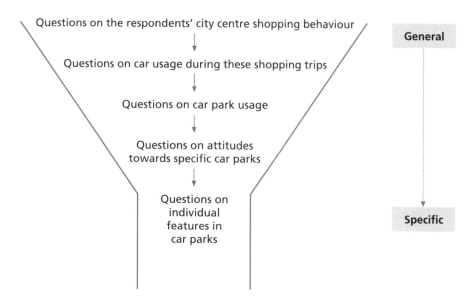

Figure 7.9 Funnel sequence of questioning

Step 5: design layout and appearance

The layout and appearance of the questionnaire is particularly important in self-administered and postal questionnaires. Response rates are likely to be higher if the questionnaire looks attractive, uncluttered and easy to understand. Even where interviewers are involved, the care and attention the interviewer gives to recording the responses is likely to be influenced by the layout and appearance of the questionnaire.

The key elements are:

- **Spacing**: attempting to make a questionnaire look shorter can result in researchers using smaller typefaces and squeezing as many questions as possible onto a page. This is counterproductive – respondents and interviewers find the questionnaire difficult to use, and as a result response rates reduce and poorer quality data is obtained. The questionnaire should look uncluttered with plenty of space between questions and for responses to open-ended questions. In multiple-choice and scaling questions, the potential answers should be sufficiently far apart so that the interviewer or respondent can easily pick the proper row or column. Splitting a question or its responses over different pages to save space should also be avoided. The typeface should be clear and of a sufficient size, with instructions to the respondent or interviewer printed in capitals or bold face type to differentiate them from the questions.

- **Quality of production**: a questionnaire that is poorly reproduced on poor quality paper may prove less expensive but can give the impression that the survey is unimportant. As a result, the quality and number of responses will be adversely affected. Questionnaires can be made to look more professional by high-quality printing, good quality paper and stapling the pages into the form of a booklet rather than simply a sheaf of A4 paper. This is particularly important for self-administered or postal questionnaires.

- **Variety**: a questionnaire that uses similar question formats or has large banks of scaling questions can look intimidating to the respondent. So the sequencing and layout of the questionnaire should seek visual variety in the look of the questions and the questionnaire. Colour, typefaces, borders and arrows can also be used to delineate different sections of questions or different skip patterns through the questionnaire.

- **Coding/analysis requirements**: although design and layout decisions are critical to effective data collection, those who will be involved in the coding and analysis of the questionnaires should also be consulted about the best layout and design requirements for efficient data processing.

There are many computer packages that can help in the design and layout of traditional and web-based surveys. In the UK examples of such software include snap, QSL/Research Machine, MerlinPlus, QPS and Quanquest. In a package such as the snap package from Mercator,[2] the researcher only needs to type in the questions to be asked and the package will produce the layout for the questionnaire, including instructions and scaling questions, in an attractive and clear manner. Following the completion of the interviews, the data can be fed back into the same package for analysis. A particular benefit of these packages is that the question-and-answer text and data definitions from the questionnaire can be taken over into the analysis and tabulation of results without requiring to be rekeyed into the computer.

Step 6: pilot test

Pilot testing (sometimes known as pre-testing) involves administering a questionnaire to a limited number of potential respondents in order to identify and correct design flaws. The potential respondents for the pilot test and for the full survey should be drawn from the same populations. The questionnaire should also be administered in the same manner as is planned for the full survey. Where interviewers are involved, they should be able to identify errors in the format and nature of questions, judge respondent reaction to the questionnaire, measure the time taken to complete the questionnaire, and determine the overall appropriateness of the questionnaire to the target population. However, where the questionnaire is self-administered, a researcher should be present during the pilot test when respondents are completing the questions. Some respondents are then asked to voice their thoughts as they attempt to answer each question. Others will be asked to complete the questionnaire in a normal fashion so that the time for completion can be noted and then they will be asked to explain their experiences with the questionnaire.

Normally, the pilot test sample is relatively small, varying between 10 and 40 respondents depending upon the heterogeneity of the target population. It is better to test the questionnaire systematically with detailed probing of a small sample rather than doing superficial testing with a large sample.

If significant changes are made to the questionnaire following the pilot test, it is recommended that the pilot test be repeated with the revised questionnaire.

> **Researcher quote:** *Pilot testing is critical if you want to make sure that the questionnaire is going to fully address your information targets.*

Step 7: undertake survey

Following the pilot test, the managers who will be using the information from the research should always be asked to finally approve a questionnaire before it goes 'live' with the respondents. This ensures that there will be no disputes at the end of the project about incorrect or inappropriate questions being asked. Once the approval has been received, the data collection can commence.

Summary

This chapter has examined the sequential stages involved in designing a questionnaire for quantitative research. The process consists of the following:

1 develop question topics;
2 select question and response formats;
3 select wording;
4 determine sequence;
5 design layout and appearance;
6 pilot test;
7 undertake survey.

Specific emphasis was placed on describing the three main types of question (open, closed and scaled response) and their usage. The different types of each were explained, including the most commonly used scaling approaches (constant sum, Likert, semantic differential, stapel and purchase intent scales). Guidelines were also provided regarding the wording, sequencing, layout and pilot testing of questionnaires.

Questionnaire design has a major influence on the quality of data gathered in any survey. It also has a major impact on the response rates in self-administered studies. As such, it is critical that a systematic and careful approach is taken to questionnaire design if research money is not to be wasted.

Discussion questions

1 Explain the concept of 'noise' in questionnaire design.

2 What factors should a researcher consider when developing question topics?

3 Why would a researcher choose to use an open-ended question?

4 What factors are critical in the development of multiple-choice questions?

5   Explain the difference between comparative and non-comparative rating scales.

6   Explain the difference between forced and non-forced rating scales.

7   What are the main differences between a Likert scale and a semantic differential scale?

8   In wording questions, what are the main faults that a researcher should attempt to avoid?

9   Explain what is meant by the funnel sequence of questioning.

10   What are the main elements that should be considered in designing the layout and appearance of a questionnaire?

Additional reading

Albaum, G. (1997) The Likert scale revisited. *Journal of the Market Research Society*, **39**(2), pp. 331–48.

Likert, R. (1932) A technique for the measurement of attitudes. *Archives of Psychology*, **140**. Also in Summers, G.F. (ed.) (1970) *Attitude Measurement*. Rand McNally, Chicago, IL, pp. 149–58.

Oppenheim, A.N. (1992) *Questionnaire Design, Interviewing and Attitude Measurement*. Pinter Publishers, London.

Reynolds, N., Diamantopoulos, A. and Schlegelmilch, B.B. (1993) Pre-testing in questionnaire design: a review of the literature and suggestions for further research. *Journal of the Market Research Society*, **35**, April, pp. 171–82.

Sudman, S. and Bradburn, N.M. (1983) *Asking Questions*. Jossey Bass, San Francisco, CA.

References

[1] For more information see www.bmrb.co.uk.

[2] For more information see www.mercatorcorp.com.

8
Sampling methods

Over 7.3 billion musical items are broadcast and publicly performed in the UK each year. The Performing Right Society (PRS) has around 33,000 members (composers, songwriters and publishers) on whose behalf it licenses the rights of organisations and individuals to publicly perform and broadcast their copyright work – music and lyrics. About 250,000 licences for premises using music (from aircraft through concert halls, restaurants, schools, shops and factories to zoos) are in existence at any one time. The charges for these licences vary but over £200 million is collected from these licences each year.

Marketing research was required to improve the fairness, accuracy and clarity of PRS royalty distributions to its members. The research had to take into account all the different ways in which music is used – live and recorded – across a large variety of venues as well as in radio and television. With regard to venues, information was required on the musical works actually being performed during a researcher's visit to an establishment in a statistically valid sample of premises across the UK, with information on the type of venue, means of performance, time of day, etc.

After a pilot study, a sample of 1,200 establishments was drawn from the PRS's own licensing database of 200,000 licensed premises. Weeks of analysis and planning were required to get the database into the format necessary from which to select the sample.

The physical sampling aside, the researchers first needed to decide which sampling method to apply. Work from the pilot study showed that there was a great deal of variation in the amount of music played between premise types; the sample selected would need to represent this. The database would therefore require at least

one level of stratification. In addition to this, PRS also wanted to identify any regional differences. Although distribution was not currently weighted regionally, the opportunity existed to test for regional differences.

One way by which venues are classified on the database is by tariff code. A venue can belong to more than one tariff. For example, if a live music venue had both popular and classical music concerts, then it would be classified under tariffs, LP (Live Popular) and LC (Live Classical). Two strata were therefore applied to the database. The first stratum was by geographical region (eight in total based upon PRS's internal regional structure), and then tariff. Premises were then selected randomly.

Should the sample be weighted in any way? To test this, sampling proportional to the number of venues within a strata/sub-stratum was considered. This was then compared with the proportion of revenue that PRS collect from each of the tariffs (part of the licence fee that a premise pays PRS is a reflection of the amount of music that a premise broadcasts). What the analysis showed was that for certain tariff types the sample was not reflective of the revenue that those tariffs generated. For instance, Wembley Stadium would be charged substantially more than the Carpenters Arms. However, sampling based upon strata numbers was not reflective of this since there are many pubs but few concert stadiums. Therefore a random sample that was proportional to the revenue was chosen.

Three tariffs (Hotels, Members Clubs and Pubs) would require a further sub-stratum to allow for the diversity of music played within these. The sub-stratum reflected the majority of the licence fee for which the premise was charged. Premises could also belong to more than one tariff but the project team from Millward Brown needed to ensure that the premise was only selected once. Although a random sample was chosen, the probability of selection was proportional to the revenue. Since the premise could belong to more than one tariff, this therefore required the probabilities to be updated after each premise had been selected. Work from the pilot study showed that the average acceptance rate onto the study was one in six. To allow for this, at least an eight times sample was required. However, this would also need to be increased due to the reliability of some of the information contained upon the database. So, allowing for the proportion of premises that could not be successfully identified, a 12 times sample (i.e. 14,400 names) was chosen and sent away to have addresses checked and telephone numbers added.

Each fieldwork visit lasted up to six hours. Researchers noted down musical work by all means of performance and data was collected from all rooms in a venue in which music was played. Other useful information regarding the numbers, styles and timings of musical events was also collected to give an extra insight into music use in the venue. A programme of research was also carried out with unlicensed venues. The results make interesting reading and the top twenty music types being played or performed are shown in the following table:[1]

	Genre	Percentage of performances		Genre	Percentage of performances
1	90s pop and rock	27.51	5	House	6.12
2	80s pop and rock	10.98	6	60s pop and rock	5.20
3	70s pop and rock	10.43	7	Funk/disco	3.86
4	Light instrumental	6.39	8	Jazz	2.57

Genre	Percentage of performances		Genre	Percentage of performances
9 Popular and light vocal	1.97		15 Classical	1.33
10 Techno	1.80		16 Hip hop/rap	1.21
11 50s pop and rock	1.75		17 Blues	0.80
12 Country	1.58		18 Latin	0.77
13 Reggae	1.36		19 Machines	0.44
14 Celtic/gaelic	1.35		20 Folk european	0.39

Learning outcomes

After reading this chapter you should:

- be aware of the steps involved in the sampling process;
- understand the concepts of population and sampling frame;
- be aware of the different types of probability and non-probability sampling techniques;
- be aware of some of the problems involved in sampling for Internet surveys;
- be able to explain how to determine the sample size for a survey;
- understand the concepts of sampling and non-sampling error.

Key words

area sampling
census
cluster sampling
confidence level
convenience sampling
data errors
disproportionate stratified random
    sampling
interviewer quality control scheme
    (IQCS)
judgement sampling
multi-stage sampling
non-probability sampling
non-response errors
non-sampling error

normal distribution
population of interest
probability sampling
proportionate stratified random
    sampling
quota sampling
sample
sampling error
sampling frame
sampling frame error
simple random sampling
snowball sampling
stratified random sampling
systematic sampling
weighting

Introduction

In quantitative marketing research, it is very unlikely that a researcher will be able to survey every person in the target market or population of interest. Constraints of time and money restrict researchers to seeking a sample of respondents that is representative of that population. The selection of that sample is critical to the accuracy with which the data that is collected reflects the reality of the behaviour, awareness and opinions of the total target market. In any study, researchers need answers to questions such as:

- What type of people do we want to survey?
- Where do we find these types of people?
- How do we select the individuals involved?
- How many individuals do we need to survey?
- How representative is the information we collect?

This chapter sets out the process involved in answering these questions through the development of a sampling plan. The major sampling approaches that are available to the marketing researcher will also be discussed, as will the sampling and non-sampling errors associated with quantitative research.

The sampling process

The process involved in developing a sampling plan can be summarised in the six steps shown in Figure 8.1. The remainder of this chapter will discuss each of these steps in detail.

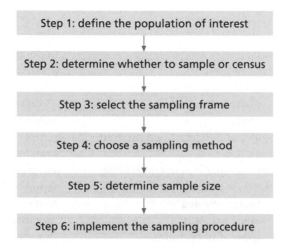

Figure 8.1 The sampling process

Step 1: define the population of interest

The population of interest (sometimes referred to as the target population or universe) is the total group of people that the researcher wishes to examine, study or obtain information from. The population of interest will normally reflect the target market or potential target market for the product or service being researched. However, accurate delineation of the population of interest is the key foundation step in the sampling process. For example, a researcher conducting a study into the potential market for an updated model of the VW Golf may need to consider a wide range of categories as potential delineators before coming to a clear definition of the population he or she is interested in.

Possible categories

- All car drivers.
- Current owners of VW Golfs.
- Current owners of mid-size hatchbacks.
- People who have previously sought information on VW Golf models.
- Those who are likely to purchase cars in the next 24 months.
- Those who are likely to purchase mid-size hatchbacks in the next 24 months.

Final definition of population

- Car drivers who are current owners of mid-size hatchbacks who are likely to purchase a replacement mid-size hatchback in the next 24 months.

It is then up to the researchers to provide explicit instructions about the qualifications for inclusion in the target population to interviewers or those responsible for developing a mailing list for a postal survey. Screening questions will then be developed to qualify which respondents should or should not be included in the research. Certain groups of the population of interest may be excluded for obvious reasons (e.g. employees of car manufacturers or dealerships may be excluded as they may work for competitors or have atypical opinions). There are no specific rules or guidelines for defining the population of interest – it simply requires careful, logical thinking about the characteristics of the target market or target audience.

Researcher quote: *You should always take time to carefully think through the nature of the population of interest.*

Step 2: determine whether to sample or census

A census occurs when data is obtained from every member of the population of interest. For example, the UK government population census, which takes place every ten years, requires every adult in the UK to provide information about characteristics such as employment, travel patterns, family relationships, etc. This is a very large, complicated and expensive data gathering exercise, which may partially explain why it can only be done on a ten-yearly basis. Censuses in marketing research are also very rare. Many populations of interest may consist of thousands or even hundreds of thousands of people. The cost, time and effort that is required to interview every single person is prohibitive for marketers and marketing researchers. The value of interviewing every person may also be questionable, as the data is likely to be only marginally better than data obtained from a carefully designed sample.

Censuses are occasionally used for research involving specialised industrial products or services where the number of customers is very small. For example, a research project looking at the use of specialised chemicals in the paper making industry may be able to gather information from all of the paper mills in the country or region being investigated. However, it should be stressed that this is only appropriate where the market is very small and specialised; for most studies a sample of the population of interest will be sought.

Step 3: select the sampling frame

The sample frame is a list of the population of interest from which the researcher selects the individuals for inclusion in the research. It can be a list of names and telephone numbers for telephone surveys, a list of addresses for mail or doorstep interviews, or a map showing local housing. It is unlikely that the list will match the population of interest exactly. If we wanted to interview every household within a town, we could use the town's telephone directory as our sample frame. However, people may have moved or died recently; some may not have their telephone number listed in the directory; some may prefer to use a mobile phone and some may not have any phone at all. The researcher will need to determine whether the residents included in the telephone directory are likely to differ markedly from those who are not included. The answer will probably be yes as those without telephones are likely to be in the poorer than average category, those using mobiles will be younger than average and those likely to be unlisted will be more affluent than average. This difference means that a sample based on the telephone directory will have sampling frame error. The nature of this will be discussed in more detail in the section on sampling and non-sampling error later in the chapter.

To reduce sample frame error, a number of lists may be added together to create the sample frame. There may be a wide range of lists available, which may relate to mailing lists of homeowners, magazine subscribers, people who have responded to previous direct mail campaigns, retail loyalty cardholders, members of clubs, etc. Similar lists exist of manufacturers, distributors, service organisations and retailers in the business-to-business research sector.

Where no lists exist, it may be necessary to use a general list of the population. Potential respondents would then be selected based on their answers to a number of filter questions which would screen them either into or out of the research. In telephone research the procedure of random digit dialling can be used, where the numbers to be telephoned are selected using random number generation software. This selects numbers in a random manner similar to the numbers being chosen for the national lottery.

As it is generally unlikely that there will be a perfect sample frame, it is important for the researcher to be aware of any shortcomings in the sample frame in order to make adjustments in the remaining steps of the sampling process.

Step 4: choose a sampling method

Sampling methods can be grouped under two headings, probability and non-probability sampling.

Probability sampling methods

These comprise samples where an objective procedure of selection is used, resulting in every member of the population of interest having a known probability of being selected. In probability sampling the researcher specifies some objective and systematic procedure for choosing potential respondents from a population. Once the procedure has been set out, the selection of potential respondents is independent of any arbitrary, convenient or biased selection by the researcher. This systematic approach enables probabilities to be assigned to (a) the likelihood of each member of the population being surveyed and (b) the extent to which the values obtained in the survey can be projected to reflect the true values held by the population as a whole. This second area relates to sampling error (the difference between the sample value and the true value of a phenomenon for the population being surveyed), which can be stated in mathematical terms: usually the survey result plus or minus a certain percentage.

Probability sampling methods

Advantages

- The survey results are projectable to the total population (plus or minus the sampling error) – the data is definitive rather than indicative.
- The sampling error can be computed.
- The researcher can be sure of obtaining information from a relatively representative group of the population of interest.

Disadvantage

- The rules for respondent selection and sample design significantly increase the researcher/interviewer costs, time and effort.

Non-probability sampling methods

These comprise samples where a subjective procedure of selection is used, resulting in the probability of selection for each member of the population of interest being unknown. A large proportion of marketing research studies use non-probability sampling methods as they can be executed more quickly and easily than probability samples.

Non-probability sampling methods

Advantages

- The cost is significantly less than probability samples to undertake.
- The less stringent procedures required in potential respondent selection mean that they can be conducted reasonably quickly.
- Sample sizes tend to be smaller.
- The researcher can target the most important respondents.

Disadvantages

- Indicative rather than definitive results.
- Sampling error cannot be computed.
- The researcher does not know the degree to which the sample is representative of the population from which it is drawn.
- The researcher needs to make certain assumptions about the groupings within the population of interest.

The most commonly used sampling methods are shown in Table 8.1.

Table 8.1 Most commonly used sampling methods

Probability sampling methods	Non-probability sampling methods
Simple random sampling	Convenience sampling
Systematic sampling	Judgement sampling
Stratified random sampling	Quota sampling
Cluster sampling	Snowball sampling

The types of probability sampling

Simple random sampling

In a simple random sample, every possible member of the population has an equal chance of being selected for the survey. If a list of the population is available, we can number each of the members of the population and select the sample either on the basis of random numbers generated by a computer or a published table of random numbers.

For example, if we wanted 5 potential respondents from a population of 25, the random number generator may select the following 5 people: numbers 3, 9, 14, 15, 24. These are the people we would approach for interview.

For a simple random sample, the probability of a population member being picked is calculated using the following formula:

$$Probability\ of\ selection = \frac{Population\ size}{Sample\ size\ required}$$

For example, if the population is 1,000 and the sample size is 200, then the probability of selection is 1 in 5. Each member of the population has a 1 in 5 chance of being selected (5 = 1,000/200).

If a complete listing of the population is available, simple random samples live up to their name and involve a very straightforward procedure. However, a complete, up-to-date population listing is extremely difficult to obtain and therefore tends to be limited to two specific situations:

1 where a company is selecting people from a population that is defined as its own database of customers. Computer programs can then select random samples from the database.
2 where random digit dialling is used for telephone interviews. So, in a survey of fixed-line telephone users being carried out in Glasgow the area code would remain constant but a computer would randomly generate all the remaining digits in the telephone number.

Researcher quote: *Simple random sampling is only possible when we can get a complete, up-to-date listing of the population of interest.*

Systematic sampling

Systematic sampling produces samples that are almost identical to those generated by simple random sampling. However, it is considered to be easier to implement, as it does not involve random number generation or tables for selection of all potential respondents.

It does require a full listing of the population, as in simple random sampling, but these do not need to be numbered. Instead a **skip interval** is calculated and the names are selected on the basis of this skip interval.

The calculation can be computed using the following formula (which is the same as the one used for calculating the probability of selection set out above):

$$Skip\ interval = \frac{Population\ size}{Sample\ size}$$

For example, using the earlier example, if the population is 1,000 and the sample size is 200, then the skip interval is 5 and so every fifth name from a list would be selected for the sample. A random starting number should be drawn to determine where the skip pattern should start. For example, the random starting point may be 4. Combining this with a skip pattern of 5 results in the following names being used in the sample: 4th, 9th, 14th, 19th, . . . 999th.

The systematic sample is far easier to construct using this approach than is the case for simple random sampling. As a result, the time and cost involved in sample design is less. There is a remote possibility that there are certain patterns in the listing of the population and by taking every *n*th person, the sample is not representative of all groups in the population. For example, selecting respondents on an aeroplane using a systematic sampling method and seat numbers may always include bulkhead and emergency exit rows, which may bias any measurement of attitudes relating to leg room. It is therefore always worthwhile to examine the selected sample to ensure that there are no obvious anomalies.

Stratified random sampling

A stratified random sample is a probability sampling procedure in which the chosen sample is forced to contain potential respondents from each of the key segments of the population.

It is created by first dividing the population of interest into two or more mutually exclusive and exhaustive subsets, and then taking random samples (either simple random or systematic sampling) within each subset. Subsets may relate to different age ranges in the population, gender, ethnic backgrounds, etc.

In many cases, stratified samples are used rather than simple or systematic random sampling because of their statistical efficiency. The sampling error (i.e. the difference between the survey result and the value for the population as a whole) is likely to be smaller for a stratified sample than for a simple or systematic random sample. This can be shown by the following example.

The following grid represents the population of interest (50 individuals, 40 per cent of whom are male (M) and 60 per cent female (F)). The researcher requires a sample of 10. A systematic sample starting at person 3 with a skip interval of 5 would select the people who are shaded (7 males and 3 females). If the purchasing behaviour of males and females is significantly different then the data from the sample will not reflect the situation within the overall population.

M	F	M	F	F	F	M	M	M	F
F	F	M	M	M	F	F	F	F	F
F	F	F	F	F	M	M	M	M	M
F	F	M	F	M	F	F	M	M	F
F	F	M	F	F	F	M	F	F	M

With a stratified sample, the population can be split into, say, the two subsets of males and females, and the importance of each can be reflected in the sample. This can be done in one of two ways: proportionate and disproportionate stratified random sampling.

Proportionate stratified random sampling

This is stratified random sampling where the units or potential respondents from each population subset are selected in proportion to the total number of each subset's units in the population. For the example above, that would mean 60 per cent of the sample would be female and the remaining 40 per cent would be male. Although this approach has better statistical efficiency than simple random samples, it does have problems where a subset makes up only a small percentage of the total population. This can result in the sample for that subset being very small, making it very difficult for the researcher to do any specific analysis that focuses on that subset alone or where comparisons are to be made between subsets.

Disproportionate stratified random sampling

This is stratified random sampling where the units or potential respondents from each population set are selected according to the relative variability of the units within each subset. This approach provides one of the most efficient and reliable samples. There are two steps involved. First, the number of units/potential respondents to be taken from each subset are determined in the same manner as for a proportionate sample. Then the numbers are adjusted to take relatively more units from those subsets that have larger standard deviations (more variation) and relatively fewer units from those subsets having smaller standard deviations. This allocates more units to the subsets where the potential for sampling error is greatest. A potential difficulty in this procedure is that the researcher may not know in advance the level of diversity that exists within each subset. Consequently, proportionate, rather than disproportionate random sampling is more commonly used. However, if there is variability and researchers are also concerned about small subsets, they may adopt the procedure of drawing samples of equal rather than proportionate size from each subset.

Cluster sampling

An adequate sampling frame may not be available to allow the researcher to adopt the random sampling approaches that have been discussed thus far. Where this is the case, cluster sampling is often used.

> Cluster sampling is a procedure in which clusters of population units are selected at random and then all or some of the units in the chosen clusters are studied.

With cluster sampling, the researcher does not need to produce a complete sample frame for the total population but instead only needs to develop sample frames for the clusters that are selected. This makes the sampling process shorter and potentially less complicated. Each of the clusters should ideally represent the total population in microcosm. This means that the make-up of each of the clusters is similar with similar levels of variability within each cluster. This is very different from the sub-sets in stratified random sampling, where the subsets had to be homogeneous and significantly different from each other. However, the ease of sample selection in cluster sampling must be balanced against the potential difficulty in forming clusters that truly reflect the total population in miniature. Cluster sampling therefore tends to be limited to situations where the population can be easily divided into representative clusters. One of the most common approaches is using names in a membership directory or telephone directory.

> A directory holds 50,000 names listed alphabetically on 500 pages with 100 names on each page. If the researcher wants a cluster sample of 1,000 names. The researcher can randomly select 10 pages and take all of the names from these pages as the sample. As the names are listed alphabetically, the sample should be representative of the total directory. This may not be the case if the area of study is influenced by ethnic factors as certain sections of the directory may be biased towards certain ethnic groups, e.g. names starting with Mc and Mac (Scottish), or common names such as Patel (Asian) or Smith (English).

There are a number of different approaches to cluster sampling:

- **One-stage cluster sampling** (sometimes known as simple cluster sampling): once the clusters have been selected by random selection, data is collected from all of the units/people in the selected clusters.

- **Two-stage cluster sampling**: once the clusters have been selected by random selection, a random sample is taken of the population units in each of the selected clusters. The two-stage approach tends to be used when the clusters are relatively large.

- **Area sampling**: a type of cluster sampling in which the clusters are created on the basis of the geographic location of the population of interest. Area sampling is probably the most widely used version of cluster sampling. A researcher undertaking a door-to-door survey may divide an area into neighbourhoods, housing blocks or streets and choose a random sample of these. After selecting the geographical clusters to be included, a sample of potential respondents will be approached in each cluster area. No sample frame is needed for the geographical clusters that are not selected. There is the possibility with area sampling that sections of the population could be excluded because the areas are not totally representative of the population as a whole. This is particularly the case when one considers that inhabitants of a particular neighbourhood are more likely to be like each other than like people in other neighbourhoods. To compensate for this and to reduce sampling errors, researchers are advised to use a large number of small clusters rather than a small number of large clusters.

Multi-stage sampling

When sampling national populations, a representative sample will be necessary but researchers may also require interviews to be concentrated in convenient areas. To achieve this a multi-stage approach in developing a sample may be needed. As the name suggests, the sample selection process involves a number of successive sampling stages before the final sample is obtained.

For example, a sample of households in the UK may be developed using the following steps:

1 List the postcode areas in the UK. The postcode areas are selected from the list so that each postcode area has a probability of being selected proportionate to the number of addresses each contains (for example, G, the Glasgow postal area, may be chosen at this stage).

2 Within each postcode area selected, all postcode districts would be listed in order of number of addresses each contains. Selection of postcode districts would also be proportionate to their number of addresses (for example, the district G4 may be selected at this stage).

3 Within each selected postcode district, individual postcode locations would be chosen proportionate to the number of households within each postcode cluster (usually around 15 homes).

4 One household would be chosen from the selected locations using systematic random sampling procedures.

This example of multi-stage sampling can be seen as a combination of stratified sampling, cluster sampling and systematic sampling. By using this combination of methods, the researcher does not need to have a full list of all the households in the UK; instead, all that is required is a list of households for each of the selected postcodes.

The types of non-probability sample

Convenience sampling

Convenience sampling is a procedure in which a researcher's convenience forms the basis for selecting the potential respondents. The researcher approaches the most accessible members of the population of interest. This may mean stopping people in the middle of a shopping street, interviewing employees that are present in an office, interviewing customers as they exit a service outlet or selecting names from a company's database. This may seem to be very biased and unprofessional. However, if the composition of the selected sample is reasonably similar to the population of interest, it can provide useful information, particularly for exploratory research purposes. Where a client is seeking an indication of what is going on in the market place, a convenience sample may provide the answers. However, care and time should be taken in thinking through the appropriateness of the particular sample to the study and the population of interest (for example, asking people waiting in a railway station about public transport may not be appropriate if the researcher is interested in the views of the population as a whole).

Judgement sampling

Judgement sampling (sometimes known as purposive sampling) refers to any procedure where a researcher consciously selects a sample that he or she considers to be most appropriate for the research study. This is different from convenience sampling, where a researcher may consider the appropriateness of a sample but will not exert any effort to make it representative of the population of interest. Judgement samples involve the deliberate choice of each sample member. For example, in business-to-business or industrial markets, certain companies may be selected to appear in the sample because they are typical of the purchasers in a particular segment (for example, Shell and BP may be included as being typical of large oil companies). In consumer research, certain neighbourhoods may be selected as representing the typical mix of the population of interest. Judgement samples are particularly appropriate where the sample size for a research project is relatively small. In small samples, a carefully chosen judgement sample may be better able to represent the mix of potential respondents in a population than even a probability sample as you can balance your sample to be in keeping with known market characteristics.

Quota sampling

Quota sampling involves the selection of cells or subsets within the population of interest. A numerical quota is established for each cell and interviewers are asked to carry out sufficient interviews in each cell to satisfy the quota. For example, a sample of 100 adults may be constructed with the following quotas covering 8 sample cells:

Age (years)	Male	Female
20–29	10	10
30–44	10	10
45–59	25	25
60 or over	5	5

Quota samples and stratified samples are often confused; however, there are two significant differences between the two approaches. First, potential respondents for a quota sample are not selected on a random basis, as they need to be for a stratified sample. In quota samples the potential respondents are selected on a subjective basis, with the only requirement being that a designated number are interviewed in each cell. Second, the factors used for determining the subsets must be selected on the basis of a correlation between the factors and the topics being investigated. In quota samples, the factors used for selecting the quotas are selected on the basis of researcher judgement only. Quota samples do allow the researcher to define the cells using a number of characteristics (e.g. sex, age, location, socio-economic group, product use, etc.) in combination rather than the one (or occasionally two) in stratified random sampling.

If the control characteristics used in designing the cells are relevant to the research questions then quota sampling is superior to judgement and convenience sampling in terms of sample representativeness. However, care must be taken to ensure that the definitions of the cells are not so complicated (e.g. having a cell that requires 10 respondents who are 20–25 years old, have an income in excess of £28,000, live in Manchester, and who have purchased a house in the last two years) that the time and effort needed to fill the cell is beyond the value of the information gained.

Snowball sampling

Snowball sampling tends to be used in low-incidence populations that make up a very small percentage of the total population (e.g. people with certain disabilities, people with unusual hobbies or interests, specialist manufacturers). It involves a sampling process where additional respondents are identified and selected on the basis of referrals of initial respondents. Where the potential respondents (e.g. people who keep reptiles as pets) are difficult to find and where screening members of the general population to identify these individuals would be prohibitively expensive, the snowballing technique may be used. It is far more cost effective to identify a small number of the low-incidence group and ask them to identify other potential respondents similar to themselves. However, researchers need to note that the final sample is likely to be biased because individuals are likely to recommend contacts and friends who generally hold similar ideas and views to themselves.

Sampling for Internet and e-mail-based surveys

Sampling of potential respondents for Internet and e-mail-based surveys generally takes the form of convenience samples. It is clearly accepted that respondents on the Internet do not accurately reflect the general population as there are large sections of the public who do not currently have access to the relevant technology. However, even for those who do have access, the problem of representativeness is exacerbated by the fact that there is no comprehensive and reliable sample frame of e-mail addresses. Reasons for this relate to people constantly changing their Internet service providers and their e-mail addresses, people having multiple e-mail accounts, and people being cautious about publishing their e-mail addresses in case they get spammed with junk mail. Some researchers attempt to recruit samples of consumers via Internet bulletin boards. However, it is unlikely that these potential respondents will be representative of anything other than membership of the bulletin board in question.

> The Taylor Nelson Sofres Internet sample represents the GB Internet user population and consists of an Internet-only panel of 2,700 individuals, who have been recruited from a random sample of the population. Contact with the panel members is via e-mail or the panel member website.[2]

Some research agencies have developed panels of individuals on the Internet who have agreed to be involved in research projects. However, these people are self-selected, meaning that they are only representative of people who respond to requests for research volunteers and are willing to spend time completing electronic questionnaires. This may make them very different from the true population of interest, in terms of being more technically oriented or being a type of 'Internet junkie'. However, it may be easier to obtain a more representative sample relating to specialist groups who are heavy users of the Internet, such as individuals in the information services or computer departments of major corporations. This will be particularly the case if the research is on software or hardware issues for a client company such as IBM, Dell or Microsoft, which can provide e-mail addresses for all of its major users. For other applications, although Internet surveys may become more significant in the future, at present there are still major concerns about the representativeness of the samples being used.

Step 5: determine sample size

One of the most difficult decisions for any young researcher is the determination of the most appropriate size of sample for a study. The process of determining sample size relates to financial, managerial and statistical issues. Although a bigger sample may reduce the sampling error associated with a project, this has to be balanced against the increased cost and time involved in the data collection process. Research costs and interviewing time are likely to increase in direct proportion to any increase in sample size (a 50 per cent increase in the size of the sample will result in a 50 per cent increase in cost and interviewer time). However, sampling error tends to decrease at a rate equal to the square root of the relative increase in sample size (so a sample that is increased by 100 per cent (i.e. doubled) is only likely to reduce its sampling error by 10 per cent). Research managers and clients need to determine the relative importance of precision against time and cost considerations. There are a number of ways in which sample size is determined.

Budget available

Frequently the sample size is determined by the amount of money that is available for the project. A marketing manager may state that he or she is willing to spend £15,000 to examine a particular aspect of a market. After making allowances for questionnaire design, data processing, analysis, etc., the remainder determines how many interviews can be undertaken. Although this may seem unscientific, it is realistic, as the resources available for marketing research in a company have to compete against budgets for promotional activity, new product development, etc. Researchers and marketers therefore need to carefully consider the value of reliable information in relation to its cost.

Sample sizes used in similar studies

Many researchers will rely on their past experience to determine an appropriate sample size. Previous studies covering similar research objectives may guide the researcher to select a particular sample size. These will give an indication of:

- **The homogeneity of the population of interest**: if there are likely to be significant differences in the views or behaviours of the population, a larger sample will be required.
- **The likely response rate**: if refusal rates within a particular population of interest are likely to be higher than the norm, then the sample of potential respondents will need to be larger.
- **The incidence rate of the characteristic being investigated**: where the characteristic being investigated is common among those in the sample frame then the sample will be smaller than will be the case if the characteristic is rare. (For example, a research study on televisions will need to approach fewer households to find TV owners than if the study was on home computers.)
- **The number of subgroups of data that are to be analysed**: the larger the number of subgroups of the sample that the researcher wishes to analyse separately, the larger the required total sample size. Individual subgroups of the sample will have larger sampling errors than the total sample. It may be difficult to determine whether there are real differences between the results from two subgroups or whether the difference is simply a reflection of sampling error.

Statistical methods

For probability samples, statistical methods are generally used to determine sample size (these are not appropriate for non-probability samples). The statistical methods require three pieces of information:

1 An estimate of the standard deviation for the population.
2 The acceptable level of precision expressed as sampling error.
3 The desired confidence level that the result of the survey will fall within a certain range (result +/− sampling error) of the true result of the population.

There are a number of different formulas for calculating simple random samples, stratified samples and cluster samples. Although the general principles of sample size calculation are similar, the formulas for stratified and cluster samples are more complicated and are beyond the scope of this particular text.

With simple random sampling, the formula chosen depends on whether the researcher is trying to measure averages (e.g. the average weekly expenditure on grocery shopping; the average number of nightclub visits made by students per month) or is trying to measure proportion (e.g. the percentage of households that have purchased a television in the last two years).

Studies involving Averages (Means)

The formula for calculating sample size for studies that involve the estimation of the mean or average value in a population is as follows:

$$N = \frac{Z^2 \sigma^2}{E^2}$$

where Z is the level of confidence expressed in standard errors, σ is population standard deviation and E is the acceptable level of precision expressed as sampling error.

Considering each of the variables in the formula with regard to a study looking at average weekly expenditure on grocery shopping:

1 **Specify the level of precision**: the client and researchers will need to decide on the level of precision that is acceptable. This is influenced by the available budget and time scales. For determining weekly shopping expenditure, a value that is within +/− £5 (σ = 5) may be acceptable whereas in the concept testing of a new product, greater precision may be needed as significant investment decisions will be dependent on the results.

2 **Determine the acceptable confidence interval**: the acceptable confidence interval is also influenced by budget and time constraints. To understand the concept of confidence levels it is important to consider the **normal distribution**.

The normal distribution

Scientists who observed that repeated samplings of the same population fitted within a common distribution of results first identified the properties of the normal distribution or normal curve in the eighteenth century. This distribution is bell-shaped and symmetrical about the mean value (see Figure 8.2). This means that in a study, 68.27 per cent of the observations fall within plus or minus one standard deviation of the mean, approximately 95.45 per cent fall within plus or minus two standard deviations and approximately 99.73 per cent fall within plus or minus three standard deviations. The exact areas contained by the normal distribution are to be found in special Z scale tables (see Table 1 in the Appendix) in most statistical textbooks. The most frequently used values in surveys are for the 95 per cent (Z value = 1.96) and 99 per cent (Z value = 2.58) confidence limits.

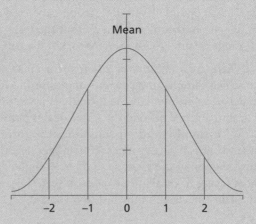

Figure 8.2 Normal distribution graph

So Z equals the level of confidence that the true mean of the sample falls into the interval defined by the sample mean plus or minus the acceptable level of E, the sampling error. For the study of grocery shopping, the researcher may decide that he or she needs to be 95 per cent confident that the true population mean falls into the interval defined by the sample mean plus or minus £5. A total of 1.96 standard errors are required to provide for 95 per cent of the area under a normal curve. Therefore the value for Z in this example will be 1.96.

3 Estimate the standard deviation for the population: It is impossible to know the standard deviation before undertaking a survey, therefore the researcher has to rely on an estimate when calculating sample size. The estimate can be based upon:

- Results from a previous study: if a study has been undertaken on a similar subject with a similar population, it may be possible to use the results of the previous study as an estimate of the population standard deviation.
- Use secondary data: secondary data may be available to assist in the estimation.
- Conduct a small pilot survey: a pilot survey could be used to develop an estimate of the population standard deviation. Such a pilot survey could also be used to test the appropriateness of questions in the questionnaire.
- Judgement: using judgement to determine the likely standard deviation.

In the grocery purchases study, the standard deviation was estimated as being £40.80. Once the survey has been completed and the true sample mean and standard deviation have been calculated, the researcher can make adjustments to the initial estimates of the confidence interval and determine the precision level actually obtained.

For the grocery purchases example the overall calculation would be as follows:

$$N = \frac{Z^2 \sigma^2}{E^2}$$

$$N = \frac{(1.96)^2 \times 40.8^2}{5^2}$$

N = 256 (rounded to the next highest number)

Therefore the sample size is 256.

Studies involving proportions

Where studies relate to proportions rather than averages or means, a different formula is used, which uses estimates of likely proportions rather than standard deviations. The formula is as follows:

$$N = \frac{Z^2[P(1 - P)]}{E^2}$$

where Z is the level of confidence expressed in standard errors, E is the acceptable amount of sampling error and P is the proportion of the population having a certain behaviour or characteristic.

If a researcher is looking at purchasing behaviour of televisions over the last two years, then the following values could be substituted: similar to the previous example, an acceptable sampling error level is set. For example, an error level of plus or minus 5 per cent (written as 0.05) is set. A Z value of 1.96 is established relating to a 95 per cent confidence level. Finally, P is the estimated percentage of the population that have bought televisions over the last two years, say 25 per cent (written as 0.25).

The resulting calculation identifies that a random sample of 289 respondents is required:

$$N = \frac{(1.96)^2 [0.25(1-0.25)]}{0.03^2}$$

$$N = 289$$

Therefore the sample size is 289.

Once the survey has been conducted and the actual proportions or sample means/standard deviations (for studies involving means) have been calculated, the researcher can assess the accuracy of the estimates used to calculate sample size. At this stage, adjustments can be made to the levels of sampling error based on the sample size and the actual sample measurements.

Adjustment of sample size for larger samples

Generally there is no direct relationship between the size of the population and the size of sample required to estimate a characteristic with a specific level of error and a specific level of confidence. The only area where sample size may have an effect is where the size of the sample is large in relation to the size of the population. The normal assumption in sampling is that sample elements are drawn independently of one another. Although it is safe to assume this when a sample is less than 10 per cent of the population, it is not when the sample is bigger than 10 per cent. An adjustment is therefore made to the sample size. This adjustment is called the **finite population correction factor**. The calculation used to reduce the required sample involves the following formula:

$$N^1 = \frac{nN}{N + n - 1}$$

where N^1 is the revised sample size, n is the original sample size and, N is the population size.

For example , if the population has 1,200 elements and the original sample size is 250, then:

$$N^1 = \frac{250 \times 1200}{1200 + 250 - 1}$$

$$N^1 = 208$$

Based on this adjustment using the finite population correction factor, a sample of 208 is required in comparison with the original 250.

Step 6: implement the sampling procedure

Once the sample size has been determined and the sampling procedure has been selected, the researcher can start selecting the members of the sample and begin the survey. However, the purpose of conducting a survey based on a sample is to make inferences about the population of interest rather than simply reporting on the characteristics of the sample. It is therefore important to know why the characteristics of a sample may differ from those of the population.

Sampling and non-sampling error

Sampling error: the difference between the sample value and the true value of a phenomenon for the population being surveyed (usually expressed as the survey result plus or minus a certain percentage).

A certain level of sampling error will always exist in studies that involve collecting data from only a part of the population. Sampling error merely reflects the extent of random chance in selecting respondents with different views and behaviours. It says nothing about the accuracy of the data collected from probability samples – it simply reflects the accuracy of estimates about the total population that can be made from that data. The higher the sampling error, the wider the confidence interval estimate for the population parameter will be. The amount of sampling error can be reduced by using a sampling procedure that has high statistical efficiency and/or increasing the sample size.

In addition to sampling error, there are a number of other errors that can occur and impact on the accuracy of survey data. These other errors are called non-sampling errors as they consist of any error in a research study other than sampling error. They tend to be classified into three broad types: sampling frame error, non-response error and data error. Whereas sampling errors can be estimated using statistics, non-sampling error results in bias that is difficult, if not impossible, to estimate. However, if researchers are aware of the potential non-sampling errors they can take steps to minimise them.

Sampling frame error

Sampling frame error is a bias that occurs as a result of the population implied by the sampling frame being different from the population of interest. For example, a telephone directory may be used to generate a list of people in a geographic area. This may differ significantly from the overall population as it will exclude people who are unlisted, people who only use mobile phones (e.g. students) and people who do not have access to a telephone. The researcher must determine whether excluding these groups of people is likely to produce significantly different results than would be the case if they were included. In other words, do the members of the population included in the telephone directory differ significantly from those not included? If they do, there may be a need to look at modifying the sampling frame or adopting an alternative sampling approach. The researcher may need to supplement the sampling frame with names from another source such as the electoral roll or may need to use an alternative sampling approach such as area sampling combined with doorstep interviews.

Non-response errors

A non-response error arises when some of the potential respondents included in a sample do not respond. The primary reasons for non-response are:

- **Refusals**: includes members of the population who fail to respond to postal surveys or who refuse to be interviewed on a subject, either because the timing is inconvenient or because of resistance to the survey. Efforts can be made to reduce refusal rates by:
  - *In postal/self-completion questionnaires*: making the questionnaire and questions short, interesting and attractive, offering incentives, sending out reminders, including reply paid envelopes.
  - *In telephone and face-to-face surveys*: making contact at times convenient to the respondent, using well-qualified interviewers, offering incentives, providing information to guarantee the authenticity of the research, careful questionnaire design.

- **Non-availability of respondents**: may result from people being on holiday when a postal questionnaire arrives or being away from home when an interviewer calls, either at the door or on the telephone. Some interviewers may be tempted to substitute another respondent for the one that is unavailable but in probability samples, there is the danger that this may cause bias because the people who are actually available are in some way different from those who are unavailable. For example, a programme of telephone interviews undertaken in the early evening may miss those who do not answer their phones because they are feeding young families at that time, they work late or commute long distances, they work shift patterns, they undertake social or hobby interests in the evening, or they are watching their favourite television programme at that time. By omitting any of these groups, researchers may be missing an important segment of the population from their sample and as a result may be biasing the survey results. Call-backs (phoning or returning to a potential respondent's address at a similar or different time) are more effective in reducing non-response error than the substitution of available respondents. Call-backs obviously add to the cost of a study, however. Many researchers will attempt three calls on a potential respondent (one original and two call-backs) to complete the interview. Only then would substitution with available respondents be used.

Non-response error can be reduced, but it cannot be eradicated from surveys. Researchers need to consider the implications of non-response for their research findings and should indicate the level of non-response in the final research report. This will enable the report's audience to take account of this when interpreting the research findings.

Data error

Data errors are any errors that occur during data collection or analysis that impact on the accuracy of inferences made about the population of interest. They can be classified into three main types:

- **Respondent errors**: respondents may inadvertently or intentionally give distorted or erroneous responses. Respondents may give erroneous answers because they fail to understand a question and do not want to admit their incomprehension.

This is difficult to control, although the guidelines for questionnaire design outlined in Chapter 7 may help to reduce this by ensuring that questions are as simple as possible and are pre-tested with representatives of the population of interest before they are used in a full survey. Even where questions are clearly expressed, respondents may give socially acceptable answers or may give answers that they think will impress or shock the interviewer or researcher. For example, respondents may inflate their level of earnings, reduce the number of cigarettes they smoke, increase the number of sexual encounters they have had, or reduce the number of incidences that they break the speed limit when driving. The respondents' distortions may be altered according to age, sex and appearance of the interviewer. Distortions of this type are far more difficult to detect and measure. Their reduction is attempted through the placing of sensitive questions nearer the end of an interview once rapport and trust have been established between the respondent and the interviewer. Rather than using open-ended questions on subjects where distortions are likely to occur, multiple-choice questions are used (see the example below). This highlights the types of answer that the interviewer is expecting rather than leaving the respondent to judge how the interviewer will respond to a particular answer. Respondents frequently do not want to embarrass themselves by giving an inappropriate or unusual answer.

Open-ended question:

What is your annual salary before tax?

£_____

Multiple-choice question:

Within which of the following categories does your annual salary (before tax) fall?

Less than £12,000 ____
£12,000–£14,999 ____
£15,000–£19,999 ____
£20,000–£29,999 ____
£30,000–£39,999 ____
More than £40,000 ____

Using a range of different types of interviewer may also balance out the impact of respondents answering to please or impress the interviewer. Beyond these measures, it is very difficult to influence respondents who are determined to distort their answers.

- **Interviewer errors:** errors can also occur as a result of interviewers recording answers incorrectly. This may be particularly evident for open-ended questions, where some interviewers may try to summarise the respondent's answer rather than writing it verbatim. A small minority of unprofessional interviewers may also partially fill out questionnaires by themselves rather than asking bona fide respondents. The keys to reducing such errors are selection, training and supervision. In the UK, the quality of these inputs is being improved through the Interviewer Quality Control Scheme (IQCS). The Market Research Society, the Association of Market Survey Organisations, the Association of British Market Research Companies, the Association of Users of Research Agencies and a number of leading research companies jointly run this scheme. Agencies subscribing to the scheme are visited by quality control inspectors who audit the research operations with the objective of maintaining and raising the standards of fieldwork. Those agencies that satisfy the inspectors are able to use the IQCS logo. Some clients will only use agencies that are approved to the IQCS standard. **Validation** of the completed interviews is also important in exposing any falsification of information by unscrupulous interviewers. After all the interviews are completed, the research agency recontacts a small percentage of the respondents surveyed by each interviewer. This is done to check on the following:

1 Was the person actually interviewed?
2 Did the person meet the sampling requirements of the survey? (e.g. If the survey related to people of a certain age range, is the respondent within that age range?)
3 Was the interview conducted in the correct location and in the required manner? (e.g. Was it undertaken in the predefined street or did the interviewer recruit people in a shopping centre or café? Were the proper showcards used?)
4 Did the interviewer ask all of the questions in the survey or did they only ask certain parts of the questionnaire? (Respondents may need to be asked a number of sample questions to verify this.)
5 Was the interviewer courteous? (e.g. Is there anything that the respondent was unhappy about?)

Such checks on the validity of the interview process are critical to ensure that the results are truly representative of the respondents interviewed.

In addition to validating the questionnaire with the respondent, the questionnaires will be checked to ensure that (1) there is consistency in the answers provided (if somebody has two children at the start of the questionnaire then later questions also relate to two rather than three children), (2) answers are recorded for all questions and (3) appropriate skip patterns have been followed. This checking is part of the **editing** process carried out prior to the data entry and analysis of the questionnaires. Where computer-assisted interviewing has been used, this will have been done automatically by the computer during the interview process.

- **Data analysis errors**: errors can occur when data is transferred from the questionnaires to computers by incorrect keying of information. Such errors can be identified and reduced by checking a sample of questionnaires against the computerised data. This will identify any keying errors. Computers can also be used to check for unexpected codes in the data and test for the consistency of data on each respondent.

> **Researcher quote:** *Non-sampling error can be reduced but it is impossible to totally eradicate it.*

Using weightings

Sample results are used to generalise about the population surveyed. If the sample is not representative of that population because of sampling errors or non-response, then these generalisations will be flawed. Equally, if some groups have been over-sampled, it will be necessary to adjust the data to reflect the proportions found in the population. This process is called weighting. There are various approaches to weighting but the simplest is to apply known proportions to the findings. For example:

| | Percentages across | |
	Men	Women
Population	49%	51%
Sample achieved	42%	58%
Weight applied	1.17	0.88

As long as demographic information about the population is known or can be reliably estimated, then weighting can help considerably to improve estimates, provided that the disparities found between the sample and the population do not arise from a lack of coverage of significant parts of the population. However when weighting is used, researchers must always provide a full description of the weighting procedures.

Summary

In marketing research it is very rare that a researcher will be able to undertake a census of every member of a particular population. Therefore a subset or sample of the population needs to be selected and surveyed. This chapter has taken you through the main steps in the sampling process. These steps can be summarised as follows:

1 **Define the population of interest**: this is the total group of people that the researcher wishes to examine and will normally reflect the target market or potential target market for the product or service being researched.

2 **Determine whether to sample or census**: as stated above, the majority of marketing research is undertaken with a sample rather than a census of the population of interest.

3 **Select the sampling frame**: obtain a list of the population of interest, from which the researcher selects the individuals for inclusion in the research.

4 **Choose a sampling method**: either a probability or non-probability sampling method can be used. Probability sampling includes the following types: simple random sampling, systematic sampling, stratified random sampling, cluster sampling and area sampling. Non-probability sampling include convenience sampling, judgement sampling, quota sampling and snowball sampling. Selection is based on the sample frame available, budgets, time scales and the precision with which the survey results can be projected to reflect the true values held by the population under investigation.

5 **Determine sample size**: the process of determining sample size relates to financial, managerial and statistical issues.

6 **Implement the sampling procedure.**

Both sampling error and non-sampling error impact upon the accuracy of survey results. Sampling error reflects the accuracy of estimates about the total population that can be made from the data. For probability samples, this can be expressed as the confidence interval that is placed on the estimate of the population parameter. Non-sampling errors relate to any error in the survey findings other than sampling error, and are usually classified as sampling frame error, non-response error and data error.

Discussion questions

1 Explain the term 'population of interest'.

2 Why does the marketing research industry undertake so few censuses?

3 What are the difference between probability and non-probability sampling errors?

4 Explain the similarities and differences between simple random samples, systematic samples and stratified random samples.

5 Why do some studies require a multi-stage sampling approach?

6 Explain the differences between quota samples and stratified samples.

7 Discuss the proposition that the determination of sample size is simply a matter of guesswork.

8 Identify the different types of sampling frame error and suggest ways in which each of them can be reduced.

9 What is the purpose of the Interviewer Quality Control Scheme (IQCS)?

10 Discuss the problems of establishing representativeness for Internet and e-mail-based surveys.

Additional reading

Bradley, N. (1999) Sampling for Internet surveys. An examination of respondent selection for Internet research. *Journal of the Market Research Society*, **41**(4), pp. 387–95.

Corlett, T. (1996) Sampling errors in practice. *Journal of the Market Research Society*, **38**(4), pp. 307–18.

Research Development Foundation (1999) Business co-operation in market research. *Journal of the Market Research Society*, **41**(2), pp. 195–225.

Schillewaert, N., Langerak, F. and Duhamel, T. (1998) Non-probability sampling for WWW surveys: a comparison of methods. *Journal of the Market Research Society*, **40**(4), pp. 307–22.

References

[1] Adapted from Pincott, G. and Anderson, T. (1999) Lost in music – analysis of music listening in the UK. *Journal of the Market Research Society*, **41**(2), April. Published with the permission of the Market Research Society.

[2] For more information, see www.tnagb.com.

9
Analysing quantitative data

Tetley and the round tea bag

In the late 1980s, Lyons Tetley were losing market share in the tea market to super-markets' own branded products. To counter this trend, the company developed a round tea bag as a possible replacement for their traditional square bag. The problem for the company was that the risk of changing shape would be very high – the brand turned over around £80 million at that time. In addition, new packaging machinery would cost several million pounds and take some time to obtain and install, and the relaunch would cost several million more. The three key questions were:

1 Would roundness increase the share of Tetley by attracting sufficient non-users to Tetley to compensate for any Tetley users who would be lost because of the change?
2 Was the novelty of roundness likely to wear out in a relatively short period of time?
3 Would the gain in share be sufficient to pay for the cost of the relaunch?

Tetley used a simulated test market to answer these questions. A panel of 240 heavy buyers of tea were recruited using the following qualification criteria:

1 the household used at least 80 tea bags in a two-week period;
2 the household regularly used one of four major national brands (Tetley, Typhoo, Quick Brew or PG Tips).

The qualified panel members were asked to attend a local briefing session at which the research project was explained to them and they were shown the packaging and a TV advertisement for round bags in the setting of packaging and advertising for the familiar principal brands. The panel was then operated by inter-viewers calling each week with an illustrated brochure of tea brands and sizes with the lowest prices pre-vailing in the best of three local supermarkets that week. Tetley's

round bags was one of the brands included in the brochure. To induce trial, the round bag was offered at a promotional price over the first two weeks.

In the total panel, 46 per cent of participants tried round tea bags and made at least one repeat purchase. Thus 76 per cent of trialists liked it sufficiently to make at least a second purchase. People preferred the product because of their perception of its improved flavour (note: the tea was the same as in the square bag; it was only the shape of the bag that was different).

The panel was originally planned to run for 12 weeks, by which time stable repeat purchasing rates had emerged. Lyons Tetley was still sufficiently concerned about possible novelty wear-out that it ran the panel on for a further 8 weeks. However, there was no perceptible erosion of the repeat purchase rate after over 4 months' exposure to the brand.

Analysing the purchasing patterns in detail and using the results to forecast potential sales patterns, Lyons Tetley decided to relaunch using the round tea bag. In spite of considerable competitive activity at the time of the launch, the relaunch was a major success. As a result, many competitors have developed their versions of round tea bags, pyramid tea bags and drawstring tea bags.[1]

Learning outcomes

After reading this chapter you should:

- understand the key steps in data entry and analysis;
- have an understanding of the statistical techniques used most frequently in marketing research.

Key words

chi-square	measures of central tendency
cluster analysis	measures of dispersion
coding	multiple discriminant analysis
conjoint analysis	multiple regression analysis
correlation	multivariate data analysis
cross-tabulations	nominal data
data cleaning	ordinal data
data entry	perceptual mapping
descriptive statistics	ratio data
factor analysis	regression
frequency distributions	statistical significance
hole counts	t test
hypothesis testing	Z test
interval data	

Introduction

Once data collection has been completed and the validation and editing (described on page 196) has been undertaken, the researcher moves on to the stage of data entry and analysis. This chapter is designed to introduce you to the three main steps involved in this phase of the research process. These are:

- Step 1: coding
- Step 2: data entry
- Step 3: tabulation and statistical analysis.

More and more components of these three steps are undertaken automatically by computers through questionnaire analysis or statistical software packages. However, researchers need to develop an awareness and understanding of these activities and statistical techniques if they are to both understand the data and present the findings in an accurate and confident manner. This chapter aims to provide that awareness and understanding.

Coding

Coding is the first step and involves translating responses into a form that is ready for analysis. To understand coding, it is necessary to understand how research responses are held in a computer file.

A computer file consists of all the responses relating to all of the respondents in a study. It is made up of a series of records, with each record containing all of the responses from one respondent. Each record is organised in the form of a number of fields, with each field representing a question in the questionnaire. Codes are the numerical data in each field representing the respondent's answer to a particular question. This is shown in the following example (Table 9.1) of a computer file relating to four respondents answering a questionnaire consisting of five questions.

Coding therefore involves the assigning of numerical codes to responses so that they can be (1) recognised by the computer, (2) stored in the data fields and (3) interpreted and manipulated for statistical and tabular purposes. For example, in a dichotomous question with a yes/no response format, 'yes' could be assigned the code 1 and 'no' could be assigned the code 2. This could then be stored for each respondent in a manner similar to that shown for field 1 in Table 9.1.

Table 9.1 An example of data in a computer file

	Field 1 Question 1	Field 2 Question 2	Field 3 Question 3	Field 4 Question 4	Field 5 Question 5
Record 1 (respondent 1)	1	5	245	1	2
Record 2 (respondent 2)	2	3	356	3	2
Record 3 (respondent 3)	2	6	32	5	3
Record 4 (respondent 4)	1	2	243	3	2

With many of the computer packages used to design questionnaires, the codes for closed questions (i.e. dichotomous questions, multiple-choice questions, rating questions) will be established prior to the questionnaire being used. Such questions are described as **pre-coded**. For open-ended questions where the responses are not known in advance, the codes are applied after the data collection phase and are therefore described as **post-coded**.

The process of post-coding responses to open-ended questions involves the following steps:

1 **Developing a list of responses**: the researcher prepares lists of the actual responses to each open-ended question. This may involve listing the responses from all of the questionnaires or doing so for a sample if the number of questionnaires is very large. Some questionnaire software packages such as snap (see the list of software packages at the end of the chapter) allow the researcher to enter the data verbatim before providing a computer listing of all the responses.

2 **Categorising responses**: a number of responses will essentially have the same meaning even though different words may have been used. These responses can be consolidated into a single category. So thousands of responses may be consolidated into a maximum of, say, 10–12 categories. For example, answers such as: inexpensive, moderate price, reasonable price, fair price, appropriate price, affordable, correct price, etc., may all be consolidated into a category entitled 'acceptable price'. There may need to be some subjective assessment, on the part of the researcher, to determine whether an answer fits into a category or whether a new category is required.

3 **Assign and enter codes**: a numeric code is assigned to each of the categories. The codes are then entered into the computer file for analysis.

In the future, such post-coding may become easier as software for automated coding becomes more common and reliable. Such software uses algorithms to search open-ended responses for keywords, phrases and patterns in order to categorise responses and assign codes. However, the reliability of such software needs to improve, as you will know from the incorrect word associations that occur when you use an Internet browser to find websites.

Data entry

With computer-assisted interviewing and web-based surveys, data is entered into the computer file automatically. In all other situations, data has to be transferred from the questionnaire either by:

1 an operator typing the responses from the questionnaires into the computer, or

2 the optical scanning of questionnaires. This can be done using appropriate scanning equipment and questionnaires that have an appropriate layout. Scanning has significantly moved on from the time when computers could only read the data if respondents used pencils to fully shade an entire square next to their response choice.

Once the data has been entered, computerised checks will be made on the data to check that there are no inconsistencies in the data and to identify if there are any unexplained missing responses. This task is called **data cleaning**. Inconsistencies may include out-of-range data values (e.g. a code of 8 on a five-point (1–5) scale), extreme values (where one respondent has a very different response from all other respondents) or logical inconsistencies (where a respondent answers a question about a service that he says he does not use). 'Missing value' is the term used to describe situations where no response to a question is recorded. These may be expected as particular respondents will have legitimately skipped certain questions; however, others may result from keying errors. Where these problems exist, the computer can be programmed to print out details of the questionnaire, record number, field number and the offending value or missing value.

Tabulation and statistical analysis

Once the data is stored in the computer and is free of errors, the researcher needs to select the most appropriate approach to tabulation and statistical analysis. Tabulation involves laying out data in easy-to-understand summary tables, while statistical analysis is used to examine the data further and identify or confirm patterns that are difficult to see or interpret. The selection of approach will be determined by the objectives of the research (what questions/problems do the research findings need to address?) and the type of measurement data that has been collected. There are four basic types of measurement data:

1 **Nominal data**. The word 'nominal' means name-like – in other words, the numbers assigned to objects or phenomena that name or classify but have no true numeric meaning. They are simply labels or identification numbers (see the examples below) that partition data into mutually exclusive and collectively exhaustive categories and as such they cannot be ordered, added or divided.

> Gender: Male (1)   Female (2)
> Type of transport used: Car (1), Coach (2), Train (3)

The only calculation or quantification possible with nominal data is the counting of the number and percentages of objects in each category; for example, 50 car users (37 per cent) and 26 train users (19 per cent). Only a limited number of statistics, all of which are based on frequency counts, are possible. These include the mode, chi-square and binomial tests (all of which are explained later in this chapter).

2 **Ordinal data**. This stems from ordinal scales and has the labelling characteristics of nominal data, but also has the ability to communicate the order of the data. The numbers do not indicate absolute quantities, nor do they imply that the intervals between the numbers are equal. Ordinal scales are used strictly to indicate rank order – the numbers are void of any meaning other than order. Here is an example of an ordinal scale.

> Please rank the following car makes from 1 to 5, with 1 being the make
> which offers the best value for money and 5 being the one that offers the
> least value for money:
>
> Ford   ——
> Renault   ——
> Fiat   ——
> BMW   ——
> Toyota   ——

If Fiat is ranked 4 and BMW is ranked 5, there is no indication as to whether Fiat has much better or only slightly better value for money than BMW. Common arithmetical operations such as addition or multiplication cannot be used with ordinal scales. As such, it is inappropriate to calculate a mean; instead modes and medians are used.

3 **Interval data**. This is similar to ordinal data with the added dimension that the intervals between the values on a scale are equal. This means that when using a scale of 1 to 5, the difference between 1 and 2 is the same as the difference between 4 and 5. However, in an interval scale, the zero point is not fixed; instead, it is an arbitrary point. This can be demonstrated in the example below, where 1 does not represent a particular level of cost effectiveness that can be defined, but simply provides an evaluation of cost effectiveness relative to the elements being compared. For example, a respondent's ratings may be allocated differently if the list of cars were to change (for example, if Skoda was added to the list). As a result calculating the ratios between different values on the scale is not valid. In other words, a manufacturer receiving a rating of 4 does not represent twice the value for money of a manufacturer that has a rating of 2.

> Please rate the following car makes on a scale of 1 to 5, where 1 represents
> very poor value for money and 5 represents very good value for money.
>
> Ford   1 2 3 4 5
> Renault   1 2 3 4 5
> Fiat   1 2 3 4 5
> BMW   1 2 3 4 5
> Toyota   1 2 3 4 5

Unlike nominal and ordinal data, arithmetic means and standard deviations can be calculated using interval data. Correlation coefficients and many statistical tests, including *t* tests, can also be used with interval data.

4 **Ratio data**. This consists of actual, 'real' numbers that have a meaningful absolute zero or origin. Actual characteristics of a respondent or a situation such as age, height, level of expenditure, number of products purchased and time taken are all examples of ratio-scale variables. Not only is the difference between 4 and

6 the same as the difference between 58 and 60, but 60 is 10 times the size of 6. The nature of ratio data means that all arithmetic operations are possible.

It should be noted that nominal and ordinal data are sometimes referred to as **non-metric data,** whereas interval and ratio data are sometimes referred to as **metric data.**

Tabulations

Holecounts and frequency distributions

Researchers often attempt to get a first feel of the data they have by producing a **hole-count**. This name originates from the days when punched cards were used to enter data into computers and holes in the cards represented the responses to each of the questions. Holecounts, sometimes known as **frequency distributions**, communicate the number of respondents who gave each possible answer to each question. Figure 9.1 sets out an example of a frequency distribution about transport usage. In addition to frequencies, such a table will typically indicate the percentage of those responding who selected each response. These percentages are normally calculated using the number of people asked as the base figure. However, unless the number of non-responses (people who refused or chose not to answer a particular question) has a bearing on the research objectives, it is often more sensible for the base to relate to the number of people asked less the number who did not respond. So using the example in Figure 9.1, a more accurate base would be 1995 (2000 − 5).

Sometimes, researchers will print out a questionnaire with the holecount numbers appearing next to each response on the questionnaire. This helps the researcher to obtain a very quick overview of the pattern of responses and may influence the next steps in terms of tabulation and analysis.

Q17 What method of transport did you use to travel to the theme park today?

	Total
Total respondents asked	2,000 (100%)
Car	1,735 (87%)
Coach/bus	206 (10%)
Train	54 (3%)
No response	5 (–%)

Figure 9.1 Example of a frequency distribution

Researcher quote: *Holecounts give an indication of what types of further analysis are likely to be useful.*

Cross-tabulations

Cross-tabulations are both simple to use and provide a powerful analysis technique. They examine the responses to one question relative to the responses to one or more other questions. Figure 9.2 shows a simple cross-tabulation that explores the relationship between the method of travelling to a theme park and the number of children within the group/party. Interestingly, the figure shows that the larger the number of children, the more likely it is that the party will have travelled by car. Three different percentages may be calculated for each cell in a cross-tabulation table: column, row and total percentages. Column percentages (used in Figure 9.2) are based on the column total, row percentages are based on the row total, and total percentages use the table total as the base.

Many statistics, spreadsheet and questionnaire packages, such as snap, Excel and SPSS, can generate cross-tabulations at the press of a button. It is also possible to cross-tabulate data in an almost endless number of ways within a survey. However, it is important for the researcher to exercise judgement to determine which cross-tabulations are appropriate in order to (1) meet the research objectives and (2) show differences that indicate patterns in the data that are significantly different from what is likely to have occurred by chance.

Method of transport by number of children

	Total	0	1	2	3	4	More than 4
				Number of children			
Total asked	2,000	200	229	422	365	568	216
	(100%)	(100%)	(100%)	(100%)	(100%)	(100%)	(100%)
Car	1,735	72	123	402	358	567	213
	(87%)	(36%)	(54%)	(95%)	(98%)	(100%)	(99%)
Coach/bus	206	88	96	17	3	0	2
	(10%)	(44%)	(42%)	(4%)	(1%)	(0%)	(1%)
Train	54	40	8	3	1	1	1
	(3%)	(20%)	(3%)	(1%)	(0%)	(0%)	(0%)
No response	5	0	2	0	3	0	0
	(0%)	(0%)	(1%)	(0%)	(1%)	(0%)	(0%)

Figure 9.2 Example of a cross-tabulation

In addition to cross-tabulations, data can be presented in a variety of graphical formats using pie charts, line graphs, bar charts and pictograms. Like cross-tabulations, these can also help in the communication of results and patterns in data. These graphical approaches are described and explained in Chapter 10.

Descriptive statistics

Descriptive statistics help to summarise the characteristics of large sets of data using only a few numbers. The most commonly used descriptive statistics are measures of central tendency (mean, mode and median) and measures of variability (range, interquartile range and standard deviation).

Measures of central tendency

Measures of central tendency indicate a typical value for a set of data by computing the mean, mode or median.

The mean

The mean is probably the most commonly used average in marketing research. It is the arithmetic average and is calculated by summing all of the values in a set of data and dividing by the number of cases. It can only be computed from interval or ratio (metric) data.

The mode

The mode can be computed with any type of data (nominal, ordinal, interval and ratio) and represents the value in a set of data that occurs most frequently. One problem with the mode is that any data set may have more than one mode (i.e. a number of categories/values may all be equal and each share the highest frequency).

The median

The median can be computed for all types of data except nominal data. When all of the values in a data set are put in ascending or descending order, the median is the value of the middle case in a series (if the number of values is an even number and therefore no single middle value exists, the two middle values are added together and divided by two). The median has as many cases on the higher side as on the lower side. The measure offers the advantage of being unaffected by extreme cases at one end or the other of the data set. It may, for example, be appropriate where a few extreme values may impact adversely on representativeness of the arithmetic mean.

The mean, median and mode for a set of ages are shown below.

Mean, median and mode

Ages of 10 respondents:

42, 45, 43, 46, 48, 49, 39, 42, 45, 42.

Mean = 44 years   Mode = 42 years   Median = 44 years

Measures of dispersion

Measures of dispersion indicate how 'spread out' a set of data is. The **range** is probably the simplest measure and is found by calculating the difference between the largest and smallest values in the data. As such, the range is directly affected by any extreme values. The range for the ages in the example above would be $(49 - 39) = 10$. The **interquartile range** reduces the impact of any extreme values by measuring the difference between the 75th and 25th percentile. To compute these percentiles, the data is arranged in order of magnitude, and the 75th percentile is the value that has 75 per cent of the data values below it and 25 per cent (i.e. $100 - 75$) above it. The 25th percentile is identified in the same manner and is then subtracted from the value of the 75th percentile to obtain the interquartile range.

The most commonly used measure of dispersion is the standard deviation of a data set. It is calculated by taking the square root of the sum of the squared deviations from the mean divided by the number of observations minus 1. The formula is shown below. Basically it tells the researcher what is the average distance that the values in a data set are away from the mean. The standard deviation of different sets of data can be compared to see if one set of data is more dispersed than another.

$$s = \sqrt{\frac{\sum_{i=1}^{n} (x_i - \bar{x})^2}{n - 1}},$$

where n is the number of units in the sample, x_i is the data obtained from each sample unit i, and $\bar{x}$ is the sample mean value, given by $\sum_{i=1}^{n} \frac{x_i}{n}$.

Statistical significance

In marketing research, it is common for statistical inferences to be made which attempt to make generalisations about population characteristics from sample results. However, in statistical inference it is possible for numbers to be different in a mathematical sense but not significantly different in a statistical sense. For example, a sample of 1,000 car drivers is asked to test drive two cars and indicate which they prefer. The results show that 52 per cent prefer one car and 48 per cent prefer the other. There is a mathematical difference in the sample results but in statistical terms what is the likelihood that this difference would also be evident in the general population? The difference is probably smaller than the level of accuracy with which we can measure attitudes in the general population using a sample of 1,000 car drivers. To understand this, it is important to consider the meaning of the following two concepts:

1 **Mathematical differences.** It is obviously a fact that where numbers are not exactly the same, they are different (e.g. 8 can be seen to be different from the number 10). This does not, however, suggest that the difference between the two numbers is either important or statistically significant.

2 **Statistical significance.** If a particular difference is large enough to be unlikely to have occurred due to chance or sampling error, then the difference is statistically significant.

> **Researcher quote:** *It is important to understand the difference between mathematical differences and statistical differences.*

Various approaches for testing whether results are statistically significant are discussed in the following section. It should be noted, however, that tests of sample precision are based on an assumption of random sampling. These tests cannot be applied to non-random samples.

Hypothesis testing

A **hypothesis** can be defined as an assumption or proposition that a researcher makes about some characteristic of the population being investigated. The marketing researcher needs to determine whether research results are significant enough to conclude something about the population under investigation. For example:

- Research undertaken ten years ago suggested that a typical family's weekly expenditure in a supermarket was €76. However, a recent survey suggests an expenditure of €82. Considering the size of the samples used, is the result significantly higher?

- The marketing manager of a leisure centre believes that 60 per cent of his customers are younger than 25. He does a survey of 250 customers to test this hypothesis and finds that, according to the survey, 51 per cent are under 25. Is this result sufficiently different from his original view to permit him to conclude that his original theory was incorrect?

These situations can both be evaluated using a statistical test. In hypothesis testing, the researcher determines whether a hypothesis concerning some characteristic of the population of interest is likely, given the evidence. To do this, the researcher needs to establish the hypothesis and then select an appropriate technique to test it.

1 **Establish the hypothesis:** Hypotheses are stated using two basic forms: the null hypothesis H_0 and the alternative hypothesis H_1. The null hypothesis is always the hypothesis to be tested and is the statement of the status quo where no difference or effect is expected, whereas the alternative hypothesis is the one in which some difference or effect is expected (i.e. a difference that could not occur simply by chance). The null and alternative hypotheses complement each other; they are mutually exclusive (i.e. they cannot both be true at the same time). For example, a marketing manager for a chain of retail grocery stores believes that the value of an average customer's shopping basket is less than €80. She conducts research based on 1,000 customers passing through the checkouts and finds the average value to be €94. For this example, the null hypothesis and the alternative hypothesis might be stated as:

Null hypothesis H₀: Mean value of shopping basket is less than €80.

Alternative hypothesis H₁: mean value of shopping basket is €80 or more.

A statistical test with these hypotheses can have one of two outcomes: that the null hypothesis is rejected and the alternative hypothesis is accepted or that the null hypothesis is not rejected based on the evidence.

2 **Select an appropriate statistical technique to test the hypothesis:** There are many statistical tests available but this book concentrates on the three most commonly used tests, the chi-square test, the Z test and the t test. Before describing these tests, it is necessary to explain three concepts that impact on the tests:

(a) **Degrees of freedom:** many of the statistical tests require the researcher to specify degrees of freedom in order to find the critical value of the test statistic. Degrees of freedom (d.f.) are defined as the number of observations (i.e. the sample size) minus one. Therefore a sample (n) has $n - 1$ degrees of freedom.

(b) **Independent versus related samples:** the selection of the appropriate test statistic may require the researcher to consider whether the samples are independent or related. Independent samples involve situations in which the measurement of the variable of interest in one sample has no effect on the measurement of the variable in the other sample. In the case of related samples, the measurement of the variable of interest in one sample may influence the measurement of the variable of interest in another sample.

If, for example, 20–30 year olds and 50–60 year olds were interviewed in a survey regarding their frequency of attending the cinema, the samples would be considered to be independent, as the response of the younger group is unlikely to have an impact on the responses of the older group. However, in a tracking study using a panel of respondents where awareness or attitudes are measured over time, measurements during each wave of the research may be contaminated by respondents thinking differently about a subject having taken part in a previous wave of the research. The samples in each wave are therefore not independent.

(c) **Errors in hypothesis testing:** hypothesis tests are subject to two general types of error, which are generally referred to as Type I and Type II errors. A Type I error involves rejecting the null hypothesis when it is actually true. This may occur as a result of sampling error (see Chapter 8). The probability of committing a Type I error is referred to as the alpha (α) level. The alpha level needs to be selected for each test and is commonly set at 0.05 (meaning that there is a 5 per cent chance of a Type I error occurring). Reducing the alpha level below 0.05 increases the probability of a Type II error occurring. A Type II error involves failing to reject the null hypothesis when it is actually false. The alpha (α) level selected should be a function of the relative importance of the two types of errors. If there are major consequences of rejecting the null hypothesis (e.g. in a clinical trial of a new drug), then the alpha level should be low (e.g. 0.01). However, for most marketing research scenarios, there is no real difference between the impact of a Type I and a Type II error and therefore an alpha (α) level of 0.05 is commonly used.

Testing goodness of fit: chi-square

Surveys regularly produce frequency tables and cross-tabulations. Researchers need to ask whether the number of responses that fall into different categories differ from what is expected. The chi-square (χ^2) test enables the researcher to test the 'goodness of fit' between the observed distribution and the expected distribution of a variable.

Chi-square test of a single sample

Consider the example of a bank that selects three bank branches of equal size for refurbishment. A different design is used in each outlet and the number of product enquiries is monitored over a three-month period and is shown below:

	Number of enquiries
Branch 1	11,154
Branch 2	10,789
Branch 3	11,003

The marketing manager needs to know whether there is a significant difference between the number of enquiries being made at each branch. The chi-square (χ^2) one-sample test is used to answer this question:

1 Specify the null and alternative hypotheses:

Null hypothesis H_0: The number of product enquiries in the different branches is equal.
Alternative hypothesis H_1: There is a significant difference in the number of product enquiries in the various branches.

2 Determine the number of product enquiries that would be expected in each category if the null hypothesis were correct. This would mean the same number of product enquiries in each of the branches (calculated by totalling the number of product enquiries and dividing by three [$(11,154 + 10,789 + 11,003)/3 = 10,982$]. Under the null hypothesis, each of the branches should have expected 10,982 product enquiries. (Note: chi-square should not be used if (a) more than 20 per cent of the categories have expected frequencies of less than 5 or (b) any of the expected frequencies are less than 1.)

3 Calculate the chi-square value using the following formula:

$$\chi^2 = \sum_{i=1}^{k} \frac{(O_i - E_i)^2}{E_i}$$

where O_i is the observed number in the ith category, E_i is the expected number in the ith category and k is the number of categories.
For the banking example:

$$\chi^2 = \frac{(11,154 - 10,982)^2}{10,982} + \frac{(10,789 - 10,982)^2}{10,982} + \frac{(11,003 - 10,982)^2}{10,982} = 6.13$$

4 Select the level of significance (α). If the 0.05 (α) level of significance is selected, the χ^2 value with 2 degrees of freedom ($k - 1$) is 5.99 (see Table 2 in the Appendix).

5 As the calculated χ^2 value (6.13) is higher than the table value, the null hypothesis should be rejected. The researcher can then conclude with 95 per cent confidence that customer response to the branch designs was significantly different. In other words, the variation among the branches is greater than would be expected by chance. However, although it confirms a difference, it does not confirm whether any design is significantly better than the others are.

Chi-square test of two independent samples

The chi-square test is also used by researchers to determine whether there is any association between two or more variables. For example, the following research results on bank branch visits appeared in a cross-tabulation:

Number of visits per month	Male	Female	Totals
1–4	180	80	260
5–8	100	180	280
More than 8	20	40	60
Totals	300	300	600

The expected frequency for each cell is calculated as follows:

Number of visits per month	Male	Female	Totals
1–4	$300 \times 260/600 = 130$	$300 \times 260/600 = 130$	260
5–8	$300 \times 280/600 = 140$	$300 \times 280/600 = 140$	280
More than 8	$300 \times 60/600 = 30$	$300 \times 60/600 = 30$	60
Totals	300	300	600

The value of χ^2 is calculated using the following formula:

$$\chi^2 = \sum_{i=1}^{r} \sum_{j=1}^{k} \frac{(O_{ij} - E_{ij})^2}{E_{ij}}$$

where O_{ij} is the observed number in the ith row of the jth column and E_{ij} is the expected number in the ith row of the jth column.

$$\chi^2 = \frac{(180 - 130)^2}{130} + \frac{(80 - 130)^2}{130} + \frac{(100 - 140)^2}{140}$$
$$+ \frac{(180 - 140)^2}{140} + \frac{(20 - 30)^2}{30} + \frac{(40 - 30)^2}{30} = 67.99$$

The tabular χ^2 value at 0.05 level of significance, and $(r - 1) \times (k - 1) = 2$ degrees of freedom is 5.99 (see Table 2 in the Appendix). Because the calculated $\chi^2 = 67.99$ is more than the tabular value, the null hypothesis is rejected and the researcher can conclude that there is a significant difference between males and females in terms of the frequency of visits to bank branches.

Hypotheses about means and proportions

Where sample data produces a mean (for example, the average value of a weekly grocery shop) or a proportion (59 per cent of the sample prefer butter), researchers may wish to test a hypothesis relating to these figures. To do this, either a Z test or a t test is used. A Z test is used if the researcher is aware of the population's mean and variance (actual or assumed) and the sample size is larger than 30. A t test is appropriate when the mean and variance of the population are not known or where the sample size is less than 30. The t test tends to be used more frequently by marketing researchers.

Z test

A mobile phone manufacturer undertook a survey of 1,000 mobile phone users examining attitudes towards different brands of phone. Each phone was rated for quality using a 1–5 rating scale. The mean rating for Nokia was 3.6. The sample standard deviation was 1.8. The client company wants to determine whether Nokia's rating is significantly higher than the average score for all of the brands of phone (3.1).

A Z test for hypotheses about one mean is used with the null hypothesis (H_0) being: Nokia's quality rating is equal to or less than 3.1. The alternative hypothesis states that Nokia does have a higher rating than 3.1.

At the 0.05 level of significance, the tabular value of Z (critical) = 1.64 (see Table 3 in the Appendix – the table for t is used because t holds the same value as Z when the sample is greater than 30). The tabular value of Z at any level of significance depends on whether a one-tailed or two-tailed test is involved. If an evaluation is required to determine whether something is more or less than something else (as is the case here), then a one-tailed test is appropriate. If an evaluation is required to test whether something is the same as something else, then a two-tailed test is appropriate.

The first step is to calculate the estimated standard error of the mean, using the formula:

$$\text{Standard error} = \frac{\text{Standard deviation}}{\sqrt{\text{Sample size}}} = \frac{1.8}{\sqrt{1,000}} = 0.06$$

$$Z = \frac{(\text{Sample mean} - \text{Population mean})}{\text{Estimated standard error}} = \frac{3.6 - 3.1}{0.06} = 8.3$$

As 8.3 is larger than the critical Z value (1.64), the client company can infer with 95 per cent confidence that Nokia's quality is higher than the average value of quality.

Alternatively, proportions may be involved. Say, for example, a survey of 300 customers found that 67 per cent of them disliked a new flavour of a well-known snack product. Before withdrawing the product, the brand manager wants to determine whether the true percentage is greater than 60 per cent. The null and alternative hypotheses are specified as:

H_0: *The proportion of the population who dislike the product is equal to or less than 60 per cent.*

H_1: *The proportion of the population who dislike the product is more than 60 per cent.*

Step 1 involves calculating the estimated standard error using the following formula:

$$S_p = \sqrt{\frac{P(1 - P)}{n - 1}}$$

where P is the proportion specified in the null hypothesis and N is the sample size.

$$S_p = \sqrt{\frac{0.6(1 - 0.6)}{300 - 1}} = 0.028$$

Calculate the Z value using the following formula:

$$Z = \frac{(\text{Observed proportion} - \text{Proportion under null hypothesis})}{\text{Estimated standard error } (S_p)} = \frac{(0.67 - 0.6)}{0.028} = 2.5$$

At the 0.05 level, the table value of $Z = 1.64$ (see Table 3 in the appendix – value for Z where d.f. = infinity, 0.05 significance, one-tail). On this basis the null hypothesis is rejected because the calculated Z value is larger than the critical Z value. The brand manager can then withdraw the product as he can conclude with 95 per cent confidence that more than 60 per cent of customers dislike the new flavour.

If the proportions in two independent samples are to be compared, for example to determine whether the number of people disliking one flavour of snack product in the UK survey is significantly different from the number disliking the flavour in a separate study in France, the procedure is similar to the test above except that the following formula is used:

$$S_{p_{a-b}} = \sqrt{P(1 - P)\left(\frac{1}{n_a} + \frac{1}{n_b}\right)}$$

where

$$P = \frac{n_a P_a + n_b P_b}{n_a + n_b}$$

P_a is the proportion in sample a, P_b is the proportion in sample b, n_a is the size of sample a and n_b is the size of sample b.

t test

Although the Z test is generally used for large samples with a sample size of more than 30, some statistical computer packages use the t test for all sample sizes. The procedures for using the t test are similar to those for using the Z test. The different formulas are as follows:

For a mean and one sample:

$$t = \frac{\text{Sample mean} - \text{Mean under null hypothesis}}{\text{Estimated standard error of the mean}}$$

Table 9.2 Statistical tests used with ordinal data

Test	Data type	Sample type
ANOVA (analysis of variance)	Interval and ratio data	Testing the means of two or more independent samples
Mann–Whitney U test	Ordinal data	Two independent samples
Kruskal–Wallis test	Ordinal data	More than two independent samples
Wilcoxon signed rank	Ordinal data	Two non-independent samples
Friedman two-way analysis	Ordinal data	More than two non-independent samples
Kolmogorov–Smirnov test	Ordinal data	Similar to chi-square (but for ordinal data)

For comparing means in two samples:

$$t = \frac{\text{(Mean from sample 1)} - \text{(Mean from sample 2)}}{\sqrt{[\text{(Standard error for sample 1)}^2 + \text{(Standard error for sample 2)}^2]}}$$

In addition to t tests and Z tests, there are a number of other tests depending on the nature of the data and the comparisons made. For example with ordinal data, the tests listed in Table 9.2 are used.

Measuring relationships: correlation and regression

Marketers are frequently interested in the degree of association between two variables such as advertising and sales, temperature and ice cream sales, square footage of retail store and sales, average queue length and customer satisfaction scores. Bivariate techniques such as correlation analysis and regression analysis are used when only two variables are involved. If more than two variables are involved then multivariate techniques are used. These are briefly described at the end of this chapter.

Bivariate analysis cannot be used to prove that one variable causes some change in another variable. It simply describes the degree of association between the two variables. Although a researcher may label each of the variables as being independent or dependent, this is not confirmed by either correlation or regression analysis. Independent variables are those variables that are believed to influence the dependent variable. As such, we can clearly assume that advertising is the independent variable and sales is the dependent variable. However, things may not always be so clear cut (e.g. in the case of credit card usage and level of household debt, does the level of debt influence credit card usage or does credit card usage influence household debt?).

Regression and correlation examine relationships in different ways. Regression analysis identifies the nature of the relationship using an equation, whereas correlation analysis uses an index to describe the strength of a relationship. To fully understand this, it is useful to look at a number of scatter diagrams (see Figure 9.3). These diagrams plot the variable that is considered to be dependent on the y axis and the

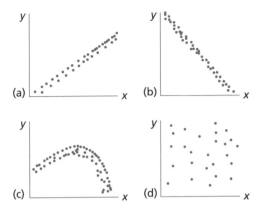

Figure 9.3 Types of relationships found in scatter diagrams

independent variable on the *x* axis (for example, advertising would be on the *x* axis and sales would be on the *y* axis. Figure 9.3(a) suggests a positive linear relationship between *x* and *y*, whereas Figure 9.3(b) suggests a perfect negative linear relationship. Instead of a linear relationship, Figure 9.3(c) shows a nonlinear relationship, and more complex appropriate curve-fitting techniques are required to describe this relationship mathematically. Figure 9.3(d) shows no relationship between *x* and *y*. The correlation and regression techniques introduced in this chapter are only designed to capture the extent of linear association between variables and will not identify a curvilinear relationship.

Pearson's product moment correlation

The Pearson's product moment correlation approach is used with interval and ratio data. It produces the coefficient of correlation (R) which is a measure of the degree of association between *x* and *y*. The value of R can range from -1 (perfect negative correlation) to $+1$ (perfect positive correlation). The closer R is to either $+1$ or -1, the stronger the degree of association between *x* and *y*. If R is equal to zero, then there is no association between *x* and *y*.

The formula for calculating R is as follows:

$$R = \frac{n\Sigma xy - (\Sigma x)(\Sigma y)}{\sqrt{[n\Sigma x^2 - (\Sigma x)^2][n\Sigma y^2 - (\Sigma y)^2]}}$$

Pearson's product moment coefficient of correlation

To illustrate the computation and interpretation of Pearson's product moment coefficient of correlation, let us consider some data gathered by a manufacturer of photocopiers on worldwide sales. The following table contains data from a sample of 16 countries for the size of the salesforce and the revenues generated by sales during a 6-month period.

Country	Number of sales personnel (x)	Sales (million euros) (y)	x^2	y^2	xy
1	45	5.85	2,025	34.22	263.25
2	32	4.06	1,024	16.48	129.92
3	16	2.09	256	4.37	33.44
4	8	1.05	64	1.10	8.40
5	33	4.31	1,089	18.58	142.23
6	18	2.33	324	5.43	41.94
7	10	1.27	100	1.61	12.70
8	3	0.38	9	0.14	1.14
9	22	2.93	484	8.58	64.46
10	23	2.79	529	7.78	64.17
11	26	3.37	676	11.36	87.62
12	24	3.12	576	9.73	74.88
13	41	5.33	1,681	28.41	218.53
14	37	5.00	1,369	25.00	185.00
15	19	2.79	361	7.78	53.01
16	11	1.30	121	1.69	14.30
Sum Σ	368	47.97	10,688	182.26	1,394.99

$$R = \frac{n\Sigma xy - (\Sigma x)(\Sigma y)}{\sqrt{[n\Sigma x^2 - (\Sigma x)^2][n\Sigma y^2 - (\Sigma y)^2]}}$$

$$R = \frac{16(1,394.99) - (368)(47.97)}{\sqrt{[16(10,688) - (368)^2][16(182.26) - (47.97)^2]}}$$

$$R = \frac{4,666.88}{4,678.20} = 1.0$$

This value of R indicates an almost perfect positive linear relationship between the number of sales personnel and the level of sales.

Spearman's rank-order correlation

Where the data is ordinal, Spearman's rank-order correlation is used. For example, if a researcher wants to examine the relationship between the rankings for advertising expenditure in an industry and the rankings for annual turnover, then the formula for Spearman's rank-order correlation coefficient should be used:

$$R_s = 1 - \left(\frac{6\sum_{i=1}^{n} d_i^2}{n^3 - n} \right)$$

where d_i is the difference in ranks of the two variables and n is the number of items ranked.

Spearman's rank-order correlation

To illustrate the computation and interpretation of Spearman's rank-order coefficient of correlation, let us consider the following table showing the rankings for 14 companies in terms of advertising expenditure and annual turnover. Note that the rank of 1 indicates the highest expenditure and highest turnover.

Company	Advertising expenditure (x)	Annual turnover (y)	Difference in ranking (d)	(Difference in ranking)^2 (d^2)
A	1	2	1	1
B	8	6	−2	4
C	2	4	2	4
D	4	3	−1	1
E	3	1	−2	4
F	10	14	4	16
G	13	11	−2	4
H	5	5	0	0
I	14	13	−1	1
J	7	8	1	1
K	12	12	0	0
L	6	9	3	9
M	11	10	−1	1
N	9	7	−2	4
			Sum	50

$$R_s = 1 - \left(\frac{6 \sum_{i=1}^{n} d_i^2}{n^3 - n} \right)$$

where d_i is the difference in ranks of the two variables and n is the number of items ranked.

$$R_s = 1 - (6(50)/(14^3 - 14))$$

$$R_s = 0.89$$

Based on this coefficient, the two rankings are positively correlated. Higher rankings on one are associated with higher rankings on the other. The value of the correlation coefficient can be tested against the null hypothesis that states there is no relationship. This is done using a t distribution for a given sample size ($n = 14$) as follows:

$$t = R_s \sqrt{\frac{n-2}{1-R_s^2}} = 0.89 \times \sqrt{[(14-2)/(1-0.89^2)]} = 6.76$$

The tabulated value (see Table 3 in the Appendix) for t with 12 $(n-2)$ degrees of freedom is 2.18 (at $\alpha = 0.05$). As the calculated t value (6.76) is higher than the tabulated or critical value (2.18), the null hypothesis is rejected and so there is a positive relationship between a company's advertising expenditure and its annual turnover.

While the Pearson and Spearman rank-order correlation coefficients are effective in uncovering bivariate associations, there is one important caveat concerning their use. A low correlation coefficient does not necessarily mean there is no association; it only implies an absence of a linear association. A researcher should always explore the possible presence of a nonlinear association, especially when intuitively the researcher feels that the variables may be related. The easiest way of identifying a nonlinear association is to plot and examine a scatter diagram.

Simple regression analysis

Simple regression analysis is similar to the procedures used to calculate the Pearson correlation coefficient. However, whereas correlation analysis focuses on summarising the degree and the direction of association between variables as a single number, the purpose of regression analysis is to generate a mathematical equation linking those variables. In other words, regression analysis attempts to describe the gradient and direction of the line that goes through the plots on a scatter diagram. The equation that provides the description of the line can be used to forecast the value of the dependent variable for any value of the independent variable within the range examined by the regression analysis (for example using past data to identify the likely sales impact of a change in advertising expenditure). When examining the association between two variables, the designation of one of the variables as the independent variable is more important to regression analysis than to correlation analysis. In regression analysis, it is only the dependent variable that is random; the independent variable is implicitly treated as a set of fixed numbers. In other words, the independent variable is seen as being set at a variety of fixed levels, at each of which the researcher observes the value of the dependent variable. This does not mean that regression analysis can prove that one variable definitely causes another. The specification of which variable is the dependent variable is done by the researcher using prior knowledge and theoretical considerations rather than by the regression technique. Similar to correlation analysis, regression analysis simply describes the relationship between the variables and does not explain it.

Least squares approach

The regression procedure that is widely used for deriving the best-fit equation of a line (see the line in Figure 9.4) for a given set of data involving a dependent and independent variable is the **least squares approach**. No straight line can perfectly represent every observation in a scatter diagram. As Figure 9.4 shows, there are discrepancies between the actual values and predicted values (value indicated by the

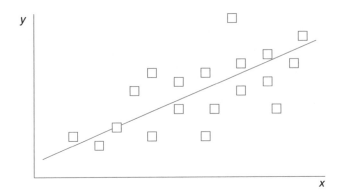

Figure 9.4 Scatter diagram showing a straight line aimed at fitting the data

line). The line does not go through every value. A number of lines could be drawn that would seem to fit the observations in the scatter diagram.

The least squares procedure identifies the line that best fits the actual data (better than any other line). The general equation for the line is $y = â + \hat{b}x$ where $â$ is the point at which the line intercepts the y axis and $\hat{b}$ is the estimated slope of the regression line, known as the regression coefficient.

The values for $â$ and $\hat{b}$ can be calculated using the following equations:

$$\hat{b} = \frac{\sum x_i y_i - n\bar{x}\bar{y}}{\sum x_i^2 - n(\bar{x})^2}$$

$$â = \bar{y} - \hat{b}\bar{x}$$

where $\bar{x}$ is the mean value of x, $\bar{y}$ is the mean value of y and n is the sample size (number of units in the sample).

The following example uses the same data as was used for illustrating Pearson's product moment correlation to calculate $\hat{b}$ and $â$.

Country	Number of sales personnel (x)	Sales (million euros) (y)	x^2	y^2	xy
1	45	5.85	2,025	34.22	263.25
2	32	4.06	1,024	16.48	129.92
3	16	2.09	256	4.37	33.44
4	8	1.05	64	1.10	8.40
5	33	4.31	1,089	18.58	142.23
6	18	2.33	324	5.43	41.94
7	10	1.27	100	1.61	12.70

Country	Number of sales personnel (x)	Sales (million euros) (y)	x^2	y^2	xy
8	3	0.38	9	0.14	1.14
9	22	2.93	484	8.58	64.46
10	23	2.79	529	7.78	64.17
11	26	3.37	676	11.36	87.62
12	24	3.12	576	9.73	74.88
13	41	5.33	1,681	28.41	218.53
14	37	5.00	1,369	25.00	185.00
15	19	2.79	361	7.78	53.01
16	11	1.30	121	1.69	14.30
Sum Σ	368	47.97	10,688	182.26	1,394.99
Mean	23	3.00			

$$\hat{b} = \frac{1,394.99 - 16(23)(3)}{10,688 - 16(23)^2}$$

$$\hat{b} = 0.13$$

$$\hat{a} = < - b\,\xi$$

$$\hat{a} = 3 - 0.13 \times 23$$

$$\hat{a} = 0.01$$

Thus the estimated regression function is:

$$y = 0.01 + 0.13(x)$$

According to the estimated regression function, for every additional 10 sales personnel, sales will increase by 1.31 million euros.

Strength of association R^2

In addition to the regression function, the researcher is frequently interested in the strength of the relationship between the variables. In other words, how widely do the actual values of y differ from the values predicted by the equation of the line?

The **coefficient of determination**, denoted by R^2 is the measure of the strength of the linear relationship between x and y. It specifically measures the percentage of the total variation in y that is 'explained' by the variation in x. If there is a perfect linear relationship between x and y (all the variation in y is explained by the variation in x and all values appear on the regression line) then R^2 equals 1. Finally, if there is no relationship between x and y, then none of the variation is explained by the variation in x and R^2 equals 0.

Country	Number of sales personnel (x)	Sales (million euros) (y)	$\hat{y}$	$y - \hat{y}$	$(y - \hat{y})^2$	$(y - \bar{y})^2$
1	45	5.85	5.86	−0.01	0.0001	8.133
2	32	4.06	4.17	−0.11	0.0121	1.128
3	16	2.09	2.09	0	0	0.825
4	8	1.05	1.05	0	0	3.795
5	33	4.31	4.30	0.01	0.0001	1.721
6	18	2.33	2.35	−0.02	0.0004	0.446
7	10	1.27	1.31	−0.04	0.0016	2.986
8	3	0.38	0.40	−0.02	0.0004	6.854
9	22	2.93	2.87	0.06	0.0036	0.005
10	23	2.79	3.00	−0.21	0.0441	0.043
11	26	3.37	3.39	−0.02	0.0004	0.138
12	24	3.12	3.13	−0.01	0.0001	0.015
13	41	5.33	5.34	−0.01	0.0001	5.438
14	37	5.00	4.82	0.18	0.0324	4.008
15	19	2.79	2.48	0.31	0.0961	0.043
16	11	1.30	1.44	−0.14	0.0196	2.884
Sum Σ	368	47.97	48.00	−0.03	0.2111	38.462
Mean	23	3.00				

Calculating the coefficient of determination using the data relating to the manufacturer of photocopiers:

$$R^2 = \frac{\text{Total variation} - \text{Unexplained variation}}{\text{Total variation}}$$

$$= 1 - \frac{\text{Unexplained variation}}{\text{Total variation}}$$

$$= 1 - \frac{\sum\limits_{i=1}^{n}(y_i - \hat{y}_i)^2}{\sum\limits_{i=1}^{n}(y_i - \bar{y})^2} = 1 - \frac{0.2111}{38.462} = 0.99$$

This is a very strong linear relationship between x and y, suggesting that almost all the variation in y is explained by the variation in x.

Multivariate data analysis

Multivariate data analysis is the term for statistical procedures that simultaneously analyse two or more variables on a sample of objects. For example, multivariate data analysis would enable the researcher to examine the relationships between advertising expenditure and number of salespeople, packaging costs and level of sales. Increased computer power has made it possible to examine complex relationships between multiple items with relative ease. The most common techniques provided by statistical software packages and used by marketing researchers are:

- multiple regression analysis;
- multiple discriminant analysis;
- factor analysis;
- cluster analysis;
- perceptual mapping;
- conjoint analysis.

Detailed explanation of the procedures involved in undertaking these techniques is beyond the scope of this book. However, the following subsections provide a brief description of the techniques and their application.

Multiple regression analysis

Multiple regression analysis enables a researcher both to understand the relationship between three or more variables and also to calculate the likely value of a dependent variable based on the values of two or more independent variables. In general, all of the variables require to be based on interval or ratio scales if they are to be suitable for multiple regression analysis (under exceptional circumstances, it may be possible to use nominal independent variables if they are recoded as binary variables). Multiple regression analysis is used for a variety of applications in marketing research including:

- estimating the impact of different marketing mix variables on sales or market share;
- estimating the relative importance of individual components of customer satisfaction on overall satisfaction;
- determining the impact of different customer characteristics on levels of purchasing.

Multiple discriminant analysis

Multiple discriminant analysis is generally used to classify individuals into one of two or more segments (or populations) on the basis of a set of measurements. For example, the grouping may relate to brand usage, with respondents being either users or non-users of a brand. Multiple discriminant analysis enables a researcher to predict the likelihood of a person being a brand user based on two or more independent variables, such as size of weekly shop, income level, age, or purchasing levels of related products. This may allow the researcher to establish a model for classifying individuals into groups or segments on the basis of the values of their independent variables. The technique can also be used to identify which variables contribute to making the classification. Overall, the objective in discriminant analysis is to find a linear combination of the independent variables that maximises the difference between groupings and minimises the probability of misclassifying individuals or objects into their respective groups.

Factor analysis

Factor analysis is a procedure that studies the interrelationships among variables for the purpose of simplifying data. It can reduce a large set of variables to a smaller set of composite variables or factors by identifying the underlying dimensions of the data (e.g. measures of 'size' and 'value' in a study may be indicators of the same theoretical construct).

Reasons for performing factor analysis can be summarised as:

- It can provide insights from the groupings of variables that emerge. These insights might have practical or theoretical significance.
- It can reduce the number of questions, scales or attributes being analysed to a more manageable number.

In marketing research, factor analysis is most frequently used when analysing data coming from rating scales. Respondents may be asked to rate a service on a whole range of attributes; within this, satisfaction with the service employee may be measured through a range of attributes such as product knowledge, empathy with the customer, speed of service, clarity of communication, etc. A researcher may want to add some of these attributes together to develop a composite score or to compute an average score for the concept. Factor analysis will determine whether and how attributes can be combined into summary factors such as 'interpersonal skills' and 'technical ability'. Different weightings may require to be applied to the original attributes to determine the summary factors. A factor is thus a variable or construct that is not directly observable but that needs to be inferred from the input variables.

The most important outputs from factor analysis are the factor loadings and the variance–explained percentages. The factor loadings are used to determine the factors and describe the correlations between the factors and the variables. The variance-explained percentage help to determine the number of factors to include and how well they represent the original variables.

Factor analysis can generate several solutions for any data set. Each solution is called a factor rotation and is generated by a factor rotation scheme (e.g. Varimax rotation). Different rotations result in different factor loadings and different interpretations of the factors. Rotation simply means that the dimensions are rotated until suitable factors are identified. This highlights a weakness of factor analysis – it is a highly subjective process. The selection of the number of factors, their interpretation, and the rotation to select the factors (if one set of factors is disliked by a researcher, rotation may be continued indefinitely until a more suitable set is found) all involve the researcher's selective judgement. In order to increase the objectivity of the analysis and to determine whether the results of the analysis reflect something meaningful rather than being merely accidental, the following approach is frequently adopted: the sample is randomly divided into two or more groups and a factor analysis is run on each group. If the same factors emerge in each analysis, more confidence can be placed in the results.

Cluster analysis

Cluster analysis refers to statistical procedures used to classify objects or people into mutually exclusive and exhaustive groups on the basis of two or more classification variables. Frequently, marketing managers need to identify consumer segments

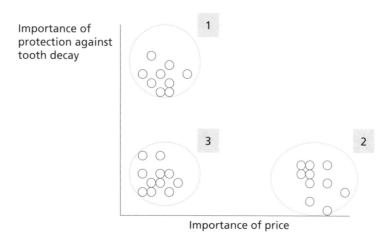

Figure 9.5 A scatter diagram showing three clusters

so that marketing strategies can be developed and tailored to each segment. Such segments can be based on lifestyles, purchasing behaviour, socio-economic characteristics, etc.

Although a number of different approaches and procedures are available for clustering, the underlying process involves determining the similarities among people or objects with regard to the variables being used for the clustering. At the most basic level this can be done plotting the characteristics of respondents on a scatter diagram and examining the patterns in the data. For example, Figure 9.5 shows the clusters relating to the purchases of toothpaste and variables relating to the importance placed on the reduction of tooth decay and the importance placed on price. The scatter diagram shows three clusters:

- **Cluster 1** includes those people who purchase toothpaste on the basis of protection against tooth decay and pay little attention to price.
- **Cluster 2** includes those people who purchase toothpaste on the basis of price and pay little attention to protection against tooth decay.
- **Cluster 3** includes those people who do not pay attention to either price or protection – they may be influenced by brand name, taste, appearance, type of dispenser, etc. (further scatter diagrams would be required to determine this).

Using scatter diagrams for cluster analysis is time consuming and can become an onerous task, particularly when considering a large number of variables or a large number of respondents. Scatter diagrams can sometimes be difficult to interpret if there are very large numbers of points plotted onto one two-dimensional diagram, never mind a diagram with three dimensions or more. However, there are computer programs available to undertake this task. The procedure they use involves algorithms that alter cluster boundaries until a point is reached where the distances between the points within the clusters is smaller than the distances between the points in one cluster and those in another. The computer will continue to assign and reassign data to clusters until it achieves the number of clusters that the researcher is seeking. The researcher will determine the optimum number by considering the

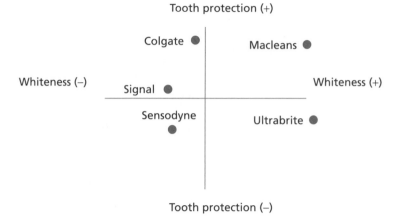

Figure 9.6 Example of a perceptual map

practicalities of using the cluster information or by looking at the pattern of clusters and the distances between the clusters generated by the computer program at each iteration.

Perceptual mapping

Multidimensional scaling involves the positioning of objects in a perceptual space. This is particularly important in determining the positioning of brands relative to their competitors. For example, toothpaste manufacturers may want to assess the position of their branded products against those of the competition in terms of protection, price, taste, modernity, freshness of breath, and level of whiteness. Respondents will be asked to evaluate each brand on these attributes and the output from the data analysis is called a perceptual map. Such a map is usually two-dimensional; although three-dimensional maps are possible they are often more difficult to interpret. Where more than two dimensions are required, a series of two-dimensional maps is generally used.

Figure 9.6 shows an example of a perceptual map for toothpaste, it shows Macleans and Colgate as being perceived as better for tooth protection than the other brands, with Macleans and Ultrabrite being seen as performing better in terms of whiteness.

Conjoint analysis

Conjoint analysis provides a quantitative measure of the relative importance of one attribute over another. It is frequently used by marketers to determine what features a new product or service should have and also how products should be priced. This is often used instead of the more expensive approach of full concept testing.

In assessing the importance placed on attributes by consumers, it is rare to find that only one attribute is important. People will buy their toothpaste on the basis of a combination of factors (e.g. price, protection against tooth decay, flavour, size of packet) rather than on the basis of one factor (e.g. flavour) only. In conjoint analysis, the respondent is asked to make trade-offs between the different attributes. Which attribute can be sacrificed? At what level of price does protection become less attractive? Sometimes the preferences may be in conflict; for example, high protection against tooth decay for a very low price. The aim is to find some form of compromise solution.

Trade-off data is collected in one of two ways: respondents are either asked to consider two attributes at a time or to assess a full profile of attributes at once.

The **full-profile approach** involves the respondents being given cards that describe a full product or service. This can best be described using a hypothetical banking product, which has only three attributes:

Interest rate	Means of delivery	Access to money
Low rate	Passbook	Immediate
High rate	Cash machine	Seven-day notice
	Internet	

For such a banking product the design would consist of 12 combinations ($2 \times 3 \times 2$) as shown below:

Profile	Interest rate	Means of delivery	Access to money
1	Low	Passbook	Immediate
2	Low	Passbook	Seven-day notice
3	Low	Cash machine	Immediate
4	Low	Cash machine	Seven-day notice
5	Low	Internet	Immediate
6	Low	Internet	Seven-day notice
7	High	Passbook	Immediate
8	High	Passbook	Seven-day notice
9	High	Cash machine	Immediate
10	High	Cash machine	Seven-day notice
11	High	Internet	Immediate
12	High	Internet	Seven-day notice

Respondents can be asked either to rank-order the profiles in order of preference, or to assign a rating scale to each profile measuring overall preference or intentions to buy. The full-profile approach is similar to real life, in that consumers tend to consider all attributes at once when purchasing a product. However, as the number of attributes increases, the task of judging the individual profiles becomes very complex and respondents have difficulties in taking account of all the variations in the attributes.

An alternative approach is the pairwise (trade-off) approach where the attributes are presented in pairs. For example, in the bank product example, this would lead to three possible pairings:

1 Interest rate/Means of delivery
2 Interest rate/Access to money
3 Means of delivery/Access to money

The pairings would be presented in grids similar to the following and respondents would be asked to put each combination in rank order of preference:

Means of delivery

	Passbook	Cash machine	Internet
Low interest rate	6	5	3
High interest rate	4	2	1

Although the pairwise approach may lack the realism of the full-profile approach, it is generally easier for the respondent to make judgements between two attributes. Care must be taken to ensure that the number of attributes is not excessive, as the task may become repetitive and boring. If there is a very large number of attributes, a two-stage approach may be adopted where the respondent first classifies the attributes into various groups relating to importance. The pairings are only set up with the attributes that the respondent considers to be at least reasonably important.

The process can also be made less tedious by allowing respondents to input their decisions directly into a specialist computer package. The package can decide on the attributes to test on a real-time basis using the respondent's previous responses to select the next attributes to assess. Where a respondent has indicated that certain attributes or levels of attribute are totally unacceptable then these will not be presented again. The computer can also monitor the degree to which the model of preference that is emerging is actually explaining the choices made – when a good enough fit emerges, the interview can be ended.

Analysis of the data produces a set of utilities (a set of values/scores) for the various potential attributes of the product or service. These may look something like the following table, where the utilities are shown in brackets:

Set of utilities for respondent 1

Interest rate	Means of delivery	Access to money
Low rate (0)	Passbook (5)	Immediate (100)
High rate (100)	Cash machine (40)	Seven-day notice (70)
	Internet (30)	

By adding the various utilities, the total utility of a proposed product/service for each respondent can be calculated. This can enable the researcher to make estimates of the potential market share for each of the potential designs of products or services. However, a word of caution: when using conjoint analysis, the researcher should remember that it may not totally reflect reality, as consumers are unlikely to approach purchasing decisions in such a rational and deliberate manner. Customers may not be fully aware of all product features when buying a product or may be strongly influenced by branding or advertising.

Summary

This chapter has attempted to introduce you to the key steps and most common approaches used by researchers when analysing quantitative data. The three main steps involve:

- **Coding**: the transforming of responses into a form that is ready for analysis.
- **Data entry**: entering of the data into a computer, either automatically or manually.
- **Tabulation and statistical analysis**: the interpretation and communication of the meaning behind the data.

Quantitative data exists in one of four forms – nominal, ordinal, interval and ratio. The nature of each of these impacts on the types of tabulation and statistical analysis that are possible.

The main forms of statistical analysis can be categorised into:

- **Descriptive statistics**: measures of central tendency, measures of dispersion.
- **Statistical significance and hypothesis testing**: chi-square, Z test, t test.
- **Measuring relationships**: correlation and regression.
- **Multivariate data analysis**: multiple regression analysis, multiple discriminant analysis, factor analysis, cluster analysis, perceptual mapping.

The author is only too well aware that many students' eyes glaze over when confronted by formulas and statistics. Thankfully many of the analysis and questionnaire design software packages (listed at the end of this chapter) remove the onerous tasks of applying formulas and calculating statistical outcomes. However, researchers do need to develop an awareness and understanding of the statistical techniques available and the meaning of their outputs. This chapter has attempted to provide this basic awareness and understanding. More detailed discussion of statistical techniques can be found in the books listed in the 'Additional reading' section below or on a website such as that run by Statsoft (http://www.statsoft.com).

Discussion questions

1 What does coding involve and how should a researcher go about post-coding responses to open-ended questions?

2 What is the difference between nominal and ordinal data?

3 What is the difference between interval and ratio data?

4 Describe the main measures of central tendency.

5 Explain the difference between mathematical differences and statistical differences.

6   Explain what is meant by the terms null hypothesis and alternative hypothesis.

7   For what purpose would you use the chi-square test. How is the chi-square test different from Z tests and t tests?

8   Explain the difference between correlation and regression.

9   Explain what is meant by multivariate data analysis.

10   Explain the difference between factor analysis and cluster analysis.

Additional reading

Devore, J.L. and Peck, R. (1997) *Statistics: the exploration and analysis of data.* Duxbury Press, Belmont, CA.

Freedman, D., Pisani, R. and Purves, R. (1998) *Statistics.* W.W. Norton, New York.

Hair, J., Tatham, R., Anderson, R. and Black, W. (1998) *Multivariate Data Analysis*, 5th edn. Prentice Hall, Upper Saddle River, NJ.

Johnson, R.A. (2001) *Statistics: principles and methods.* John Wiley, New York.

Koosis, D.J. (1997) *Statistics: a self-teaching guide.* John Wiley, New York.

Moore, D.S. (2001) *Statistics: concepts and controversies*, 5th edn. W.H. Freeman, New York.

Salkind, N.J. (2000) *Statistics for People Who (Think They) Hate Statistics.* Sage, New York.

Wilcox, R.R. (1996) *Statistics for the Social Sciences.* Academic Press, London.

Quantitative analysis/questionnaire design software suppliers
Apian (SurveyPro): www.apian.com
CfMC (Mentor): www.cfmc.com
Creative Research Systems (The Survey System): www.surveysystem.com
FIRM (Confirmit): www.confirmit.com
Mercator (snap): www.snapsurveys.com
Merlinco (MERLIN): www.merlinco.co.uk
P-STAT: www.pstat.com
Pulse Train (STAR): www.pulsetrain.com
QPSMR: www.qpsmr.ltd.uk
SPSS: www.spssmr.com
VOXCO (StatXP): www.voxco.com

Reference

[1] Adapted from Phillips, A., Parfitt, J. and Prutton, I. (1989) Developing a rounder tea, *Market Research Society Conference Proceedings*, pp. 289–308. Published with the permission of the Market Research Society.

10
Presenting the research results

Levi Strauss: disseminating findings in an unorthodox manner

Levi Strauss, the maker of jeans, uses a Youth Panel to understand the trends in the clothing market. The panel is a regularly refreshed qualitative consumer panel focused on the segments of the market most likely to have greatest impact on the dynamics of change within the casual apparel market. The panel has been built up in each of the most fashion-significant European cities (Berlin, Milan, Paris, Barcelona and London) and comprises between 50 and 100 of the most fashion-forward-looking members of the youth market. The panellists are hand selected individually from the art/media/photographic schools of each city by stationing recruiters in the bars, clubs, shops, etc., that they frequent. The panel is convened twice per year to fit into the company's design development calendar prior to the season's first sketches being laid out. In the past a major challenge was getting fashion designers to listen to main-stream consumers and marketing research. The company experimented with a few different techniques to ensure panel learning was professionally interpreted and appropriately communicated. Research findings were put on multimedia CD-ROMs. However, they became occasional reference documents when what was needed was a living tool. The inspiration in the fashion industry revolves around style mag-azines, so the research department decided to package their knowledge as a style magazine. The internal magazine YP was created and is now into its 6th edition with an internal print run of over 500. This unorthodox marketing research communication and presentation tool means everybody who needs to understand the consumer in the company has an accessible bag-sized reminder of where the market is moving and what the key challenges are for the Levi Strauss brands.[1]

Learning outcomes

After reading this chapter you should:

- be aware of the need to understand your audience when doing a presentation or when writing a report;
- be aware of the key elements and format of the final report and oral presentation;
- understand some of the key guidelines for undertaking presentations;
- be aware of the main types of tables and graphs;
- be aware of some of the common dangers encountered in reporting and presenting.

Key words

audience's thinking sequence
bar chart
doughnut chart
line graph
oral presentation

pictogram
pie chart
research report
tables

Introduction

The communication of the research results in the form of a research report or a verbal presentation is the culmination of the research project. This step is particularly important, as the clarity and relevance of the communication is critical to the client's final satisfaction with the marketing research project. A marketing manager may question the overall value and accuracy of the research if it is presented in a confusing and unconfident manner. The report provides a lasting impression of the quality of the research long after the project is finished. As such, it will play a big part in determining whether the researcher obtains further work from the client. This chapter provides guidelines for report writing in terms of structure, writing style, graphs and tables. It also discusses the preparation required for oral presentations. The pitfalls in both of these areas are also explored.

Understanding the audience

Researchers need to put themselves in the shoes of the clients and think through the specific information that the clients want to hear and also the likely manner in which they will want it communicated. One way of doing this is to consider the audience's thinking sequence, the sequence of thoughts that people go through when they are being communicated with. These can be illustrated as shown in Figure 10.1. Each of these thoughts has implications for the researcher:

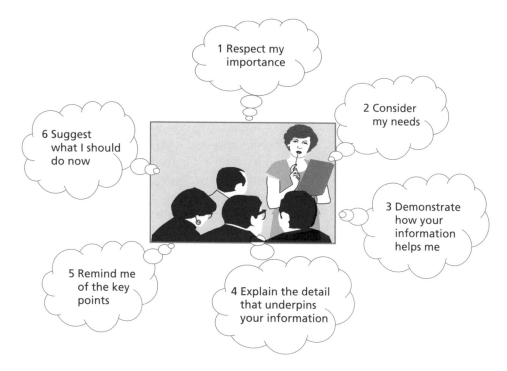

Figure 10.1 The audience's thinking sequence

1 **Respect my importance:** no matter how big or small the research project, the audience are giving up their valuable time to read the researcher's report or attend the researcher's presentation. Members of the audience do not want to waste their time reading or listening to material that:

- is poorly presented (poor quality paper and poorly proofread);
- is unnecessarily long;
- is unclear and confusing;
- does not address the objectives set;
- is structured for the ease of the researcher rather than the needs of the audience.

Client quote: *It is difficult to have confidence in a report if it is full of typographical and grammatical errors.*

2 **Consider my needs:** the report or presentation should clearly provide evidence that the researcher is aware of the rationale for the research and is addressing the original research objectives. Relating the research findings to the marketing decisions that have to be made is critical. The material should take account of the reader's technical sophistication and their likely interest in different parts of the material.

3 **Demonstrate how your information helps me**: the audience wishes to see how the research addresses each of the research objectives and marketing decision areas. They are less concerned about different parts of the questionnaire but instead are more interested in what the findings mean to them and their organisation.

4 **Explain the detail that underpins your information**: the audience needs to be convinced that what is written or presented is accurate. They will therefore want to see the charts, tables and actual respondent quotes that support the findings. Researchers should be anticipating the likely questions that the audience will have and should be attempting to pre-empt them in the report or presentation.

5 **Remind me of the key points**: no matter how long or short the presentation or report, there needs to be a summary of the key points. This concurs with the following maxim for communicating with an audience:

- **you should tell them what you are going to tell them** (explain the agenda of the report or presentation);
- **tell them** (i.e. the findings);
- **tell them what you have told them** (summarise and repeat the key points).

6 **Suggest what I should do now**: although the clients will be responsible for taking any marketing decisions resulting from the research findings, the researchers will normally be expected to provide recommendations about possible courses of action and issues to be addressed.

In addition to these immediate needs of the audience, it is important to realise that the report is a reference document. Long after the research has been completed, decision makers may return to the report as an input to further decisions or as a baseline or template for a follow-up research study. The report must therefore be self-explanatory and capable of being interpreted by a future audience who have had no involvement in the research project.

Understanding the current and future audiences for the research findings is critical to the successful preparation and planning of the report and presentation.

The research report format

The exact format of research reports may vary from one research agency to another and also in response to specific client requirements. However, the majority of reports typically have the following components.

1 title page
2 table of contents
3 executive summary and recommendations
4 introduction and problem definition
5 research method and limitations
6 research findings
7 conclusions
8 appendices.

The following subsections consider each of these in more detail.

Title page

The title page should include the title of the research study, information (name, address and telephone number) about the researcher or research agency, the name of the client, and the date of preparation. The title page should provide sufficient information to enable those who were not directly involved in the research to identify and contact those who were (either on the client or research side).

Table of contents

The table of contents should list the major headings and subheadings in the report with the appropriate page numbers. There may also be a list of tables and graphs.

Executive summary and recommendations

This section is very important as it may be the only section that is read by all of the senior decision makers in the client organisation. Certain managers may not have the time or inclination to read all of the report. This section should be no more than a few pages long and should normally be written after the other sections in the report have been completed. The summary should briefly describe the objectives of the study, the method adopted and the key research findings. The implications of the findings should also be explained, along with the researcher's suggested recommendations. Some clients may request researchers to exclude recommendations as the researcher may not be fully aware of the internal and external factors impacting on the decision area.

> **Researcher quote:** *Although the writing of the executive summary may be undertaken at the end, it should not be rushed, as it is the one area that will definitely be read by the most senior managers in the client company.*

Introduction and problem definition

The introduction should set out the rationale and the detailed objectives for the study. In many ways, this will be similar to the background and objectives sections of the proposal. Some researchers simply copy these sections from the proposal and change the tense.

Research method and limitations

This section should set out details of the research approach adopted for the study. As such, it should cover the research method, questionnaire/discussion guide design, sampling approach and method of data analysis. Justification should be provided for the specific research approach adopted. Any limitations relating to a skewed sample, low response rate, timing of study, etc., should be highlighted as these may have a bearing on the study's findings and conclusions. In general, this section should not be any more than 4–5 pages long, with further technical details being placed in an appendix.

Research findings

This is the main part of the research report. The material should be divided into sections and structured in relation to either:

1 **the research objectives**, with each section describing the findings in relation to the information targets for each objective, or

2 **the customer segments being examined**, with each section describing the research findings in relation to different subsegments of the population. For example, one section may describe the results that relate to young couples, whereas another may focus on families and yet another may focus on the retired segment.

The findings should *not* be structured to reflect the different questions in the questionnaire. This may reflect the researcher's thinking process and analysis procedures, but it is unlikely to reflect those of the marketing decision maker. The structure should be logical and coherent, reflecting the original information needs and taking account of the audience's thinking process. The researcher should be trying to tell a story with a linked line of argument, which builds into a complete picture of the area under investigation. Key information should be supported with tables and graphs (guidelines for these are discussed later in this chapter). For qualitative research, quoting the verbatim responses of the participants can bring the findings to life and increase the reader's interest and understanding.

Conclusions

The researcher should interpret the findings in the light of the research problems and identify the main implications for the client. The conclusions should be concise, highlighting the key findings and implications, and providing justification for these without going into excessively lengthy discussions.

Appendices

The questionnaire or discussion guide (and any showcards) should be included in the appendix, as should any tables or other material that is complex or specialised or not directly relevant to the research objectives. In other words, any material that may be of interest to the client but that may interrupt the flow and coherence of the document if it is included within the main body of the report should be placed in the appendices. If the researcher has used a large amount of secondary data, a reference list should appear in an appendix identifying the data sources, past studies, articles and books. When only a few citations are involved, these can simply be referenced in footnotes on the pages where they appear.

The oral presentation format

Making an effective oral presentation is sometimes seen as more difficult than writing a good report because of the direct interaction with the audience. It is certainly true that any lack of confidence during an oral presentation will result in the audience having doubts about the research results. This will be evident through more questions being posed and data being challenged. Therefore careful planning of an oral presentation is essential. Planning will revolve around the client's thinking sequence, which was highlighted earlier in this chapter.

The basic structure for a presentation should be as follows:

1 **Introduction**
    - thanking the audience for attending;
    - introducing the team doing the presentation (and any other members of the research team present);
    - explaining the format and structure of the presentation;
    - explaining the rationale for the study and the objectives of the project.

2 **Methodology**
    - a brief description of the methodology including the data collection method, sample, time scales and any limitations.

3 **Key findings**
    - a brief presentation of the findings that are key to the objectives of the study, supported by graphs and tables;
    - the material should be aggregated into sections (possibly relating to individual objectives) as this will make it easier for the audience to assimilate.

4 **Conclusions and recommendations**
    - reiterating the key points to emerge from the research and their implications for decision making;
    - setting out recommendations;
    - inviting questions and comments from the audience.

5 **Questions**
    - handling questions posed.

A wide range of software packages, such as Microsoft's PowerPoint, are now available to enable researchers to make high-quality computer-controlled presentations or to make professional quality overheads. Whichever technology or package is used, the researcher should always ensure that it is compatible with the facilities and layout of the room where the presentation will be done.

> **Researcher quote:** *There is no point turning up with a lap-top computer and projector if there is no blank wall or window blinds.*

Even with new technology, there are a number of basic presentation guidelines that the researcher needs to follow if quality communication is to be delivered:

- **Maintain eye contact:** the researcher should avoid reading detailed notes or staring at either the computer or presentation screen. Instead, regular eye contact should be maintained with the audience. This:

- shows concern for the audience and their needs;
- enables the researcher to note the reactions of the audience and possibly respond to these (speeding up or slowing down, providing further explanation);
- maintains the interest of the audience (it is difficult to stay alert when you are constantly looking at the presenter's back or the top of their head);
- builds trust or confidence in what the researcher is saying.

If the researcher is concerned about forgetting something, cue cards can be used. These are index type cards setting out brief notes that the presenter can hold in his or her hand.

- **Seek variety**: the researcher should avoid speaking in a monotone, using the same volume and pitch throughout. The audience will drift away and think about other things. For the same reason, variety should also be sought in the visuals used, mixing lists of bullet points with graphs and tables. Use pauses to break up the presentation and allow the audience time to digest the material.

- **Keep it simple**: over-complex visuals that are cluttered with elaborate diagrams or many words lead to confusion and boredom. Wording should be limited to the key words. The visuals are prompts for the researcher and the audience, and should not be seen as a proxy for the researcher's script. The typeface and graphics should be large enough to be viewed by everyone in the presentation room.

- **Check understanding**: throughout the presentation, researchers should regularly check with their audience that the material is clear and understood. If the researcher waits until the end to do this, he or she may find that the audience has not listened to the end of the presentation as they were so busy puzzling over the material on slide three. This becomes even more important when the presentation is being undertaken using video conferencing, if only to find out if all the members of the audience are still receiving a communication signal.

- **Provide handouts**: the provision of handouts saves the audience from taking notes, freeing the listener to pay attention to and participate more fully in the presentation. Many presentation software packages enable handouts to be produced at the same time as the visuals.

> **Researcher quote:** *I like to put the client's logo on the handouts and presentation charts – it makes it look more professional.*

- **Act natural**: researchers concerned about their mannerisms or what their hands are doing are likely to look more awkward and less trustworthy than those who focus on what they are saying. Most people do not have mannerisms that are so distracting that they annoy an audience.

- **Finish on a high note**: the researcher should attempt to finish on a final summarising statement or key point rather than simply saying 'That's all I have to say, any questions?'. The emphasis should be on winding *up* the presentation and not winding it *down*. What is the lasting impression that the researcher wishes to leave with the audience?

- **Rehearse**: the researcher should rehearse the presentation and time it. Compare the time taken with the time available, allowing sufficient time for discussion and questions (possibly as much as an extra 25–30 per cent). Be prepared to be flexible: recheck the time available at the start of the presentation, and if an important decision maker is leaving early, ensure that the key points are communicated before he or she departs.

- **Clarify questions**: before answering questions, the researcher should pause to think carefully about what was asked. Frequently confusion in presentations results from researchers acting defensively and jumping in to answer questions that are slightly different from the ones that are being asked. A good technique is to write the question down. This indicates to the audience that the researcher is taking their points seriously. If the researcher is confused about what is being asked, they should seek clarification.

Using tables and graphs

There is a saying that a picture is worth a thousand words. This is particularly true in the communication of research results. Tables and graphs can aid understanding by communicating the contents of written material in a very succinct and effective manner. They can also maintain the interest of the audience by providing breaks in the blocks of text or dialogue.

There are an infinite number of ways that tables and graphs can be produced and used. This section will set out the guidelines for the most popular: tables, pie charts, line graphs, bar charts and pictograms.

Tables

There are a number of fundamental elements in a table that impact on its effectiveness at communication. Figure 10.2 shows an example table on the purpose of customer satisfaction measurement to illustrate some of these elements.

- **Title**: every table should be numbered and have a title. The number enables the table to be referred to in the text and the title should briefly describe the table's contents.

- **Base**: the base figures for the sample and subsamples should be shown. This is particularly important when percentages are being used in the table as a figure of 50 per cent may be less important when the base is 6 respondents in comparison to 6,000 respondents.

- **Ordering of data items**: wherever possible, data items in a table should be ordered with the largest items appearing at the top of the table. In the example in Figure 10.2, the elements are ordered in relation to the percentages appearing in the Total column. This enables the audience to quickly recognise the most important and frequent responses. The columns can also be ordered in this way with the

Table 10.1: Purpose of Customer Satisfaction Measurement Analysed by Industry Sector

	Retail	Hospitality sector	Financial services	Total
BASE	64	48	48	160
	%	%	%	%
To monitor customer attitudes and the organisation's performance in general	93	87	90	90
To identify particular problem areas in service delivery	86	64	76	76
To benchmark against data on competitors	36	45	30	37
To determine individual and team rewards/bonuses	36	23	50	36
To compare the performance of individual outlets	29	10	45	28
To feed into staff appraisals	14	20	23	19

Source: Strathclyde University (2001) Customer Satisfaction Report, p. 31

Figure 10.2 An example of a table

segment that has the biggest subsample being in the first column. Although such a layout eases understanding, this should not be done at the expense of a more logical ordering, such as time period (Monday, Tuesday, etc.) or size category (0–14 litres, 15–29 litres, 30–44 litres, etc.).

- **Layout:** the table should incorporate plenty of space around each cell of data, and lines or boxes are also useful to distinguish between the different categories and figures. Any additional explanations or comments should appear in footnotes to the table (letters or symbols should be used for these footnotes to avoid additional confusion).
- **Source:** if the data comes from a published source, this should be cited at the bottom of the table.

Pie charts

A pie chart is a circle divided into several slices whose areas are in proportion to the quantities being examined. It is particularly useful for showing the decomposition of a total quantity into its components (Figure 10.3). However, there should be no more than 6 or 7 components, otherwise the chart becomes very cluttered and difficult to read. If there are many small categories (as was the case with the pie chart

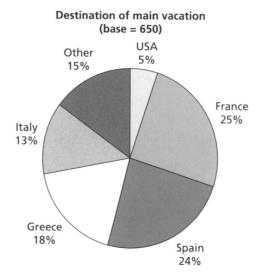

Figure 10.3 An example of a pie chart

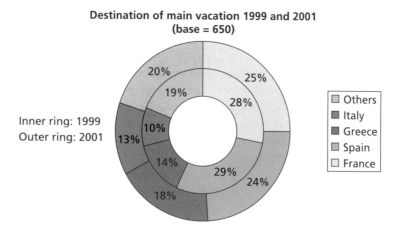

Figure 10.4 A doughnut chart

in Figure 10.3), these can be lumped into an 'Other' category to avoid overcrowding the chart. Using different colours or shading for the various slices improves the chart's effectiveness. As pie charts will normally show percentages, it is important that the base or sample size is shown. Also, the percentages for each segment should be included as some of the audience may have difficulty in determining the relative difference between segments.

A variety of pie charts are possible. For example, Figure 10.4 shows a derivative of the pie chart which takes the form of a 'doughnut'. The doughnut chart can be used to show different sets of data. For example, Figure 10.4 shows 1999 data in the inner doughnut and 2001 data in the outer doughnut. With many of the data processing packages that are now available, three-dimensional pie charts are also possible. These look impressive but can sometimes be difficult for the audience to interpret.

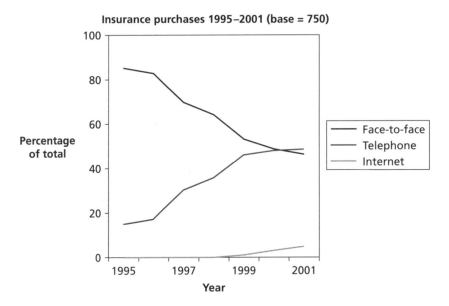

Figure 10.5 An example of a line graph

Line graphs

A line graph is a two-dimensional graph that is typically used to show movements in data over time. Several series of data can be compared on the same chart using lines of different colours or format. A glance at Figure 10.5 shows the dramatic change in the way respondents purchased their insurance products over the period 1995–2001. Similar to pie charts, the base should be shown and the number of lines should be limited (with a maximum of around 4–5) otherwise the graph becomes cluttered and confusing.

Bar charts

A bar chart consists of a series of bars that may be positioned horizontally or vertically to represent the values of a variety of items. Figure 10.6 shows a bar chart representing the same data as shown using the pie chart in Figure 10.3. This raises the question as to when bar charts rather than pie charts should be used. The rule of thumb is that pie charts are better for illustrating relative data or percentages (e.g. market shares) where the number of items is less than 6 or 7 components. Bar charts are more appropriate for illustrating actual or absolute numbers such as sales figures or where the number of items is more than 7. Stacked bar charts as shown in Figure 10.7 tend to be used instead of multiple pie charts when space within the report or presentation is limited.

Pictograms

A pictogram is a special type of bar chart which uses pictures (such as bottles, cars, money) of the items rather than bars. An example of this is shown in Figure 10.8 relating to apples. Pictograms can be more interesting and appealing where the audience

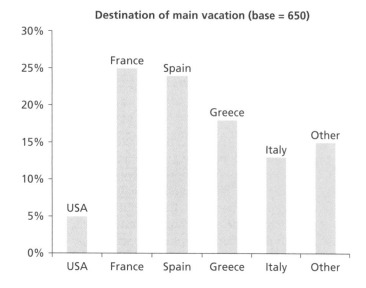

Figure 10.6 An example of a bar chart

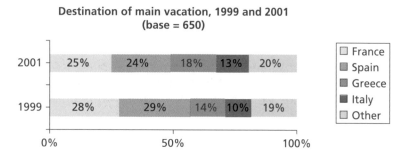

Figure 10.7 An example of a stacked bar chart

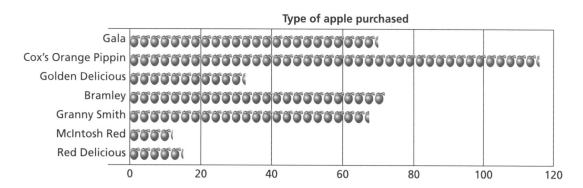

Figure 10.8 An example of a pictogram

is unused to using statistics and graphs. This is one of the reasons why they are commonly used in newspapers and television programmes aimed at the general public.

Common dangers in the reporting and presentation of results

There are a number of areas where new researchers regularly fail to take account of the decision maker's thinking sequence. These are:

- **Assuming understanding**: some researchers will present tables and graphs in reports and presentations with very little commentary as to how the figures should be interpreted. The researchers may simply put up a visual of the data and repeat the numbers shown. It is dangerous to assume that the audience will interpret the data in the same manner as the researcher. It can be very tedious for the audience to read page after page of data without any explanation of what they mean. The audience will simply skip pages in the report or lose attention and start dreaming in the presentation.

- **Excessive length**: exceedingly long reports or lengthy presentations may give researchers the opportunity to demonstrate their extensive knowledge on a subject. However, they annoy decision makers as the key points get lost in the excessive detail and the results are devalued. Excessive length suggests a lack of clear thinking on behalf of the researcher.

> **Client quote:** *Some researchers go on and on. They don't consider the fact that we have other meetings to attend and decisions to make. We therefore don't concentrate on what they are saying.*

- **Unrealistic recommendations**: providing naïve recommendations which are beyond the financial capabilities of the client organisation or which do not take account of their organisational structures and overall strategy.

- **Spurious accuracy**: as computers may produce data to two or even three decimal places, some researchers also present them to this level. On many samples, particularly where the sample size is below 200–300 respondents, such accuracy is meaningless. For example, one recent marketing research report quoted figures of 47.08 per cent on a sample of 80 respondents. What does 0.08 per cent mean? It is around 1/15 of a respondent. Such spurious accuracy is totally misleading as it gives credibility to the data, which cannot be justified, particularly on a sample of 80. In the main, researchers should stick to whole numbers.

- **Obscure statistics**: some researchers may use obscure statistical techniques to cover up the fact that the data shows very little. This is becoming more common as a result of computer analysis being able to throw up all types of statistical measures (many of which involve very complex procedures) at the touch of a button. Although the researcher may believe that this will impress the client, it may result in a non-technical marketing manager rejecting the report, branding it as being too academic.

- **Too much gloss and no substance**: producing charts or an oral presentation which are very eye catching, colourful and entertaining but fail to communicate the information that the decision maker requires. For example, a PowerPoint presentation using animated features, sound, video clips and 3D effects may impress the client or may raise questions as to how much time was spent on the presentation rather than the data gathering and analysis. The client may miss the key points because he or she is too engrossed in examining the visuals. Alternatively, the visuals may not work as intended. For example, the projector, computer, lighting or the layout of the room may limit the effectiveness of any glossy presentation. With reports, these may be photocopied by the client, resulting in poor quality (or black and white) reproductions of complex graphics being seen by key decision makers.

Presentations on the Internet

The report or presentation can also be placed on the Internet or on a company's intranet, enabling decision makers to access the presentation, regardless of where they are in the world or when they need to access it. The presentation can take exactly the same format as it does when being done in a boardroom or meeting room. Reports can be provided as PDF files, which will provide the same graphical and layout format as the physical document, or can be turned into an interactive document where the reader can click on particular tables or sections to obtain further, more detailed information. Sound and even video clips from focus groups can be added. It should be noted, however, that the principles and guidelines outlined in this chapter are as relevant to communication via the Internet as they are to the more traditional methods of communication.

Summary

Report writing skills and presentation skills are very important to the marketing research process. Researchers need to think from the reader's or audience's perspective and consider what it is that the clients want to hear, as well as the likely manner in which they will want it communicated. Understanding the audience's thinking sequence will assist with this. Research reports, presentations and Internet reports should be structured and prepared in a style which eases understanding, maintains interest and follows a logical sequence. Modern software has made the creation of impressive presentations available to almost everyone, but even with such technology, there are a number of basic presentation guidelines that the researcher needs to follow if a quality presentation that results in quality communication is to be delivered. These include maintaining eye contact, varying elements of the presentation, minimising complexity, checking understanding, providing handouts, acting naturally, finishing on a high note, rehearsing and clarifying questions.

A variety of tables and charts can be used to enhance the clarity and effectiveness of communication. This chapter has identified those that are most commonly used (tables, pie charts, line graphs, bar charts and pictograms) but there are an infinite number of possibilities. However, care must be taken to ensure that these ease understanding and do not cause confusion or mislead readers.

The chapter finished with a description of some of the most common flaws seen in the communication of marketing research results. Awareness of these should ensure that good research is not undermined by poor communication.

Discussion questions

1 In what ways should the content of a presentation differ from that of a report?

2 What are the key guidelines for producing tables?

3 By what criteria would you evaluate a research report? Develop an evaluation form for assessing these.

4 By what criteria would you evaluate an oral presentation? Develop an evaluation form for assessing these.

5 Why is the executive summary such a critical component of a research report?

6 Distinguish between findings, executive summaries, conclusions and recommendations.

7 In presentations, why is eye contact so critical?

8 Go through a quality Sunday newspaper and pick out any three graphical illustrations. Explain what types of charts they are and critically evaluate their strengths and weaknesses.

9 Describe the audience's thinking sequence and identify its implications for the researcher.

10 Think about all the good presentations that you have witnessed. What made them so good?

Additional reading

Hague, P. and Roberts, C. (1994) *Presentation and Report Writing*. Kogan Page, London.

Reference

[1] Adapted from Thygesen, F. and McGowan, P. (2002) Inspiring the organisation to act: a business in denial, *MRS Research Conference*, March, Brighton.

Marketing research in action: case histories[1]

Case 1
Skoda – *researching brand values*

Case 2
AIR MILES – *researching advertising effectiveness*

Case 3
Medical research on hypertension – *researching behaviour*

Case 4
Birmingham Airport – *researching customer satisfaction*

Case 5
Age Concern – *researching policy issues*

Case 6
BT Cellnet – *researching new services*

Case 7
Glasgow Underground – *researching customer characteristics*

Case 8
Allied Domecq – *researching lifestyles*

Case 9
Carlsberg-Tetley – *communicating research to the board*

[1] These case histories were originally published in *Research*, and have been reproduced here with the permission of the Market Research Society.

Case 1
Skoda – researching brand values

Human Touch[1]

Skoda's fortunes improved after market research helped to turn a brand that was a laughing stock into something that people could warm to, says Simon Lidington.

Seven years ago, when Skoda UK commissioned Quadrangle to help it develop a five-year strategy to transform the brand, Skoda was a joke. Literally. Over a period of six months we conducted almost 30 group discussions with owners, non-owners and rejecters up and down the country. Without exception, respondents would spend at least the first 20 minutes telling 'Skoda jokes'.

Early quantitative research revealed a 98 per cent prompted awareness of the name, but less than a 1 per cent awareness of the models. It was not a car brand, but a cultural phenomenon – just like mothers-in-law. The task was to transform what *Campaign* magazine reckoned to be the lowest rated brand for any product in any sector, into a brand with a positive image. Skoda posed us a number of key questions:

- are there any potential positives in Skoda's brand values that can be built upon?
- what core values do we want people to associate with the new Skoda?
- what is the potential for the brand if we successfully change its image?

This presented us with a serious research problem: we could not simply analyse what defined Skoda currently. What mattered was what Skoda could become, rather than what it was.

We used our qualitative approach, Open Research, designed to reveal potential opportunities in the market rather than simply reflecting and recording the accumulation of history. Nearly all of the work was done using three to four hour group discussions. There was no topic guide or any specific questions. Respondents did not know the research was for Skoda until near the end of the discussion.

This proved vitally important in comparing open and unqualified discussion of their lives – the part cars play in them, brands (in general), car brands, Skoda (if it came up) – with discussion of Skoda when introduced three hours into the discussion, posing questions such as: How interested were they in Skoda? Did they know anything about Skoda? Was there any warmth towards the brand? Did they know about Volkswagen's ownership?

This sociological approach placed the emphasis on hearing about the way people lead their lives: their frustrations, prejudices, likes, dislikes, desires, what they despise and admire. It also meant ignoring much of the surface noise. Importantly, consumers were not asked to 'play brand director'. As research consultants we had the responsibility to deploy a method that enabled them to paint a landscape in which to place Skoda then, and Skoda in the future.

From the Open Research we identified key elements of Skoda's brand image that would drive change. It was vital to know the dimensions on which Skoda had to change to become credible, those that were susceptible to change in consumers' perceptions, and those that were already latently positive in the Skoda brand.

We identified that Skoda's values are not car values, they are to do with people who have life in perspective, are interested in community and friends, who value a 'what you see is what you get' approach, and who are not interested in flashiness. Skoda's values are to do with people and the way they lead their lives.

From this research they developed a clear set of values defined as 'The Human Touch': honesty and integrity; friendliness; accessibility; genuine value; sense of humour; people; rapid and sustained improvement; credibility; and modernity. Clearly, the last three were a consequence of change. But they were also the vital indicators used by consumers to articulate success. For that reason alone they had to be integral to the definition of Skoda's transformation in the public psyche.

Then there was the stark finding that the overwhelming majority of the car-buying public said that they would never, under any circumstances, consider buying a Skoda. The strength of the negative brand image came as little surprise to the Skoda management team. But the potential was far richer than expected. We recommended a strategy that involved:

- Targeting the susceptibles: using TGI, it was found that about 17 per cent of the car-buying population identified with an interlocking set of questions based on the values set out above. Together with the findings from the Open Research this strongly suggested that there was a group of consumers whose latent affinity to Skoda could be targeted.

- Using Volkswagen: consumers needed to believe that Skoda could be credible. Volkswagen's ownership provided an instantly recognisable seal of improvement, quality, and modernity.

- Creating a perception of change: the qualitative research had shown that the difference between Skoda being seen as good value for money rather than cheap and nasty was directly linked to consumer's perceptions of real and sustained improvement.

- Using exposure marketing: the entrenched prejudice against Skoda meant that susceptibles would be more effectively reached 'in the metal' rather than simply via any advertising medium.

- Developing the brand based on 'The Human Touch': building on Skoda's values in everything it did and said about itself.

The new Felicia was launched in the summer of 1995. A comparison of the image ratings most closely related to the key values measured pre-launch, six, and twelve

Table 1 Skoda image ratings.

	May 95	Sep 95	Jun 96
Offers modern designs	−39%	−31%	−11%
Produces good quality cars	−11%	−6%	+3%
An honest and down to earth company	+20%	+30%	+31%
Is a trustworthy company	+6%	+30%	+31%
Cars have improved recently	−7%	+38%	+46%

Source: Quadrangle Research.

months post-launch, shows the gains made during this crucial period. Figures for the first four statements (see Table 1 above) are consistently based on the net difference between those agreeing and those disagreeing with each of the statements. The figures for 'cars have improved recently' are based on a slightly different scale for May 1995, but the principle of 'net strength' is consistent.

Much of the movement in image can be attributed to the arrival of the Felicia itself, and to increasing awareness of Volkswagen's ownership. But marketing played a crucial part. The launch advertising was designed to jolt the 'susceptibles' out of their 'accepted wisdom' perception of Skoda. 'We've changed the car, can you change your mind?' was based on a strategy of straight talking, no hype, confident but not arrogant communication. It was intended to create a perception of dynamism, change and improvement.

A concerted trade and consumer PR campaign also helped Skoda gain unprecedentedly wide coverage, with a message designed to emphasise the Volkswagen link, credibility, change, improvement, and modernity. Both the advertising and PR effectively tapped into the susceptibles' sense of fair play.

While the image ratings had moved, consideration levels were relatively unchanged. Nor was there any immediate leap in sales. In 1992 Skoda sold 8,000 cars. In 1995 it sold 11,000. During the next two years, however, Skoda's sales started to accelerate. A continued focus on converting the susceptibles through test drive campaigns, exposure marketing and consumer PR, reaped sales rewards.

Our view is that Skoda's impressive growth has been the result of identifying a clear set of values, establishing credibility, and unlocking the latent potential among the susceptibles, rather than focusing on the rejecters, who are a much longer term challenge.

Since the launch of the Octavia in 1998, Skoda's image has further improved. Rising sales have also continued. In 1999 Skoda is on track to sell 24,000 cars.

Simon Lidington is joint managing partner at Quadrangle.

[1] This case history appeared in the October 1999 edition of *Research*, pp. 33–4, and is published with the permission of the Market Research Society.

Case 2
AIR MILES – researching advertising effectiveness

Loyal air force[1]

A multimedia approach to research helped AIR MILES to develop its latest campaign, report Sarah Hayward, Helen Mennis and Bethan Cork.

AIR MILES, founded in 1988, is the pioneer of customer loyalty schemes. Although hundreds of loyalty schemes have been introduced subsequently, including, more recently, online schemes, AIR MILES remains the UK's leading brand in this market with 6 million customers and 90 per cent awareness of the brand among its target audience – ABC1 adults aged between 25 and 54. The company has built up its business by forming partnerships through well-known companies through which customers collect AIR MILES.

The Who Joins Wins campaign was developed by ad agency Bartle Bogle Hegarty. Anybody who joined the AIR MILES scheme during the campaign was entered into a prize draw, and was guaranteed a prize, ranging from a cinema ticket to one million AIR MILES. The marketing objective was to increase new registrations by 250,000 during the campaign.

The target audience for the campaign was ABC1 adults aged between 25 and 54. The campaign budget was in the region of £1m, so TV was not an option. Instead radio and press were used with additional point of sale material at petrol station forecourts and supermarkets. Radio advertising was used to arouse interest and generate excitement; press executions, which followed later, were designed to give more detail. Titles and stations were chosen to give greatest coverage of the target audience. Forty radio stations with an estimated coverage of 65 per cent of the target audience and 7.1 OTH (opportunities to hear); seven daily papers and six Sunday supplement magazines with an estimated coverage of 75 per cent of the target audience and 8.5 OTS (opportunities to see) were used.

Research was used to evaluate the advertising at all stages, from testing creative concepts through to analysis post launch.

Forrest Associates undertook the qualitative research during campaign development. The objectives at this stage were twofold:

- to ascertain whether the key message was clear and understood;
- to gauge whether or not people felt a sense of 'you'd be mad not to take part'.

More specifically the following elements were tested:

- did individual executions involve, communicate and motivate?
- was the prize draw itself understood and did people feel it was relevant to them?
- was the campaign promoting the AIR MILES brand as fun, exciting and enjoyable?

Forrest ran eight focus groups: five groups of non AIR MILES collectors (but non rejecters of loyalty schemes) and three groups of current 'passive' AIR MILES collectors, who only currently collect with one AIR MILES partner. The primary purpose of the campaign was to increase the number of new AIR MILES collectors but it also wanted to prompt 'passive' collectors to start collecting with another partner.

As a result of this work, AIR MILES gained an understanding of which executions had the greater appeal, and was able to structure the media buying to reflect this. BBH was also able to make changes to the radio ads.

Once the campaign had been finalised AIR MILES needed research to evaluate its effectiveness:

- Were people aware of it?
- What impact was it having on future behaviour?
- What was the effect of specific ad executions?

BMRB International was commissioned to undertake this stage of the advertising evaluation. There were a number of issues that we needed to address before designing the research.

A critical consideration for AIR MILES was sufficiently robust sample sizes to allow for analysis of key groups, in particular current and potential collectors. The former accounted for 11 per cent of the adult population and the latter, defined as people who either shopped at Sainsbury's, owned a NatWest credit card, owned a Vodafone or bought Shell petrol/diesel (key partners in the scheme), accounted for 34 per cent.

Within these groups, it was important to provide enough people who recalled the advertising. Previous research conducted by AIR MILES had produced very low levels of recall with sample sizes too small to permit reliable sub-group analyses.

Finally and true of almost every research project the client had a restricted budget!

We decided the best solution was to conduct the research among a nationally representative sample of adults aged 18+ within the UK and not to restrict the sample to people who fell into the key groups only. This enabled us to compare the advertising effects among the target groups versus the rest of the population. We collected the information via a face-to-face omnibus survey enabling us to cost-effectively screen a large number of people to identify the 'niche' groups, with fieldwork costs shared by all the clients who had questions on the surveys used.

In order to maximise recall of the advertising we opted for multimedia technology for the interviewing. This is only marginally more expensive than traditional CAPI, with a small administration charge for the costs of preparing/editing ad clips, pressing them on to CD and despatching to the interviewers.

While the most obvious benefit of multimedia data collection is for TV advertising, here we felt there were advantages in integrating the radio ads into the computerised questionnaire and playing them to respondents via soundcards:

- a number of different executions needed to be tested. We were able to guarantee effective rotation and hence eliminate any order bias;
- it avoided the expense of producing multiple tape copies and sending interviewers portable cassette players;
- it avoided the use of a free-phone number and the reliance on respondents agreeing to call it.

Three waves of research were conducted, before, during and after the campaign. A total of nine radio executions (six in Great Britain and three in Northern Ireland) and five press executions were tested at the second and third waves (mid and post campaign) of research. Each respondent was played three radio ads and shown three press ads towards the end of the interview. These were rotated (within media) so that each execution had an equal chance of being heard or seen first. In the words of Bethan Cork, research manager at AIR MILES: 'This is the most successful ad campaign research project we have ever undertaken. Armed with this research we will be able to develop clearly defined and targeted ad campaigns in the future.'

The key points that came out of the research that AIR MILES will take on board when developing future campaigns were that the role of the different media worked well to stretch the reach of the campaign; findings echoed what had been seen in earlier research, i.e. that a major barrier to collection is still a perception that AIR MILES can only be used for free air travel; and in terms of future intentions to collect AIR MILES, the greatest increase throughout the campaign was among 18 to 24 year olds, a group which had never before been identified as potential collectors. If we had opted to research the target groups only and not recommended extending sample coverage to all adults this would not have been discovered.

The overall key learning from this research was that the messages used in future campaigns need to be kept as simple and clear as possible.

So was the advertising successful? Yes, in terms of meeting the marketing objective. The research showed that 14 per cent of adults not currently registered with the scheme would be likely to collect AIR MILES in the future. It was also successful by using two media that effectively complemented one another.

The main learning point, for AIR MILES and the ad agency, was the realisation that it is possible to cost effectively develop a robust and effective measurement of a multimedia campaign (be it a relatively modest one at £1m!), with careful thought and planning. One of the reasons it worked so well was the collaborative effect – all parties, the ad agency, the client and the research agency – worked closely together at every stage, from the development of the first creatives, to the final stage of the post campaign tracking. And not only was the research effective, but 350,000 new customers registered to collect AIR MILES, over the period of the campaign.

Sarah Hayward and Helen Mennis are research consultant and director respectively at BMRB International. Bethan Cork is research manager at AIR MILES.

[1] This case history appeared in the August 2000 edition of *Research*, pp. 37–8, and is published with the permission of the Market Research Society.

Case 3
Medical research on hypertension – researching behaviour

Hard to swallow?[1]

A recent study examined the reasons why patients don't always take their medicine. Roger Brice looks at the results.

This article summarises the background, methodology and the main conclusions of an international study to improve knowledge of the reasons for non-compliance with drug therapy for hypertension. MR methods were chosen to assess the viability and value of investing in a more expensive and time-consuming longitudinal clinical study. The work also led to important conclusions in its own right.

Hypertension – high blood pressure – is a major risk factor for stroke, cardiovascular and renal morbidity and mortality. Control of high blood pressure reduces the incidence of these complications. Yet adequate blood pressure control occurs in only around one-quarter of patients, with inadequate treatment adherence being a major problem. In other words, the majority of people either do not continue to take their medicine, or vary their consumption of it.

The ability of physicians to identify which patients will not comply is also limited. A better understanding of the relationship between patient perceptions and hypertension treatment compliance was desirable, therefore, to identify factors that can be addressed by the physician. Ideally, this should be through the treating physician being able to identify, in advance, a patient's likelihood of not complying with therapy – continuing their treatment – and understand the reasons for it. This would enable an individually tailored compliance strategy to be devised.

The ideal method of studying the problem would be to conduct a clinical observational study. However, this approach would involve both significant cost and time: a seven-figure sum, and up to three years, would have to be allowed for data collection and analysis. It was decided that a feasibility study was required. It was with this goal and also with the expectation of, in itself, adding to the understanding of non-compliance and how to affect it that the current research exercise was conducted.

Objectives

The quantitative research summarised here followed two earlier qualitative studies, comprising in depth individual interviews and focus groups with hypertensive patients, their partners, and treating physicians.

This early research identified that, while treatment experiences can be similar, individual reactions to treatment, plus varying understanding of hypertension control, results in differing compliance behaviours. A separate group of hypertensive patients was also observed who were essentially asymptomatic or whose symptoms (of whatever nature) had been recently relieved. These people were likely to think of themselves as being cured.

The quantitative study, therefore, included exploring the role of self-reported health status as an influence on compliance behaviour in hypertension. Self-reported health status was assumed to be a proxy measure of patients' perceptions of their clinical condition. We also examined whether patients reporting fewer or no symptoms of ill-health were likely to be non-compliant with their therapy. If so, this might be based on an incorrect assumption that continued pharmacotherapy was unnecessary.

Methods

In the interests of time and economy, respondents were identified through a number of different sources including general practice records, responses to newspaper advertisements, and from leisure, retirement and unemployment centres.

A sample of 730 hypertensive patients was recruited from France, Germany, Italy, Canada and the United States. These patients had been newly treated patients (within the previous 3–18 months) diagnosed with hypertension, but lacking cardiovascular conditions such as angina or heart failure.

Identification of compliance was based on self-reporting, using the question 'Which of the following statements best describes you?' The response choices were as follows, with items 1 and 2 being combined to define non-compliers:

1 I have been prescribed medication for my high blood pressure, but I have never taken it.
2 I have taken medication for my high blood pressure in the past, but I am not taking the medication now.
3 I am currently taking medication for my high blood pressure, but I am not taking it exactly as instructed by my doctor (e.g. I could be taking less of the drug or not taking it regularly, among other things).
4 I am currently taking medication for my high blood pressure, and I am taking medication exactly as the doctor instructed.

An additional question, 'How often have you taken hypertension medication in the last four weeks?', was included to serve as a response consistency check.

Health status was measured through a standard self-reporting scoring system of physical and mental functioning. The Physical Component Score (PCS) includes two physical functioning items, two items on role limitations related to physical functioning, one item about bodily pain and a final item about general health.

Variables included in the final model were specified following univariate and sequential multivariate analyses, and also hypotheses around their association with compliance from the qualitative research. These variables were:

- risk factors (smoking, alcohol, family history)
- blood pressure
- various socio-economic parameters
- healthcare service satisfaction
- healthcare service expectations.

Responses to the two compliance questions were compared. Subjects who provided inconsistent responses to these questions were excluded from further analysis.

Conclusions

The analysis of the data supported the hypothesis that health status is associated with compliance. Non-compliers also reported a lack of satisfaction with assistance from healthcare providers and a desire for the physician to inspire trust. It is tempting to interpret these results as indicating that a lack of satisfaction with the healthcare delivery is a predictor of non-compliance. Such interpretation from cross-sectional data is dangerous and potentially misleading. It has been identified that a lack of satisfaction with the medical services could also be a post-event rationalisation, emerging after the decision not to comply.

This possible interpretation of the results demonstrates that further, large-scale research is required to explore the role of patient perceptions on compliance. The need for physicians to measure their own success beyond the short term lowering of blood pressure is also demonstrated. Should this lead to a patient perception of success, this very 'success' with treatment may, in itself, lead to non-compliance with drug therapy necessary for the long term goals of hypertension treatment. It can be argued, therefore, that physicians need to be extra vigilant in these situations and that the implied necessary extra time would be more efficiently allocated if the more likely non-compliers could be identified.

Roger Brice is research director at The Adelphi Group.

[1] This case history appeared in the January 2000 edition of *Research*, pp. 40–1, and is published with the permission of the Market Research Society.

Case 4
Birmingham Airport – researching customer satisfaction

Airport Blues[1]

How do you measure the moods and emotions of all types of airport passenger? By a particular form of group discussion, says Tim Baker.

Birmingham International Airport (BIA) has enjoyed consistently high levels of customer satisfaction since measurement began. Passengers have always rated BIA more highly than its nearest serious competitors – Manchester, Heathrow and Gatwick – on all key measures: ease of access, staff attitudes, speed of processing, and the provision of facilities.

BIA has become the airport of choice for many in the West Midlands and from further afield.

The measurement of customer satisfaction has been taken in the traditional UK airport way: specially trained and security-passed interviewers circulate in the airport, interviewing a representative sample of passengers, asking them to rate their satisfaction with each factor. All major airports in the UK operate exclusive fieldforces, providing a data collection facility for internal purposes that remains consistent and sensitive to the special circumstances of airports and their customers.

It became clear, however, that BIA risked becoming a victim of its own success. Increasing numbers of passengers were keen to use BIA as their preferred gateway, airlines had seen the benefits of offering services direct to the UK's second city, and the local authority which controlled the airport at the time was keen to benefit from the increased revenue opportunity such expansion offered. This was a compelling case, and plans for expansion were made.

The airport was to get an additional terminal building, the existing building was to be enlarged, and there were to be expanded car parking areas and increases in all the supporting infrastructure needed to facilitate a growth from around six million passengers a year to more than double this figure. Services inside the terminal buildings would also need to be developed – check-ins, security gates, catering, customer services, retail facilities, and so on. This would clearly signal a significant change in the character and atmosphere of Birmingham Airport.

Proud of its excellent customer satisfaction record, this projected expansion presented the authorities with two key service challenges:

- How to maintain the high ratings through the development process and as the new airport emerged. While it was inevitable that there would be disruption and inconvenience in the short term to customers (and staff), BIA needed to check for the roots of any dissatisfaction as the works progressed.

- How to ensure that satisfaction was being measured on the right criteria, using the right vocabulary. Through the changes, perhaps other, 'new' issues would become more important to customers. This might also be the case once the developments were completed. It was clearly important that the ongoing quantitative measure remained flexible and could reflect the core issues. To this end, MRSL was commissioned by BIA to conduct a series of Insight On Site™ qualitative sessions with airport users.

Insight On Site™ is a unique qualitative research method developed by MRSL to allow group discussions to be conducted with respondent types that may be difficult to reach through conventional means. Originally designed for use at airports, the method is now used at exhibitions, visitor attractions and other places where people congregate to use the products or services under discussion.

Each session lasts between two and two-and-a-half hours, during which time between 16 and 30 respondents attend the discussion. Respondents are recruited at the time of the research by experienced interviewers. The method allows MRSL to gain the types of qualitative insight that are normally only available from group discussions, from people that would not normally be available or inclined to attend these discussions.

The sessions first commissioned provided a qualitative review of the departure process, from arriving at the airport through check-in, security, the use of the facilities, and so on. A corresponding view of arrivals was also obtained. Critically, we were able to provide a view to BIA management of the mix of moods and emotions felt by all types of passenger as they actually 'experience' the airport. A quite different view will be given (by, say, a commuting business passenger who cannot get a fresh breakfast) when the airport facilities are being discussed on site rather than being discussed at some later stage in a conventional group discussion. In addition to the regular quantitative analysis, management were thus given first-hand experiences from passengers of all types. This provided a more detailed understanding of response, and the reasons why ratings vary.

Passengers in airports are in a stressful situation. Typically, a passenger is not at rest until seated in the departure lounge. And many passengers will not visit an airport more than twice a year (indeed the bulk will visit only once or less often) and this effectively means that the passenger is rediscovering the experience each time. They may be sent to BIA by a travel company, or they may have chosen BIA as their preferred departure point. In either case, they will talk to friends, family and colleagues about the experience of BIA and this will affect the actions of many other potential visitors. The same can be said to be true of more frequent flyers: while they will accept mistakes that are corrected, they will be intolerant of continuous poor service, and will eventually vote with their feet. Importantly, they will also try to influence other flyers.

The Insight On Site™ sessions were conducted at regular intervals through the development process and continue to provide a regular dipstick monitor of customer moods. Specific areas where BIA has been able to respond quickly and effectively to customer needs include:

- Provision of information through the development process. Leaflets and other information about the development, the stages it would go through and the ways it would immediately inconvenience and ultimately benefit passengers had, of course, been made available to all visitors to the airport. We were able to quickly determine the most appropriate ways to communicate this information. In addition to leaflets that would need to be picked up by the customer, posters were put up showing various stages of the work and giving artists' impressions of the final phase. Other vantage points were also used to give customers information, so that BIA was perceived to be proactive, giving information rather than simply expecting customers to get the information for themselves.

- Determining the most appropriate retail mix in the departure lounge. Many customers had specific requirements of BIA which would help the airport maintain its distinct, personal and friendly character. Rather than simply emulate other airports, BIA has been able to build on particular customer responses and needs. This has been doubly important as duty free sales in the EC have ended and shops needed to offer a more tailored and attractive service.

- As a result of the group work, our quantitative surveys showed an increase in customer satisfaction for both retail and catering choice, with catering showing a 6 per cent increase in satisfaction and retail showing a 12 per cent increase.

- Identifying the key stress points for customers as they move through the airport. This identification gives a better understanding of the pressure points, why they exist and the specific needs of the customer as they go through them. This in turn helps to identify the need for specific staff training and leads to improved customer relations.

- A similar result has been obtained in security, one of the most stressful areas when passing through an airport. This area has shown a 6 per cent increase in satisfaction.

- A major cause of customer frustration at airports is not being able to find their way. This is a particularly complex issue. Both externally and internally, our work has helped BIA understand which signs work less well, where signs are needed so that they direct customers at the key points (that is, where does the customer pause and look for information and where do they simply carry on?), and the information that is needed on the signs.

These and other issues have been addressed for BIA so that the new airport is sensitive to customer needs and responsive to their issues. Our work has continued since the completion of the airport developments, providing board level feedback and insight into: all currently identified customer service issues; the vocabulary used by passengers; the changing needs of customers; and competitive performance.

In the old days we had to rely on conventional quantitative surveys and feedback from passengers. Now, qualitative feedback from on-site work provides first-hand information on both the negative and positive aspects of the airport, and we have been able to address these issues with the knowledge that we are satisfying our customers' needs.

Tim Baker is joint MD of MRSL.

[1] This case history appeared in the December 2000 edition of *Research*, pp. 35–6, and is published with the permission of the Market Research Society.

Case 5
Age Concern – researching policy issues

Helling the aged[1]

The challenge was to survey 500 delegates and have the findings ready during a high-profile policy conference. Chris Watson and Caspar Tearle explain.

In the first few decades of the new millennium the UK population structure will be transformed, with fewer young people and more older people. The dramatic implications of this historically unprecedented change will affect everything from housing, transport and pensions to health, community care, public attitudes and the labour market.

The Debate of the Age committee was formed to look into public perception and some issues surrounding the impact of this change. Co-ordinated by Age Concern, The Debate of the Age was formally launched by Tony Blair in March 1998, with three specific goals:

- to raise awareness about the ageing society
- to provide a forum where people of all ages and walks of life could debate the implications of this change
- to influence public policy in matters relating to demographic ageing.

The debate championed a huge research effort involving two nation-wide surveys, numerous focus groups, citizens' juries and the UK's first citizens' forum. The research programme involved a number of partners both in research and other sectors. BMRB Direct was commissioned to process and analyse the responses to questionnaires from the public, and also to deal with the collation and dissemination of key findings from the final conference.

Nearing the end of the work of the debate, the research had identified 35 issues that public opinion deemed worthy of government investigation. These issues created the agenda for the final conference of the debate, which was held at Greenwich in December 1999.

The conference was attended by over 500 people, drawn from business, charities, education and government.

The participants, as part of the day, were asked to consider the 35 propositions that had been generated during the last two years and rate them in terms of importance.

Final research

The research challenge was to gather, process, analyse, report and present the views of the participants – all within a deadline of just two hours. The results would then feed directly into an address to the delegates being given by the chairman of the Financial Services Authority, Howard Davies. The project was scheduled to run as follows:

- 12.50: delegates begin filling in questionnaires
- 1.15: completed questionnaires begin to come in and are fed through scanner
- 2.15: final questionnaires arrive, scanning completed and data transferred out of system
- 2.20: analysis run and data reported
- 2.40: presentation delivered to client on disk, ready for Howard Davies to present.

In fact, the delegates did not start completing the questionnaire until 1:15. There was a team of fully briefed facilitators whose role was to advise on the questionnaire, and ferry the completed forms to the waiting scanning team. In all, 403 completed questionnaires were returned, a response rate of over 80 per cent.

To be able to return the results in the allotted time required a fully operational scanning system set up on the premises. The portable equipment had been pre-tested and installed the day before. Howard Davies needed to have a simplified and ranked set of proposals to ensure that he could present the results cogently.

The data from the scanned questionnaires were processed and quickly outputted to a common format. The raw data were then interpreted and reported on laptop by a waiting researcher, and having been fed into a set of presentation charts, they were handed on disk to the speaker.

The results

The questionnaire required the delegate to consider the 35 propositions and decide whether each required 'immediate action', whether it was something for 'mid-term action' or 'less immediate action'. These were given a weight of 100, 50 or 0 respectively and the weighted results for the highest scoring proposals can be seen in the table.

Questionnaire results: propositions for an ageing society (base: all respondents – 403)

Proposal	Ranking Score
Proposal 30: The government should introduce equal opportunities legislation enshrining the principle of age neutrality so that individuals can no longer be denied access to health care, employment, financial services and other support simply on the grounds of age	83.88
Proposal 11: To improve the take-up of benefits the government should produce more straightforward application forms in appropriate languages and publicise their availability through a wide range of networks and outlets	83.21

Proposal	Ranking Score
Proposal 35: The government's resolve to listen to older people's views and reflect them through a 'joined-up' approach to policy at a national and local level is welcome. This needs to be sustained and strengthened in future as our society ages.	81.79
Proposal 13: The state pension should be immediately uprated to the same level as the Minimum Income Guarantee and thereafter both should be uprated in line with economic growth	78.24
Proposal 3: Rationing of health care should not be made on the basis of age but through a transparent system where an individual clinical assessment is made, including consideration of the likely quality and length of a patient's life after they receive the treatment	76.92

The publication

Age Concern wanted the findings of the Debate of the Age to be made public as a matter of urgency on the day of the conference. The audience to be informed was drawn from government, public and related sectors. In total there were over 3,500 parties to be notified, including:

- UK MPs – at their constituency address or at the House of Commons
- members of Welsh, Scottish and Northern Ireland Assemblies
- members of the House of Lords – at home/place of work or at the House of Lords
- heads of local authorities
- heads of education and housing for local authorities
- heads of health authorities and NHS trusts
- regional development agencies
- Age Concern organisations.

To handle the complex task of distributing these findings, BMRB Direct worked with specialist agency Telescope, which sourced contact information and handled the implementation of the delivery programme. Due to the urgency of notification needed the information was distributed using (in order of preference): email, fax and post. Sensitive parts of the distribution list were screened by the Mail Preference Service and Fax Preference Service to ensure conformity with data protection requirements.

The results were emailed and faxed immediately after the final conference so that they would be available on desk or PC the following morning.

Subsequent email replies were captured and forwarded to the client. Any errors encountered were checked and re-tried. If the problem recurred, these individuals were contacted by another method. Faxes were tried three times during the evening and any failures were retried the next morning. Finally, if email or fax contact failed, the results were posted.

The future

'Agenda for the Age', the debate's final report, is due to be presented to government in May this year. This will present key findings from debates around the country and incorporate recommendations from the policy symposium, from interim reports and from the Greenwich conference.

The agenda is likely to have three main sections:

- priorities for individuals – drawn from all the public responses
- priorities for organisations – drawn from the experience and research of all our hundreds of debate partners
- priorities for government – drawn from all the research, discussion and debate activity.

The aim of the debate was to employ research to uncover the considered opinions of the public, and to use that information to help inform government in addressing policy issues.

Chris Watson and Caspar Tearle are director and senior associate director respectively at BMRB Direct.

[1] This case history appeared in the March 2000 edition of *Research*, pp. 35–6, and is published with the permission of the Market Research Society.

Case 6
BT Cellnet – researching new services

Mobile moods[1]

Finding out what consumers really want from new technology is all the harder when you are dealing with the fast-moving mobile phones sector. Claire Thomas describes how the old-fashioned dictaphone played a part in an innovative research programme.

Working in a market where technology is moving ahead rapidly poses challenges for research. It is difficult to get a reliable steer on what consumers would like to be able to do in the future. The best we can hope for is a series of 'what if' scenarios. There is also an ever more pressing need to offer clients guidance on how to move forward and to provide insight into their target market.

This was the situation we faced when we recently conducted a programme of qualitative research for BT Cellnet exploring consumers' wants from future mobile technology. Included in the research were areas such as mobile internet and WAP phones. In this scenario, traditional qualitative research struggles to facilitate respondents to anticipate their future desires and behaviour. On the one hand, responses in research sessions tend to be limited by what respondents know and have experienced. This makes research particularly difficult when the technology is innovative and beyond their experience.

On the other hand, respondents can get excited about 'good ideas' in developmental research sessions that in the cold light of day may not really fit into their lives.

Another issue we needed to think about was how to communicate complex new services to respondents in a meaningful way during the research. Rarely are there examples of fully operational devices that respondents can use to get closer to the technology. In the absence of anything tangible, respondents can find future technology beyond their grasp, if not intellectually then certainly experientially.

Such fast-moving markets also put a big strain on time schedules. So we needed to find ways to feedback findings to marketers who were having to make decisions while the research was in progress. As launch dates were brought forward in response to market activity, this was a real test of whether the research process could meet BT Cellnet's needs.

Methodology

Our approach needed to deliver against the following criteria:

- enable us to get close to the reality of consumers' daily lives
- ensure respondents could grasp the benefits of the technology and assess how it might fit into their lives
- include a built-in reality check
- provide BT Cellnet with flexibility in terms of feeding back findings, e.g. regular updates.

We realised that a straightforward series of groups would not be appropriate. We designed a staged research programme involving pre and post tasks, reconvened sessions and follow-up telephone indepth interviews. To get respondents to imagine what they would like to be able to do in the future, they were given dictaphones that they carried with them and used over a typical week to record things they would like to be able to do as they thought of them.

They tended to think of the dictaphone as the proverbial 'genie' that could grant their wishes and seemed to find it easy to come up with many opportunities for mobile services. By recording ideas as they went about their daily lives, their suggestions were based on genuine needs and wants unlike some of the 'good ideas' that can come up in group discussions.

Karen Armes from BT Cellnet brand and market planning commented: 'This innovative method provided us with informed, reliable information about when and what services the customer would use. This would be impossible to gauge accurately with traditional research.'

The output from this exercise was useful not only in developing new services, but also in terms of how to communicate the benefits.

We were able to create 'week in the life' portraits of key customer types that would enable the advertising agency to understand the context in which new services were likely to be used. Rather than these portraits simply painting a stereotypical picture of, for example, a young professional adult, we were able to provide details of actual moments when the services might be relevant.

The benefits of reconvened sessions

After working on some of the respondents' ideas with BT Cellnet and matching these with the available technology, we presented ideas back to the same respondents in reconvened group discussions. Interestingly, they were less enthusiastic about some of the ideas they had come up with. This indicated that the pace of change they could accommodate was more gradual than the dictaphone exercise alone would have suggested. We also came away with a strong steer on those ideas that they were relatively close to accepting and those that still felt quite far away.

Typically, it is inadvisable to ask respondents to be both developmental and evaluative within one research session as they can get attached to ideas and cannot stand back. Giving respondents time between sessions allows them to take a more objective stance. They have time for their thoughts to develop between generating ideas and critically assessing them.

Furthermore, as their ideas were presented back to them in a synthesised form, it wasn't clear who had generated the ideas, and respondents did not feel obliged to defend them as they can do in a traditional group discussion.

Staging the research enabled us to take into consideration the fact that respondents often struggle to imagine how new and complex products and services might fit into their lives. They need time to do this effectively. Additional time allows respondents to change their minds or amplify their views during the course of the research. Such a research process can give some indications about the likely decision-making process.

For example, one particular target audience was less enthusiastic about mobile internet in the initial sessions but later became much more receptive and could see a role for it in their lives. Having more than one opportunity to talk to respondents ensures that both their spontaneous reactions and their more considered responses are included in the research findings. The latter are typically missing from traditional group discussions.

We planned from the outset to drip feed findings back to BT Cellnet to enable them to make pressing decisions. We built in an interim meeting and emailed findings in sections, so they could be circulated to the relevant parties. As BT Cellnet understood the rationale for the research process, it was possible to manage their expectations and they were aware that the findings might evolve.

Benefits to the respondent

We were astonished by the commitment to the research project shown by many of the respondents. They let us into their lives, particularly through the dictaphone exercise when they were surprisingly unselfconscious. Because we were seeking a higher degree of commitment (multiple sessions, pre or post tasks etc.) and co-operation than usual, we consciously treated respondents as equals.

Group discussions were set up carefully, explicitly stating the research objectives at the start and asking them what outcomes would be good for them. In following up the groups, they were given a number of different ways of corresponding with us including email so they could use the best method for them.

The feedback from those respondents who had participated in research before suggested that this was a very different and significantly more rewarding experience.

Conclusions

It is possible to do the kind of qualitative research that is genuinely useful and not compromised, even in markets that are fast-moving. The research agency, the client and respondents all need to buy into the process and commit to it.

Research agencies need to work hard at devising a process that meets the needs of all parties at the front end and ensure that expectations are set throughout the project. It's more than good client servicing, it's about everyone having a good experience.

Claire Thomas is MD of Mosquito Research.

[1] This case history appeared in the September 2000 edition of *Research*, pp. 34–5, and is published with the permission of the Market Research Society.

Case 7
Glasgow Underground – researching customer characteristics

Clockwork time bomb[1]

The runaway success of the Glasgow Underground left its operator with a system that could go out of control. Sandy Ochojna undertook a research task that had to be done at breakneck speed.

Strathclyde Passenger Transport (SPT) operates the Glasgow Underground. The circular rail service links the city centre with its southern and western inner suburbs through 15 stations. The service was opened in 1897 and is the third-oldest underground railway in the world.

It was fully modernised in 1979: it was at this time that its new, orange liveried trains earned the service its local name of the Clockwork Orange. And since its reopening patronage has increased steadily such that today the system carries more than 14 million passengers per annum and is stretched to capacity at peak times.

In 1998, SPT set up a comprehensive review of every aspect of the operation of the railway, with a key commercial objective to spread the peak traffic and increase off-peak use. Early into this review it became clear that the success of the system meant that little or no effort had been spent in the recent past in trying to understand the marketplace within which the Underground was operating. SPT was facing two vital questions to which it had no answers:

- Who are the Underground's passengers?
- Who could be the Underground's passengers?

Without such information there could be no robust justification for any strategic, tactical or marketing propositions.

SPT turned to Taylor Nelson Sofres Harris in Manchester because of its experience in public transport research and particularly passenger surveys for clients like London Underground, First North Western Trains, ScotRail, Eurostar and Greater Manchester PTE. Time was of the essence: confidence in the ability of any survey agency to deliver was of paramount importance.

The surveys

Commissioned on 30 April 1998, the fieldwork was conducted by Harris in mid-May and a full presentation of results was held in Glasgow on 7 July. Two separate surveys were undertaken to answer the two vital questions that SPT needed answering.

Over a number of weekdays and a weekend, Harris interviewers were allocated to specific stations or platforms (depending on whether the station had side or island platforms) for pre-determined time slots. They sought to interview as many boarders as possible while patrolling their platform(s). All survey periods were covered at the the busiest stations, while at others interviewers would cover two or three stations in hourly or half-hourly rotation. The system-wide picture was produced by weighting the interviews achieved using simultaneously collected all-day station and platform traffic counts collected either by the automatic barriers or by observation.

Via a short questionnaire, some 2,100 passengers were questioned about the trips they were making and the highest price they would be willing to pay for the journey.

Clearly, as a city centre carrier with direct links into central bus and rail stations, the Underground's potential catchment area could be drawn very wide. To confine the issue and deliver an effective yet manageable survey, the potential marketplace was defined to be everyone who uses Glasgow city centre and lives in Strathclyde region, barring the North East of the region because that area is least well served by the Underground as a city centre distributor.

As a result, interviews were carried out on street level in several city centre locations and the sample was quota-controlled by age and sex.

Respondents were asked about how they came into the city on the day of the interview, their awareness of the operating hours and fares of the Underground, and the feasibility of using the service on the city-bound route on that day. In all, some 1,078 interviews were achieved between 7am and 6pm on a Thursday, Friday and Saturday.

The results

The main findings were:

- Awareness and knowledge of the system is good.
- Roughly 10 per cent of city centre trips utilise the Underground to some degree, and this proportion could theoretically rise to a maximum of 20 per cent, so there is potential for growth.
- The Underground is seen to be frequent, reliable, good value for money, but buses and trains are perceived as offering better levels of personal safety.
- Current passengers are predominantly young and would like the service to operate later into the evening.
- There is a willingness to pay significantly more to use the service, especially for longer trips.

The survey exercise went extremely well. The co-operation of the public and passengers was excellent and this was no doubt due to the questionnaires being very short and sticking very closely to the issues involved. This could be done because SPT recognised the benefits of simplicity. This is an important observation: a complicated data need can be met successfully by using simple survey methods.

The actions

The research was carried out at a crucial stage in determining the future of the Underground. The privatisation of the national rail network and the proposed changes in the organisation of London Underground emphasised the need for the Glasgow Underground to become more commercially aware and customer focused. The Underground operates in a highly competitive market where bus, suburban rail, car and walking are viable alternatives for many Underground journeys. It was essential for SPT to better understand its market, how to serve it and how the market might react to changes in service provision.

The research gave SPT the confidence to take some budget decisions:

- Operating hours are to be extended by almost one hour on week-day evenings. This has a significant cost and requires the maintenance regime to be reconfigured to allow for the shorter night time period when trains do not run.
- A fares increase well above inflation is being introduced. Based on the research, SPT is confident that there will be little long-term reduction in patronage as a result of this increase.
- New fares have been introduced targeted at specific market segments to increase off-peak use.
- A project is underway to upgrade the CCTV coverage of the system to address the concerns over personal safety.

This piece of research was extremely effective because it provided answers to the key questions which enabled SPT to proceed with confidence in taking some difficult decisions affecting the long-term future of the railway; and it was carried out to a very tight timescale.

Though SPT has not been a regular research buyer in the past, as a result of the success of this piece of work SPT has commissioned further research to look in more detail at how people use St Enoch Station, and expects to make greater use of market research in the future.

Dr Sandy Ochojna is a director at Taylor Nelson Sofres Harris.

[1] This case history appeared in the July 1999 edition of *Research*, pp. 32–3, and is published with the permission of the Market Research Society.

Case 8
Allied Domecq – researching lifestyles

Getting to Know You[1]

Adult emergent drinkers are a vital market for the alcoholic drinks industry. Shirley Acreman and Bill Pegram explain how Allied Domecq commissioned an innovative study to understand this group, and how the findings made an impression on the drinks company's business managers.

Markets are becoming ever more competitive, with new brands competing for a share of consumers' hearts and minds. Building a relationship with consumers is a challenge facing all organisations, but particularly so in the case of 'emergent drinkers' – those of legal drinking age up to 25. These consumers are highly experimental, and our only safe assumption is that their consumption habits will probably not follow on from those of preceding generations.

In 1997 Allied Domecq Spirits & Wines (ADSW) recognised the danger of being distanced from this crucial group, particularly across geographical markets. We were not looking to understand a current user group per se, but rather to gain insight into the factors influencing brand adoption as these young drinkers mature.

Working with Pegram Walters International (PWI), a unique programme of research was created. The objectives went far beyond an exploration of their current usage and attitudes towards spirits, and encompassed an exploration of their personal values, their feelings about their lives, their universe, their hopes and dreams. The project required a willingness to think beyond current market conditions and business objectives.

The broad objectives of the research – covering an elusive respondent set – clearly required an approach that would be both informal and unconventional. It needed to venture beyond 'traditional' MR in order to maximise the quality of data. Moreover, because of the innovative nature of the project, it required a high level of openness, communication and trust between client and agency, to ensure that the information was both usable and relevant. In research terms, there were two clear challenges:

- gathering information from this difficult to access consumer group
- integrating the information back into the organisation.

Gaining access to the adult emergent drinker

We believed that, to gain real insight into the emergent drinker community we would have to take into consideration two realities: nobody can understand a community better than the community itself; and information alone cannot provide valuable insight, which can only be developed from the blending of community understanding with external analysis.

Access to the community was provided via the development of the 'information gatherers' (IGs) concept. IGs would be representatives of the adult emergent drinker target group. They would participate in the research in order to interpret the dynamics of their own community for us.

To accomplish this, we recruited adult emergent spirits drinkers, who were required to understand the objectives of our research project and to be able to communicate concepts. In this way, they would not only provide feedback on their own needs and actions but, more importantly, would also be able to gather and interpret information from their peer group. IGs would become, effectively, both respondents and researchers, with the ability to provide us with rich, value-added insight.

We believe that one of the key successes of this programme was our policy of maintaining honesty at all stages of the programme. By being completely open about what we were setting out to do with the participants, by sharing our hopes and expectations with them, we empowered the IGs to have a stake in our project. As a result, they felt as committed to gaining valuable insight as we did. However, the recruitment of IGs also required both ADSW and the research agency to step away from established comfort zones and let go of control – two key ingredients to any programme of innovation.

Overall there were three stages to the research design in each market. In the first instance we conducted one-hour depth interviews. There were three clear objectives for this stage of research: to understand personal viewpoints on marketing and lifestyle issues; to clarify and/or narrow down topics for subsequent exploration at the workshop stage; to recruit appropriate 'information gatherers' (IGs). Depth interviews were conducted to understand what was happening in respondents' lives. We invited them to undertake 'homework' such as essays on their lives, and to bring along items of personal importance to stimulate discussion. From this stage we began to formulate hypotheses on issues such as how they saw themselves and their future, relationships, self-discovery, and opting in or opting out of the system. In each market, from 20 depth interviews, 10 respondents were retained as IGs to accompany us through the rest of the programme. We believed that it was important to conduct the bulk of the research in the environments in which alcohol was consumed. We rented out leading edge bars where we invited 50 adult emergent drinkers to participate in workshops.

From the time the participants entered the venue, the role of ADSW and the research agency became purely observational, with the IGs leading the discussion throughout. We designed a task guideline, empowered the IGs with an understanding of our needs, and left them to it. As an additional record, the workshops were video-recorded. Because of the way in which they had been recruited, the IGs felt a real responsibility to get the right information. The participants felt comfortable within their peer group and, in the more natural bar environment, fed back real, relevant and honest information. Moreover, both respondents and IGs respected the process, allowing them to 'buy into' the research. On the night following the workshops, we reconvened focus groups with the IGs to discuss what actually happened, and their interpretation of what it actually meant. In this way, we were able to collect concentrated data: what we observed, what the consumers said, how it was reported back to us, and an initial understanding of what it all might actually mean.

Communicating the findings within ADSW

To infuse the exercise with knowledge, learning and a sense of adventure, we invited ADSW business teams to spend a day of discovery with us. We began the day by holding breakout sessions that included ADSW marketing and sales personnel, and their key agencies. The purpose was to gauge current assumptions about adult emergent drinkers, and where necessary to dispel some myths. Then we 'met' the generation. We felt that the best way to do this was to create fictional characters for the adult emergent drinker generation. These would enable ADSW marketing managers to visualise the consumers when developing NPD or communication strategies. The personalities we created were brought to life using actors from the generation. In France, for example, the clients were able to meet Matthias, Stephanie, Seb, Justine, and Stan.

These five characters symbolised the richness and the diversity of the generation. They were not meant to represent a segmentation of the market – rather, they were intended to reflect a collage of adult emergent drinkers in order to help business managers enter into a relationship with this consumer group.

Each of the characters engaged with the audience via dialogue, discussing for example their lifestyle, behaviours, in/outs, values, concerns and expectations for the future, as well as their current attitudes towards alcohol. In addition, the audience was presented with workshop 'souvenirs', notebooks with pictures and 'bios' of the character types where they could take notes during the presentation. We then reconvened the work groups to summarise learning. The effect was immediate: with the bar as a cue, business managers were able to step into a new world and easily meet and interact with their consumers. Moreover, their 'consumers' were eager to explain what was and wasn't important to them. This multi-media/multi-layered presentation of findings allowed information to be assimilated both visually, audibly, and kinaesthetically.

In order to ensure that the information remained topical, useful and easily accessible, we felt it was important to create a vehicle for on-going communication and dialogue with the audience. To achieve this, we created a high impact 'magazine' to bring the research to life after the presentation. We refer to this as a magazine and not a research report, to reflect the lifestyle of the consumer group in question: it contained images, layouts and fonts typically associated with the generation. This magazine, together with the videos containing live footage of the actors and the workshop, was distributed throughout ADSW.

On-going innovation

We believe that this was an important exercise in terms of combining creativity of process and reportage with real business needs. We often state the need to 'get into consumers' minds', and we use creative/projective techniques to really understand what consumers are thinking. However, where, as researchers, we fall short is that we too frequently forget to devote the same amount of time to understanding and to the context of our clients' businesses.

Such was the success of the research format that the research agency developed CommunityInsight – an information-gathering process that aims to access primary target groups. CommunityInsight is based on the same two very simple premises:

- nobody can understand a community better than the community itself
- information alone cannot provide valuable insight, which can only be developed from the blending of community understanding with external analysis.

We now have successfully replicated this model in other markets and continually look for new opportunities to innovate.

Shirley Acreman is insight director, Allied Domecq Spirits & Wines, UK. Bill Pegram is managing director, Pegram Walters International.

[1] This case history appeared in the November 1999 edition of *Research*, pp. 36–41, and is published with the permission of the Market Research Society.

Case 9
Carlsberg-Tetley – communicating research to the board

Pulling power[1]

Research is looking to go all the way to the top at brewer Carlsberg-Tetley, reports Mike Savage.

Market research has never been a topic to rouse the passions of most company directors. While many will have a vague notion that a certain investment in MR is probably good for business, few feel it is a subject that should be aired at a boardroom meeting.

In one company however, brewer Carlsberg-Tetley, this could be all about to change. C-T's senior research manager James Howes is determined not just to teach the board the value of research but to place his department at the forefront of everything Carlsberg-Tetley does.

Table 1 Beverage consumption in the UK.

	Per capita consumption (litres)		Share of alcoholic drinks consumption (%)		Share of total drinks consumption (%)	
	1989	1999	1989	1999	1989	1999
Beer	115.4	103.9	83.7	77.3	17.1	15.0
Wine	12.7	17.3	9.2	12.9	1.9	2.5
Spirits	4.4	5.0	3.2	3.7	0.7	0.7
Cider	5.4	8.2	3.9	6.1	0.8	1.2
Total Alcohol	137.9	134.4	100.0	100.0	20.5	19.3
Soft drinks*	141.0	173.5			20.9	25.0
Hot drinks	276.0	271.8			40.9	39.1
Milk	119.4	115.0			17.7	16.6
Total drinks	674.3	694.7			100.0	100.0

*Soft drinks includes packaged water, carbonates, fruit juice, fruit drinks & dilutables, iced tea and sports & energy drinks.
Source: Canadean Beer Service

'We work hard to justify our existence and make it clear we have a real role to play in the business,' Howes explains. 'That role extends to working towards providing that business with leadership, through both market intelligence and knowledge, and giving opinion as the consumer champion.'

MR is entitled to a place at the top table. The proof lies in a report Howes drew up, outlining the threats to the traditionally inward-looking beer industry from other alcoholic drinks such as wine. The report worked its way to C-T's board, which responded with key strategic decisions on the strength of Howes' analysis. After this indirect endorsement, Howes decided it was essential to let the board know what MR is capable of.

'They receive information but do not always appreciate it comes directly from myself and my team. The challenge is to develop direct relationships with them. That really is fundamentally about putting ourselves about. It means going to present at board level. It means trying to understand their requirements better, making it clear what it is we can do for them, what role we can provide; and when we get that opportunity, make sure we can deliver.'

As part of his drive to promote the credentials of the inhouse researcher, Howes has pushed at the boundaries of traditional research, weaving diverse data sources into MR findings. 'Our role is much broader than just providing research,' he says. 'In a sense we are all-rounders.'

In a recent competitor report on rival firm Interbrew, Howes drew on data from a variety of sources, including analysts' reports, Interbrew's website and ad tracking and ad spend information. 'I'll look as broad as it needs to be to find information and then I'll pull that together.'

This holistic approach is a working method Howes feels is outside the scope of most agencies. Agency researchers who yearn for life on the clientside so they can see their research findings implemented have a 'very simplistic view of how the process works'. Once the researchers have finished their presentation and have hopped back on the train to London, Howes takes the findings and moulds them into something the business can use. 'That is not always a straightforward process.'

Agencies don't give much thought to what happens to the research post-presentation, Howes feels, and aren't aware of what they can contribute. Howes finds agencies remarkably reactive, rarely issuing a thoughtful challenge to a brief or suggesting new areas for Carlsberg-Tetley to look at. The initiative lies with the clientside researcher.

The role of the inhouse researcher has undergone profound changes in recent times. When Howes first joined Allied Breweries, just over ten years ago, he found himself one member of a 25-strong research and information bulwark. Before its move to Northampton in 1998, Carlsberg-Tetley employed five market research managers. Now it employs two, Howes and consumer insight manager Lisa Rendell, with two support staff – a research assistant/secretary and a placement student.

'It's not the biggest team in the world and we've got an awful lot of ground to cover,' he remarks. 'Each person really has to pull their weight and be clear about their own area of responsibility.'

This includes the support staff, who are encouraged to muck in with information support as well as the admin.

Heavily reduced MR departments are a relic of the ruthless downsizing prompted by the economic downturn at the beginning of the 90s. Increased efficiency provided by increasingly adept computer software means that a leaner, more flexible clientside resource is probably here to stay.

'In the old days of research departments you had to have a lot of people because you had great mountains of printout and half the battle was just getting the numbers together,' Howes recalls. 'We're not about that anymore. We've got quite sophisticated computer packages that take a lot of the pain out of getting hold of information.'

Howes has introduced computer software across Carlsberg-Tetley that enables C-T staff to perform basic analysis on Nielsen data, freeing up C-Ts' researchers to devote more time where their contribution is really felt across the business – in adding value.

Howes sees the MR department's function within C-T metamorphosing from information gatekeeper to a new role that's part-research, part-business planner and part-analyst, involving a broader range of skills and disciplines. Howes' report on Interbrew, which, pending government approval, became a major rival almost overnight by buying the brewing assets of both Whitbread and Bass, is a sign this change has already begun.

No matter how far marketers and other people within the business are empowered, not just to conduct their own analysis but to run their own surveys using DIY web research packages, Howes feels that he and his team will always be in demand for their impartiality and their expertise. He is hoping to expand C-T's research operation further but fears his department may have become a victim of its own success. 'People say we're doing a good job with the resource we have and it's a battle to try and expand on that. Hopefully that will be addressed in due course.'

Table 2 The UK beer market.

Leading brewers in UK 1999	Market share (%)
Scottish Courage	27
Bass	23
Whitbread	14
Carlsberg-Tetley	13
Guinness	6
Others	17

Leading brewers in UK after Interbrew acquisitions	Market share (%)
Interbrew UK (Bass/Whitbread)*	33
Scottish Courage	27
Carlsberg-Tetley	13
Guinness	6
Others	21

*Interbrew UK excludes Heineken volumes (now included in Others)
Source: Canadean Beer Service

Howes has around £1m to spend on continuous research: market surveys from industry body The Brewers and Licensed Retailers Association and ACNielsen audits; ad tracking from Millward Brown and ad spend measurement from ACNielsen; Infratest Burke's Alcovision survey for consumer measures; and Taylor Nelson Sofres' Liquor panel for brand and category dynamics.

C-T's ad hoc research needs are paid for by its internal clients, mainly brand and trade marketing, but increasingly, Howes hopes, from other departments and from the board itself. Sometimes sponsors need talking out of research, particularly on details of packaging that mean nothing to consumers but everything to brand managers.

Although research is always there to back up the multi-million pound investments Carlsberg-Tetley makes in advertising and sponsorship, Howes is no fan of researching everything to death. 'Market research should not be a crutch for people. It should be illuminating, providing guidance and direction. You should rely on your own decision-making ability sometimes.'

As clients become increasingly concerned with placing their research money where it counts, it is a perennial sentiment to which agencies should pay fresh attention.

[1] This case history appeared in the August 2000 edition of *Research*, pp. 20–1, and is published with the permission of the Market Research Society.

Current issues in marketing research[1]

Issue 1
Marketing research versus customer insight

Issue 2
Merging marketing research with customer databases

Issue 3
Declining response rates

Issue 4
Challenges of business-to-business research

Issue 5
Difficulties in achieving representative samples

Issue 6
Researching difficult minority groups

Issue 7
Innovation in advertising research?

Issue 8
Branding research products

Issue 9
Clients going direct to respondents

[1] These articles on issues were originally published in *Research* and have been reproduced here with the permission of the Market Research Society.

Issue 1
Marketing research versus customer insight

In sight of change[1]

Is the renaming of clientside market research departments just a cosmetic exercise or does it point to a fundamental shift in the role and status of MR? Ken Gofton investigates.

As new members introduced themselves at April's meeting of the Association of Users of Research Agencies, one thing stood out above all else: the wide range of job titles now in use on the clientside of the industry.

Today, inhouse professionals are as likely to be called consumer insight managers, customer insight managers or planners, as they are research managers – so much so, that AURA plans to investigate the extent to which the inhouse research function is being restructured and repositioned.

The move is one more sign of what is arguably a fundamental change under way in client companies. A number of recent 'Clientside' features in Research – General Mills, GuinnessUDV, Van den Bergh – have highlighted the increased importance now given to the 'consumer insight' function within MR buyers.

Andrew Grant, European and marketing insights manager for Ford, puts this more dramatically when he suggests it is a case of change or die for inhouse research departments. 'The clientside researcher must innovate or die. The encroachment of data suppliers and insight consultants could squeeze the clientside research function altogether.'

However, management styles and corporate structures are very prone to fashion swings, so is the move to 'consumer insight' just a relabelling exercise? Professor Tim Ambler of London Business School believes the change undoubtedly includes a certain amount of rebadging. 'I'm not against that,' he adds. 'It can be helpful, and market research people do need to market themselves better internally. But that's second prize. First prize is rethinking how consumer insight fits into the company as a whole.'

Andrew Marsden, category marketing director, Britvic Soft Drinks, says: 'We changed our consumer research team to consumer insight four years ago. Having extended that thinking to the trade research side, we now have a category insight department. It is far more than a change of name.

'I grew up with market research managers who spent their lives writing action standard documents, and whose business was buying data. They have to become strategic contributors. Insight to me is exactly what it says – it gives strategic direction to the knowledge the business requires.' Raoul Pinnell, head of global brands at Shell, agrees that the industry is seeing a basic shift. 'Market research managers used to be the deliverers, the people who ensured that the processes were proper and thorough. They are now being asked to contribute to the analysis. It means they are not just managing the process, but managing the information, which in modern life is where the power lies. It is a genuine contribution to boardroom thinking, where they want to know what conclusions you draw.'

The rapid adoption of the consumer insight idea means that there is both some uncertainty about its origins, and some variation in the terms used. But AURA chairman Leslie Sopp is convinced it is not mere fashion. He sees it as a reaction to a genuine business need.

'To a large extent it reflects pressure on businesses to deliver and develop – in other words, it's driven by shareholders and customers,' he says. 'If there's a further element, it's the growth of IT, which makes the task more difficult because there are so many streams of information coming into the organisation.'

There's broad agreement that the concept embraces the bringing together of the many sources of information available to a company, of which market research is just one strand.

Consultant Peter Mouncey, formerly responsible for customer relationship strategy development at the AA, says: 'In the 1970s the only real source of consumer data was market research in its various forms. Today, it's only one of many, alongside customer and lifestyle databases, scanner data, loyalty schemes and geodemographics.

'The dilemma is to know how to pull all these sources together, understanding the strengths and weaknesses of each. It requires a much wider application of the researchers' skills, and the need to be able to have influence – an internal consultancy role if undertaken properly.'

The insight teams at some companies have programmes in place to help their marketing colleagues develop skills in identifying consumer insights for themselves. The key requirements in the consumer insight approach are an ability to assimilate information from a much wider range of sources, to adopt a much more proactive role, and be able to contribute to strategy development.

And the reason for it all, according to Mouncey, is that 'the source of competitiveness in today's world is the brand, customer service and the breadth and depth of the relationship with the customer. All of which presupposes a well developed understanding of consumer needs, attitudes and behaviour'. Or as Ambler puts it: 'Consumer insight is what marketing is all about.'

When the Royal Bank of Scotland acquired NatWest, it was decided to retain the two brands and separate marketing teams. However, the research functions were merged a year ago to form a customer and market insight department.

Everyone now works across both brands, explains the department's head, Maryan Broadbent. Segment managers are responsible for developing understanding of areas such as small business, or customer categories such as young adults. A much flatter structure has been adopted, with an increase in the number of research managers, now rebranded 'planners', and fewer support staff.

There's an emphasis, too, on adding more value. Routine work like designing questionnaires is now farmed out to the company's agencies, while the team undertakes much more analysis of competitor activity.

'We are trying to convey that we don't just sit here and wait for our internal clients to ask us to do a survey. We are not a post box. We should be proactively looking at the organisation's information needs,' adds Broadbent.

A slightly different slant on the changed role comes from Andrew Grant of Ford. 'Insight,' he says, 'allows us to viscerally understand our consumers rather than know they are 35–49 and male. Producing products, services and advertising targeting a specific consumer yields better loyalty and affinity.

'We're looking more for the "aha" than for the two decimal places of statistical significance, or the 20 reasons why two data sets are not directly comparable.'

The changes within client companies, even where they result in new challenges for suppliers, are welcomed by some on the supplyside. Andrew Vincent, managing director of Business & Market Research, says it's a positive development because it reflects a wish on the part of clients to get more out of their market research and to understand its role in the context of other sources of knowledge.

For example, it has become more common for clients to ask what the research actually means, even to demand, 'What would you do if it was your decision?'. This is more of a consulting role, says Vincent, 'and some agencies are not comfortable with that'.

Clive Nancarrow of Bristol Business School questions whether all the researchers involved in 'consumer insight', internal and external, have a sufficiently deep appreciation of marketing issues. 'There are major human resource issues to be thought through for consumer insight to be a reality – a culture change rather than just a name change.'

[1] This article appeared in the May 2001 edition of *Research*, pp. 20–1, and is published with the permission of the Market Research Society.

Issue 2
Merging marketing research with customer databases

Raiding the databank[1]

Clients are increasingly merging their market research and database marketing functions in a bid to get more out of their data. Noëlle McElhatton investigates a major dilemma for the MR industry.

When the Royal Bank of Scotland wanted to revise its customer contact strategy last year, the UK's seventh largest bank interviewed a representative sample of customers about their contact preferences. Would customers support or oppose being phoned with an offer of a customer service review – in other words, a meeting to discuss their finances? Two thirds said 'yes, please'.

Nothing unusual about this exercise, you might think. Not unusual, but just how useful? Crucial to the finance industry, and any service industry for that matter, is the concept of customer value management, or the ability to segment and target a company's most profitable customers.

Which is why, for the above project, the Royal Bank of Scotland then added information from its internal database on product holding and gender, together with derived data like contribution, a profitability measure the bank uses. By overlaying one data set on top of the other, it discovered that the customers making the bank the most money – 93.56 per cent of contribution – overwhelmingly supported the idea of being offered a review.

Welcome to the world of merging MR and databases, a practice fast-becoming the norm for client companies with large transactional databases and relationship marketing strategies. Banks, retailers and utilities, among others, now believe that overlaying internal MR surveys onto databases is vital to improving response rates from direct marketing through the greater consumer understanding that MR can provide. While databases have volume, so the argument goes, they lack the depth of the MR study. By putting MR data on to databases and finding individual matches, clients get to know their customers better at an aggregate level.

With current or threatened competition in many markets – finance and utilities especially – clients need to extract the most value out of their databases, prompting them to take MR-overlaying extremely seriously.

'It has to happen – it's a natural progression of database development,' says Tom Kerr, head of analysis and research at Bank of Scotland (no relation to Royal Bank of Scotland). 'We're moving into an age of "customer first", and all organisations have a responsibility to utilise information they have access to without further bothering the customer for non-essential information to provide the service he or she demands.'

Moves to overlap database marketing and market research are stepping up a gear, as companies like Boots, Royal Bank of Scotland and Sun Life of Canada restructure to integrate the disciplines more closely, from shifting the furniture so that teams sit together to full integration of database and research databases. Many are conducting the overlay themselves and redefining the role of MR in the process. Meanwhile, the ethical arguments rage on.

Five years ago, Carola Southorn was group marketing services manager at travel and financial services company Saga and foresaw this trend. She spearheaded the development of guidelines for researchers handling databases, a milestone at the time. Now, she says, 'the Market Research Society ethos on the two being very separate has been overtaken by events'.

The merger process involves matching up customer databases to internal MR. Names and address are then stripped off and models are developed to predict into what segment a customer or prospect falls. In particular, clients are looking for groups for whom their share is small, but the opportunity is big.

Berry Consulting is one of the few agencies selling the practice to clients. Julian Berry, md, explains the lure of MR for database managers: 'What client databases lack is anything beyond their own customers' transactions. But if you can attribute somebody to a particular segment and you know how that segment is behaving in the market, then you've got quite a different marketplace. The only way you can do this is by modelling MR data onto databases.'

Clients say the urge to merge is being driven from the top. Marketing directors are concerned with the quality and relevance of market data, not its source. At Royal Bank of Scotland both the head of marketing information and research, Maryan Broadbent, and her database counterpart, Tim Crick report to the bank's director of retail marketing, Ian Henderson. 'It's no good me telling Ian what customers think, and Tim telling him how they behave,' Broadbent explains. 'We need to understand how attitudes and behaviour are related. Ian asks us not to give him independent views – to go away and give him a consolidated picture.' One notable example of structural integration is found at Whitbread, the leisure and restaurant group, where the database team reports to Martin Callingham, the group head of MR. Callingham agrees this set-up is not the norm: it's the result of his own initiative two years ago to bring Whitbread's many brand databases in-house.

Because MR was the most numerate and computer literate department in the company, it was the natural site for the databasers. However it's organised such that the database unit could easily be demerged from MR, in that external database suppliers report directly to John Belchamber, database marketing manager, and the function is separately funded.

The lesson from Callingham's experience is that senior management support is essential to cut through any politics surrounding the integration. He needed the support of his main board to overcome resistance from the group's various marketing directors. Likewise Kerr believes support by Bank of Scotland at the highest levels was vital to gaining approval for the merger of the bank's customer database and external MR database.

Without senior buy-in, ethical nervousness and good, old-fashioned turf wars can stymie cooperation. Jane Goldsmith is client director at First T, a joint venture between database marketing consultancy Dunn Humby and BMRB to sell applications of MR products to databases.

She says: 'Where MR and database marketing are two very separate functions it's difficult to get representatives from both departments to buy in, or even attend meetings together. There are instances where you go in to speak to one side and they won't pass the information on to their colleagues.'

The last two years have seen the evolution of customer insight groups charged with getting a customer view which combines knowledge from databases and MR. Goldsmith cites the UK's largest grocer, Tesco, as a clued-in proponent of the joint discipline. 'Tesco's customer research unit is made up of people with database expertise and a full understanding of their behavioural and transactional data. All the information in that group is shared.'

In May, Bank of Scotland brought database marketing into its strategic analysis unit alongside MR. 'It's so much more closely knit,' says Kerr, who has moved from being a researcher into involvement in all aspects of database development.

Goldsmith believes that given the tensions likely to exist between database and MR teams, some sort of guidelines should be drawn up as to how to work together. At Royal Bank of Scotland, cross-disciplinary teams meet to tackle specific issues like customer retention, where all participants agree and sign off terms of reference before they start.

Clients like John Buckle, MR manager at Alliance & Leicester, and Kerr say they are baffled by the turf wars that occur in some companies. 'We do have more to gain from working with each other,' Buckle says.

'Database marketing is very broad brush. If response rates of 2–3 per cent are deemed to be highly successful, it still suggests that there's 97 per cent who are still being hit inappropriately with the wrong product or at the wrong time. That's where the extra insight of MR will be called upon to refine the process.'

Buckle believes a purist stance by MR would be a strategic mistake. 'MR has a problem in that it's not seen as the commercial side of marketing, whereas database marketing has the ear of senior marketeers because it appears more actionable.' MR can't afford to be a brake on the marriage process, or otherwise databasers will go elsewhere for their data, lifestyle companies being the obvious alternative source.

Years ago, while he was at NOP, Kerr found it strange that the power of research should not be used within database marketing. Now as a client he says it is something that research cannot afford not to do. After he joined Bank of Scotland four years ago, he implemented the concept of integrating external and internal data into a standalone marketing 'workbench'.

'You can't underestimate its power,' he says. 'If research doesn't exist within that, then its value will further diminish and could effectively become obsolete.'

[1] This article appeared in the September 1999 edition of *Research*, pp. 28–31, and is published with the permission of the Market Research Society.

Issue 3
Declining response rates

Critical response[1]

Attracting both interviewers and respondents is becoming ever more difficult. Noëlle McElhatton asks leading client and agency figures what can be done to prevent a crisis on the front line of MR.

Research: Just to put the issue in context, what evidence exists that response rates are declining here in the UK?

Richard Windle (Director of Ipsos-RSL): It's difficult to be definitive, because surveys change in nature over time. Interview length increases, the subject matter changes, research methods change. But within the UK the main index is the National Readership Survey and that's shown a decline going back 20 to 30 years. In the 1950s they got a response rate of over 80 per cent and that's down to just over 60 per cent now. The Office for National Statistics is also experiencing similar problems on some of its major continuous surveys, particularly over the past three or four years.

Research: Project forward 10 years – what is the response rate likely to be on the NRS?

Windle: That's the crucial question! If response continues to fall at the same rate it will be down to 50 per cent, say, and once you get to that level you begin to question whether it's worth doing random surveys at all.

Research: Is there a sense of urgency among agencies about the problems of response rates?

Sharon Miller (Field Director at NOP): There is an issue for those of us still doing random probability sampling and there are only a few agencies that do. It's no secret that NOP, having carried on with probability sampling on its omnibus longer than any other agency, has just this year decided to give up this unequal struggle. Our main face-to-face general population omnibus is now carried out using an interlaced quota sample in pre-selected sampling points, because of the additional time it's taking the interviewers to find random probability samples – having to make four or five call backs and the related cost of drawing from electoral registers.

Research: To what extent are UK clients aware that there is a problem?

RUTH BETTS (Research Manager at one2one): I can only talk personally. I'm being increasingly pulled away from the coal face of research. I try to go out with interviewers, but I'm under pressure from internal clients and my line management to push such technical considerations on to the agencies and to focus more on our marketing issues.

Research: Would agencies prefer clients to be more aware of the response rate problems?

Windle: I think so, because if we do over-fish in the sea and respondents dry up, then everyone will suffer eventually.

Research: Does the industry agree on the causes of declining response rates? For instance, at MRS Conference this year, Peter Hayes described interview length as 'the most pernicious, debilitating thing in market research'.

Betts: It's a very simplistic analysis of the problem. I don't think there's any scientific way of predicting how long you're going to be in a lady's front room talking about Fairy Liquid. If interviews are timed in a field office, who's to know that the respondent isn't going to want to keep the interviewer there three times as long.

Windle: Peter Hayes was right to express it in those terms because it makes people sit up and listen. But it's not just interview length – it's to do with the subject matter of the survey, the relation between the interviewer and the respondent, and the fact that some government and social surveys can be one or two hours in length and are completed quite happily by the respondent because it's a subject matter they feel is important.

Research: CMOR, the US MR lobbying association, now has a full-time executive examining co-operation issues for the American industry. Is the UK industry being proactive enough by comparison?

Miller: We know the MRS is putting a lot of effort into publicising the benefits of research to the business community but I think we could be doing a lot more, particularly in terms of how much we're publicising the benefits of research to members of the public. We all remember the 'Your Opinion Counts' PR campaign 10 years ago – it was very effective. Of course there's the issue of money and where it's going to come from to maintain a campaign like that.

Research: Would clients help fund a PR campaign aimed at boosting response rates amongst the general public?

Betts: Most clients would find that quite difficult. Not because they wouldn't be willing to back their colleagues in agencies on an important issue, but because of the way our budgets are managed these days. We don't have money just slopping around to put towards any old project, it's all accounted for in terms of doing MR. It is something we have started to talk about in AURA because we were approached by the Marketing Market Research Committee for funds. The feeling was that finance for promoting MR should come out of agency overheads. From a purely practical point of view, not many clients could explain to their internal finance departments what was deliverable to the company.

Research: Are incentives a solution?

Windle: Incentives would add to costs greatly, for no benefits. There are lots of people who would happily take part anyway. Also, if you offer incentives the potential is there for you to influence responses. If you've been paid to take part in the interview then you're more likely to be more compliant.

Miller: We don't want to go down the same road the health care MR industry was forced to go down, where we are paying for each minute of a doctor or consultant. I don't think we can judge how much a respondent is worth – how do you put a value on a housewife's time as opposed to another member of the public who happens to be a financial director? But the reality is it's not respondents who expect incentives, rather it makes the interviewer feel better, slightly more professional, in that they would be offering some compensation for taking up the respondent's time.

Windle: It would be a difficult situation if one agency said, we'll give £10 and another said £5, and the client says 'we'll go with you because you're cheaper'.

Miller: It is a highly competitive market out there and most clients go out to tender to two or three companies. You design a survey, confident that you're recommending the right methodology, and you don't want to ruin your chances of getting the job. It's about considerations of cost, because clients have a finite budget.

Research: If it was proven that incentives would boost response rates, would clients be willing to pay for them?

Betts: In our company that would be a project-by-project decision, not a matter of policy. But if adding one per cent to the budget is going to mean that work is going to be conducted more professionally and we get a better result at the end, then I'm sure clients wouldn't rule out spending the money.

Research: Are respondents given enough information about the background to the research project?

Betts: It depends on the project and on the client. Clients often have good reasons for not divulging their identity, the most important being the danger of biasing responses to an idea.

Miller: It would be more effective to up the level of information about what the participation in the interview is going to involve. It's giving respondents an agenda – some warning of the format of the interview. Things like, stressing that it isn't a test, that there are no right or wrong answers and when they can free flow.

Research: But that's not going to secure you an initial response – that just paves the way for future cooperation.

Betts: That's why it's important that the industry gets going on monitoring people's satisfaction with the interview experience. The sooner we can start finding out whether interview length or revealing the client's identity makes a difference, the sooner we can start finding solutions. Don Beverley, the chairman of the Respondent Interviewer Interface Committee (RIIC), came to present to AURA recently about its efforts to produce more rigorous information on what motivates respondents. Everyone was very encouraging. Personally, I went back and called my brand tracking agency and told it to feel free to add questions useful to the RIIC, such as 'how pleasant was this experience for you?' and 'would you do it again?'.

Research: How well are interviewers being trained in interpersonal skills, to overcome that initial refusal?

Miller: That's the key thing for us – because respondents do make up their minds quickly. And if interviewers feel demotivated, the next door they knock on, they'll get another refusal. Technology takes the onerous task of administrating the interview off the interviewer and it enables them to concentrate on building that rapport and motivating the respondent. At NOP we're putting a lot more emphasis on interpersonal skills during training, now that we've taken away the burden for administering the interview by using technology.

Betts: Last time I went out with an interviewer the agency was using state-of-the-art lap tops that the interviewer could write on and which played video. This made it interesting for both respondent and interviewer, even though it was a relatively long, repetitive interview.

Miller: NOP does face-to-face interviewer briefings for the more complex research projects. It helps response rates if the interviewer has much more of an understanding of the task expected of them – they feel more comfortable about taking a respondent through what may seem a very long and boring interview.

Research: But you can only train and brief an interviewer so much. Is the industry recruiting the right type of interviewer to begin with?

Windle: I don't think it's a question of targeting recruitment on particular types of people. Sometimes older people are better interviewers because they're more mature and can deal with problems. And sometimes it's good to have youngsters and students because they're enthusiastic.

Miller: Fifteen years ago we attracted a lot of housewives who were between careers and raising a family. Now the optimum time for door-to-door interviews is late afternoon, evenings and weekends, so we need to attract different types of people, and are attracting a lot of older people, the over-50s – people who no longer have the same family commitments and are able to work unsociable hours. For some respondents, seeing an older person at the doorstep might be more reassuring.

Research: So what's next? Is the will there to action what findings the RIIC comes up with?

Miller: I tried many years ago when I was chairman of the field committee to bring response rates on to the agenda. We discussed how we field the many calls the agencies get from respondents – like the standard 'why did you have to find out what the occupation of the chief income earner was' – and how we should put out a consistent message. We produced some standard responses for agencies, but I'm sure they ended up in some dusty cupboard. We should be putting out a very consistent message throughout the industry about common issues that respondents raise again and again. Perhaps the RIIC could take up that as an issue.

Windle: I still think we're left with the two key people here – the interviewer and respondent. If we can get them both feeling good about the experience, it will improve the response rate next time round.

Betts: I fully support the collection of information for RIIC. I don't know if having empirical evidence will solve the problem, but it will at least tell us whether or not we do have a problem. I agree that the answer lies in having well motivated, trained and equipped interviewers, so we can get word of mouth going.

[1] This article appeared in the October 1999 edition of *Research*, pp. 24–7, and is published with the permission of the Market Research Society.

Issue 4
Challenges of business-to-business research

Mind your own business[1]

Business-to-business research presents challenges not only to the client but also to the researcher. Peter Shreeve discusses the ins and outs of poking your clipboard into other people's business.

It is a marketer's dream to understand customers on a one-to-one basis and to provide tailored communication, and products and services. Most consumer business research provides data at the aggregate level, offering guidance on segment-based strategies, while permission marketing techniques allow marketers to push marketing messages and move closer to the one-to-one goal.

In some types of research, such as customer satisfaction, gaining permission from customers to allow their details and views to be passed to the client moves organisations towards the one-to-one relationship goal. In business-to-business research this is characterised through key account research where attributed account profile information is reported. With this in mind, let's look at the steps required to provide data that businesses can act upon and take into their organisations to drive customer commitment.

Samples vs client base

Using a representative sample of a business-to-business market can present a serious challenge to researchers. Business listings are all well and good, but difficulties inevitably arise. There is little or no homogeneity in the business world; people with a number of different job titles may perform the same function; and what counts as a decision-maker, anyway? Time must be taken to make sure the source sample reflects the needs of the research.

On the other hand, agencies might be tasked with researching the client's own business customers or channel partners. The challenge arises when companies rely on a relatively small number of customers for the bulk of their revenue. You are then potentially researching the whole client base rather than a small sample representative of a much larger set.

This provides researchers with a chance to produce information that can impact on the bottom line. If you're asking questions of the actual customers, then responding to the answers they give must directly impact on your business. This kind of research takes on a different role within the business than standard sample-based surveys.

Engaging the client

There are arguments against doing this type of research. Clients may say that they have a key account management system or that key account managers provide them with feedback.

It's possible to see the research as a threat rather than a complementary tool. A key account manager, by definition, will provide a subjective viewpoint of their clients and might only identify issues they think are important.

Researchers do not offer the Holy Grail but a means to help clients understand their customers through an objective appraisal of the relationship. The researcher has a different end goal and can pull together the views of all key accounts. Research is critical to get a good understanding across a customer base. It doesn't replace a key account management structure, but key account managers cannot carry it out.

Not all companies have a research function, and this can sometimes lead to a lack of recognition about the benefits of research. And of course, those people that benefit most from this kind of research are rarely the research buyers themselves.

Finding budget for a survey of this nature is about engaging all of the stake-holders. The project has to obtain the wholehearted buy-in and support from the customer-facing teams to have the desired effect.

It is well recognised that business decision-making processes are different from those of consumers. But as researchers we can still provide the client with meaningful and actionable information based on these processes. In an organisation there will always be an understanding of how or why purchasing decisions are made, the information we provide is complementary.

Engaging the customers

Engaging the customers in the research to elicit the highest possible response rate is the next stage. We are reliant upon accurate customer databases. While this task should be relatively easy because we are dealing with a smaller number of establishments, we find that most organisations still do not have up-to-date listings of the key contacts.

Much of the information is stored informally with sales mangers and key account managers in electronic and paper-based systems. This in itself can be revealing. One such example uncovered data that was three years out of date, stopping the project in its tracks before it had even started and informing the organisation it needed to change. Where projects span many countries the potential inconsistency escalates.

Depending on the nature of the project, co-operation could be required from both decision-makers and users. Either way, pre-notification, where practical and possible, can greatly improve response rates. Co-operation rates are usually above 50 per cent and can reach 75 per cent–80 per cent in some cases.

There is always some refusal to be interviewed on the grounds of company policy or time pressures. But it may also be an indication of their feelings towards their supplier – are they just another supplier of products and services or a strategic partner? Given this, and the fact that the pool from which to draw samples is smaller, our clients tend to want to understand more about the reasons for refusal than those in general consumer research.

One of the key differences between this type of research and sample survey research is that data can be used to drive both strategic and tactical individual account changes. Within the pre-notification process and the questionnaire we tell respondents that the company wishes to identify them as individuals for the development of individual account plans. Communicating the client's intentions at the start helps us increase the likelihood of obtaining respondent attributable data.

Doing the research

If a business is new to carrying out this kind of research into their own customer base, a qualitative stage amongst a selection of key accounts should be used. This will drive the focus, content and terminology used in the quantitative stage of the research.

As with most research, the choice of data collection method is dependent on a number of issues. Even if your client has a strong relationship with their clients, a postal-based methodology does not always elicit a high enough response rate, particularly for this type of research. And this can often fail to communicate the importance of a survey. There are similar problems with web-based surveys, aside the obvious problems of access to the web. Budget availability is a primary consideration. Face-to-face interviewing of key accounts through a semi-structured interview should glean the most detailed information, but the unclustered nature of respondents and subsequent costs usually prevent us from suggesting this as an approach for this type of quantitative research. More often than not our research tasks involve multicountry studies. This tends to indicate the centrally controlled CATI-style research. The benefits of CATI in this instance are the ability to:

- Double check that the respondent is the correct person, and keep a tighter control on sample, quota control and routing, thus ensuring and improving the quality and accuracy of the data collected
- Speed up the turnaround from implementation to completion
- Expedite changes to questionnaires in response to client or agency suggestions
- Make appointments and carry out interviews at the convenience of the respondent
- Allow the interviewer to probe during the one-to-one interaction, if necessary.

The primary focus of this type of research is the measurement of current performance and the identification of areas for improvement or for new service offerings. We can put this in the context of competitor organisations' performance (actual or perceived). We can measure all the key factors that impact on the relationship with each key account rather than just satisfaction per se.

Once we've done all this, and having engaged the key stakeholders in the research at the beginning of the process, we need to report the data in a way that maintains their interest whilst the research is being carried out and beyond the reporting.

Feedback

The transparency of the research allows instant client feedback on customers' attitudes towards them based on several criteria. If a customer has anything they wish to discuss with the client that is urgent it is identified.

While this information can be collected and passed to the client (if permission is granted) the key thing is that the client is set up to respond. The research normally involves questions identifying whether the customer is at risk. Other techniques include the need to report when scores on key questions drop below an agreed level.

The debrief needs to provide the stakeholders with a number of different things: an overview; the key differences between customer types; the key issues; the strengths and weaknesses identified on elements that form the dynamics of the relationship; and performance improvement planners.

The session should be like a workshop. Let the clients ponder on the implications. How are they going to make some of these changes? Do the results surprise them? Do they confirm what they knew already but are surprised at the impact on the relationship?

The results at this stage are shown in aggregate form. Electronic reporting can engage users of the information whether they were in attendance at the debrief meeting or not. Through the use of dynamic reports users can examine data by different cuts at their leisure, to let them explore the points made in the presentation in more detail, usually through a few sheets rather than pages and pages of slides. The data then becomes even more actionable through the use of profiles on an account-by-account basis in an attributable rather than an anonymous way. This enables key account teams to produce targeted performance improvement: exactly what is it that customer X wants and how does this compare to the average response?

While the use of individual account profiles based on the survey data clearly has its benefits for account management, if these are combined with internal data the power of the data is so much greater. Companies who properly account-manage will have information relating to the account's importance to the organisation, defined in terms of revenue or profitability.

At the strategic level, research can be used to understand the triggers for likely defection, or simply where competitors are rated more highly.

Once this is combined with the importance of a specific customer the organisation gets to understand how much of its business is at risk and which accounts it needs to target to ensure they stay committed. The next stage is crucial. After the survey clients should communicate with each key account in a creative and positive manner what action will be taken as a result both within that account and throughout the organisation. In most cases, it does not need to do this through advertising as with the broader markets – it can tell them directly.

This style of research then lends itself to periodically repeated studies to measure how customers view the performance of the organisation – have they recognised the changes made? However, this is a bit 'chicken and egg', as they need to see change to be convinced of the benefits of taking part again.

Key to the success of this type of business-to-business research is communication. Internal and external customer expectations need to be managed carefully. It also points to including research needs as part of CRM-based strategies. We are still a long way from research featuring at the core of CRM, but we have to start somewhere. At least with key account research the task, in theory, should be easier.

Peter Shreeve is client service director at Maritz Research.

[1] This article appeared in the May 2002 edition of *Research*, pp. 30–5, and is published with the permission of the Market Research Society.

Issue 5
Difficulties in achieving representative samples

The data dilemma[1]

Do tumbling response rates and shrinking turnaround times make a mockery of representative samples? Mike Savage hears why MR must make a stand.

Research: In today's climate of falling response rates and clients wanting data turned round ever more quickly, are we deluding ourselves when we still try to seek representative samples?

Corrine Moy (Director of Statistics, NOP): Sure, clients want data turned around ever more quickly but there is absolutely no question that they are still seeking, and expect, representative samples. Our job is to make judgements on how best to deliver representative samples given the conditions of any project we undertake.

Ken Baker (Statistical Consultant): Without representative samples we don't have an industry – we are no different from the data collecting methods adopted by database marketing companies. We shouldn't be deluding ourselves – we should be attempting to represent the population, and moreover, we have tools to represent the population better than we had 20 years ago.

Research: To what extent do you think response rates and commercial pressures from clients undermine the quest for true representativeness?

Baker: It's difficult to do a strict probability sample with time pressures because you need call backs. That puts the onus on getting a high class quota sample. With the new tools at our disposal, such as geodemographic systems, we should be able to get something like representation without taking the time a probability sample would. There's no earthly reason why these things are incompatible, given that you design your survey well enough.

Moy: In terms of designing samples to produce representativeness, I would argue we are better than we have been in the past. We have more resources, our knowledge has increased from all the development work that has gone on. The demographic information we have about the population at large makes it easier to produce balanced samples which improve the quality of what we are trying to do.

Baker: The problem is you never know whether you've got systematic bias in your sample with non-probability means. Where is the non-response coming from? Up to a point we can set quotas to counter that, but declining response rates are a worry because they may be creating hidden systematic bias. We can put so much more structure on our actual survey designs but if there is any systematic bias, declining response rates will increase the error.

I am worried about declining response rates. At least the tools that we've got have increased in quality. Sampling techniques have improved quite a lot over the last 20 years. Whether everybody is taking advantage of these improvements, I don't know.

Research: What are the other issues that prevent the industry from attaining representative samples?

Baker: If you're not in a probability situation you've got differential probabilities of likelihood of being in to be interviewed; you've then got the problem of over-researched people not wanting to give you an interview, and so on. Aside from that, the only real issue is: are research companies prepared to pay the price for good quality, non-probability sampling? If they are, they should be able to redress the balance up to a point.

Moy: There's always a cost pressure. If a client wants to carry out a survey for half the cost of a perfect survey then you've got to make some decisions. In a sense it doesn't cost a lot more to produce a decent sample than a poor one. There are inevitably cost pressures but the real issues are response rates and time available.

Research: If the benefits are much greater, shouldn't agencies be able to persuade clients to pay a bit more?

Moy: Sometimes what happens is that clients go to competitive tender for a job and you will see a price differential which is the result of different methodologies. It may well be the cheaper bid will win out but the methodology may not be quite so sound. Now, maybe the client has taken an informed decision about trading off accuracy or purity for cost, or maybe they just don't know. Some clients don't have the knowledge to make the judgement but I have to say I think the majority of them do – that's a relatively infrequent occurrence.

Research: How big an issue is awareness of statistical methods among research buyers? There are more pressures and broader responsibilities for clientside departments, who pay less attention to the details and rely more on trust.

Baker: Why should the onus be on the research buyer? They should be able to buy on trust. It's up to the research provider to make sure their systems are well founded for the problem in hand.

Moy: We have some highly skilled, highly informed clients who know exactly what they are doing. They may not necessarily be good statisticians but know about the issues that produce good research. Equally we have clients who are less well informed, often primarily because research isn't even their main function. There, if you've got a relationship of trust they can lean on the agency for advice. It's slightly more difficult when they go out for competitive bid because they are having to make decisions based on the knowledge they have.

Research: There's also an issue with the scope of the data user – it's not just the research department anymore. How far is it possible to educate all the data users?

Moy: This is where finding a balance between rigour and practicality becomes important. We can't afford to sit in our ivory towers and pontificate about how a perfect survey should be conducted. The bottom line is, if it's not available to the client when they need it, it's not going to be of any use to them. Ultimately they're either not going to buy it, or, even if they buy it, they won't be able to use it, and that will compromise their choice when they think of doing research the next time. Research buyers come from disparate backgrounds. Our task is to find the balance between giving the information they need to make informed decisions, and not overwhelming them or trying to turn them into researchers. That's a business skill and in our industry the most successful people are those who blend business and research skills.

Research: There is a worry that research buyers are not fully aware of the strengths and weaknesses of data on which they base commercial decisions. Data can appear authoritative on a computer screen.

Baker: It does seem to give it a degree of credibility. Sampling is just one issue behind the data you see. A more fundamental issue is the questioning technique. I can't prove this but if I were to say 'where's the main source of error in market research?', it wouldn't be sampling error at all – it would be simply the wrong question at the wrong time in the wrong place, over-fatigued respondents answering by rote and therefore not saying what they mean at all – they just want to get rid of you – and so on. That leads to a much more fundamental issue. How can we keep our respondents interested in the subject and how can we avoid making the fundamental mistakes of questionnaire design? That is where the major problems lie, rather than in sampling error.

Research: What would you say are the main alternatives to representative sampling?

Baker: There is a bad alternative to probability sampling – a poorly designed quota sample. Maybe it is cheaper but I doubt whether it's that much cheaper to justify doing it. Some of the alternatives for minority products are things like snowball sampling, where you try and find maybe a shop where they sell this minority product and you stand outside until you've found somebody, and try and interview them and see if they know anybody else. These sorts of techniques are rather like using databases – you've got no idea what the probability is. You don't even know what the universe looks like. These techniques are only useful when there's virtually no alternative. As long as we try, whenever practical, to represent the population as well as possible, that's what we should be doing.

Research: Even though the internet is not representative of the population it is an attractive medium for data collection. The lure of that may push the industry away from statistical representativeness.

Moy: For some people I'm sure it will, but hopefully whichever agency is doing research for those people will be able to inform them of the trade-off they are making. There is no doubt that the internet is sexy at the moment. If you're looking for views from business people or early adopters the internet is a good vehicle. However, as coverage is not yet universal, it will not produce good representation of the general population. If you're looking for a rounded view of that general population, then it may well be in a year's time we are looking at the digital TV route and the interactivity there, effectively carrying out what we perceive as internet surveys over TV sets. That may turn out to be a much quicker way of getting a representative sample, rather than over the internet.

Baker: You can also set up a panel of internet people where you actually give them a PC and access to the net and show them how to use it and so on. Things like that might be the way forward with net research.

Moy: We can learn a lot from our colleagues in the States because they're ahead of us in this game, given that internet penetration is much higher there. There's a lot of experience there that can inform how we do things. There's also quite a lot of work being done here that looks at bias that comes from using internet samples and how to deal with that. If the internet is the only way that gives you data in the time frame that you need, then we have to accept that and find ways to accommodate our objectives within an internet sample. The only thing I would add to that is you could do an overnight telephone survey and that may well be a better solution in some cases. It really does depend on the situation.

Research: The other issue with the internet is that it moves the research agency away from the client. It can be automated, removing the opportunity to educate the client or warn them about the data they are using. Is this a danger?

Baker: I think this is a major danger. The more we communicate with our clients about the limitations of what it is we are doing, the better.

Moy: We carry out a lot of large surveys where we harness the processes to set up very sophisticated web delivery systems. This clearly tends to be for bigger clients but there they will have a very deliberate, well thought out policy of dissemination within their organisation. There's actually quite a lot of thought that goes into those kind of processes when we set up web delivery of data. That's one side of the argument. I suppose the other end of it is there is so much data available on the web for people to get their hands on. We can't be expected to police the whole world.

Baker: I think as an industry we should be setting the standards for what it can and can't do via industry bodies such as the Market Research Development Fund, which in the 80s looked at hot methodological issues such as telephone research and data fusion. We should be doing the same things on internet research, but it seems to me that there are far too many busy people to volunteer their time than there were 10 to

15 years ago. That is an industry problem. But this is what we ought to be doing – have an industry body saying: what are the problems with this? What are the recommendations? What's good about it? What can it do, what can't it do? I'd like to see the industry looking into things like this.

Research: Do you think this is feasible? We live in a time-poor age.

Baker: We certainly do, but there are some outstanding brains floating around who may be willing to do this – people who have theoretically retired but maintain a big connection with the industry. Perhaps we should be recruiting those people to look into the technical problems rather than expecting very, very busy people to give more of their time. Perhaps we should slightly change tack about the way we go about it, but the thing is, it needs to be done.

Moy: There is less collaborative work going on. Having said that it doesn't mean there's no collaborative work going on. As I said earlier, a lot of work has been published from the States. Because the internet is such a big issue, there is a commercial imperative which wasn't there with the advent of telephone research. There are a lot of technological issues now with internet research which didn't really exist with telephone research. The combination of the pressure of work on people's time and, to an extent, more commercial pressure to keep developments under wraps, means there is less collaboration in research into research. But there's still quite a lot of stuff going on. It's the responsibilities of researchers to keep themselves up to date with that kind of work.

Research: What form will representativeness take in the future?

Baker: The industry is changing but representative sampling has got to keep up with it. The moment we start to decline in standards in terms of representation then what's our product? What are we selling?

Simply, we have to find more and more ingenious ways to represent the population as well as you can. It is so important to keep in touch with our roots. At the moment we seem to have a whole series of developments like net research going on without any concerted industry investigation. I am not talking about a witch hunt or anything like that, I'm just saying, now we've been in this for some time, can we establish the rules?

All the time the internet universe is changing anyway. What the rules are today may not be the rules in five years' time. But the need for representation will always be there.

Moy: What we've managed to do as an industry is convince ourselves and our clients, despite the arguments to the contrary of some academics, that it is possible to produce representative samples, and therefore reliable data, based on quota sampling. I don't think that's going to change. It may well be harder to achieve those samples and there may be larger issues around non-response bias if response rates continue to fall, but it's the responsibility of the industry to arrest that trend. There will undoubtedly be more panel research going on. That will service a particular need. The emphasis is still on achieving that holy grail – the representative sample.

The challenge for us is: what different mechanisms do we need in our changing environment to achieve what has been the constant aim from 60 or 70 years ago when market research was in its infancy? I don't think the ultimate aim has changed and I don't think for the majority of research it will ever change.

[1] This article appeared in the September 2000 edition of *Research*, pp. 20–5, and is published with the permission of the Market Research Society.

Issue 6
Researching difficult minority groups

Children in Need[1]

Working with children is a challenge in itself. But when the youngsters involved come from a difficult background, researchers have to find new ways of communicating with them, says Barbie Clarke.

Carrying out research with children and young people can be a challenge. It means communicating with those who may be less than enthusiastic participants, who may view all adults as too sad to be taken seriously or as a threat, and who are desperately conscious of how they appear to their peers.

Research with children cannot be merely an extension of the research methodologies used with adults. It calls for a different and innovative approach, especially when dealing with 'sensitive' issues.

Those of us involved in child and youth research regularly know it can create far more problems than research with 'grown ups', but it can also be far more rewarding, entertaining, surprising and, as a consequence, satisfying. It is challenging simply because most young people do not hide behind a facade of politeness and a basic social etiquette. Children and young people can be incredibly forthright, and wonderfully honest. They can give direct and straight answers that make us re-think and re-examine our language, phraseology and objectives constantly. As researchers we have to work doubly hard to think up creative, fun and probing techniques that tell us what kids really mean – techniques that allow for kids who are not skilled in the three Rs, and who might be tempted to agree with their peers, simply because an alternative opinion can place them in an isolating and vulnerable position.

NOP has always handled social and political research, and NOP Family gets approached frequently to look at issues such as crime, drugs, alcohol, and child abuse. Our team has wide experience of working with young offenders, kids who have been excluded from school, children who admit to taking drugs, committing crime, and who are generally labelled as the disaffected. It amazes us that such children, rejected by many adults and lacking in trust can, with an experienced moderator in a non-judgmental and gentle forum of a group, or an indepth interview, reveal much of what they do, how they do it, and some of the reasons for doing it.

Our team involved in such research is a highly trained bunch of individuals with a background in child and family therapy, child psychology, teaching and counselling.

The work can be tough; children are supposed to have a warm, protected, and joyful time up to adulthood. But of course we know, by reading newspapers or just being with kids that this is not always the case, and sadly many children do not fit into the stereotypical picture that we would wish to conjure up for them.

Much research is based on the assumption that children can be opinion-formers, make decisions, use 'pester power', have a degree of autonomy, and indeed happily this is certainly the case for much of the youth marketing mix we are involved in. It is also the case, however, that some clients will need to look at what drives children not to conform, not to listen to their teachers or parents, and to find out how they can be protected and made safe anyway.

Many clients in this category fall into governmental and public sectors. We have worked recently for several government departments, charities, local authorities, educational authorities and academic institutions, all of whom need to look closely at what motivates children to act and behave in the way they do.

We carried out work for a local authority among young people who were homeless, jobless, and in many cases severely depressed. Talking to these young people, many of whom had been labelled as 'trouble makers', was harrowing. Many had suffered verbal, physical or sexual abuse at home. They took to the streets, and even if they had a job to start with, they rapidly gave in to the peer group behaviour of drug or alcohol abuse, which meant they were unable to maintain the discipline of a regular job. Although they were offered sheltered housing, they sometimes found themselves in a worse situation than they had experienced at home, with bullying, crime and even physical attack rife as they struggled with the drug and alcohol culture. The research gave the local authority a real insight into the way of life and motivations of these young people; we were asked to present the results to several other agencies, including social services, police, community workers, teachers and young people's charities.

What happens though when the research sets out to find out not so much what the experience of troubled young people is, and how this can be improved, but how to prevent young people behaving in a way that might be dangerous or even fatal to other people and themselves?

Research carried out by NOP Family on behalf of a government organisation among young male offenders looked at ways in which warning and safety messages could be heard and seen by such a hardened audience. Go into any male young offenders' institution, and a tough, testosterone-driven world is found, where bullying is rife, suicide or attempted suicide is not uncommon, and anger is acted out in every conceivable way. Research to find out how these young people could be encouraged to pause and consider their actions, was a challenge.

The discussion groups and indepth interviews we carried out with young offenders called for great skill on the part of the moderators. Young offenders tend to be suspicious of adults, especially any they perceive to be in authority. Recruiting the respondents in itself was a particular challenge; imminent court cases, visits to probation officers and community work placements had to be taken into consideration, and several respondents were re-arrested before the research could take place!

We had to communicate to young offenders that we were there to understand, and to help make sense of their behaviour, not to be judgmental or tell them how they should behave. It is an important lesson to learn when carrying out any research with children. Most children want to conform, and need to be given the confidence by the researcher, whether conducting qualitative or quantitative research, that their opinions do matter and what they say counts; to make them feel that we as adults do not always know ourselves what is right, and that they as children and young people can contribute to our understanding.

Working with stimuli material of pictures, CD-roms, and video footage, we worked in discussion groups, paired interviews and individual interviews to find out how powerful prevention messages could reach the sub-conscious of these kids; what would make them stop, and consider the consequence of their action. While client confidentiality means the answers cannot be disclosed, what is important is how successfully the methodology worked. A group of disparate, disaffected male adolescents, who thought nothing of trashing property, writing graffiti, stealing cars, and mugging people on the street, were visibly moved by some of the images and attached messages they were shown.

With research such as this, and other work on sensitive issues, we make extensive use of projective techniques, much of it using methods drawn from family and child therapy, including drawings, modelling and collage making. These work well in allowing children and young people to express their feelings and their attitudes that otherwise might be difficult to facilitate.

An analogy for using this type of technique might be a child who has experienced severe trauma, for instance the death of a parent. Sometimes these difficult and painful experiences can be hard to express, the emotions are complex and might include anger, blame, guilt, as well as extreme sadness and sense of loss. By finding ways to express these feelings, other than in words, the child can be given an opportunity to indicate what she is feeling, even if it seems to her inadmissible to voice them. In the same way, questions on how young people really react to issues such as drugs, crime or homelessness, can be difficult for them to answer. Using projective techniques gives us a more accurate picture of their behaviour, motivation and opinions.

But we are not running counselling sessions, and boundaries have to be set firmly in place to ensure that the children and young people do not feel threatened or disturbed by what they have revealed.

Working at this level calls for trained and experienced researchers. Respondent confidentiality is paramount, and we must ensure that they do not feel that the honesty with which they have responded to our research is going to be used against them in any way. Working with children is sometimes extraordinary, but always revealing. Working on research of a sensitive nature with children can teach us much about how we communicate with children generally, the research methods we use, and the extent to which we ensure that our young respondents are given the opportunity to express their true opinions. Children are not young adults, and there is no reason to assume that the methods we use with them should merely be an adaptation of the methods we use with adults. Research with children and young people demands a creative and flexible approach, one that ensures that their needs are met, and that makes it clear that we take their opinions entirely seriously.

Barbie Clarke is director of NOP Family.

[1] This article appeared in the November 1999 edition of *Research*, pp. 46–7, and is published with the permission of the Market Research Society.

Testing times[1]

Researchers recently came under attack from the advertising industry for showing little innovation in qual or quant. Two ad planners and two researchers put on the gloves, watched over by Mike Savage.

Research: Rupert Howell, president of the Institute of Practitioners in Advertising, used a keynote speech to the recent MRS Conference to launch a fierce attack on the research industry, accusing it of failing to innovate. Was this speech deliberately provocative or was it a heartfelt and genuine reflection of the views of the advertising industry?

Jon Leach (Planner, HHCL and Partners): It was deliberately provocative in the sense that all industries need to innovate. It was an appeal to the research industry to help the advertising industry by innovating. Not enough helpful innovation has come our way.

Sid McGrath (Planner, HHCL and Partners): One of the frustrations that Rupert has, and that both of us share, is that over the past 10 years or so, around 99.9 per cent of researchers have come back following a briefing saying: 'to meet this objective we'd recommend either focus groups or one-on-one depth interviews'. It is always the same approach. In the advertising industry we're constantly attempting to innovate – where's the innovation from market research?

Terry Prue (Senior Partner, The HPI Research Group): There are constant innovations. It's a matter of degree. The UK has the best advertising in the world and it probably has the best advertising research in the world. The models we use are more sophisticated than what you'd get out of a German agency or an American agency. Partly why innovation seems slow is that some of it is genuinely difficult and quite expensive. If you start looking at the time lag before advertising effects kick in or start trying to work across combinations of different media, it is quite hard. There are new approaches. Both we and other research agencies can cite individual cases where we've done interesting things but, I agree, they are individual cases.

Leach: The two big inventions in advertising testing have been that you can put numbers on it and you can do group discussions on it. Since then, structurally no-one has achieved a breakthrough idea. The market research industry says: 'Well, we're still doing group discussions but we do cute things like bubble diagrams or get them to fill in diaries beforehand or we've got this real power question.' But it's still structurally the same thing.

Geoff Payne (Senior Partner, The HPI Research Group): It has always been evolutionary. The forum may look the same but the way in which groups are done and interpreted, leaving aside what bells and whistles people put on, is radically different to when I started in the industry over 20 years ago. We dip into the market with our own client and prospect monitor every few years and certainly five years ago people seemed to be quite pleased with the innovations on ad pre-testing. There's been quite a step change there.

Leach: There is a sense of wanting to carry on working within the same format. The idea that maybe doing ad pre-testing in people's homes or in halls is just fundamentally flawed, is a really scary thought to the research industry but it's that kind of scary thinking which would then force it to come up with a third way. I don't know what that third way is, but perhaps it requires a certain ability to think the unthinkable. No more living rooms, no more halls, what are we going to do? That's the plea to you guys because you probably have the ability to think of the technology or the idea.

Research: What factors could be holding back innovation in research?

Leach: I'm a bit worried that clients are perfectly happy with what they've got. When we speak about the problems of research, clients might say that some suppliers are better than others and that fundamentally there isn't a problem.

Prue: When it comes down to the individual briefs we get on individual jobs, they tend to be constrained by price and time. The way you get a more original design is when you get a more original problem or developmental work. We did research for the Miller Time ad, which took the whole break on Channel 4 going out at I think 11.30 on a Friday night. If you did it qual it was such a hit between the eyes – people were often fazed by it. But then we did it quant under the guise of programme research, because they'd already made the first two films. We recruited people to say they were going to be assessing Crapstone Villas and they watched it live on Friday night in the normal way. When we went out and interviewed them the next day they loved the ads.

Payne: We learned that if you did any more qual then we had to do it when these guys and girls had been on the booze. It's just impossible doing it in a viewing facility on a Monday night after one warm can of Fosters. The whole method was built around the medium of ad consumption – watching the Johnny Miller show chilled out after a night of beer.

McGrath: The medium you use can often be as surprising or as important as the message itself. That sounds like a great innovative step forward. I don't know whether you've interrogated a classic youth brand since then. Have you been able to use the same sort of approach? If you haven't, why haven't you? Because if what you found is something critically fundamental in the way people may digest communication based on conceptually where it was situated, why doesn't that become part of the industry standard? It seems that was an innovation for a specific client and then we'll settle back to how we've always worked previously.

Prue: It was partly the fact that we've found it an exception. When we've done other things we haven't found any difference. When we've done research in a hall on an ad and we've subsequently interviewed in the home about the ad we've got the same basic results. You can see exceptions and other times you can see it doesn't matter.

Payne: There hasn't been a paradigm shift in the terms of how qualitative ad research is done, and yet I think there's been a lot of healthy evolution. I suppose one passively thinks that if it ain't broke don't fix it. It's quite difficult to think of a third way for doing it when evolution in the second way seems to work. At the end of the day it's all about talking to, observing and interpreting people.

Leach: The advertising industry in general still seems to be complaining as much as it was 20 years ago. Wouldn't it be great if you did create the paradigm shift and suddenly the advertising industry said: 'Wow, this is great, this is something fantastically new, this is competitive.' You guys can improve the product but fundamentally the whingeing or the bitching continues.

Prue: Some of the whingeing and bitching is for other reasons. There is an inherent tendency for us to be whinged at. In some agencies there is a structure that research is used to deliver bad news. The team surrounding the advertising is very close to it and enthusiastic, and the term 'it's bombed-out in research' can be used as a cop-out because there's not been any other judgement or filtering up to that point.

McGrath: Did you find that there's not as much dialogue between planners and researchers as there should be? If that is ever the case, is that ever driven by the ad agency and/or planner or is it driven by the client? When I've been excluded from the research process it's at the instruction of the client. What can be done to overcome that?

Payne: We desperately want long-term client relationships. We want continuity and more accountability. The problem with the industry is that the buying patterns in research are repertoire-based and there is often a lack of continuity. It seems much better if you're part of the tri-partite team, you fully understand what the strategy is, you understand the creative intention, you've got a grown-up relationship with everybody involved. You end up getting far more out of research.

Leach: To make this tri-partite thing work – and accountability is something you want to make happen – how would you change your remuneration patterns to achieve that? If companies like ours are willing to be paid partly on performance of the communication we produce, why can't researchers be partly paid in the same way? Rather than coming on to a project, arriving at a set of conclusions and then leaving, the researchers will be investing something more than their time. Where the communication is successful they receive a bonus, where not, they only receive part-payment. This is what will genuinely foster a sense of partnership, where the research will be considered as an equal partner. Would that be difficult? Are you guys prepared to countenance this?

Payne: It could be the reticence of research but we're not often asked to sit on the top table.

Leach: It's to do with objectivity and subjectivity. Once the researchers have given their objective view, they think they can go. But that's a very naïve view. To say you are subjective but highly experienced and talented people is a much more honest thing. The whole tri-partite thing is subjective but let's bring in people with an expertise about using research to get opinions and insights and information and let's keep them there. When our collective bet gets placed they should benefit or lose collectively.

Research: When the planners talk of the big idea, the researchers talk of evolution. So do researchers actually believe in the big idea?

Payne: I would love to think there was a big idea and I'd love to think we might help give birth to it. It seems to me somehow at the end of the day it's all about observing, talking to and interpreting consumers. I think we would see consumers in the research process as a resource. The great thing in qual is you can use them as that. We bounce things off them, we take that away and we cross-reference that against all our other learnings of advertising new products and then we come back with some findings.

Leach: This isn't the idea but given the amount of interactive technology out, you can get somebody watching an ad and sending an email, you can send an email about the ad you're watching, literally. There seems to be a number of pre-testing opportunities. You could narrrowcast an ad into a thousand homes, possibly for a week or so to allow this bedding in. You can get feedback, you can get it quant and qually, you can phone them up and have a chat – that would be a structural shift.

McGrath: I don't think we can evolve what we've got. We need to start from a new place – a radical re-interpretation of the way we want advertising research to work and to ensure that what we're looking for is the right way of evaluating the performance of our advertising. Everyone seems to try to evolve, but not to a satisfactory conclusion – so perhaps we need to wipe the slate clean, look elsewhere and start again.

Prue: On one level I find it very easy to agree totally with that. I feel a bit defensive in saying I don't think it's as broke as you are implying, but I think that a lot of advertising research is good and that's why a lot of advertising is good. But there are bound to be as many variations in this industry as there are in any other. On the other hand it's very exciting to think about new developments and new ways of doing ad research. We need to have the stimulus of working with other people to get there.

McGrath: What's great about this session, and hopefully there will be more sessions like this, is that we're raising the issue now. You're absolutely right, it's not completely broke but there is an opportunity for improvement. Let's get that momentum going and let's improve, whether that's evolution or revolution or whatever.

Research: This is a perennial topic in the sense that it is much discussed, but little seems to come of it. What will it take to move this debate on?

McGrath: It's down to someone to seize the initiative. It's down to someone to change the rules of the game and come up with a different way of doing it, and all I can say as a final word is watch this space.

Payne: I think it's much more likely if there's a tangible problem where the client organisation, the agency and someone like us says invest in this so we can all live off this as a case history that moves things forward. It just strikes me that the experience of having these joint industry bodies will just be a load of waffle. There won't be an industry body in advertising that is going to fund it, the Account Planning Group won't have the money, AQRP won't, the MRS won't, so I think it's either going to be a case of 'seize an opportunity or make one'.

McGrath: We don't want Kilroy-style discussions where all everyone does is debate things. It's a question of how proactive people are. You can come up with great ideas but are you willing to follow through on them? People need to begin to follow through.

[1] This article appeared in the June 2000 edition of *Research*, pp. 20–3, and is published with the permission of the Market Research Society.

Issue 8
Branding research products

Battle of the brands[1]

Agencies produced a torrent of branded research products last year, despite evidence that many clients are unhappy with such off-the-peg solutions. Ken Gofton surveys the scene.

A recent *Research* survey of clients suggested that the people who pay the industry's bills are, at best, ambivalent about off-the-shelf branded products from market research agencies.

The survey, devised by Research International and published in last month's *Research*, covered a sample of 100 marketing directors in the UK. Responding to the statement 'branded research techniques are increasingly likely to be our preference over ad hoc solutions', a third of the sample were firmly in favour of branded products, and a similar number were firmly against them, while the remainder (29 per cent) were neutral. This indicates that, among clients, the jury is out on branded MR products.

This could be a cause for concern, given the growing importance many agencies place upon branding their wares. As the box shows, last year saw a torrent of branded products. The box, covering UK launches during 1999, is the result of a straw poll among some of the biggest research companies. Taylor Nelson Sofres managed an average of one branded product per month through the year. NOP and Millward Brown were not far behind.

The US provides the model for many developments in the market research industry. Product branding became a trend on that side of the Atlantic in the late 70s and early 80s, taking off a decade later, according to Larry Gold of Inside Research in the US. Market research came late to branded products, he says.

'Research people are not marketers. The motivation, then and now, for naming individual products is to establish a simple connection between the name of the product and what it does. Research people woke up to the fact that, with the proliferation of services on offer, it was hard to impress upon a potential user a remembrance of a product or service that didn't have a brand name.'

The Added Value Company

Brainpool, a four-stringed approach to mapping, measuring and making sense of societal changes

BMRB International

Digital Viewer Survey, six-monthly comprehensive survey of digital TV viewers

Access to Multi-Media, omnibus survey with ability to play digitally manipulated (e.g. 'debranded') video clips

Information Resources

Analyzer Publishing, an add-on tool for automatically updating PowerPoint presentations of Oracle sales data

Census Infoscan, combining sample and census data for retail tracking

Infratest Burke/BJM

NFO Marketmind, brand tracking service, marketed by both NFO subsidiaries

Ipsos-RSL

Satisfactor Plus, actionable data on customer satisfaction

Brandfx, brand, ad tracking and ad hoc studies with CapiVision multimedia laptops

Therapy Tracking Studies, syndicated usage and attitude studies among patients and medics

Millward Brown

ATP, Advanced Trading Programme measures advertising performance

BrandAction, qualitative research technique

BrandDynamics, brand equity measurement tool

Link, ad copy testing system

MORI

MORIfutures, a partnership with strategic research consultancy Market Dynamics

e-public panel, regular online survey of internet users

e-directors panel, online research panel of UK's biggest spending IT decision makers

e-travel tracker, consumer research panel for the travel trade

e-entertainment, tracking growth of digital TV, online music, and gaming

NOP

The Employer Brand, applying brand management thinking to the employment experience

BrandShape, measuring brand health

SmallTalk, syndicated survey of 5–15 year olds

The Youth Agenda, syndicated survey of 16–24 year olds

Next Generation, syndicated survey of financial attitudes among 14–24 year olds

Omnibus MicroMatch, motivational segmentation tool

ADD+IMPACT, ad test to complement the creative

Teen Track, teenage life in the 21st century

NOP Internet Exchange, research in internet cafes

ORC

NHS Talkback, syndicated employee research in the NHS

Employer Equity, brand image survey that determines how an organisation is seen as a place to work

ORC Interactive, evaluating, monitoring, and improving web business

Research International

Webclinics, focus groups and other techniques harnessed to improve website effectiveness

Loyalty Driver, advanced model for strategic management of customer loyalty

Brandsight Gallery, internationally validated portfolio of visual prompts

Purchase Pulse, category purchase behaviour segmentation tool

Storemind, category management toolbox

Simon Godfrey Associates

Promotions Filter, determines optimum promotions for a brand, and consumer susceptibility to promotions

Taylor Nelson Sofres

BuildUp, multimedia software tool for NPD research

Sandwich Trak, first continuous research on sandwich market

Adjust, multimedia software tool for pre-testing ad concepts

AntibioticsMonitor, comprehensive survey of antibiotics in general practice

International Omnimed, international omnibus survey of GPs

International Omnibus, international consumer survey

Kids' MealTrak, one-off three month survey of children's eating habits

BeautyPanel, continuous tracking of cosmetics, fragrances, and skincare purchases

Coverview, researching the contribution of video to ad campaigns

Miriad, interactive analysis tool, integrating all tracking data into one database

Transact, detailed weekly sales data for pharmaceutical wholesalers

NeedScope System, identifies psychological drivers behind consumer brand choice

The Research Business International

Talking Shop, employee satisfaction

Vision, advertising pre-testing

The box appears to confirm Gold's point about research proliferation – look at all the new products relating to internet research, for instance – and it also shows just how much companies need to differentiate their offerings.

Other arguments are often advanced to support the introduction of branded products, including a demand from global clients for consistency, both geographically and over time. The growth through takeovers of international research networks is also leading to their spread.

In some areas, such as new product development, the use of a consistent approach over a long period of time results in a database of hundreds, even thousands, of case studies. The advantage is that clients are able to see the research results in the context of their own industry.

The bigger research companies often grumble, also, about poor margins at the commodity end of ad hoc research. They see branding as a means of getting away from what they dub the 'vanilla ice cream' business.

Finally, it is sometimes held that, in a crowded industry, it is difficult to win new clients if all you can offer is basic research. Having a relevant branded product to talk about helps to get a foot in the door.

Not surprisingly, clients have difficulty with some of these arguments. Dick Whittington, London-based vice-president for international research with American Express, says bluntly that he never buys branded products. 'When we look for ad hoc solutions to problems, it is very rare that I find a "canned" or branded product that provides what we need,' he adds. 'In our experience, the point about consistency across borders is true of people and the teams you might approach. I buy the company, or the individual within the company.

'On the face of it, I'm not prepared to accept the idea that, because a service is branded, it is going to give you more consistency, higher quality, or whatever. The only situation I see where branding makes a lot of sense is in the omnibus or panel sector.'

Diana Brown, head of marketing and sales information at Royal Mail and until recently chair of the Association of Users of Research Agencies (AURA), is also cynical about the consistency argument. She accepts that there may be a case for a branded approach when doing a lot of multi-country work. Even here, if the field-work and data collection aren't both of a sufficiently high standard, then it is still a case of 'garbage in, garbage out'. Brown says she has no problem with branded products as such, and believes a large part of the problem may be presentation. At the core is the fact that every client likes to believe that their situation is unique.

'There's just a perception that people [researchers] are not listening to what the problem is,' she explains. 'You [the client] may raise the question of brand equity, or whatever, and they immediately leap in and say, "Ah, yes, this is our solution, and it's called whatever". They are into solution mode almost before they hear what the problem is.'

She adds: 'If it was like buying a mass-produced Ford rather than a hand-made Rolls-Royce, we could see it was better value for money, but I can't see that these off-the-shelf products cost any less. We're getting something that isn't tailor-made, and we're paying a premium for it.'

And there's the rub. Research agencies see branded products as a route to better margins; clients claim that standard approaches should mean lower costs. Despite these differences, some believe that branded products will continue to grow. 'As in most things, it is a question of balance,' says Simon Orton, deputy managing director of BMRB International. 'It is vitally important to recognise when a standard research product is appropriate, when an adaptation of it is necessary, and when an original tailored solution is required, if the objective is to provide the very best research support. A full understanding of the client's specific problem must always be the starting point.'

Research International's marketing director, Dave Phillips, agrees. Branding any old approach just to sell more research is a nonsense, he says. A proper, branded product ought to be good for its stated purpose, and flexible enough to be refined to meet the needs of specific clients.

For instance, a major client for RI's Equity Engine insisted that a particular question be put to its target audience; it was possible to run the survey with and without the question. 'It's things like that which tend to defuse this whole argument.'

That may be true, but it does not eliminate the fact that research buyers in the UK appear more resistant to branded products than their counterparts in the US.

'I have not heard of any resistance in the US – just the opposite,' says Larry Gold. 'Research managers here, unlike the UK, are not seeking totally customised solutions. They understand that brands and systems and products, if they have a consistency, are better understood by their marketing managers. There is a more general acceptance of them.'

---

[1] This article appeared in the February 2000 edition of *Research*, pp. 24–6, and is published with the permission of the Market Research Society.

Issue 9
Clients going direct to respondents

Direct approach[1]

An increasing number of clients are cutting out the research 'middle man' and talking directly to their customers. Mike Savage looks at the growth of 'direct-to-consumer' programmes, and the implications for MR suppliers.

When Microsoft UK set up special forums for its staff to meet their customers, it did so as a direct result of research – the software giant's customers were complaining that they had had enough of it. 'They didn't want to be surveyed by people over the web,' reveals Microsoft UK's customer loyalty manager, Valerie Bennett. 'They wanted to come and talk to Microsoft face-to-face.' Now they can, on 'Theme Days' organised by Bennett to talk over issues of common concern with Microsoft personnel.

Market research is no longer seen as the de facto solution to business problems; and Microsoft is not the only company that views the days when MR alone could interpret customer behaviour as over. With its roots in retail, where managers were encouraged to mingle with customers on the shop floor, the practice of going direct to the consumer has now spread in various guises to companies as diverse as Ford, Birds Eye Walls, Barclays and BSkyB.

Often these programmes are run by the research department, which has had to adapt to a new role. No longer the sole intermediary between a company and its customers, inhouse researchers are taking a step back to co-ordinate customer contact and tie the results of these meetings in with existing research programmes.

'We are primarily facilitators of consumer insight with responsibility for identifying those which can be most powerfully harnessed to drive our brands,' explains Bill Parton, market research controller for Kraft Foods. 'Ultimately, however, it is our brand and customer marketers who must translate insights into strategy and execution. To do this it is not enough to intellectually understand the insight; they need to feel it. The only way they can do this is through direct experience.'

Kraft Foods first introduced direct-to-consumer techniques in November 1998, with the initial aim of helping to build broader understanding of its consumers' lives. It has since become part of the company's culture. Parton says that the biggest challenge for researchers and marketers alike is to go beyond behaviour, to understand what really motivates consumers. To do this Kraft is trying to help its people develop some of the skills employed by research. 'It's not about the future of research,' Parton states. 'It's about the future of marketing. They are the guys who have to come up with the ideas.'

Meeting people who place their choice of instant coffee near the bottom of life's priorities can provide a much needed change of view for marketers who steep themselves in a category day after day. 'It's a good reality check,' comments Gavin Emsden, beverages research manager at Nestlé. 'Even going to groups and sitting behind the glass is not the same as sitting down with the consumer and talking with them.'

'It is tremendously powerful in getting your store to think about the customer,' enthuses Asda's head of market research, Darryl Burchell, who is teaching staff how to get the most out of focus groups and accompanied shops. 'If you work in a store day in, day out, you see the store from an operational perspective, rather than a customer's perspective. What better way to see the customer's perspective than to accompany them on a shopping trip?'

Direct-to-consumer programmes also spread the experience of customer insight to a far wider audience than is reached by traditional market research, Burchell points out. The majority of MR may still be done by Burchell and his team, but they alone do not have the resources to research each of Asda's 227 stores.

While direct-to-consumer programmes could be described as a 'quick and dirty' way of getting research done, few clientside researchers regard these as threatening the work of MR suppliers. Kraft Foods conducts many direct-to-consumer studies at early stages of development long before it becomes economically sensible to commission MR. Bill Parton believes this early work-out for fledgling ideas leads to better briefs for research projects.

The aims of Van den Bergh Foods' direct-to-consumer programme, 'Consumer Connexion', are very different to the learning it gets from market research data, points out group insight manager Stephen Donaldson.

'This programme is subjective by its design and nature. This is not an objective piece of market research.' The three-year-old programme hasn't affected Van den Bergh's appetite for basic MR data, Donaldson stresses. 'Market research still plays the role of the voice of the consumer in our business decision making. This [Consumer Connexion] is making you more aware of your customers and giving you a better understanding of them, so you make better decisions.'

Donaldson believes companies that encourage direct customer contact will thrive and is hoping that Van den Bergh's parent, Unilever, will use his experiences as a model throughout the entire group. However, direct-to-consumer programmes are not easy to introduce. Time-consuming get-togethers that have no immediate benefit are not easy to initiate in companies working to a goal-driven culture. The programmes also have to be carefully managed, to make sure managers lacking in research experience don't jump to the wrong conclusions, and to maintain the freshness that gives the programmes their value.

Despite the hurdles, direct-to-consumer is growing. It is one way of maximising learning from a tightly controlled budget. Management buy-in is easier to come by if the board has adopted a philosophy of customer focus. Direct-to-consumer offers an edge over the competition in a market where customers are increasingly perceived to be calling the shots.

'This kind of approach will only become more common,' observes Karen Wise, joint md for Martin Hamblin's consumer and business division. 'Our clients are looking for additional insights and involvement with their end users and we appreciate that this practice can do this. However, there's a strong argument that without the professional skills that an agency has, a lot is lost.' Wise suggests convening three-way workshops where the client, its customers and the research agency all work together. 'Through encouraging our clients to meet their customers face to face, we will involve them more in the research process and be able to engage them further in the findings – crucial for the success of any project.'

Even if companies are not operating schemes on the scale of Asda or Van den Bergh Foods, contact with consumers has become a common component of company induction and training programmes. The market research industry is also seeing a growth in the use of methodologies which bridge traditional MR and direct-to-consumer techniques, such as extended focus groups where traditionally passive viewers emerge from behind the mirror after a group to address issues they are interested in directly to the participants.

However, the growth of direct-to-consumer techniques also sounds a note of warning that research buyers are no longer satisfied with traditional research. Although some clients say direct-to-consumer programmes have not dented research budgets, agencies should also take note of companies like Microsoft UK, where the take-up of direct-to-consumer techniques forms part of a more fundamental shift in attitudes to research. The growth of new ways of interrogating the consumer will not eat into research budgets only as long as MR can keep proving its worth.

Companies move closer to their consumers:

Asda – Customer Listening Programme

How long has it been running?

About eight years

Who manages it?

Co-ordinated/facilitated by the market research department

Who takes part?

All managers within the business, both at Asda House and instore

How often is it run?

Frequency varies by department, but typically at least once a month

What methods are used?

The programme includes focus groups, moderated by Asda personnel, with a mixture of professionally recruited respondents and customers who had complaints or suggestions, and accompanied shops. Customer suggestion cards reviewed weekly

Van den Bergh Foods – Consumer Connexion

How long has it been running?

Since 1997

Who manages it?

The consumer insight department (formerly called market research) with an external agency, QRS

Who takes part in it?

All departments – marketing, R&D, sales, etc.

How often is it run?

Ad hoc, depending on individual needs

What methods are used?

Methods include but not limited to: in-home visit; store visit; cooking sessions; friendship pairs; mini-groups; and others

Nestlé – Unnamed informal, ad hoc use

How long has it been running?

There has been marketing/sales contact with consumers going back many years. This has become more regular over the last two years

Who manages it?

Market Intelligence – whoever is responsible for the product area the approach is being used on

Who takes part in it?

Market Intelligence, marketing and, as appropriate, staff from the category, technical, sensory departments

How often is it run?

No fixed time scale

What methods are used?

Generally group discussions or depths – usually accompanied shops or in-home interviews, but use other methods as well, such as accompanied visits to coffee shops

[1] This article appeared in the October 2000 edition of *Research*, pp. 38–9, and is published with the permission of the Market Research Society.

Glossary

Accompanied shopping
A specialised type of individual depth interview, which involves respondents being interviewed while they shop in a retail store and combines observation with detailed questioning.

Alternative hypothesis
The hypothesis where some difference or effect is expected (i.e. a difference that cannot occur simply by chance).

Ambiguous question
A badly constructed question which results in respondents and researchers reading different meanings into what is being asked, resulting in inappropriate or unexpected answers.

Animatics
A type of stimulus material where key frames for a television advertisement are drawn or computer generated with an accompanying sound track.

Annotation method
An approach taken to analyse qualitative data using codes or comments on the transcripts to categorise the points being made by respondents.

ANOVA
Analysis of variance. A test for the differences among the means of two or more variables.

Area sampling
A type of cluster sampling in which the clusters are created on the basis of the geographic location of the population of interest.

Audience's thinking sequence
The sequence of thoughts that people go through when they are being communicated with.

Audits
An examination and verification of the movement and sale of a product. There are three main types: wholesale audits, which measure product sales from wholesalers to retailers and caterers, retail audits, which measure sales to the final consumer, and home audits, which measure purchases by the final consumer.

Bar chart	A chart which uses a series of bars that may be positioned horizontally or vertically to represent the values of a variety of items.
Beauty parades	The procedure of asking a number of agencies to present their proposals verbally to the client company. The procedure is used to assist clients in selecting the research agency that will undertake a research project.
Brand mapping	A projective technique which involves presenting a set of competing brand names to respondents and getting them to group them into categories based on certain dimensions such as innovativeness, value for money, service quality and product range.
Brand personalities	A projective technique which involves respondents imagining a brand as a person and describing their looks, their clothes, their lifestyles, employment, etc.
CAPI	Computer-assisted personal interviewing. Where lap-top computers or pen-pad computers are used rather than paper-based questionnaires for face-to-face interviewing.
Cartoon completion	A projective technique which involves a cartoon that the respondent has to complete. For example, the cartoon may show two characters with balloons for dialogue. One of the balloons sets out what one of the characters is thinking or saying, while the other is left empty for the respondent to complete.
CATI	Computer-assisted telephone interviewing. CATI involves telephone interviewers typing respondent's answers directly into a computer-based questionnaire rather than writing them on a paper-based questionnaire.
CATS	Completely automated telephone interviews which use interactive voice technology and require no human interviewer. Respondents answer the closed-ended questions with their touch tone telephone.
Causal research	Research that examines whether one variable causes or determines the value of another variable.
Census	Research which involves collecting data from every member of the population of interest.
Chat rooms	An Internet-based facility that can be used for online focus groups where individuals are recruited who are willing to discuss a subject online usually using text.

Chi-square	A statistical test which tests the 'goodness of fit' between the observed distribution and the expected distribution of a variable.
Closed question	A question that requires the respondent to make a selection from a predefined list of responses. There are two main types of closed questions: dichotomous questions with only two potential responses and multiple response questions with more than two.
Cluster analysis	A statistical technique used to classify objects or people into mutually exclusive and exhaustive groups on the basis of two or more classification variables.
Cluster sampling	A probability sampling approach in which clusters of population units are selected at random and then all (one-stage cluster sampling) or some (two-stage cluster sampling) of the units in the chosen clusters are studied.
Coding	The procedures involved in translating responses into a form that is ready for analysis. Normally involves the assigning of numerical codes to responses.
Coefficient of determination	Measure of the strength of linear relationship between a dependent variable and independent variables.
Concept boards	A type of stimulus material which uses a set of boards to illustrate different product, advertising or pack designs.
Confidence level	The probability that the true population value will be within a particular range (result +/− sampling error).
Conjoint analysis	A statistical technique that provides a quantitative measure of the relative importance of one attribute over another. It is frequently used to determine what features a new product or service should have and also how products should be priced.
Constant sum scales	A scaling approach which requires the respondent to divide a given number of points, usually 100, among a number of attributes based on their importance to the individual.
Content analysis	The analysis of any form of communication, whether it is advertisements, newspaper articles, television programmes or taped conversations.

Frequently used for the analysis of qualitative research data.

Content analysis software

Software used for qualitative research which basically counts the number of times that pre-specified words or phrases appear in text.

Contrived observation

A research approach which involves observing participants in a controlled setting.

Convenience sampling

A non-probability sampling procedure in which a researcher's convenience forms the basis for selecting the potential respondents (i.e. the researcher approaches the most accessible members of the population of interest).

Cookies

Text files placed on a user's computer by web retailers in order to identify the user when he or she next visits the website.

Continuous research

See Longitudinal research.

Correlation

A statistical approach to examine the relationship between two variables. Uses an index to describe the strength of a relationship.

Critical path method (CPM)

A managerial tool used for scheduling a research project. It is a network approach that involves dividing the research project into its various components and estimating the time required to complete each component activity.

Cross-sectional research

Research studies that are undertaken once only involving data collection at a single point in time providing a 'snapshot' of the specific situation. The *opposite* of longitudinal research.

Cross-tabulations

Tables that set out the responses to one question relative to the responses to one or more other questions.

Customer database

A manual or computerised source of data relevant to marketing decision making about an organisation's customers.

Cut and paste method of analysis

A method for analysing qualitative research data where material is cut and pasted from the original transcript into separate sections or tables relating to each topic. Cutting and pasting can either be done physically using scissors or using a word processing computer package.

Data analysis errors

Non-sampling errors that occur when data is transferred from questionnaires to computers by incorrect keying of information.

Data analysis services	Organisations, sometimes known as tab shops, that specialise in providing services such as the coding of completed questionnaires, inputting the data from questionnaires into a computer and the provision of sophisticated data analysis using advanced statistical techniques.
Data cleaning	Computerised checks made on data to identify inconsistencies in the data and to check for any unexplained missing responses.
Data conversion	The reworking of secondary data into a format that allows estimates to be made to meet the researcher's needs.
Data elements	The individual pieces of information held in a database (e.g. a person's name, gender or date of birth). These elements mean little independently but when combined they provide information on a customer or group of customers.
Data entry	The transfer of data from a questionnaire into a computer by any of the following means: either directly in computer-assisted interviewing, by an operator copy-typing the responses from questionnaires, or by the optical scanning of printed questionnaires.
Data errors	Non-sampling errors that occur during data collection or analysis that impact on the accuracy of inferences made about the population of interest. The main types of data error are respondent errors (where respondents give distorted or erroneous answers), interviewer errors and data analysis errors.
Data mining	An activity where highly powerful computers are used to dig through volumes of data to discover patterns about an organisation's customers and products.
Data protection legislation	Legislation created to protect against the misuse of personal data (i.e. data about an individual person).
Database	A collection of related information that can be accessed and manipulated quickly using computers.
Deduplication	The process through which data belonging to different transactions or service events are united for a particular customer. Software will be used to either automatically eliminate duplicates or identify potential duplicates that require a manual inspection and a decision to be taken.
Degrees of freedom (d.f.)	The number of observations (i.e. sample size) minus one.

Depth interview	*See* Individual depth interview.
Descriptive research	Research studies that describe what is happening in a market without potentially explaining why it is happening.
Descriptive statistics	Statistics that help to summarise the characteristics of large sets of data using only a few numbers. The most commonly used descriptive statistics are measures of central tendency (mean, mode and median) and measures of dispersion (range, interquartile range and standard deviation).
Dichotomous questions	Questions with only two potential responses (e.g. Yes or No).
Directories	A listing of individuals or organisations involved in a particular activity. May be available in printed format, CD-ROMs or on the Internet.
Discussion guide	*See* Topic list.
Disproportionate stratified random sampling	A form of stratified random sampling (*See* Stratified random sampling) where the units or potential respondents from each population set are selected according to the relative variability of the units within each subset.
Double-barrelled question	A badly constructed question where two topics are raised within one question.
Doughnut chart	A form of pie chart which allows different sets of data (e.g. for different years) to be shown in the same chart.
Editing	The process of ensuring that questionnaires were filled out correctly and completely.
E-mail survey	A self-completion survey that is delivered to pre-selected respondents by e-mail. The questionnaire can take the form of text within the e-mail or can be sent as an attachment (either as a word processor document or as a piece of software which runs the questionnaire).
Executive interviews	Quantitative research interviews with business people, usually undertaken at their place of work, covering subjects related to industrial or business products and services.
Experimental research	Research which measures causality and involves the researcher changing one variable (e.g. price, packaging, shelf display, etc.), while observing the effects of those changes on another variable (e.g. sales) and controlling the extraneous variables.

Exploratory research	Research that is intended to develop initial ideas or insights and to provide direction for any further research needed.
External data	Secondary data that is sourced from outside the organisation requiring the research to be conducted.
Face-to-face survey	Research which involves meeting respondents face-to-face and interviewing them using a paper-based questionnaire, a lap-top computer or an electronic notepad.
Factor analysis	A statistical technique that studies the interrelationships among variables for the purpose of simplifying data. It can reduce a large set of variables to a smaller set of composite variables or factors by identifying the underlying dimensions of the data.
Field agencies	Agencies whose primary activity is the field interviewing process focusing on the collection of data through personal interviewers, telephone interviewers or postal surveys.
Focus groups	*See* Group discussions.
Frequency distributions	*See* Hole counts.
Full service agencies	Marketing research agencies that offer the full range of marketing research services and techniques. They will be able to offer the entire range of qualitative and quantitative research approaches as well as be capable of undertaking every stage of the research from research design through to analysis and report writing.
Funnel sequence	A sequence for ordering questions in a questionnaire based on moving from the generalities of a topic to the specifics.
GANTT chart	A managerial tool used for scheduling a research project. It is a form of flowchart that provides a schematic representation incorporating the activity, time, and personnel requirements for a given research project.
Geodemographic profiling	A profiling method which uses postal addresses to categorise different neighbourhoods in relation to buying power and behaviour.
Group depth interviews	*See* Group discussions.
Group discussions	Also known as focus groups or group depth interviews. These are depth interviews undertaken

with a group of respondents. In addition to the increased number of respondents, they differ from individual depth interviews in that they involve interaction between the participants.

Group dynamics

The interaction between group members in group discussions.

Group moderator

The interviewer responsible for the management and encouragement of participants in a group discussion.

Hall tests

Research undertaken in a central hall or venue commonly used to test respondents' initial reactions to a product or package or concept. Respondents are recruited into the hall by interviewers stationed on main pedestrian thoroughfares nearby.

Hidden observation

A research approach involving observation where the participant does not know that they are being observed.

Holecounts

The number of respondents who gave each possible answer to each question in a questionnaire. Sometimes known as frequency distributions.

Hypothesis

An assumption or proposition that a researcher puts forward about some characteristic of the population being investigated.

Hypothesis testing

Testing aimed at determining whether the difference between proportions is greater than would be expected by chance or as a result of sampling error.

Implicit assumption

A badly constructed question where the researcher and the respondent are using different frames of reference as a result of assumptions that both parties make about the question being asked.

Independent samples

Samples in which the measurement of the variable of interest in one sample has no effect on the measurement of the variable in the other sample.

Individual depth interview

An interview that is conducted face-to-face, in which the subject matter of the interview is explored in detail using an unstructured and flexible approach.

Information explosion

The major growth in information available in a wide range of formats from a wide range of sources. This growth has principally resulted from improvements in the capabilities and speeds of computers.

In-home/doorstep interviewing	Face-to-face interviews undertaken within the home of the respondent or on the doorstep of their home.
Internal data	Secondary data sourced from within the organisation that is requiring the research to be conducted.
Internet monitoring	The measurement undertaken by web-based retailers and suppliers to monitor the number of times different pages on their sites are accessed, what search engines bring people to the site, what service provider browsers are used as well as tracking the specific time at which the site is accessed. Using cookies, the retailers may also be able to identify when users revisit the site.
Interquartile range	A measure of dispersion that calculates the difference between the 75th and 25th percentile in a set of data.
Interval data	Similar to ordinal data with the added dimension that the intervals between the values on a scale are equal. That means that when using a scale of 1 to 5, the difference between 1 and 2 is the same as the difference between 4 and 5. However, the ratios between different values on the scale are not valid (e.g. 4 does not represent twice the value of 2).
Interviewer bias	Bias and errors in research findings brought about by the actions of an interviewer. This may be influenced by who the interviewer interviews, how the interview is undertaken and the manner in which responses are recorded.
Interviewer errors	*See* Interviewer bias.
Interviewer guide	*See* Topic list.
Interviewer Quality Control Scheme (IQCS)	A quality control scheme for interviewers in the UK. The scheme is aimed at improving selection, training and supervision of interviewers and is jointly run by the Market Research Society, the Association of Market Survey Organisations, the Association of British Market Research Companies, the Association of Users of Research Agencies, and a number of leading research companies.
Judgement sampling	A non-probability sampling procedure where a researcher consciously selects a sample that he or she considers to be most appropriate for the research study.

Leading question
A badly constructed question that tends to steer respondents toward a particular answer. Sometimes known as a loaded question.

Least squares approach
A regression procedure that is widely used for deriving the best-fit equation of a line for a given set of data involving a dependent and independent variable.

Lifestyle databases
Databases that consist of data derived from questionnaire responses to 'lifestyle surveys'. Such surveys make it clear to respondents that the data is being collected for the creation of a database rather than for marketing research purposes.

Likert scales
A scaling approach which requires the respondent to state their level of agreement with a series of statements about a product, organisation or concept. The scale using the descriptors Strongly agree; Agree; Neither agree nor disagree; Disagree; Strongly disagree is based on a format originally developed by Renis Likert in 1932.

Line graph
A two-dimensional graph that is typically used to show movements in data over time.

List brokers
Organisations that sell off-the shelf data files listing names, characteristics and contact details of consumers or organisations.

Loaded question
See Leading question.

Longitudinal research
A study involving data collection at several periods in time enabling trends over time to be examined. This may involve asking the same questions on a number of occasions of either the same respondents or of respondents with similar characteristics. Sometimes known as continuous research.

Mall intercept interviews
See Street interviews.

Marketing concept
The proposition that the whole of the organisation should be driven by a goal of serving and satisfying customers in a manner which enables the organisation's financial and strategic objectives to be achieved.

Marketing decision support system (MDSS)
An interactive computerised information source designed to assist in marketing decision making.

Marketing research
The collection, analysis and communication of information undertaken to assist decision making in marketing.

Marketing research process	The sequence of activities and events involved in undertaking a marketing research project.
Mean	The arithmetic average which is calculated by summing all of the values in a set of data and dividing by the number of cases.
Measures of central tendency	Measures that indicate a typical value for a set of data by computing the mean, mode or median.
Measures of dispersion	Measures that indicate how 'spread out' a set of data is. The most common are the range, the interquartile range and the standard deviation.
Mechanised observation	A research approach involving observation of behaviour using automated counting devices, scanners or other equipment.
Median	When all of the values in a data set are put in ascending order, the median is the value of the middle case in a series.
Metric data	A name for interval and ratio data.
Mode	The value in a set of data that occurs most frequently.
Multiple-choice questions	Questions which provide respondents with a choice of predetermined responses to a question. The respondents are asked to either give one alternative that correctly expresses their viewpoint or indicate all responses that apply.
Multiple discriminant analysis	A statistical technique used to classify individuals into one of two or more segments (or populations) on the basis of a set of measurements.
Multiple regression analysis	A statistical technique to examine the relationship between three or more variables and also to calculate the likely value of the dependent variable based on the values of two or more independent variables.
Multi-stage sampling	A sampling approach where a number of successive sampling stages are undertaken before the final sample is obtained.
Multivariate data analysis	Statistical procedures that simultaneously analyse two or more variables on a sample of objects. The most common techniques are multiple regression analysis, multiple discriminant analysis, factor analysis, cluster analysis, perceptual mapping and conjoint analysis.
Mystery shopping	A form of participant observation which uses researchers to act as customers or potential

customers to monitor the processes and procedures used in the delivery of a service.

Newsgroups

Internet-based sites that take the form of bulletin boards/discussion lists on specific topics. They involve people posting views, questions and information on the site.

Nominal data

Numbers assigned to objects or phenomena as labels or identification numbers that name or classify but have no true numeric meaning.

Non-metric data

A name for nominal and ordinal data.

Non-probability sampling

A set of sampling methods where a subjective procedure of selection is used resulting in the probability of selection for each member of the population of interest being unknown.

Non-response errors

An error in a study that arises when some of the potential respondents do not respond. This may occur due to respondents refusing or being unavailable to take part in the research.

Non-sampling error

Errors that occur in a study that do not relate to sampling error. They tend to be classified into three broad types: sampling frame error, non-response error and data error.

Normal distribution

A continuous distribution that is bell-shaped and symmetrical about the mean. This means that in a study, 68.27 per cent of the observations fall within plus or minus one standard deviation of the mean, approximately 95.45 per cent fall within plus or minus two standard deviations, and approximately 99.73 per cent fall within plus or minus three standard deviations.

Null hypothesis

The hypothesis that is tested and is the statement of the status quo where no difference or effect is expected.

Observation

A data gathering approach where information is collected on the behaviour of people, objects and organisations without any questions being asked of the participants.

Omnibus surveys

A data collection approach that is undertaken at regular intervals for a changing group of clients who share the costs involved in the survey's set-up, sampling and interviewing.

One-way mirrors

Used in qualitative marketing research to enable clients and researchers to view respondent behaviour during a discussion. Behind the mirror is a viewing room, which consists of chairs for the observers and may contain video cameras to record the proceedings.

Open-ended questions	Questions which allow respondents to reply in their own words. There are no pre-set choices of answers and the respondent can decide whether to provide a brief one-word answer or something very detailed and long. Sometimes known as unstructured questions.
Ordinal data	Numbers that have the labelling characteristics of nominal data, but also have the ability to communicate the rank order of the data. The numbers do not indicate absolute quantities, nor do they imply that the intervals between the numbers are equal.
Paired interviews	An in-depth interview involving two respondents such as married couples, business partners, teenage friends or a mother and child.
Panel research	A research approach where comparative data is collected from the same respondents on more than one occasion. Panels can consist of individuals, households or organisations, and can provide information on changes in behaviour, awareness and attitudes over time.
Participant observation	A research approach where the researcher interacts with the subject or subjects being observed. The best-known type of participant observation is mystery shopping.
Pearson's product moment correlation	A correlation approach that is used with interval and ratio data.
Perceptual mapping	An analysis technique which involves the positioning of objects in perceptual space. Frequently used in determining the positioning of brands relative to their competitors.
Photo sorts	A projective technique which uses a set of photographs depicting different types of people. Respondents are then asked to connect the individuals in the photographs with the brands they think they would use.
Pictogram	A type of bar chart which uses pictures of the items being described rather than bars.
Pie chart	A chart for presenting data which takes the form of a circle divided into several slices whose areas are in proportion to the quantities being examined.

Pilot testing

The pre-testing of a questionnaire prior to undertaking a full survey. Such testing involves administering the questionnaire to a limited number of potential respondents in order to identify and correct flaws in the questionnaire design.

Placement tests

The testing of reactions to products in the home and where they are to be used. Respondents are given a new product to test in their own home or in their office. Information about their experiences with and attitudes towards the products are then collected by either a questionnaire or by a self-completion diary.

Population of interest

The total group of people that the researcher wishes to examine, study or obtain information from. The population of interest will normally reflect the target market or potential target market for the product or service being researched. Sometimes known as the target population or universe.

Postal surveys

Self-administered surveys that are mailed to pre-selected respondents along with a return envelope, a covering letter and possibly an incentive.

Primary data

Data collected by a programme of observation, qualitative or quantitative research either separately or in combination to meet the specific objectives of a marketing research project.

Probability sampling

A set of sampling methods where an objective procedure of selection is used, resulting in every member of the population of interest having a known probability of being selected.

Professional codes of conduct

Self-regulatory codes covering acceptable practices in marketing research developed by the professional bodies responsible for the research industry (e.g. the Market Research Society or ESOMAR).

Profilers

Organisations that gather demographic and lifestyle information about consumers and combine it with postal address information. They take this base information and use it to segment an organisation's database of existing customers into different lifestyle and income groups. They may also be used to identify additional prospective customers whose characteristics match those of an organisation's existing customers.

Programme evaluation and review technique (PERT)	A managerial tool used for scheduling a research project. It involves a probability-based scheduling approach that recognises and measures the uncertainty of project completion times.
Projective questioning	Sometimes known as third-party techniques, this is a projective technique that asks the respondent to consider what other people would think about a situation.
Projective techniques	Techniques used in group discussions and individual depth interviews to facilitate a deeper exploration of a respondent's attitudes towards a concept, product or situation.
Proportionate stratified random sampling	A form of stratified random sampling (*See* Stratified random sampling) where the units or potential respondents from each population subset are selected in proportion to the total number of each subset's units in the population.
Purchase intent scales	A scaling approach which is used to measure a respondent's intention to purchase a product or potential product.
Qualitative research	An unstructured research approach with a small number of carefully selected individuals used to produce non-quantifiable insights into behaviour, motivations and attitudes.
Quantitative research	A structured research approach involving a sample of the population to produce quantifiable insights into behaviour, motivations and attitudes.
Questionnaire design process	A stepped approach to the design of questionnaires.
Quota sampling	A non-probability sampling procedure which involves the selection of cells or subsets within the population of interest, the establishment of a numerical quota in each cell and the researcher carrying out sufficient interviews in each cell to satisfy the quota.
Range	A measure of dispersion that calculates the difference between the largest and smallest values in a set of data.
Ratio data	Actual 'real' numbers that have a meaningful absolute or zero. All arithmetic operations are possible with such data.
Regression	A statistical approach to examine the relationship between two variables. Identifies the nature of the relationship using an equation.

Related samples	Samples where the measurement of interest in one sample may influence the measurement of the variable of interest in another sample.
Research brief	A written document which sets out an organisation's requirements from a marketing research project. This provides the specification against which the researchers will design the research project.
Research proposal	The submission prepared by the research agency for a potential client specifying the research to be undertaken. On the basis of the research proposal, the client will select an agency to undertake the research. The proposal becomes the contract between the agency and the client company.
Respondent errors	Non-sampling errors that are caused by respondents inadvertently or intentionally giving distorted or erroneous responses. Respondents may give erroneous answers because they fail to understand a question and do not want to admit their incomprehension.
Role playing	A projective technique which involves a respondent being asked to act out the character of a brand.
Sample	A subset of the population of interest.
Sampling error	The difference between the sample value and the true value of a phenomenon for the population being surveyed. Can be expressed in mathematical terms: usually the survey result plus or minus a certain percentage.
Sampling frame	A list of the population of interest from which the researcher selects the individuals for inclusion in the research.
Sampling frame error	A bias that occurs as a result of the population implied by the sampling frame being different from the population of interest.
Scaling questions	Questions that ask respondents to assign numerical measures to subjective concepts such as attitudes, opinions and feelings.
Scanner-based research	Collecting sales information using electronic scanners reading barcodes at the checkouts of retailers and wholesalers. The information collected feeds into audits.
Screening questionnaire	A questionnaire used for identifying suitable respondents for a particular research activity, such as a group discussion.

Search engines	Internet-based tools for finding web addresses which contain collections of links to sites throughout the world and an indexing system to help you find the relevant sites. Examples include AltaVista, Yahoo! and Lycos.
Secondary data	Information that has been previously gathered for some purpose other than the current research project. It may be data available within the organisation (internal data) or information available from published and electronic sources originating outside the organisation (external data).
Self-administered surveys	Surveys where the respondent completes the questionnaire with no help from an interviewer. The questionnaire can be delivered to the respondent via the mail (postal surveys), by hand, by fax or online (e-mail, web surveys).
Semantic differential scales	A scaling approach which requires the respondent to rate a brand or concept using a set of bipolar adjectives or phrases (e.g. helpful and unhelpful; friendly and unfriendly). Each pair of adjectives is separated by a seven-category scale with neither numerical nor verbal labels.
Sentence completion	A projective technique which involves providing respondents with an incomplete sentence or group of sentences and asking them to complete them.
Shelf impact testing equipment	*See* Stand-out equipment.
Simple random sampling	A probability sampling method where every possible member of the population has an equal chance of being selected for the survey. Respondents are chosen using random numbers.
Simulated test markets	A research approach used to predict the potential results of a product launch and to experiment with changes to different elements of a product's marketing mix. Rather than testing in retail stores, simulated test markets rely on simulated or laboratory-type testing and mathematical modelling.
Snowball sampling	A non-probability sampling procedure where additional respondents are identified and selected on the basis of referrals of initial respondents. It tends to be used where the population of interest is small or difficult to identify.
Spearman's rank-order correlation	A correlation approach for ordinal data.

Specialist service agencies	Marketing research agencies that do not offer the full range of services (*See* Full service agencies) but tend to specialise in certain types of research. For example, a specialist agency may only do research in a specific market sector such as the automotive sector or children's products, or in a geographic region of the world. Alternatively, the agency may be a specialist in terms of the research techniques it undertakes, focusing on telephone research or qualitative research.
Spider-type diagrams	Diagrams used to organise data in the analysis of qualitative research data.
Standard deviation	A measure of dispersion that calculates the average distance that the values in a data set are away from the mean. The standard deviation of different sets of data can be compared to see if one set of data is more dispersed than another.
Stand-out equipment	Sometimes known as shelf impact testing equipment, this is used to determine the visual impact of new packaging when placed on shelves next to competitors' products.
Stapel scales	A scaling approach which is a variation of the semantic differential scaling approach. It uses a single descriptor and 10 response categories with no verbal labels.
Statistical significance	If the difference between two statistical measures is large enough to be unlikely to have occurred due to chance or sampling error, then the difference is considered to be statistically significant.
Stimulus materials	Materials used in group discussions and individual depth interviews to communicate the marketer or advertiser's latest creative thinking for a product, packaging or advertising to the respondents.
Storyboards	A type of stimulus material where key frames for a television advertisement are drawn consecutively, like a comic strip.
Stratified random sampling	A probability sampling procedure in which the chosen sample is forced to contain potential respondents from each of the key segments of the population.
Street interviews	Interviews where respondents are approached and recruited while they are shopping or walking in town centres. In North America, these are known as mall intercept interviews.

Structured observation	A research approach where observers use a record sheet or form to count phenomena or to record their observations.
Systematic sampling	A probability sampling approach similar to a simple random sample but which uses a skip interval (i.e. every nth person) rather than random numbers to select the respondents.
t **test**	A hypothesis test about a single mean if the sample is too small to use the Z test.
Tabular method of analysis	A method for analysing qualitative research data using a large sheet of paper divided into boxes.
Target population	*See* Population of interest.
Telephone interviewing	Quantitative research where the interviewing is undertaken over the telephone.
Television viewing measurement	The procedures used in the measurement of the number of viewers watching a particular television programme. In the UK, around 20,000 households have electronic meters attached to their television sets to register when the set is turned on and to what channel it is tuned.
Text analysis software	Software used for data analysis in qualitative research. Such software helps segment the data and identify any patterns that exist.
Third-party techniques	*See* Projective questioning.
Topic list	Sometimes known as an interviewer guide. It outlines the broad agenda of issues to be explored in an individual depth interview or group discussion. It may also indicate the points at which stimulus material or projective techniques should be introduced.
Triangulation	Using a combination of different sources of data where the weaknesses in some sources are counterbalanced with the strengths of others. The term triangulation is borrowed from the disciplines of navigation and surveying, where a minimum of three reference points are taken to check an object's location.
Type I error	Rejection of the null hypothesis when it is actually true.
Type II error	Failing to reject the null hypothesis when it is actually false.
Universe	*See* Population of interest.

Unstructured questions	*See* Open-ended questions.
Validity	Whether the subject requiring to be measured was actually measured.
Video conferencing	The bringing together of a group of individuals using a video link and telecommunications. Can potentially be used for group discussions, particularly where the respondents are located in various parts of the world.
Viewing rooms	Specialist facilities/locations for group discussions. They are set out in the form of a boardroom or living-room setting with video cameras or a large one-way mirror built into one wall. Some are owned by research agencies, but the majority are independent and available to anyone willing to pay the hourly room-hire rates.
Web survey	A self-completion questionnaire which is delivered via the Internet. It may appear on the computer screen as a standard questionnaire where the respondent scrolls down the page completing each question. Alternatively, it can take the form of an interactive questionnaire with questions appearing on the screen one at a time.
Weighting	The process of adjusting the value of survey responses to account for over- or under-representation of different categories of respondent. Weighting is used where the sample design is disproportional or where the achieved sample does not accurately reflect the population under investigation.
Word association tests	A projective technique that involves asking respondents what brands or products they associate with specific words. In addition to the direct outputs regarding brand imagery, it is also a very useful technique for building rapport within a group discussion and getting everybody contributing and involved.
***Z* test**	A hypothesis test about a single mean where the sample size is larger than 30.

Appendix

Statistical tables

1 Standard normal distribution: *Z* values

2 Chi-square distribution

3 *t* distribution

Table 1 Standard normal distribution: Z values

Values in this table give the area under the curve between the mean and Z standard deviations above the mean. For example, for $Z = 1.75$, the area under the curve between the mean and Z is 0.4599.

Z	0.00	0.01	0.02	0.03	0.04	0.05	0.06	0.07	0.08	0.09
0.0	0.0000	0.0040	0.0080	0.0120	0.0160	0.0199	0.0239	0.0279	0.0319	0.0359
0.1	0.0398	0.0438	0.0478	0.0517	0.0557	0.0596	0.0636	0.0675	0.0714	0.0753
0.2	0.0793	0.0832	0.0871	0.0910	0.0948	0.0987	0.1026	0.1064	0.1103	0.1141
0.3	0.1179	0.1217	0.1255	0.1293	0.1331	0.1368	0.1406	0.1443	0.1480	0.1517
0.4	0.1554	0.1591	0.1628	0.1664	0.1700	0.1736	0.1772	0.1808	0.1844	0.1879
0.5	0.1915	0.1950	0.1985	0.2019	0.2054	0.2088	0.2123	0.2157	0.2190	0.2224
0.6	0.2257	0.2291	0.2324	0.2357	0.2389	0.2422	0.2454	0.2486	0.2518	0.2549
0.7	0.2580	0.2612	0.2642	0.2673	0.2704	0.2734	0.2764	0.2794	0.2823	0.2852
0.8	0.2881	0.2910	0.2939	0.2967	0.2995	0.3023	0.3051	0.3078	0.3106	0.3133
0.9	0.3159	0.3186	0.3212	0.3238	0.3264	0.3289	0.3315	0.3340	0.3365	0.3389
1.0	0.3413	0.3438	0.3461	0.3485	0.3508	0.3531	0.3554	0.3577	0.3599	0.3621
1.1	0.3643	0.3665	0.3686	0.3708	0.3729	0.3749	0.3770	0.3790	0.3810	0.3830
1.2	0.3849	0.3869	0.3888	0.3907	0.3925	0.3944	0.3962	0.3980	0.3997	0.4015
1.3	0.4032	0.4049	0.4066	0.4082	0.4099	0.4115	0.4131	0.4147	0.4162	0.4177
1.4	0.4192	0.4207	0.4222	0.4236	0.4251	0.4265	0.4279	0.4292	0.4306	0.4319
1.5	0.4332	0.4345	0.4357	0.4370	0.4382	0.4394	0.4406	0.4418	0.4429	0.4441
1.6	0.4552	0.4463	0.4474	0.4484	0.4495	0.4505	0.4515	0.4525	0.4535	0.4545
1.7	0.4554	0.4564	0.4573	0.4582	0.4591	0.4599	0.4608	0.4616	0.4625	0.4633
1.8	0.4641	0.4649	0.4656	0.4664	0.4671	0.4678	0.4686	0.4693	0.4699	0.4706
1.9	0.4713	0.4719	0.4726	0.4732	0.4738	0.4744	0.4750	0.4756	0.4761	0.4767
2.0	0.4772	0.4778	0.4783	0.4788	0.4793	0.4798	0.4803	0.4808	0.4812	0.4817
2.1	0.4821	0.4826	0.4830	0.4834	0.4838	0.4842	0.4846	0.4850	0.4854	0.4857
2.2	0.4861	0.4864	0.4868	0.4871	0.4875	0.4878	0.4881	0.4884	0.4887	0.4890
2.3	0.4893	0.4896	0.4898	0.4901	0.4904	0.4906	0.4909	0.4911	0.4913	0.4916
2.4	0.4918	0.4920	0.4922	0.4925	0.4927	0.4929	0.4931	0.4932	0.4934	0.4936
2.5	0.4938	0.4940	0.4941	0.4943	0.4945	0.4946	0.4948	0.4949	0.4951	0.4952
2.6	0.4953	0.4955	0.4956	0.4957	0.4959	0.4960	0.4961	0.4962	0.4963	0.4964
2.7	0.4965	0.4966	0.4967	0.4968	0.4969	0.4970	0.4971	0.4972	0.4973	0.4974
2.8	0.4974	0.4975	0.4976	0.4977	0.4977	0.4978	0.4979	0.4979	0.4980	0.4981
2.9	0.4981	0.4982	0.4982	0.4983	0.4984	0.4984	0.4985	0.4985	0.4986	0.4986
3.0	0.4986	0.4987	0.4987	0.4988	0.4988	0.4989	0.4989	0.4989	0.4990	0.4990

Table 2 Chi-square distribution

Entries in the table give chi-square values, where α is the area or probability in the upper tail of the chi-square distribution. For example, with 10 degrees of freedom and a 0.05 area in the upper tail, chi-square = 18.307.

Degrees of freedom	Area in upper tail									
	0.995	0.99	0.975	0.95	0.90	0.10	0.05	0.025	0.01	0.005
1			0.001	0.004	0.016	2.706	3.841	5.024	6.635	7.879
2	0.010	0.020	0.051	0.103	0.211	4.605	5.991	7.378	9.210	10.597
3	0.072	0.115	0.216	0.352	0.584	6.251	7.815	9.348	11.345	12.838
4	0.207	0.297	0.484	0.711	1.064	7.779	9.488	11.143	13.277	14.860
5	0.412	0.554	0.831	1.145	1.610	9.236	11.071	12.833	15.086	16.750
6	0.676	0.872	1.237	1.635	2.204	10.645	12.592	14.449	16.812	18.548
7	0.989	1.239	1.690	2.167	2.833	12.017	14.067	16.013	18.475	20.278
8	1.344	1.646	2.180	2.733	3.490	13.362	15.507	17.535	20.090	21.955
9	1.735	2.088	2.700	3.325	4.168	14.684	16.919	19.023	21.666	23.589
10	2.156	2.558	3.247	3.940	4.865	15.987	18.307	20.483	23.209	25.188
11	2.603	3.053	3.816	4.575	5.578	17.275	19.675	21.920	24.725	26.757
12	3.074	3.571	4.404	5.226	6.304	18.549	21.026	23.337	26.217	28.299
13	3.565	4.107	5.009	5.892	7.042	19.812	22.362	24.736	27.688	29.819
14	4.075	4.660	5.629	6.571	7.790	21.064	23.685	26.119	29.141	31.319
15	4.601	5.229	6.262	7.261	8.547	22.307	24.996	27.488	30.578	32.801
16	5.142	5.812	6.908	7.962	9.312	23.542	26.296	28.845	32.000	34.267
17	5.697	6.408	7.564	8.672	10.085	24.769	27.587	30.191	33.409	35.718
18	6.265	7.015	8.231	9.390	10.865	25.989	28.869	31.526	34.805	37.156
19	6.844	7.633	8.907	10.117	11.651	27.204	30.144	32.852	36.191	38.582
20	7.434	8.260	9.591	10.851	12.433	28.412	31.410	34.170	37.566	39.997
21	8.034	8.897	10.283	11.591	13.240	29.615	32.671	35.479	38.932	41.401
22	8.643	9.542	10.982	12.338	14.042	30.813	33.924	36.781	40.289	42.796
23	9.260	10.196	11.689	13.091	14.848	32.007	35.172	38.076	41.638	44.181
24	9.886	10.856	12.401	13.848	15.659	33.196	36.415	39.364	42.980	45.559
25	10.520	11.524	13.120	14.611	16.473	34.382	37.652	40.646	44.314	46.928
26	11.160	12.198	13.844	15.379	17.292	35.563	38.885	41.923	45.642	48.290
27	11.808	12.879	14.573	16.151	18.114	36.741	40.113	43.194	46.963	49.645
28	12.461	13.565	15.308	16.928	18.939	37.916	41.337	44.461	48.278	50.993
29	13.121	14.257	16.047	17.708	19.768	39.087	42.557	45.722	49.588	52.336
30	13.787	14.954	16.791	18.493	20.599	40.256	43.773	46.979	50.892	53.672
40	20.707	22.164	24.433	26.509	29.051	51.805	55.758	59.342	63.691	66.766
50	27.991	29.707	32.357	34.764	37.689	63.167	67.505	71.420	76.154	79.490
60	35.535	37.485	40.482	43.188	46.459	74.397	79.082	83.298	88.379	91.952
70	43.275	45.442	48.758	51.739	55.329	85.527	90.531	95.023	100.425	104.215
80	51.172	53.540	57.153	60.392	64.279	96.578	101.879	106.629	112.329	116.321
90	59.196	61.754	65.647	69.126	73.291	107.565	113.145	118.136	124.116	128.299
100	67.328	70.065	74.222	77.930	82.358	118.498	124.342	129.561	135.807	140.169

Table 3 t distribution

Entries in the table give t values for an area of probability in the upper tail of the t distribution. For example, with 10 degrees of freedom and a 0.025 area in the upper tail, $t_{.025} = 2.228$.

Degrees of freedom	Area in upper tail				
	0.10	0.05	0.025	0.01	0.005
1	3.078	6.314	12.706	31.821	63.657
2	1.886	2.920	4.303	6.965	9.925
3	1.638	2.353	3.182	4.541	5.841
4	1.533	2.132	2.776	3.747	4.604
5	1.476	2.015	2.571	3.365	4.032
6	1.440	1.943	2.447	3.143	3.707
7	1.415	1.895	2.365	2.998	3.499
8	1.397	1.860	2.306	2.896	3.355
9	1.383	1.833	2.262	2.821	3.250
10	1.372	1.812	2.228	2.764	3.169
11	1.363	1.796	2.201	2.718	3.106
12	1.356	1.782	2.179	2.681	3.055
13	1.350	1.771	2.160	2.650	3.012
14	1.345	1.761	2.145	2.624	2.977
15	1.341	1.753	2.131	2.602	2.947
16	1.337	1.746	2.120	2.583	2.921
17	1.333	1.740	2.110	2.567	2.898
18	1.330	1.734	2.101	2.552	2.878
19	1.328	1.729	2.093	2.539	2.861
20	1.325	1.725	2.086	2.528	2.845
21	1.323	1.721	2.080	2.518	2.831
22	1.321	1.717	2.074	2.508	2.819
23	1.319	1.714	2.069	2.500	2.807
24	1.318	1.711	2.064	2.492	2.797
25	1.316	1.708	2.060	2.485	2.787
26	1.315	1.706	2.056	2.479	2.779
27	1.314	1.703	2.052	2.473	2.771
28	1.313	1.701	2.048	2.467	2.763
29	1.311	1.699	2.045	2.462	2.756
30	1.310	1.697	2.042	2.457	2.750
40	1.303	1.684	2.021	2.423	2.704
60	1.296	1.671	2.000	2.390	2.660
120	1.289	1.658	1.980	2.358	2.617
infinity	1.282	1.645	1.960	2.326	2.576

Index